43111

24·50

We feel that the state of the art of management by objectives as applied to public relations is one of the hottest topics being discussed in the profession today, both pro and con . . . . We have to learn that we're ple and organizational people and that whatever we do fits goals and objectives of our companies.

W. Thomas Duke, 1983 Chair, Corporate Section
Public Relations Society of America

This book

10. MAY

27. JAN

15.

07 JAN 09

TO RENEW
071 - 514 74

Don Gresswell Ltd., London, N.21 Cat. No. 1207

D1136161

PUBLIC RELATIONS
MANAGEMENT BY OBJECTIVES

THE LIBRARY
LONDON COLLEGE OF FASHION

Norman R. Nager
T. Harrell Allen

UNIVERSITY
PRESS OF
AMERICA

Lanham • New York • London

Copyright © 1984 by Longman Inc.

University Press of America®, Inc.
4720 Boston Way
Lanham, Maryland 20706

3 Henrietta Street
London WC2E 8LU England

All rights reserved
Printed in the United States of America
British Cataloging in Publication Information Available

Reprinted by arrangement with
The Longman Publishing Group,
White Plains, New York.

Library of Congress Cataloging-in-Publication Data
Nager, Norman R., 1936-
Public relations: management by objectives /
Norman R. Nager, T. Harrell Allen.
p.   cm.
Originally published: New York : Longman, ©1984.
1. Public relations.   2. Management by objectives.
I. Allen, T. Harrell (Thomas Harrell), 1942- .   II. Title.
[HD59.N18   1991]   659.2' 068' 4—dc20   91-23451CIP

ISBN 0-8191-8330-X (pbk. : alk. paper)

43111
659.2 NAG

26. MAY

The paper used in this publication meets the minimum requirements of
American National Standard for Information Sciences—Permanence
of Paper for Printed Library Materials, ANSI Z39.48–1984.

CONTENTS

PREFACE

This book was written to break new ground in the growing public relations profession. It is the first published attempt to apply management by objectives (MBO) systematically to public relations practice.

It is hoped that this book will fill a critical gap in the public relations literature. Thorough books exist that explain public relations principles, record history, discuss particular tools, and present case studies. What is missing is an actual method for managing public relations.

Tomorrow's public relations professionals need a book that takes a detailed, *theoretically grounded and pragmatic how-to approach.*

The stimuli for this book came from the professional side of public relations. Increasingly, managers and directors of various organizations from corporations to government agencies are demanding that the public relations practitioner be results, rather than activities, oriented.

Through our consulting work and professional contacts in the field, we heard over and over again the challenge to the public relations practice to become more oriented to hardened objectives and tangible results. *Public Relations Management by Objectives* (PR-MBO) is aimed at arming the public relations professional to plan and follow through as a more effective *manager of change* who may command more respect, resources, and support from board and top management.

Some leaders in our field call it public relations management by results. Some counselors prefer the term public relations management by evaluation. Because a number of chief executive officers (CEOs) and board members identify with "management by objectives," however, we use that name throughout the book. For PR-MBO incorporates the critical focus on results achieved and means to evaluate them so that you may learn how to improve upon program effectiveness and relations with other members of the management team.

In an era of rapidly increasing complexity and accountability, public relations professionals find themselves under increasing pressure to strengthen problem prevention and solution skills. One way to do this is to adapt powerful, proven approaches from other professions.

In this book, we share with you the visions of leaders in the field:

- Winners of Public Relations Society of America (PRSA) Silver Anvil awards for professional excellence who loaned us their files
- Executives of leading public relations agencies and corporate, institutional, and governmental organizations who invested their ideas and shared their findings
- PRSA, Women in Communications, Inc. (WICI), and International Association of Business Communicators (IABC) leaders and staffs who contributed to our research
- Educators from Maryland to Syracuse, from Austin and Houston to Madison, from Gainesville to San Diego, from Athens to Seattle, from Boston to Norman, Oklahoma, teachers whose research, writings, and interviews stimulated and interacted with our own ideas
- Public relations practitioners whose names may not yet be widely known, but who challenge the state of the art by asking *why* on that which most of us may have accepted as givens of practice, and by asking *why not* as they and the profession of public relations break new ground

They spur the spirit of inquiry and the flow of creativity in us all.

Finally, we wish to acknowledge the contributions of our editors and reviewers. We credit Petra Nager for going beyond proofing to copyediting and critique. We cite Joan Matthews for her guidance as Longman's managing editor. We particularly wish to thank Gordon T. R. Anderson and Ray E. Hiebert for their expert counsel and help in making this book a reality.

Norman R. Nager
T. Harrell Allen

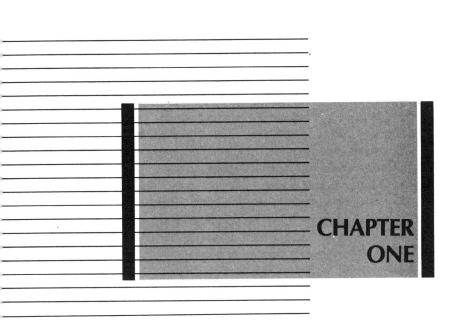

CHAPTER
ONE

INTRODUCING PR-MBO

TRENDS TOWARD MANAGERIAL ACCOUNTABILITY

A new period of significance has arrived for the public relations profession. To a degree never seen before, executives are looking to public relations professionals to become full members of the management team. With this comes an expectation to provide research, planning, communication, follow-through, counsel, and other managerial skills at higher levels.

A sense of the progress of professionals in assuming greater managerial responsibility is reflected in surveys of the Public Relations Society of America (PRSA) and International Association of Business Communicators (IABC). Sixty percent of PRSA respondents said they already were engaged in public relations *management* by 1978. A third of IABC respondents said they had more significant roles in policy making in 1983 than they did in 1981.[1]

Top Management Expectations

The trend to acquire greater management skills stems from two basic sources: top management and the public relations profession itself. Chief executive officers (CEOs) around the nation are saying, in essence: "We need and want your advice on policy issues. And, if you are going to be part of the first team, you have to think like we do."

A survey published in the Fall 1981 issue of *Public Relations Review* found senior management officers demanding "more diversified public relations practitioners" to "become an integral part of day-to-day affairs as corporations attempt to deal with the growing pressures of sophisticated consumers, government regulation, competition, internal corporate needs, and employee demands." Moreover, the incentives could include "increased public relations budgets" and "an end to PR people being the 'last hired and the first fired.' "[2]

Similarly, the December 1982 issue of *Public Relations Journal* cited results from a survey of senior public relations executives at *Fortune* 300 companies and noted the trend since a comparable study a decade earlier to increasing involvement of public relations executives from the beginning in the decision-making process through participation in top management meetings:

> Close to 80 percent of respondents feel public relations has become more important to management during the past five years. Moreover, nearly 70 percent think public relations involvement in the management process will continue to grow during the next five years.[3]

As a manager trying to guide an organization through a turbulent socioeconomic environment with its diverse publics, you are being asked to focus sharp attention on *results* of any managerial decision.

It is not an accident that by the early 1980s, the most sought after business degree emphasized finance. This degree, with its orientation to the managing of resources, suggests the attitude any public relations professional must acquire before giving counsel to top management. It is a period in which each expenditure must show the gain, if any, that results from it. The focus on finance follows—and builds upon— earlier emphases on business degrees specializing in management and marketing.

Moreover, not only in the United States but abroad as well, top management increasingly evidenced more interest in and responsibility for public relations in an era epitomized by what the *1982 Gold Paper* of the International Public Relations Association (IPRA) termed the "power of information . . . instantaneous, global, more technical, and complex."[4]

The increased involvement of top management in communication and environmental concerns will continue to pose new challenges to the public relations profession, the IPRA Education and Research Committee found:

> To public relations managers this implies that their future depends on staying ahead of senior management's needs; they must keep looking at the *next* area of concern, translating today's issues of concern into future opportunities by injecting this knowledge into corporate policy consistent with public opinion and translating it into public relations programs of action. . . .
>
> The ability to comprehend the overall business strategy, the corporate policy, the market place, the external environment, is vital.[5]

Given these realities in a period of scarcity, CEOs demand that all managers be held accountable for what they produce. This is true of all departments. Public relations is no exception.

Instant Communication, Narrower Publics, and PR Profession

The second source of factors in the historical trends toward greater managerial skill relates to the increasingly difficult nature of public relations responsibilities.

In a global society that seems to shrink with each new electronic form of communication, the audiences for public relations become larger and more immediate. In the past, an organization could be viewed as a fairly self-sufficient outpost that needed to communicate successfully with only a few publics to stay in business.

That has changed. The modern organization finds itself almost overwhelmed by the need to communicate instantly with multiple publics. Such words as "customer," "employee," or "government" really do not begin to capture the true nature of the organization's publics. Rather than think in terms of large homogeneous publics, each has to be divided into many mini-publics. Each of these will have different demands, expectations, and personal characteristics. To communicate with them, messages have to be tailored to these narrower groups of individuals. (But the messages have to be broad enough to be consistent with previous statements aimed at larger publics.)

Elected and appointed officers plus the staffs of federal, state, county, and city legislative bodies and regulatory agencies have become an important cluster of publics that must be given constant attention by the public relations professional. The governmental sphere has become, to many public relations staffs, the audience that demands most time. In fact, public relations careers can be based entirely on learning to communicate with powerful governmental publics.

For a long time, employees could be—and were—taken for granted. Contemporary public relations professionals have recognized that as a prescription for disaster. The "employee public" has to be broken down into the reality it is: multiple publics of employees with different job expectations, education and training, and career goals. Different employee publics require different communication strategies.

In summary, never has it been so easy and yet so difficult to communicate with your publics. Easy because of electronic networks, computer banks of quickly retrievable data, and the narrow focus permitted by cable television and special-interest publications. Difficult because your publics are quite diverse in expectations and makeup. And this increases the complexity and responsibilities to plan and organize your public relations thrust so as to achieve maximum results for your organization.

Of course, top management constitutes your most important internal public because of its power to allocate the resources for public relations, consider the options you counsel, approve the programs and changes you propose, and follow through upon your counsel.

These days, CEOs and public relations professionals identify among the most important publics the financial community, members of your own governing board, government officials, employees, middle management, distributors/dealers, customers, community activists, consumer advocates, environmentalists, other members of your field of enterprise, opinion leaders and gatekeepers of the media, and more. And all must be reached with demonstrative results.

Otto Lerbinger, professor of public relations at Boston University, reflected the management mood this way:

> We now have a management-by-objectives [MBO] mentality. MBO demands are being made of PR practitioners the same as with other staff and line officers. CEOs used to be satisfied with press clippings. Now they're saying, "How is this helping?"[6]

Clients of public relations agencies, as well as executives to whom public relations officers report, are behind the trend toward increased accountability and MBO-like concentration on results, according to Counselor Chester Burger, APR:

> There is increasing insistence on the part of clients that their public relations agency relationships be conducted in a businesslike manner. They're asking for much more time accountability on projects. They want to know not just how the time was spent but how efficiently it was spent.[7]

What we have attempted to do in the previous discussion is to show how the management challenge has reached the public relations profession. We have mentioned major sources for the trends and reasons why they will continue. But before discussing management by objectives in depth and indicating how PR-MBO works, we need to offer a definition of public relations.

PUBLIC RELATIONS: A DEFINITION IN TRANSITION

The very definition of "public relations" has been in a state of flux in recent years. Patrick Jackson, APR, co-publisher of the *PR Reporter*, principal of Jackson, Jackson & Wagner, and past PRSA president, put it this way in correspondence for this book:

> In order to apply MBO or to evaluate public relations activities or programs, both an organization and the individual practitioner must stipulate certain givens:
> 1. Exactly what public relations can contribute to the particular bottom line of that organization;
> 2. What is the proper scope of activities, the "role" of the practitioner?[8]

It appears that most public relations professionals readily accept the need to become more managerial or "businesslike." And the definition of public relations has come to incorporate more of an emphasis on managerial responsibilities. As Joseph F. Awad, APR, general director of public relations for Reynolds Metals Co., and 1982 PRSA president, said: "We *are* management":[9]

> [Public relations] always has and always will be . . . looking and working in two directions at once—inwardly, on the organization, and outwardly, on the sociosphere.

It always has been and always will be grounded in action and communication, said in one breath, as one indissoluble concept.

It always has been and always will be both a policy counseling and communication function, and the two are as inseparable as the two sides of a single coin. . . .

A widely accepted formal definition from the Foundation for Public Relations Research and Education follows:

Public relations is a distinctive management function which helps establish and maintain mutual lines of communication, understanding, acceptance and cooperation between an organization and its publics; involves the management of problems or issues; helps management to keep informed on and responsible to public opinion; defines and emphasizes the responsibility of management to serve the public interest; helps management to keep abreast of and effectively utilize change, serving as an early warning system to help anticipate trends; and uses research and sound and ethical communication techniques as its principal tools.[10]

What is not so readily apparent is *how* to accept the challenge. Management expects more than well-meaning advice. Public relations counsel increasingly is grounded in traditional management principles and based on solid empirical data. *Results, rather than the activities to produce those results, form the cornerstone of managing public relations.*

This new role for public relations professionals makes more and more of your colleagues indispensable to their organizations. How quickly they and you become comfortable with this new role depends on how fast managerial philosophy and skills are acquired.

The quest for *the* definition of public relations has never stopped. Each new generation of attempts, however, has led to more emphasis on the management role.

In their collaboration on the manuscript for the 1983 edition of *Practical Public Relations*, Sam Black, 1982 president of the International Public Relations Association, and Ball State University's Melvin L. Sharpe incorporated the import of:

The review and analysis of organizational goals, objectives, policies and procedures for the purpose of identifying lack of harmony between the organization and its publics or social environment and the potential short and long range effect.[11]

In their 1984 book on *Managing Public Relations,* James E. Grunig of the University of Maryland and Todd Hunt of Rutgers University defined the direct involvement in the setting of goals and objectives as more of a systematic part of public relations practice.[12]

Although the Public Relations Society of America (PRSA) had resisted over the years capsule definitions of public relations that would tend to oversimplify this complex function, the PRSA National Assembly in November 1982 adopted its first statement in 35 years about the profession, one that focuses on public relations as a management function. As part of that statement, carried in full in the concluding chapter of this book, the PRSA reached out beyond review and analysis of organizational goals and objectives to: "Setting objectives, planning, budgeting . . . managing the resources. . . ."[13]

One pervasive system, management by objectives, is widely used in business and other organizations. Because of its success and familiarity among so many managers, MBO has become a foundation for public relations management, in short, PR-MBO. For the public relations professional about to move up to the role of management, PR-MBO will help develop a philosophy and style that will allow you to manage everything from the most basic publicity campaign to the most sophisticated research-based consultation to higher management.

For the remaining part of this chapter and the rest of this book, we counsel you on the use of management by objectives to effectively manage your public relations efforts.

MANAGEMENT BY OBJECTIVES: THE CONCEPT

In 1943, Peter Drucker, one of the nation's most influential business consultants, was approached by General Motors to undertake a study of GM's management. His book, *Concept of the Corporation,* resulted from that study. Arjay Miller, former president of Ford, recalled:

> When I left the Army Air Force to join Ford Motor Company in January 1946, Drucker's *Concept of the Corporation* had just appeared and I found it extremely useful in forming my own judgments regarding what was needed at Ford.[14]

Out of his work at General Motors and additional thinking, Drucker wrote *The Practice of Management.* From this book, the idea of management by objectives was introduced to the managerial world. Richard

H. Buskirk of the School of Business Administration, Southern Methodist University, said:

> His [Drucker's] emphasis upon the results of managerial actions rather than the supervision of activities was a major contribution, for it shifted the entire focus of management thought to productivity—output—and away from work efforts—the inputs.[15]

In essence, Drucker was responding to the old inadequacies of management: a concentration on activity. Drucker, with his MBO concept, shifted the focus to *the purpose* of activity, rather than activity per se. Under MBO, Drucker said that the manager must be held responsible for results.

With this idea in mind, many businesses began to turn to MBO for guidance during the 1960s. And, it was in this time period that the first book with the title *Management by Objectives* was published. Its author, George S. Odiorne, is probably the best known of all MBO writers in the United States today.[16]

The evolution of MBO has led to two major areas of influence. On the one hand, MBO can be viewed as a philosophy for management to use in guiding an organization. On the other hand, MBO has come to mean a particular set of techniques for achieving results for the organization. These two areas of influence are reflected in the hundreds of books, articles, and seminars devoted to the application of MBO.

While Drucker wrote about MBO in his 1954 book, George Odiorne, "the father of MBO," was beginning to exert his influence in the adoption of MBO.[17]

According to Jack N. Kondrasuk, business professor and MBO consultant, Odiorne in 1955 held executive seminars for four Minneapolis companies in which MBO was a major topic. The four companies were General Mills, Daytons, Northwest Bank Corp., and Honeywell. Kondrasuk noted that Odiorne was instrumental in helping General Mills install MBO internally.[18]

Although it is difficult to point out an exact starting date for the adoption of MBO at individual companies, approximate times can be offered: General Electric, 1953; General Mills and Honeywell, 1955–1960; Univac, 1959; and Control Data, 1964–66.[19] The public sector was also involved in MBO concepts in the mid-1950s with the California State Training Office adopting "results" as an orientation for managers.

MBO is now used in countless organizations. A sense of how widespread the concept has become was indicated in a discovery by Odiorne that a Canadian scholar prepared a 55-page list of literature in the area of MBO, "consisting of over 700 books, articles, monographs, dissertations and theses."[20]

You can get some idea of its acceptance from the actual use of MBO in such organizations as Times Mirror Co., General Motors, 3M, United Airlines, Monsanto, State Farm Insurance, General Electric, St. Regis Paper, Canadian Post Office, U.S. National Park Service, U.S. Navy Supply Systems Command, Burson-Marsteller, Memorial Hospital Medical Center of Long Beach, and government agencies, school systems, and volunteer organizations.

Where is MBO today?

A 1982 national survey of public and private organizations suggested that MBO is alive and well. The survey by two business professors, Stephen R. Ruth and William W. Brooks, involved 320 organizations from industry plus state and local governments.[21] According to this survey, about 60 percent of respondents were using MBO. Nearly 90 percent of MBO users were favorably disposed toward MBO.[22]

The survey suggested that MBO support is found at all levels of the organization; although support wanes at the lower levels. Of the reporting organizations, 91 percent of top management favored MBO, and 72 percent of middle management supported it.

Survey respondents showed strong perceptions of the role of MBO as successfully changing individual as well as organizational performance. Apparently these organizations found that MBO can function as a positive *change agent* leading to increased organizational effectiveness. The survey also revealed that 60 percent of respondents who were not yet using MBO favored adopting it in their organizations.

In November 1982 the 10th annual State of the Art Conference of the International MBO Institute attracted Drucker, Odiorne, and a number of corporate, government, and nonprofit organization executives to Long Beach, California, to discuss "Goal Driven Organizations, the American Strategy for Managing."

The adoption of MBO has continued to spread rapidly because of its success in solving chronic problems in such areas as profit declines, worker evaluation, employee discipline, collective bargaining, motivation, and communication breakdowns. Today, organizations in Japan, Europe, England, and Australia, as well as the United States, operate on the principles of management by objectives.

In every phase of its historical development, MBO has been exhaustively tested by academic researchers, managers, consultants, and behavioral and social scientists, making it one of the most thoroughly researched management concepts, as the extensive literature on the subject indicates.

Although MBO, as the practice of public relations, has operated under a number of different names, the basic approach has survived a test of more than a quarter century of use, while a number of managerial fads have come and gone. This is not to say that MBO will instantly work in your organization. It has to be thoroughly understood as a management philosophy and it has to be carefully implemented. As a tool, like any other, it is subject to human error. Just as a computer word processing system does not guarantee effective writing, MBO may not work in situations lacking necessary policies, training, and other factors.

PR-MBO DEFINED

As public relations assumes a more managerial role, the time has come to explain the fine points of how to blend the actual practice of public relations with management by objectives.

In essence, that is what this book is about. The authors have attempted to take the management technique of MBO and show how to apply it to the practice of public relations. The remaining chapters reveal through discussion, procedures, and examples how this is done.

MBO may be defined formally as a *total management system* that *focuses on results* rather than activities *for performance evaluation*. With this definition in mind, consider these questions concerning the practice of public relations:

1. Why is public relations vital to your organization's management?
2. What does public relations do for the organization?
3. How are public relations priorities set?
4. How is the public relations department evaluated?
5. How effectively are public relations resources utilized?
6. To what results can the public relations department point?
7. How does the public relations department support and contribute to the organization's goals?

If you can give specific answers to these questions, chances are you are practicing public relations management by objectives to some extent already. But if you have difficulty answering any of them, then you are not using PR-MBO. Why? Because, in a phrase, PR-MBO means achieving measurable results. Well-formulated objectives provide specific milestones for the actual practice of public relations. Stated as a definition, *an objective is a specific description of an event (result) to be accomplished.* An ideal objective will tell who will achieve what and when and how.

Goals, which are written before objectives, give the *why*. By definition, goals are much broader in scope than objectives and point to the general aims of your public relations program. *Goals tell you the general direction and objectives give you your destination.*

PR-MBO is similar to the business concept of zero-based budgeting in that it requires each public relations activity to be evaluated against results that demonstrate the *return on investment of resources.* Because something has been done in the past is not a sufficient reason for doing it now, according to both zero-based budgeting and MBO principles.

Just because a newsletter was published last year does not assure automatically that the same investment plus additional increments to adjust for inflation should be made for the next year. (In zero-based budgeting, managers literally start with a zero budget, rather than pick up from where the last budget left off. The value to the organization of proposed expenditures must be demonstrated anew and not taken for granted.)

Table 1.1, "Comparison of PR Roles," illustrates zero-based budgeting and PR-MBO thinking by comparing traditional public relations behaviors with PR-MBO strategies for given management tasks.

10 CONDITIONS OF OBJECTIVES

To grasp the meaning of objectives in the special case of management by objectives as applied to public relations, consider 10 conditions that apply here:

1. Objectives are results in the interests of the public relations client or employer and its publics.

CASE EXAMPLE: NBC-TV Consumer Advocate David Horowitz, a frequent critic of business practices. gave testimony on the air about

Table 1.1
Comparison of PR Roles

Management Task	Traditional PR	PR-MBO
Major aim of PR program	Involved with many activities	Oriented to meeting objectives
Focus	Narrow, on PR department only	Entire organization
Managing public relations department	Day-to-day	Future-oriented
Setting priorities	Unclear, changes daily and weekly	Priorities established and followed
Planning	Short term	Long term
Job descriptions	Subjective	Objective
Evaluation	Based on little (if any) general feedback (such as clippings counts)	Based only on results
Communication in the organization	One-way, flowing from management down	Two-way flow among all levels of employees plus lateral (among departments)

how a supermarket chain's in-store campaign to provide consumers with point-of-sale nutritional information on meats or products can produce results in the interests of both client and customer public:

> Personally, I hope this idea pays off for Market Basket, not just in image points, but in real dollars and cents, because if this is really as good an idea as it seems to be, if it helps us all eat better and buy more wisely, then even a small added profit on the bottom line might encourage other stores to follow suit.[23]

2. Moreover, they are results so precisely defined that they are free of ambiguity and you can readily determine whether or not they are met *and* to what degree.

CASE EXAMPLE A: When the MGM Grand Hotel was opened in Reno, Nevada, the public relations person retained for the campaign set as her primary objective getting the media to publicize the opening, both before and during the event, so as to create an aura of mystery and excitement. Secondary objectives included attracting unspecified numbers of easterners, high rollers from neighboring states, and recreational vehicle owners.[24]

Although the secondary objectives come closer to the results many a client would rank most important, they are ambiguous in not indicating what numbers of each group should be attracted over what periods of time.

The primary objective contains ambiguity in not qualifying, let alone quantifying, which media would cover what aspects of the opening for which publics with what elements of content. Beyond that, specificity could be sought on results of the media coverage. For instance, how well did it do in predisposition of members of publics to want to go to the hotel during or after the opening. Furthermore, surveys could have indicated the degree of likelihood of going to the hotel.

CASE EXAMPLE B: Contrast the primary objective of the hotel campaign with that of the Clay County Jail Bond Campaign, represented by Fleishman-Hillard. After nine previous defeats of measures to build new jail facilities, the agency mounted an effort to target positive voters and get them to the polls in sufficient numbers to gain a two thirds vote of approval. (The actual results—approval by 83.6 percent with voters in every precinct passing the issue by at least two thirds majority.)[25]

3. You must have a date—a time certain, as some CEOs say—as the target for attainment of the results. Of course, those who plan for contingencies also may include fallback positions with "if this happens, then the date will be delayed (or advanced) by this many days."

CASE EXAMPLE: New York Telephone won the highest PRSA award in 1981 for customer relations based on its time-certain, six-month campaign to secure customer cooperation in converting over to "One Plus Dialing" (dialing the number 1 before the phone number when placing calls outside the 212 area code). The campaign was tied to the November 22, 1980, cutover to the new system.

The objective was to bring about an overnight change in the dialing habits of the nearly eight million people who live or work in New York City, and do so at minimal cost. This was achieved within a $70,000 budget.

The big test for the telephone network came on November 24, the first business day after "One Plus Dialing" began. By noon that day, more than two thirds of all "One Plus" calls were being dialed directly by customers . . . with an even higher percentage in the business district.[26]

But although the date of cutover started November 22, the company provided an additional 15 days in its planning for the conversion of customer behavior.

4. The results sought are hardened and concrete rather than abstract. This means that an objective will not be developed in terms of generalities or superlatives but in measurable terms, preferably quantitatively. But as it will be developed later, without *benchmark or baseline data* (a foundation of previous measurements), this may require some compromises initially.

CASE EXAMPLE: As part of the research phase of the campaign for Conti Commodity Services, Daniel J. Edelman incorporated a 1978 benchmark study (initial data foundation) of *Wall Street Journal (WSJ)* readers by researchers Erdos and Morgan. The study not only indicated the key criteria for investors in selecting a futures broker but also showed that investors "tended to call on established 'wire houses' like Merrill Lynch and Bache, who also had commodity departments, instead of the recently established commodities-only firms like Conti." When Erdos and Morgan performed a follow-up study in 1980, one of the reverses achieved was in frequent commodity traders rating Conti's research department above Shearson's and Bache's.[27]

To operationalize part of their purpose "to raise local awareness of the firm," Conti and Edelman set out to strengthen attendance at weekly local seminars, particularly in areas of poor reach for the *WSJ*. Follow-up studies "credited our publicity with generating 30 to 50 percent of seminar attendance."

5. Within themselves, objectives contain sufficient specifications for measurement so that you may know how to evaluate the public relations program as a whole, as well as the tools, strategies, budget, time line, and other parts.

CASE EXAMPLE: Although the statements in the objectives section of the public relations program summary tended to general directions, such as "create a comprehensive environmental education program" and "develop a pilot program that can serve as a national model,"

Johnson Wax and the Burson-Marsteller agency built formal evaluations into the Living Planet film program.

One of the criteria set was demand for showings at New York's Ziegfeld Theater. (Within two weeks, 14,000 students and 500 teachers participated in 11 presentations and an additional 200 schools could not be accommodated but had to be provided films later.)

A majority of the teachers said they would give positive ratings to the value of the film as a teaching tool and called for the program to be accepted. (Teacher evaluations resulted in 90 percent giving the film "excellent" marks and 96 percent registering approval of the entire program as "a complete teaching tool.")[28]

6. Projected results/achievements must be realistic and attainable within the time frame estimated and the conditions prevailing. They should neither be so high as to be out of your reach with the resources and constraints involved (what researchers refer to as *situational variables*), nor should they be so low as to appear seriously below the needs and capabilities of the organization.

CASE EXAMPLE: The basic objective was simple and concise— "increase prune sales" based upon a campaign to generate "positive awareness" of the nutritional, recipe, health, snack, and taste values. For many organizations, a mere increase would not be enough, and it might be hard to separate the public relations activities impact from that of advertising.

Yet, the modest objective of an increase without quantification was sufficient for an industry that had just experienced five years of declining sales. The California Prune Board, represented by Botsford Ketchum Public Relations, produced a program that was given credit for a sales gain of 4 percent during a year in which no generic (nonbrand name) advertising was involved.

A test promotion to persuade retailers that sales would increase if they used point-of-sale materials (posters, recipe tear-off pads, etc.) saw participating units gain immediate increases ranging from 114 to 556 percent.[29]

7. Public relations objectives may support or be identical to other organizational objectives, such as increases in sales, productivity, funds raised, legislation passed (or tabled in committee), retention of employees, and attraction of new investors.

CASE EXAMPLE: Olin's Robert A. Kelly, vice president for public relations and communication, contributed Table 1.2 "Direct Support of Business," to show how public relations may support corporate business purposes:[30]

Table 1.2
Direct Support of Business

Corporate	Public Relations
1. To achieve continuing long-term growth in earnings and a record of financial stability that attracts to the company the capital (equity and debt) required to support growth.	1. Effectively communicate the company's strengths and objectives to financial and business communities, especially capital markets.
2. To concentrate efforts in business and product areas in which the company realistically can expect to achieve a leadership position and this leadership will be rewarded.	2. Effectively communicate the company's strengths and objectives to all appropriate business and financial publics, and to all current and prospective customer groups.
3. To offer our products and services wherever in the world the company's operations can be consistent with all its objectives.	3. Effectively communicate corporate, product, and service capabilities to all appropriate publics, with particular emphasis on targeted areas.
4. To have working environment in which each individual is treated with fairness, that encourages and rewards excellence, and stimulates maximum growth of the individual.	4. Maintain effective two-way communication with employees, determining their views and presenting them with management policies and plans; then counsel management with regard to employee opinions, morale and expectations.
5. To anticipate the needs of the future sufficiently well to develop the human talent to be and remain a leader.	5. Project the company's identity internally and externally and thereby attract and maintain the kind of work force essential to the company's continued growth and industry leadership.
6. To be a responsible corporate citizen.	6. Counsel management on the public impact of operational decisions, anticipating and analyzing emerging political and social trends; and communicate the company's range of policies and corporate ties to relevant publics.

(Courtesy of Robert A. Kelly)

8. Public relations objectives may pertain to impact upon awareness, understanding, acceptance, expectations, attitudes, and other considerations involved in the actions of the organization's external and internal publics.

CASE EXAMPLE: The ICPR agency developed a microwave oven marketing campaign for Whirlpool's entry into the field to encourage wholesale distributors to aggressively merchandise the new product, Whirlpool dealers to want to purchase and inventory the line, and consumers to be predisposed to buy it. Corporate marketing management credited the campaign with making "significant contribution to the company's successful entry to the market" and reported to ICPR that "ambitious sales plans were met or exceeded in all areas in spite of heavy competition in the microwave market."[31]

9. This condition may appear somewhat redundant with condition 1, but it is too important to just mention at the head of the list: Objectives will not be what the public relations person does in using the tools of the profession, but *what is accomplished with those tools for the short- and long-range good of the organization and its publics.*

CASE EXAMPLE: Capitol Records found itself besieged by media, fans, other record companies, and distributors in the wake of the gunning down of John Lennon in New York, December 8, 1980. The answering of queries was not the objective per se. Nor was the placement of memorial advertisements in such publications as *Variety* and *Billboard.* Nor were the written directives disseminating information to employees. Nor were the press releases to trade and news media. The company looked ahead to a memorial tribute album that would follow about a year after Lennon's death. The press and publicity department counseled management and followed through to help in the maintenance of normal production and flow in the marketplace and in maintaining both Lennon's and the company's reputation while avoiding the taint of being perceived as trying to exploit his death.[32]

10. And just as you approach "objective" as if it were a word in another language with its own set of meanings different from conventional use, also keep in mind that "goal" and "objective" may be synonymous in everyday use, but not in the language of MBO and PR-MBO.

The semantics are important here because they structure organization of planning, priorities, strategies, and follow-through, including evaluation, adaptation, and back-up and fallback systems.

In the operational language of MBO and PR-MBO, goals are the immeasurable aspirations and visions toward which you move. And objectives are the milestones, the actual achievable payoff for the investment a client or employer makes in a public relations person and for the investment you make in your continuing education and work.

CASE ILLUSTRATION: MOTORCYCLE SAFETY RESULTS

When the Motorcycle Safety Foundation distributed "My Men Wear 'Em" poster photos of "Dallas" TV series actress Charlene Tilton, "We Wear 'Em" glossy prints of "CHiPs" TV series actor Larry Wilcox, and other materials to the electronic and print media, the objective was *not* to secure publicity for the Carl Byoir & Associates agency client. And bringing "glamor and a macho image to helmet use" were merely tactics accompanied by the "We Wear 'Em" nonauthoritarian campaign "to enable young riders to emulate the behavior of famous people."[33]

For the Motorcycle Safety Foundation subscribes to "management by objectives [that] requires extensive and frequent measurement and evaluation of results." And when the foundation stresses "planning results that contribute to objectives . . . we are interested in *results*, not efforts. . . . Although not a profit making organization, maximizing the return on investment is our operating motto."[34]

Byoir and the foundation won a PRSA Silver Anvil for their voluntary helmet use campaign. They won with a campaign anchored to the twin purposes of:

1. "substantially broader helmet use as measured by helmet sales increases exceeding motorcycle sales during the same period" and

2. "a clear demonstration that voluntary helmet use campaigns are effective so that government funding for the expansion of such programs would be available."[35]

The media program succeeded in exposure to a gross audience (including multiple exposures to some individuals) of 320 million. Public service advertising reached 550 million. Although this would have been considered sufficient as results in an earlier era of public relations, Byoir and the foundation indicated that this exposure was merely a means (activities) to these ends (results):

1. The Motorcycle Safety Foundation program contributed to a dramatic increase in helmet sales. During this same period, motorcycle sales declined about 2 percent and motorcycle registrations also declined.

2. The National Highway Traffic Safety Administration included support of educational programs that promote voluntary helmet use in its 1981 budget. This is the first time that federal funds have been made available for such programs.[36]

Note how these results compare with their objectives. And yet the Motorcycle Safety Foundation subsequently hardened the definition and operationalization of objectives for the 1982 draft of its statements of goals and objectives:

> While goals give us direction, they are not attainable as stated. . . . Objectives, however, grow from the goals, tell staff exactly what to do in the next program year and *why*. Objectives have a single outcome, are measurable, attainable, and set in a time frame. . . . As the year's program is taking place, evaluation of that work and progress helps staff refine and upgrade objectives for the future.[37]

14 OBJECTIVES FOR ANALYSIS

In presenting 14 examples of 104 Motorcycle Safety Foundation objectives for 1982 through 1986, we invite readers to analyze what each statement does in meeting the criteria:[38]

A. Assist four states each year to incorporate sharing the roadway information into their regular drivers' handbooks for a total of 35 states by 1986.

B. Increase the number of Motorcycle Rider Course graduates per year to 100,000 by 1986.

C. Assist in the passage of three major state rider education or licensing bills each year beginning in 1982.

D. Conduct individual department project evaluations on a continuing basis each year to streamline activities and ensure project goals are being met.

E. Institute the adoption of the *Motorcycle Operator Manual* in 10 states by 1986.

F. Expand efforts to reach the general public and improve their view of motorcycling through a 5 percent increase in placements in newspapers, general interest magazines, trade press, and television/radio programs each year.

G. Conduct an International Motorcycle Safety Conference in 1986 to report research since the 1980 conference and set goals for future research activities.

H. Establish Motorcycle Safety Foundation "800" telephone number in 1983 to provide information on rider education courses to 3,000 callers and local course sponsors; continue through 1986 with 5 percent call increase per year.

I. Produce a cable or public broadcasting program on Motorcycle Safety Foundation and motorcycle safety in 1985; distribute to 75 television stations in 1986.

J. Develop incentive plans to increase the number of participants in rider education programs.

K. Increase manufacturers' compliance with voluntary advertising guidelines to achieve 100 percent compliance on proper gear and 75 percent compliance on all other guidelines by 1986.

Wear A Helmet When You Ride

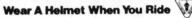
Wear A Helmet When You Ride

(Courtesy of Motorcycle Safety Foundation.)

L. Encourage the adoption of the Motorcycle Operator Manual Knowledge Test and accompanying slides for automated testing equipment.

M. Develop and distribute a brochure to publicize and promote the test to state and federal licensing officials each year.

N. Produce booklet on recommended model legislation for rider education and licensing bills and plan for its distribution in 1982.

8 GOALS FOR MATCHING SELF-TEST

As a self-test of understanding of the match of objectives with goals they support, the authors invite readers to examine the following goals considered by the foundation and pick one or more of the above objectives that could be used to support and measure the goals:[39]

You may check your analysis with the key at the end of this chapter.

1. To increase the number of riders receiving quality motorcycle safety education.

2. To increase the number of license applicants participating in quality motorcycle testing programs.

3. To collect, develop, and disseminate motorcycle safety information.

4. To promote and participate in quality motorcycle safety research.

5. To represent the safety interest of the motorcycle industry in governmental activities.

6. To continually upgrade motorcycle program and personnel standards.

7. To cooperate with other organizations in pursuit of the Motorcycle Safety Foundation's mission.

8. To communicate to the public and private sectors the rights, responsibilities, and needs of motorcyclists and motorists.

NOTES

1. James A. Morrissey, "Will the Real Public Relations Professional Please Stand Up," *Public Relations Journal*, December 1978, p. 25. *Profile/83* (San Francisco: IABC, 1983), p. 3.
2. Walter Lindenmann and Alison Lapetina, "Management's View of the Future of Public Relations," *Public Relations Review* 7 (Fall 1981): pp. 3–4.

3. Matthew M. Miller, "Corporate Public Relations Update," *Public Relations Journal*, December 1982, pp. 21–24.
4. IPRA *Gold Paper No. 4: A Model for Public Relations Education for Professional Practice* (Dorset, England: International Public Relations Association, 1982), p. 8.
5. Ibid., pp. 9–10.
6. Otto Lerbinger, quoted in *Business Week*, "The Corporate Image: PR to the Rescue," January 22, 1979, p. 54.
7. Chester Burger, quoted in Edward Langley, "Preview: Managing the PR Firm," *Public Relations Journal*, December 1978, p. 10.
8. Patrick Jackson, correspondence to Norman R. Nager, February 5, 1982.
9. Joseph F. Awad, "Taking Charge of Change" speech to the 34th National Conference of the Public Relations Society of America, Chicago, November 9, 1981.
10. Foundation for Public Relations Research and Education.
11. Printer's proofs provided by Sam Black and Melvin L. Sharpe, *Practical Public Relations* (Englewood Cliffs, N.J.: Prentice-Hall, 1983), p. 5.
12. Telephone interview with James E. Grunig, December 20, 1982, on James E. Grunig and Todd Hunt, *Managing Public Relations* (New York: Holt, Rinehart, and Winston, 1984).
13. PRSA National Assembly, transcript of adopted motion, San Francisco, November 8, 1982. (Statement reproduced in full in Chapter 9 of this book.)
14. Arjay Miller, quoted in John J. Tarrant, *Drucker: The Man Who Invented the Corporate Society* (Boston: Cahners Books, 1976), p. 32.
15. Richard H. Buskirk, quoted in Tarrant, *Drucker*, p. 77.
16. George S. Odiorne, *Management by Objectives* (New York: Pitman, 1965).
17. Jack N. Kondrasuk, "Management by Objectives: Past, Present, and Future," *Managerial Planning*, May/June 1982.
18. Ibid.
19. Ibid.
20. George S. Odiorne, "MBO: A Backward Glance," *Business Horizons*, October 1978, p. 14.
21. Stephen R. Ruth and William W. Brooks, "Who's Using MBO in Management?" *Journal of Systems Management*, February 1982, pp. 16–17.
22. Ibid.
23. David Horowitz, Southern California NBC-TV Evening News, January 28, 1982. The public relations agency was Berkhemer & Kline; the account executive, Darlene Lynch.
24. Susan Harris, cited in "MGM Grand Hotel Opening" (case study by Lynn D. Bright for advanced public relations methods class, California State University, Fullerton, December 17, 1981).
25. 1981 PRSA Silver Anvil Notebook of Clay County Jail Bond Campaign with Fleishman-Hillard.
26. 1981 PRSA Silver Anvil Notebook of New York Telephone.
27. 1981 PRSA Silver Anvil Notebook of Conti Commodity Services and Daniel J. Edelman, Inc.
28. 1981 PRSA Silver Anvil Notebook of Johnson Wax and Burson-Marsteller.
29. 1981 PRSA Silver Anvil Notebook of California Prune Board and Botsford Ketchum Public Relations.

30. Robert A. Kelly, from "A Generic PR-MBO Plan," March 1981; and correspondence to Norman R. Nager, June 26, 1981.
31. Cliff Dektar, correspondence to Norman R. Nager, December 31, 1981.
32. Stephen Gelber, cited in "John Lennon's Death from a Public Relations Point of View" (case study by Joseph Taubman for advanced public relations methods class, California State University, Fullerton, December 17, 1981).
33. 1981 PRSA Silver Anvil Notebook of Motorcycle Safety Foundation and Carl Byoir & Associates.
34. Board of Trustees, Motorcycle Safety Foundation, Draft of Five-Year Plan, January 1982.
35. 1981 PRSA Silver Anvil Notebook of Motorcycle Safety Foundation.
36. Ibid.
37. Draft of Five-Year Plan, Motorcycle Safety Foundation.
38. Ibid.
39. Ibid.

KEY TO MATCHING SELF-TEST

Goal 1—Objectives B and J.
Goal 2—Objectives A, E, L, and M.
Goal 3—Suggest your own objective.
Goal 4—Objective G.
Goal 5—Objectives C and N.
Goal 6—Objective D.
Goal 7—Suggest your own objective.
Goal 8—Objectives F, H, I, and K.

Table 2.1
Systems Concepts Overview

Concept	Definition	Corporate	PR Example
System	Set of interrelated components with a common boundary	Corporation Personnel role Employee	PR agency Campaign News releases
Component	Subsystem or part of a system	Sales division Budget Products	PR proposal Internal PR Annual report
Interrelated	Interdependency of parts or components of system, each part affecting the others	Manufacturing, R & D, sales, marketing in new products	Working with legal and personnel in labor survey
Boundary	Area between one system and another, differentiating them	Responsibility and function of each dept.	Differences that define your publics
Suprasystem	Mother system or a controlling system that may include multiple systems	Trade assn. Conglomerate Trustees, CEO Stockholders	PRSA, IABC Agency head Goals Corporation
Wholes	System greater than sum of its parts; looking at parts as they interact rather than fragmented units	The economic environment — poverty, rates of interest, and inflation	Organization reputation for products, services, and policies
Interact	Components or parts affecting one another in a way that creates a new, dynamic system	Product demand and new markets; competition and new objectives	Video, print, interpersonal campaign materials
Levels	Perspective on where you choose to enter a system; beginning point for examining a system; view of a system as hierarchy	Publics chosen by degree of intensity of opinion on an issue	Publication Graphics Written text Theme Evaluation Results
Feedback	Information that is systematically sought or randomly obtained and used for control purposes	Sales reports Market surveys Focus groups Investor data Trend analysis	Opinion polls Field test Interviews Pre/posttest Reader survey

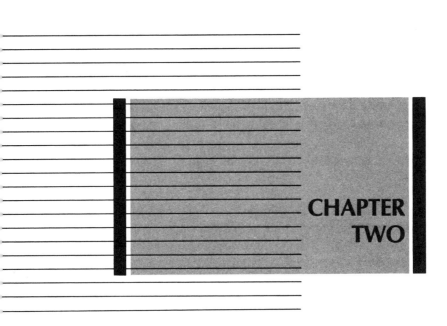

PR-MBO AS A
MANAGEMENT SYSTEM

THE ECONOMIC AND SOCIAL CLIMATE

*As we move toward the beginning of the twenty-first century it becomes
increasingly apparent that the public relations profession has arrived at
a watershed in its history. Public relations is being asked to contribute
its full share to the growth and—sometimes—survival of the organization.*

In a period of turbulent social environments and economic uncertainty, organizations from corporations to universities have had to adapt
to a world of limited funds. This kind of climate is characterized by
declining revenues; limited growth; obsolescence of once modern operations; fierce competition in domestic and overseas markets; new demands
from government and special-interest groups; and upheavals in social
values that have an impact on investors, customers, and employees.
All this has placed an enormous burden on the communication systems
of any organization.

For example, an organization must find a way to communicate with credibility to stockholders the reasons why top management believes sales and, ultimately, profits will increase. Or a manufacturing plant must discover a way to combat crippling rumors that massive layoffs are planned. Or managers must develop new communication strategies for boosting morale and productivity among employees.

From such examples, it is evident that communication will play an even more central role in the managing of organizations. Naturally, public relations increasingly is expected to provide more expertness to top management in the form of research findings and counsel.

To be able to give pragmatic, sound counsel, the contemporary professional strives not only to understand causes and potential impacts of problems facing the organization but also to offer advice in such a managerial context that it is easily understood—and accepted—by top management.

The challenge is to find the most effective strategy to grasp the essence of the problem and then communicate viable options for its solution in such a way that a policy maker can take immediate action.

THE SYSTEMS APPROACH

You may discover a body of knowledge—general systems theory—that can be quite useful. Theory is simply used here as a practical device for thinking about your problems in a common-sense way. You can think of general systems theory as a road map to guide you through a complex system of alternate paths to your desired destination. This chapter presents a short course in understanding how the symbols on that general systems road map are used.

TWO WAYS TO APPLY SYSTEMS

We use general systems theory in two ways: First, we use systems concepts to help you discover the causes of your employer's public relations problems. Second, we use these same concepts to help you communicate your solutions to management in a way that is meaningful to them. This shows how late-twentieth-century public relations management by objectives is actually based on systems concepts. In fact, your success in using PR-MBO depends on a good understanding of systems.

As a practicing public relations professional, you can easily get drawn into a whirlwind of activities that consume much time and energy. And after all this is done, the results of your public relations efforts may be relatively negligible in comparison to what you and top management may expect of public relations.

Much of the high effort–low productivity syndrome likely stems from an incomplete understanding of the problems today's public relations professionals face. Perspective could be too limited by what is not anticipated. It is easy to find energies concentrated upon working on only a portion of the problem, or possibly even a symptom. Worse, you may find the same problems returning again and again in slightly different guises to consume your valuable time and drain your creative drive.

The strategy is to treat a problem's causes rather than symptoms. A beginning point for doing this is to get a broader perspective. This is done by focusing on the *whole* problem, not just the part you see in front of you.

An important systems concept is: *General systems theory stresses the importance of the whole.* Systems theory says that to really understand the whole problem, you strive to determine the root causes. For example, if an organization suffers from a poor image (in the sense of reputation for product or service, how the publics perceive the organization), and if you are to really understand why, you must try to discover all the important factors that contribute to this poor image. If you do that, then you have a whole or comprehensive understanding of the problem.

A DEFINITION OF SYSTEMS

A system is a set of *components* that are *interrelated* and have a *boundary*. A corporation serves as a model of this systems definition.

A corporation includes a board of directors, departments, people, budgets, and so on. All these parts (components) interact and depend upon one another to produce the corporation's products or services. Any corporation, like any system, has a boundary that separates one system from another, just as General Motors is separate from Ford.

Components Defined

Systems theory offers you, as a public relations professional, the power to decide which *components*, or parts, to concentrate upon in analyzing systems. For example, you might focus on the interactions of the board of directors and top management in examining their communication problems. Or you could focus on the budget process by looking at each department's budget as a component of the corporation's overall budget.

As parts of a system, components can be used to refer to any number of things, from people to airplanes to news releases.

In a sense, what is a component (a synonym is *subsystem*) also can be viewed as a system in its own right if it consists of a collection of smaller parts. For instance, a corporation may be composed of three major divisions: manufacturing, sales, and research and development. Each is a component, or subsystem, that can be looked at for analysis. In turn, each can be broken down into smaller components. The sales division may be broken into management team, marketing personnel, support staff, and sales personnel. Or you may go down another level to sales people in a particular line of merchandise or geographical district. This illustrates the versatility, utility, and power of systems use of components.

Interrelated Defined

Interrelated, in the systemic sense, means that each component affects and is in turn affected, to varying degrees, by every other component in the system. This notion of interdependency has important implications for problem solving.

To illustrate, consider the communication exchanged among departments or individuals within the organization: A sales person in the field gets a request for a particular kind of product and relays this information to the research and development department. If the R & D people think it is feasible, they may approach sales executives or marketing to do a further analysis of the potential. And if the idea seems worthwhile, the manufacturing division will be consulted and, eventually, will receive specifications on what to produce. Finally, the sales person who generated the original idea will go out in the field to sell it.

This full-circle example illustrates interdependency. Actually, you'd probably see the creation of a committee or task force representing these divisions to form the whole new product system. The ARCO case study near the end of the chapter illustrates this.

Boundary Defined

The *boundary* of a system is that area between it and another system. On a simple level, the walls of a room, the borders of neighboring countries, or your skin constitute a boundary.

When two systems overlap, a new, or third, system has been created. For instance, advertising and public relations normally are separate functions. However, institutional advertising may present an area of overlap between the two departments—a system of joint advertising–public relations responsibility (see Figure 2.1).

For another perspective of boundaries, consider this university example: One way to look at boundaries is to identify the various departments. For instance, the history department is separate from the busi-

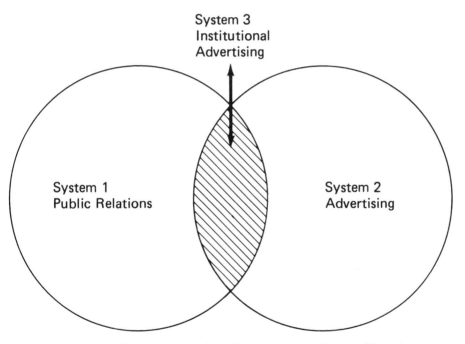

FIGURE 2.1 Illustrating Interface. Two systems such as public relations and advertising may overlap, as they do in this illustration of how institutional advertising represents an area of interface between the two original systems. The overlap of the two systems also creates a third system—part advertising, part public relations, but really a separate system with its own unique set of characteristics and boundaries.

ness division. Each has its own curriculum, majors, requirements, faculty, administration, different responsibilities, functions, and purposes. The dividing lines *are* the boundaries.

The real utility of a systems perspective is to enable you to look at the world from a particular viewpoint and make some sense of its complexity. It also enables you to look at complicated problems and see them as wholes rather than unrelated parts. And it helps you to avoid overlooking an important factor (component) before moving to a solution.

PUBLIC RELATIONS AS A SYSTEM

The PR Department as an Organizational Model

You can look at a public relations department as a system or just as easily view it as a component, or part, of the larger system of the organization. If you view it as a system, the employer organization could be called a *suprasystem* or a collection of related systems.

The public relations department operates in relation to a number of other divisions or systems of the organization. It might be considered a component of a system that includes staff services together with legal and other departments that are not a direct part of production and distribution of the employer's products or services.

Public relations may be seen as a component in a system in which marketing, advertising, and industrial relations form the other components. Public relations is interrelated with these and other systems of the organization.

The funds public relations spends come out of a corporate budget that is limited. So what another department is allocated may affect what all others can receive.

If public relations creates a videotaped news-and-feature production aimed at improving productivity, retention of employees, or quality-control efforts, that role represents interrelations with a number of other systems within the company. But that same video production may be seen on another systemic level as a point of *interface*, the place where two systems come into contact.

Consider the systemic impact on the time and other resources invested in the audiovisual system. And consider the impact on every other system of the company that provides locations or personnel to be filmed (and thus is disrupted), and on the organization as a whole if each employee is taken away from other activities to spend 15 minutes watching the production.

Other Perspectives of a PR System

In looking at the public relations functions of an organization, a department could be divided into components by areas of responsibilities or skills or levels of employees. Similarly, activities could serve as systems or components, such as the annual report system, the newsletter system, the media relations system, and the governmental relations system.

You can look beyond the company itself and conceive of the other organizations in that field as systems of a greater suprasystem.

Competition and cooperation provide interrelations. And members of an entire industry (suprasystem) are affected by legislation, scandals that hurt one company and end up having an impact on the reputation of all, or progress that reflects well on the suprasystem.

Or you can view an employer as part of a community system, state system, regional system, national system, or world system. That is where a number of publics come into play in their interrelationship with your system. The boundaries may at times be obscure in dividing the interests of the publics with which your client interacts.

Or you could think in terms of systems of public relations problems and programs.

SYSTEMS CONCEPTS

Several concepts of systems may illustrate the utility of systems thinking to public relations practice. Table 2.1 at the beginning of the chapter provides an overview of these concepts.

Wholes

Any problem that is fairly complex tends to have many causes. The task of the problem solver is to discover these causes. Rather than attempt a piecemeal approach, the real effort must focus on the whole.

A *wholes* perspective not only incorporates all causes that can be identified but also focuses on how those factors interact to affect or cause the problem. News releases, for instance, may do nothing to change the poor reputation of an organization whose product has been recalled. The product is simply defective. And this causes the bad image, regardless of the quality of the news releases. Now, if the news releases follow upon the actual improvement of the product and service to consumers, then the public relations professional is taking steps to solve the problem from the *wholes* perspective.

When you deal with the tasks at hand, you must see as many components, or parts, of the problem (system) as possible. This is known as the descriptive phase of problem solving, and the more complete it is, the better the chance of generating effective solutions. Pragmatic considerations may make it impossible to completely analyze every possible system or component and the process of interaction that may be involved in a given problem. Computerized information processing may provide a great deal of help.

The key point to remember is that by developing a greater sensitivity to describing the whole, the professional lessens the chances of inadequate description. And description provides the foundation for investigation and analysis.

Greater sensitivity may be gained in at least two ways:

1. Understand that most problems are extremely complex and that the first "shoot-from-the-hip" description may be too simplistic. Many problems are nonseparable. That is, *problems are more than the sum of their parts; the parts, working together, create a dynamic whole.*

Common problems such as poverty, inflation, human rights, pollution, and energy use are nonseparable, as beleaguered policy makers now realize. This is not to say such problems cannot be solved. But to solve them requires that you have a good grasp of the parameters of the problem—what it includes and what it does not include. It is easy to overlook an important element or forget to rule out a particular characteristic that may not be present in a particular case.

2. Another way to become more sensitive to describing wholes is to use the analogy of the pebble dropped in a pond. First, draw a circle around what you consider the core of the problem—such as a poor perception of your organization by consumers. Now draw a larger circle around this one in which you begin to list what is causing this poor image—such as lack of awareness of what your firm actually produces. Now draw another circle describing the cause of this. Con-

tinue to ask, "What causes this?" until you have exhausted all possible reasons.

Many problems have multiple causes, and these may have to be taken into consideration in developing objectives, strategies, research, consultation, and evaluation.

Interaction

Unfortunately, after you have done the hard work of adequately describing the problem as a whole, more hard work remains. Because systems are more than just the simple product of addition, their parts must be studied as they interact rather than as separate entities.

An electric typewriter or computer terminal is made of many parts, but when you start it and press the letters on the keyboard, those parts begin to interact to create a whole with a force all its own. And so it is with most real-world problems.

It is easy to forget this principle of systems. When it is forgotten, "solutions" that fail abound. An indication of this is found when seemingly effective solutions are generated by managers at one level in the organization and fail to work after they are passed to another level for implementation.

That happens because implementation requires *interaction*, and interaction factors such as communication and motivation are vastly different from the neat descriptions of so-called independent parts managers may supply. For instance, a well-written news release may be quite different from the story that actually appears in tomorrow's edition.

A key point to remember: *You can never do only one thing in a system without affecting other parts of it.*

For example, suppose executives think only one group of employees reads the internal newsletter. All other components of the organizational system, other employee groups, executives, board members, and even visitors may read it. Information is disseminated to all parts of the system, whether intended or not. Ideally you would have separate editions for different subpublics. Pragmatically you may not have the resources to define the target publics as much as you would like. But at least you sensitize yourself to the diversity of readers exposed.

Sometimes an editor who needs an executive's approval before going to print may think of only the one system—how that executive will react—rather than the objectives for the greater publics for which the publication is written. Obviously you also have to be concerned with this public of one. Public relations professionals are concerned with internal, as well as external, publics. This may require interpretation to an executive of the why and how of communication to others.

Levels

One of the most powerful concepts from systems theory is the notion of *levels*. Real-world systems can be exceedingly large and therefore difficult to describe. A beginning point is to view systems imbedded in other systems, much as an onion is composed of one layer on top of another. You may discover a hierarchy to a system in which you find different components at different levels.

Suppose somebody wanted you to conduct an attitude survey of the "general public." On closer examination that person would find that the general public is not so "general" after all. It may consist of opinion leaders on different subjects for different groups of individuals, and many other distinct publics, including disinterested citizens.

In rethinking objectives for doing the attitude survey, you realize that what is really wanted is the information from a particular public of opinion leaders. Now you draw your sample and phrase questions to elicit the information from this group. You have succeeded in categorizing the vague, all-encompassing "general public" system into a hierarchal system and have focused on one level of it. In so doing, you have analyzed one component of the system while not losing sight of the whole.

This systemic concept of levels gives you great flexibility when you attempt to deal with a complex problem because it allows you to enter the system at that point where it is most advantageous to your purposes. For example, if your client experiences problems in gaining coverage in the local media, you may approach the situation at several levels:

- Is the problem related to the quality of writing?
- Could your client and the local media be operating under different definitions of what constitutes news or feature value?
- Might local media style or deadlines be inadvertently over-

looked because of pressure to issue all-purpose releases to a diversity of media?

- Does the problem lie in timing your backgrounders, news conferences, or releases on heavy news days?

This is a "levels" question in the sense of where the problem originates. Once that is identified, you enter at the causal level to generate a solution.

Assume the primary cause may be what the media gatekeepers perceive as content that does not meet their needs. Then the corrective step is to enter the problem at this level and diagnose and provide counsel on improvement of the writing.

Probabilistic Causes

One of the effects of systems theory on the scientific community and, more recently, on the management world is to do away with simple cause-and-effect explanations. Only the simplest systems can be described to behave in clear predictable ways, such as "A causes B to happen."

The systems with which professionals have to cope in public relations cannot be predicted in such deterministic fashion. In fact, systems can only be predicted to probably behave in a certain way, so you refer to them as *probabilistic* systems.

Much of this is due to the principle of interaction. The components have ranges of behaviors they may adopt: for example, a survey respondent may "strongly agree" now, but "agree somewhat" at a later date. Similarly, what worked in one product promotion campaign may not in another.

Rarely, if ever, does a single cause account for the behavior of a complex system. Usually many causes work in some combination that forces a system to assume its current posture. Labor strife or inflation does not stem from a single cause.

This is not to say that systems are unpredictable. In fact they are predictable, but *not* with complete certainty. For complex systems, it makes sense to discuss only what will probably happen. In the uncertain world in which public relations professionals have to function, this notion of probabilistic systems is extremely important because of the power it brings to analysis and counsel.

Conversely, if you want to cause something to happen, as in persuasion for attitude change, the situation will likely take more than one stimulus.

It seems so commonsensical to talk in terms of probabilities rather than absolutes. Yet think back to a recent conversation in which someone said, "All you have to do is this, and that will happen." Something very similar to this way of thinking occurred in public relations for years with some people saying, "If you want to persuade or change attitudes, issue a press release or distribute a newsletter or brochure."

Feedback

Multiple causes of most public relations problems make *feedback* especially important. Feedback can be used to suggest root sources of the problem and where to make corrective adjustments so that communication and action programs are on course. Feedback in problem solving and prevention can be used as a diagnostic and prescriptive tool.

Most important, professionals systematically solicit feedback rather than wait for random, fragmented, unexpected information. And that feedback is systematically analyzed. This is the difference between a poll of a cross section of publics and a scattering of letters or calls from unhappy consumers.

The trend in public relations is to quantitative prediction in terms of numbers and percentages. It is one thing to tell a CEO that there is a market out there and another to define the market and project its patterns. That is what CEOs mean when some say they want better information from their public relations directors concerning public predispositions to behavior.

To the typical CEO, this means you are responsible for all that your department does or fails to do. To manage such a system, you use reliable feedback to exercise any control.

The *output*, the product of public relations work, is compared with some standard or goal and the variance, if any, is fed back to the producing unit to correct the discrepancy. You make corrections over time as feedback indicates they are needed.

Newcomers to public relations sometimes have difficulty with the notion that feedback analyses and adjustments constitute a continuous, ongoing process, not an occasional or end-of-project operation.

Feedback Loop

To progress in systems thinking for public relations, consider the concept of *feedback loop* and this analogy: Recall that NASA typically controls space vehicles by short bursts of trajectory rockets to keep them on course. But Mission Control needs feedback to do this.

First, NASA must program acceptable limits for trajectory and have controls built into their space systems to continuously monitor how they are doing in staying on course. Then, Mission Control requires data to alert it to needed corrections. And once the corrections are sent across space, Mission Control must have additional feedback to assure that the corrective bursts work as they should.

This continuing feedback forms a loop, much as the feedback you wish to have when you counsel change, plan communication with critical publics, and follow through.

SYSTEMS AND PUBLIC RELATIONS ROLES

Multiple causality (the combination and interaction of a number of causes in given problems) together with increased demands within the modern organization lend themselves to the wedding of PR-MBO and systems thinking.

To manage today's public relations department requires a planning process that will help you choose with greater clarity where you are going, where you need to go, and how to get there. Both management by objectives and a systems perspective are needed.

CEOs view such a perspective—with planning, stated objectives, and measured outcomes—as indicators of professional management of public relations. Executives reward men and women who are capable of assuming new responsibilities and levels of managerial proficiency.

The PR Profession as a System

This perspective requires viewing of the profession, as well as daily public relations activities, as part of a larger system. To borrow a systems concept, this means not only doing things right but, on another level, also doing right things.

Modern professionals who view their employers as systems in which all parts interact are helped to most effectively harness and apply resources to accomplish objectives. It is unfortunate when a newcomer views the public relations department as independent of the organizational system and the public relations role as "simply to do my own thing" in daily activities—without sensitivity as to how these efforts affect other departments and the total organization. More than one CEO told us: "I don't consider any activity as either good or effective until its effect on the total system is understood."

It is not the intent of this chapter to present a full-scale description of general systems theory. The reader is directed to several references.[1] Rather, we aim here to emphasize the importance of systems concepts and give you sufficient orientation to help you build an adequate philosophical base for coping with complex problems. For, without the proper philosophical grounding, attention is soon focused on narrow daily issues and the result may well be inadequate for long-term solutions.

MBO AS A SYSTEM

The question that troubles some public relations professionals is not so much whether they want to assume a more managerial role but how this can be accomplished effectively. What strategies, methods, and tools are available to help make the transition?

The *management by objectives system* provides a useful tool. In essence, MBO provides a systematic means of achieving desired ends. This section explains how PR-MBO actually creates a management system within an organization. The M and the O in MBO are really system components in the overall management system philosophy.

M Stands for *Management*

A common practice when considering management by objectives is to focus attention only on the objectives. Equal attention should be given to the word, "management."

This emphasis is underscored because MBO is both a management technique and a philosophy. When there is no understanding that *MBO is a philosophy for managing the entire organizational system*, this useful tool loses much of its power.

O Stands for *Objective*

Today there remain managers whose managerial philosophy often has been described in the literature as the "fly-by-the-seat-of-the-pants," or subjective, approach. A closer look at the word "objective" indicates that it is the opposite of "subjective." It seems reasonable to conclude that Peter Drucker had such a distinction in mind when he first used these two terms. [2]

Drucker, and many other management experts who embraced the objective-subjective dichotomy in MBO, meant that a person must manage by *measurable (objective) criteria rather than personal thoughts or instincts (subjective)*. This approach emphasizes precisely stated and verifiable-by-systematic-evaluation results as opposed to rationalization based on personal feelings.

The modern organization, with a multitude of forces coming from a turbulent environment, is much too complex to be managed by the unsystematic swings of mood and thought so common to the subjective style. Under an objective approach, MBO has come to mean a style that attempts to compare a set of formal organizational procedures with a set of performance criteria. In fact, Dallas T. DeFee concluded: "Advocates of MBO assert that it is to management what the scientific method is to research—a guiding framework for the conduct of management activities." [3]

As a philosophical guide, MBO is in phase with the complex and often crisis-laden times. Forced to make managerial decisions, today's public relations professionals need all the help that can be secured to function successfully. And that management system must be sensitive to sudden change. The manager in the last few years of the twentieth century will acquire an increasingly anticipatory behavior rather than just respond to events.

4 COMPONENTS OF THE MBO SYSTEM

Although components of the MBO system may be labeled under different names by various writers, their functions are rather universal. An MBO writer, Dale D. McConkey, has identified them succinctly. And with slight modification, we present his four crucial components: [4]

1. Goals and objectives
2. Plans for implementation
3. Control
4. Feedback

Nager and Allen have adapted McConkey's verbal concepts to a graphic symbolization of their interaction in Figure 2.2.

Goals and Objectives Component

The goals and objectives component of the system represents statements by the manager on what he or she plans to accomplish in a given time period. Such statements reflect whatever priorities management believes the organization's internal publics must focus on.

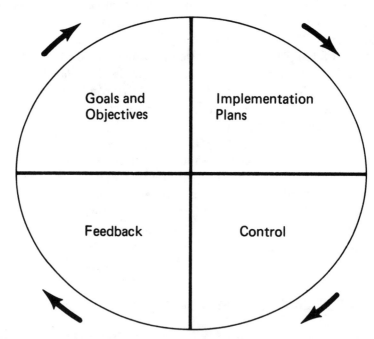

FIGURE 2.2 How Four Components Interact in MBO System. As indicated by the arrows, the components interact to create the working MBO system. Goals and objectives spring from feedback and lead to implementation of your plans and that leads to controlling mechanisms that lead full circle to feedback.

Well-formulated objectives provide direction for management as specific descriptions of events to happen, results to be accomplished. *An ideal objective will tell* WHO *will achieve* WHAT *and* WHEN *and* HOW. *The goal that an objective supports provides the* WHY.

Plans and Implementation Component

The plans and implementation component focuses on the actions you must take to achieve the objective. A set of well-written objectives can do nothing on their own; the manager must plan how to actually implement them—what must be done to turn the objectives into action.

Control Component and Measurement

Measurement is at the crux of the third component, control. Even if good implementation plans get the objectives in motion, the effective manager must maintain control over the process. There must be some means of determining how, if at all, the action is moving toward the stated target.

Feedback Component

Unless the state of progress in attaining the objectives is fed back to the manager in the form of relevant information, no corrective action can be taken to get back on target.

C. West Churchman has defined a system as a "set of parts coordinated to accomplish a set of goals."[5] In the realm of public relations practice, this means that you could have difficulty in meeting your objectives unless you coordinate the four components of the PR-MBO system.

We have developed a graphic illustration of the diamond core and the suprasystem whole of PR-MBO systems in Figure 2.3.

INFLUENCE AT TWO LEVELS

As a management system, MBO exerts its influence at two levels of the organization—macro and micro—and both are important to the public relations professional.

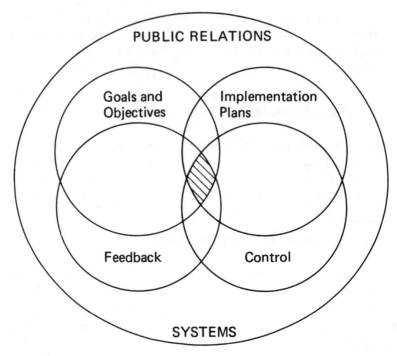

FIGURE 2.3   PR-MBO Suprasystem. The shaded or diamond area represents the overlap of all four components as they form the MBO system. The
larger area outside the four circles (components) illustrates the public relations
suprasystem. Without any of the four components, MBO as a system is actually
incomplete. If one of the four components is missing, the operation of the
system will be ineffective. Notice how each of the components is embedded
in a larger system as well as interacting with all others.

Consistent with our earlier discussion, the presence of MBO is
felt at what social scientists call the macro level, the level of the organization as a whole. If we define an "ideal" organization as a set of
individuals working for a common goal, such as earning profits or
providing services, then it is easy to see the necessity for any organized
group of individuals to understand and agree upon the goals and objectives—the purposes—before them.

However, it is quite common for an organization, on undertaking
PR-MBO, to discover that groups often have contradictory purposes,
and many of these are in conflict with the overall organizational goals.

Working Together for Common Goals

Some organizational theorists argue that an organization can best be understood as a hierarchy of goals and that management's main task is to organize work activities to accomplish the objectives that support these goals. The role of PR-MBO in such a view is to make sure that all work activities do support these stated goals and that a particular department or division does not pursue contrary results.

PR-MBO's purpose is to develop an organization-wide team concept. Goals become components of the organizational system and are interlocked with one another. From this perspective, PR-MBO as a managerial philosophy is saying that although it may be best for your particular goals "to do your own thing," it may be detrimental to the organization as a whole. A major strength of a system of managing by objectives, then, is the clarification of organizational goals.

PR-MBO exerts its influence at the second level—the micro, or small unit level—where the primary concern is with you as an individual, the public relations person performing in a managerial capacity. From this viewpoint, we are concerned with how your behavior using PR-MBO can be supportive of the organizational goals. In other words, how do you fit into the overall scheme of things? It is common sense that individuals who understand their own roles well tend to perform more effectively.

Working Together in Creating Objectives

PR-MBO helps provide clarity of role and mission by establishing an environment that induces people to plan and communicate together. Because objectives are not written in isolation but are normally worked out with the executive to whom you report, this means that close interaction may take place.

Out of this interaction, you have a chance to learn as well as to communicate the role of public relations in the organization. This is crucial if you are to assume the expanded role envisioned by the CEO. To do this, you must know the results you are expected to produce and how they will contribute to the organization's overall mission. For instance, to perform effectively in a new effort to boost employee morale, you will want to know the organization's policy on unionization, cost-of-living adjustments, promotions from within, handling of grievances, and so much more.

On the micro—or individual—level, PR-MBO can be extremely useful to you in trying to run your office more effectively. PR-MBO makes it clear that the only yardstick for measuring performance is results (not activities).

For the practitioner burdened by excessive paperwork, PR-MBO argues that paperwork is rarely a measure of effectiveness. As you implement or strengthen your PR-MBO systems, you get away from paperwork for the sake of paperwork.

On the individual level of role development and more job efficiency, you use PR-MBO to decide what someone in your position is required to achieve. In actual practice, you may apply PR-MBO to help your executive discover that you are currently held responsible for important duties for which you do not have the resources (time, staff, funds, etc.) or authority. That is not a guarantee of aid, but it is a necessary beginning.

THE ARCO PR-MBO SYSTEMS MODEL

To illustrate the systems concepts and the marriage of management by objectives and public relations, we present an original case study on ARCO—Atlantic Richfield Co. This case shows how an organization puts PR-MBO into practice.

The case centers on an attempt by the corporation to create a new issues management suprasystem, a collection of relatively well defined and closely related systems that would combine the resources of four major public relations divisions within ARCO.

By way of background, consider that ARCO ranked 15th among the *Fortune* 500 with more than 45,000 employees producing in excess of $20 billion in sales a year for the diversified energy and minerals corporation when then-President Thornton Bradshaw (subsequently, RCA board chairman) gave fresh impetus to new directions in public relations.

The corporation in 1980 had begun a creative audit and new thrust in strategic public relations planning and issues identification. An internal report to ARCO public relations management concluded:[6]

It will be important to begin a more systematic process to identify needs, formulate PR tools and assess or evaluate the impact of PR programs. With increasing frequency, management will demand that we quantify the impacts and benefits of our efforts.

It will be important for PR to demonstrate to the operating companies and other corporate units that we are as concerned about productivity and efficiency in our areas as they are in theirs.

This will require the establishment of priorities on possible measures of effectiveness, including a strong linkage between analysis and action. This involves relating external factors to the internal dynamics of the company, a function of planning which must also relate closely to all PR functions. Such a process should help us decide what programming projects . . . and which expenditures will be most effective. . . .

One of the difficult and elusive concepts for PR involves developing measures of effectiveness. *A basic starting point for a more systematic process of program development and assessment is to identify objectives and priorities for each of the PR functional areas.* In addition to evaluating existing programs, of course, efforts should be directed to future programs and activities in advance of implementation.

To assure credibility and effectiveness, the planning process must establish a framework for the orderly development and assessment of new programs, including use of attitude surveys, assessment of the external environment and issues tracking and analysis. . . .[7]

In just about a decade, the professional public relations staff had more than quadrupled to over 100. During the same period the overall number of ARCO employees had doubled.

Through the early 1970s "the modus operandi, the way of doing public relations, had been pretty traditional, maybe reactive, but growing in sophistication," Special Projects Manager Manuel Jimenez explained.[8] The signs were clear enough that Jimenez returned to college. He earned his MBA in 1982.

A Formal System for Objectives and Strategies

For ARCO, sophistication meant the creation of a new multidisciplinary issues management task force and a new position of manager of planning and analysis–public affairs as opening steps.

Norman H. Emerson, who was appointed to that position, previously served with the U.S. Secretary of Transportation, did policy analysis for a joint committee of the California State Legislature, and headed the Los Angeles mayor's policy and research office. In commenting on his intensive study of ARCO and other corporate systems needs, Emerson said:

> There was a certain level of accountability that other departments had, a recognition of budgetary restraints on the horizon. There needed to be some sort of formal system in place for objectives to achieve and strategies to achieve them.[9]

To initiate the new ARCO Issues Management System, the four managers of public relations were invited to the first meeting and then each nominated up to three persons from their respective groups to participate in future sessions. The committee of these nominees formed the new suprasystem. Then the other related organizational systems of government relations and planning were brought into the picture.

Special Projects Manager Jimenez explained the building block process this way:

> The initial challenge was in trying to determine who we should be, who else outside of public relations should be involved, how high we could go in involving upper corporate management. We wanted to go as high and as broad as possible.[10]

According to Planning and Analysis Manager Emerson, the initial thrust was to lay out external environment risks and opportunities and outline how public relations and government relations could serve to reinforce opportunities as well as strategies for coping with hostile conditions.[11]

In a report to the Corporate Planning division, Emerson reviewed the objectives of the corporation and its operating companies and the assumptions used in development of ARCO's five-year plan for meeting these objectives. He set up a series of meetings with the public relations field staffs (Denver, Philadelphia, Anchorage, Louisville, Dallas, Chicago, Houston) and Los Angeles headquarters staff.

Emerson described what happened:

> With the field offices, we were trying to get them to provide public relations field perspective on the plans of operating companies and have them identify specific trends and issues in their areas and regions of operation. . . .

Using corporate, field staff, and our resources, we sought to explore opportunities, risks, and strategies and then move internally to activities of operating companies requiring public relations support.[12]

Emerson's own group analyzed trends of the media, calling upon media relations and other experts. They focused on 14 national issues that could have an impact on ARCO. And they provided "a snapshot of regionalized issues." Public opinion was examined as part of each issue. Examples of issues: the nationally growing concern for toxic waste disposal, the state government trends toward funding operations, and the local imposition of refinery taxes.

They examined trends in demographics as a setting for trends in public opinion, including such factors as an aging population and an increase in the proportion of Hispanics.

Their work was based on surveys to which ARCO subscribes. These include:

Opinion Research Corp.
Cambridge Reports
Roper
Yankelovich, Skelly and White

By July 1981 the plan was being used as a back-up for the budgeting process. By 1982 budgeting required much more justification based on operating companies' objectives, corporate objectives, and some of the trends in the external environment. A permanent planning council of representatives from each public relations unit was established to develop more consensus on objectives and strategies, leading to more general agreement on objectives, program, and budget.

The Emerson group also began doing an in-depth survey analysis among key publics to determine why and how they held and changed attitudes in shaping their mental images of ARCO, its operating companies, and issues of concern.

Objectives and Priorities High on the Agenda

Specific agenda items for the Corporate Public Affairs Council included establishing objectives and priorities, securing placement of public relations field staff on respective operating companies' planning committees, and identification of areas where operating company management could assess or critique selected public relations programs.

The report to management started with public opinion trends and analyses and continued with societal trends including demographics and social/political environment. [13]

Matrix Approaches for Systems Analysis

In their discussion of critical issues, ARCO's planning strategists used several matrix approaches. This is similar to the systemic levels concept discussed earlier in this chapter. A matrix uses rows and columns (that you may think of as "levels") to identify the resulting interaction when systems come together.

One matrix, for instance, looked at the interaction of issue status, general impact, outlook, specific impact on company units, and proposed public relations response. Still another matrix provided an overview of corporate priorities and activities in relationship to available public relations resources.

In a particular operationalization, the report examined the energy pricing issue and reduced domestic production and suggested identification of areas for cooperation and liaison; development of consistent theme and messages about the issue; and use of communication channels including "Energy Update," speakers bureau, and executive committee. It recommended scheduling ongoing briefings with editorial boards, thought leaders, and other influential individuals.

PR-MBO AND THE C-R-E-A-T-E SYSTEM

Taken together, PR-MBO and application of principles from general systems theory provide a potent approach for the public relations person responding to the management challenges of the 1980s and '90s. PR-MBO itself may be viewed as a system, and so may the organization, its publics, problems, needs, opportunities, and environmental variables.

To show how PR-MBO and systems theory may profitably combine with the most prevalent public relations activity, writing, *Public Relations Management by Objectives* presents the logic and detailed use of this book's 10-step public relations writing by objectives system in a later chapter.

The 10-step PR-MBO writing system actually is a subsystem of the C-R-E-A-T-E system for public relations management that is graphically depicted in Chapter 3 (Figure 3.3).

C-R-E-A-T-E is an acronym for:

Communication
Research
Evaluation
Action
Time/resources planning
Energy

In Chapters 4 and 5, we discuss Communication as a system within a system, sharing in common with the PR-MBO suprasystem the central role of objectives in the form of results for both clients and publics. In Chapter 6, we bring together C-R-E-A-T-E's Research and Evaluation, into a system called Research-Evaluation, an integral part of the public relations role. In Chapter 7, we examine the remaining Action, Time/resources planning, and Energy of this PR-MBO system.

In Chapter 8, components of the C-R-E-A-T-E PR-MBO system are discussed in reviewing crisis management. And Chapter 9 reviews implementation of the system.

Before leaving this chapter, however, you are invited to apply the concepts of PR-MBO and systems thinking by listing the systems, components, and areas of interface of public relations with other parts of the organization with which you are most familiar. And you may wish to note important systems outside this organization as parts of a greater suprasystem.

You also may build analytical strengths by working with the PR-MBO self-test on systems.

THE PR-MBO SELF-TEST

How Does PR Interact With Other Systems?

To check your understanding of systems concepts as applied to PR-MBO, try filling in the columns in this chart. The left-hand column provides examples of other systems that interact with the public relations system in your organization. Space is provided for you to write in another important public and another important department with which the public relations system interacts. The middle column asks you to suggest objectives in which the interests of the public relations department and other systems named overlap, objectives that serve their mutual interests. The right hand column calls for behavior (activities or services) public relations persons would provide in support of objectives.

Other Systems	Overlapping Objectives	Supportive Behavior
News media		
Stockholders, taxpayers, or donors		
Government agencies		
Consumers		

Other Systems	Overlapping Objectives	Supportive Behavior
Community leaders		
Activist groups		
Board of Directors		
Top management		
Middle management		
Union officials		
Fill in key public:		

Other Systems	Overlapping Objectives	Supportive Behavior
Marketing department		
Industrial relations		
Legal department		
Fill in key department:		

NOTES

1. See F. K. Berrien, *General and Social Systems* (New Brunswick: Rutgers University Press, 1968); L. von Bertalanffy, *General Systems Theory* (New York: Braziller, 1968); Ervin Laszlo, *The Relevance of General Systems Theory* (New York: Braziller, 1972); T. H. Allen, *New Methods in Social Science Research* (New York: Praeger, 1978); and James G. Miller, *Living Systems* (New York: McGraw-Hill, 1978).
2. Peter Drucker, *The Practice of Management* (New York: Harper & Row, 1954).
3. Dallas T. DeFee, "Management by Objectives: When and How Does It Work?" *Personnel Journal*, January 1977, p. 37.
4. Dale D. McConkey, *MBO for Nonprofit Organizations* (New York: AMACOM, 1975), p. 13.
5. C. West Churchman, *The Systems Approach* (New York: Dell, 1977), chap. 3.
6. ARCO, internal management report, December 1981.
7. Ibid.

8. Manuel Jimenez, interviews, July 29, 1981; December 5, 1981; and February 4, 1983, Los Angeles and Westminster, California.
9. Norman H. Emerson, interview, July 29, 1981, Los Angeles.
10. Jimenez, interviews.
11. Emerson, interview.
12. Ibid.
13. ARCO, internal report.

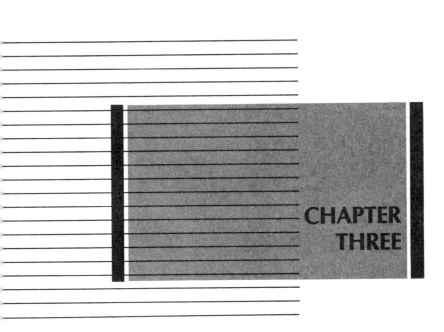

CREATING GOALS AND OBJECTIVES

CLEARING AWAY CONFUSION

This chapter focuses on two key terms from the PR-MBO system, goals and objectives, and how to write them. PR-MBO goals and objectives are written to provide a common language for public relations professionals, their CEOs, and other top management personnel. By adapting the how-to guidelines of business administration for writing MBO goals and objectives, you provide for more effective communication with those you supervise and persons to whom you report, as well as with other departments in the organization.

TERMS NOT INTERCHANGEABLE

Adopting PR-MBO requires careful thinking and a clear focus on what you want to accomplish. The organizational and business literature is full of ambiguous statements made by those trying to articulate their goals and objectives. Actually, the writing of goals and objectives is not too hard once you understand the purposes behind each term.

A major area of confusion results from using "goals" and "objectives" to mean the same thing. The terms are distinct concepts and should not be used as synonyms for one another.

If you hear someone say, "I met my goal," then you have actually heard someone confuse a goal with an objective. A goal—in the language of MBO and PR-MBO—is more than a specific situation that you would like to see occur. A goal is a broad statement that points you or your organization in a particular direction.

A simple analogy may be drawn between north on a compass and a goal. Just as the compass needle points north, so do goals indicate the direction toward which an organization, department, or person is moving or attempting to move. You never arrive at "north." Conversely, you need to follow the direction to drive 200 miles up the highway to your destination or objective.

Direction = goal; destination = objective. Goals actually guide the development of objectives. Even though goals cannot be fully attained, they give direction or purpose to the organization or manager. That is why they are so important.

"I want to present the best image of my organization to the community," for example, is reasonable as a goal. But it cannot be met because there is always something under the heading "best" that can be added.

The critical point in writing goals, then, is to keep asking, Where does this lead?

HOW TO WRITE GOALS

Identify Responsibilities

A natural place to begin when writing goals is to identify the major responsibilities of the job. Although someone in public relations must respond to unexpected situations or problems, many tasks are handled on a regular basis. These become fertile areas for goal setting.

Goals may be generated from a particular job activity. For instance, the publishing of a company newsletter may be viewed from the perspective of future, but needed, improvements. However, it can also be judged from the perspective of maintenance activities in which careful attention is needed to keep it running satisfactorily. The appropriate goal statement may be phrased with either improvement or maintenance in mind.

Time is also important to keep in mind when writing goals. Usually goals are written for 1, 5, or even 10-year periods, but they could be written for much shorter periods.

Goals may be divided into two major types, organizational and personal. Organizational goals refer to statements that reflect the broad concerns of the public relations department and client. These are interdependent and support one another. Personal goals reflect your individual aims as a public relations professional. Personal goals refer to the directions in which you wish to move.

There is no reason why organizational and personal goals should contradict each other. Personal goals should actually support the broader organizational goals. For instance, a public relations agency might have as a goal "increase agency business during the next year." This could be supported by a counselor in the agency having a personal goal to "increase my client load during the next year." (Once the agency and counselor set the minimal acceptable level of increase for the 12-month period and specify the kinds of business and load, they move from goals to objectives.)

Examples of Public Relations Goals

Here are some examples of public relations goal statements:

- Improve the organization's reputation in the local community.
- Provide better service to agency clients.
- Increase morale among company employees.
- Promote favorable media coverage of the organization.
- Establish more effective government relations.
- Strengthen the company's image among potential investors.
- Operate the public relations department effectively.
- Position the public relations division more in the center of corporate communication.
- Generate cost-effective measures for your projects.
- Build evaluation criteria into all client accounts.

Chart Your Personal Professional Goals

To strengthen understanding and build skills in writing goals, it would be helpful to practice on a personal level. In the chart of "Personal Professional Goals," we have created typical situations that a public relations professional encounters. To cope with the situation, you need to write a personal goal.

To get you started, we have given you some possible goals as examples. After examining the situations, try writing your goals in the blank space provided. Later, you may wish to advance to a higher stage of developing personal professional situations and the goals to accompany them.

Continuing education programs of both the PRSA and IABC provide materials and training in this area. We also wish to recommend the seminal work for public relations professionals: *Your Personal Guidebook: To Help You Chart a More Successful Career in Public Relations*, written by Kalman B. Druck, APR, and Ray E. Hiebert, APR, for the National Professional Development Committee of the PRSA.[1]

Personal Professional Goals Self-Test

Situation	Your Goal Statement
You perceive need to more effectively communicate with top management.	To talk same language as management. To read literature that top management reads. To attend the same professional meetings, such as American Management Association. To attend professional seminars on management. To take extension courses in management or courses toward an MBA or equivalent degree. To study background of managers. More ideas?
You wish to secure more recognition of your PR programs.	
You want to increase your understanding of research strategies.	
You wish to become better known among peers in the profession.	

You wish to be seriously considered for promotion.
You are bored with routine activities and want more creative responsibility.

Silver Anvil Winners' Goals

Here are examples of actual goal statements from winners of the Silver Anvil, the highest award for public relations professional achievement from the Public Relations Society of America:

- "Stimulate public cooperation in the murder investigation [of a score of black children] and increase police support generally"—from Atlanta Bar Association with Manning, Selvage & Lee in the "Give Our Police a Hand" public service campaign.

- "Create a positive, accurate image and keep this image highly visible with all the hospital's publics. With a change of public image, attract usage of hospital services"—from Herrick Hospital and Health Center "New Image Public Relations Program" in the nonprofit organization field of competition.

- "Make the general public aware of home ownership opportunities"—from Harshe-Rotman & Druck (before merger with Ruder & Finn) in its community relations/public information program for the U.S. Department of Housing and Urban Development.

- "Demonstrate the gas industry's sincere commitment to energy conservation"—from the Natural Gas Council of Minnesota entry in the trade associations division of community relations.

- "Heighten general awareness of the necessity for good listening and of Sperry's commitment to it"—from Sperry Corp. institutional program.

- "Improve the image of accredited schools" in the aftermath of Federal Trade Commission ruling that produced "negative publicity portraying unscrupulous practices at certain trade schools"—from Daniel J. Edelman, Inc., and National Association of Trade and Technical Schools institutional campaign.

• "Call attention to and create excitement for The Bahamas Ministry of Tourism in four primary marketing areas which had shown signs of 'softening' in advanced bookings"—from The Bahamas Ministry of Tourism and N W Ayer Public Relations Services "Salute of Sail" special observance.

• "Generate awareness among PhoneCenter employees of the Bell System's evolving marketing stance; and generate awareness and excitement among PhoneCenter employees of their changing role in the home communication market"—from Southwestern Bell employee staff/communications program.

After you have reviewed these model public relations goals, take a moment to write a strong goal statement for the most important public relations program currently under way in your organization.

CRITERIA FOR OBJECTIVES

If PR-MBO goals are by their nature unattainable, you need some means of determining if you are on course, progressing satisfactorily in the direction of your goals. Objectives provide you with that determination.

Before you write public relations objectives, it is important to discover particular qualities that powerful, effective objectives possess. Here are four such criteria:

1. *Specific results operationally defined.* An objective establishes a specific result to be achieved. And it does this in clear language that leaves no doubt about exactly what will be required.

When you use language that allows no room for ambiguity on what is required, and if you take pains to do this so your executive or other persons will be able to understand it as you do, then you are *operationally defining your objectives.*

2. *Tells who does what, when, and with which results.* An objective contains specific information. Similar to a simple news story lead, an objective should tell *what* and *when.* The "what" refers to the end result or outcome to be achieved and the "when" to the deadline or time period allowed for doing this. If the responsibility for meeting the

objective rests with someone other than you, then the objective should state the *who*.

Of course, a basic news lead serves only to attract or focus attention, guide the reader, and/or relate some of the more essential details that establish the significance of the story. But an objective serves as a hardened target. This requires the public relations department to channel critical resources and to develop strategies and tactics. So the objective may require more precision and depth than a news lead can provide.

3. *Measurability as a criterion.* An objective should be measurable. In most cases, measure refers to a quantitative (numerical) criterion. That is, an objective should contain words that describe *how much* or another measure indicative of whether the minimum level agreed to by public relations and higher management is reached and, if so, by how much surpassed. This is needed to gauge the effectiveness of everything from overall campaign strategies and allocation of budget and staff time to use of particular tools and tactics.

If an objective cannot be measured, then you really have no way of determining if you have met it. If you have an objective that cannot be measured, then it is likely that you have written a goal statement rather than an objective.

Measurability and evaluation are explored in greater depth later in this book.

4. *Most important, make clear the benefits.* Another criterion for PR-MBO objectives statements should be the clarity of the value of the results to the overall public relations program and to the client's success in the marketplace. It bears repeating that the results sought not only should be shown to be productive, tangible benefits for the client but also for publics and the social environment.

MAKING OBJECTIVES SPECIFIC

Options for Wording

Two schools of thought concern the actual wording of objectives. The first argues that objectives should be written in a particular format—the infinitive: the objective begins with "to" followed by a verb and then the rest of the phrase. The second school takes a much more open approach and suggests that an objective may be phrased in any style as long as it meets criteria for effectiveness.

Both schools have merit, and the authors do not actually prefer one style over another. If you or a member of your staff are just beginning to write objectives, you may find it helpful to use the "to"-verb format. After gaining experience in writing objectives, you may want to switch to the more open style.

Aim for Quantification

In attempting to make your objectives specific, assume that you can quantify them. Your measures should use words that indicate how much. These would include numbers, percentages, averages, ratios, and index or baseline numbers. At a somewhat higher level of sophistication, you may wish to write objectives, or seek help in so doing, that incorporate correlations, standard deviations, and other statistical measures.

If at all possible, you should give your objectives the precision of quantitative measures. Precision can be your greatest asset when you build your supportive case for allocation of valuable public relations and organizational resources. Management will be much more open to persuasion if they can tell precisely what you are doing or plan to achieve with next year's budget and additional staff.

Counsel on Budgets

Public relations budgeting requires quantitative objectives. "Assume you have no staff, no programs" and start with the proverbial clean piece of paper in setting out to budget and provide the specifics for results and evaluation of results, public relations professionals were advised in *The Dartnell Public Relations Handbook*.[2]

"A surprising number of companies do no evaluation at all" in their public relations budgeting, according to Richard W. Darrow, former CEO and board chairman of Hill and Knowlton, and Dan J. Forrestal, former director of public relations for Monsanto Co. And they warned:

When a budget is about to be cut or an internal communication device threatened, then someone will say, "I wonder who'll miss it."

The question does not have to be "keep the [employee] newspaper or cashier it?" Instead, a better question is: "Keep it as it is or try to improve it in terms of effectiveness?"[3]

And if internal communication managers on public relations staffs are to justify budget approvals, they not only have to train, educate, and motivate but they also have to prove to management that they can achieve the necessary results, Darrow and Forrestal wrote.[4]

Similarly, they cautioned that those who deal in marketing publicity (which they equated with fund-raising publicity for hospitals, universities, and health and welfare agencies) should plan in terms of quantification when evaluating their effectiveness: "The marketing publicity specialist works toward objectives that quantify sales quotas, profitability and advertising investment."[5]

THE LANGUAGE OF SPECIFICITY

One of the best ways to add the needed specificity to your objectives is to avoid wording them with general terms. Such generalities may sound impressive but actually lack the specificity many CEOs and public relations professionals demand. Consider these worthwhile goals:

- Greatly improve efficiency.
- Develop highest standards.
- Maintain good communication.
- Increase sales.
- Increase media contacts.
- Improve public image.
- Achieve highest possible.
- Attain maximum efficiency.
- Decrease client complaints.
- Improve staff morale.
- Achieve highest quality.
- Coordinate requests.

Instead, substitute potent verbs that at least point in the direction of accomplishing something specific. For example, use these verbs, suggested and inspired by *Effective Management by Objectives*, by W. J. Reddin:[6]

Approve	Assign
Authorize	Calculate
Complete	Correct

Decide	Delegate
Determine	Distribute
Draft	Hire
Interview	Locate
Make	Notify
Organize	Outline
Plan	Prepare
Provide	Recommend
Record	Release
Request	Require
Review	Revise
Schedule	Select
Start	Submit
Summarize	Supply
Tabulate	Teach
Tell	Trace
Train	Verify
Write	

Unlike Reddin, Robert Jameson was not giving counsel on effectiveness in management by objectives but on effectiveness of professionals in obtaining job interviews and offers of positions that meet their objectives. And in *The Professional Job Changing System*, the placement expert advised readers to fill out questionnaires that had a familiar MBO ring to them:[7]

> *Significant accomplishments:* relate to sales/profits/cost savings where possible.
> Describe any *original* reports, papers, documents that you prepared or originated under your direction.
> List any of your *administrative* or procedural recommendations which were implemented.
> List *major management decisions* not covered so far or *organizational changes* in which you actively participated. . . .[8]

Accompanying the detailed questionnaires on strengths and achievements was a list of words that Jameson asked applicants to check against their own performance on present and past jobs. With the exception of words that duplicated several in the Reddin list, here are Jameson's:[9]

Administered	Analyzed
Arranged	Cataloged
Conceived	Conducted
Contracted	Controlled
Coordinated	Created
Designed	Developed
Directed	Disapproved
Enlarged	Established
Examined	Expanded
Governed	Grouped
Guided	Harmonized
Implemented	Improved
Indexed	Investigated
Managed	Moderated
Negotiated	Presented
Presided	Recruited
Rectified	Reshaped
Revised	Sorted
Straightened	Strengthened
Supervised	Systematized

If You Had to Apply for Promotion

This prompts a fascinating scenario: Imagine that you had to apply for a promotion—or to retain your present position—and place yourself in the position of the executive who would make the decision. What reliable, preferably measurable, indexes of achievement would that executive want? What could be done in the future to build in projection and measurement of effectiveness and results in your programs? Would the same approach serve to gain access, authority, staffing, budget, vital information, approvals, and other valuable resources for your programs and your work?

Using Models

Although it takes painstaking work to write objectives and build in the essential, specific measures of achievement, you can look to the models of others in the profession who have succeeded and borrow and adapt their ideas in your proposals, budgets, program planning, follow-through, and progress reports.

James F. Tirone, AT&T public relations director, for instance, has frequently shared his strategies and techniques at professional development seminars and in published reports, such as his discussion of how the Bell System went about measuring public relations.[10]

STANDARDS OF ACHIEVEMENT

One of the more difficult questions to answer when using PR-MBO is, How will I know when I have actually met my objective? The easiest way is to describe results in ways that are measurable. Here are four typical measures:

1. *Quantity: Strive for numerical measures.* Quantity is discussed more in depth after this book takes up PR-MBO system applications to public relations writing, but, in a phrase, the objective should have a numerical measure in it.

2. *Time: Set a target date.* Time is another measurement dimension of achievement. Here is an example: "Attract 10 percent more letters inquiring about the tax advantages or other benefits of life income gifts to my client's fund development director or CEO by December 30." A specific time or date is set for accomplishing the result.

3. *Costs: Aim for dollar or percent reductions.* Costs, particularly their reduction, can be used for measurement criteria. For instance: "Reduce annual printing costs for the next fiscal year by 7 percent (without sacrificing other objectives for the printed materials)."

In a period of inflationary spirals, real reductions may be in the form of holding the line or maintaining costs at the same proportion of business income.

4. *Quality: Even "better" can be quantified.* Quality measures are concerned with how well something was done. Qualitative criteria are more difficult to measure than quantitative criteria, and this is why the authors stress *how much better* over *better*.

Improvements in how investors perceive the capabilities of the management, the soundness of their securities, and the profitability for the future can be measured.

Improvements in how patients perceive the speed with which nurses respond to their calls, the warmth of the admitting personnel, the fairness of billing policies, and the preventive health practices of a medical center can be measured. So can their overall opinions of service and their responses to appeals for donations a year after hospital discharge.

Numbers for Numbers' Sake?

There are instances when the only way to measure an objective is with limited quantification, such as when you have to rely on interviews rather than surveys or the analysis of fairly objective auditors. This may be the case when baseline or comparative data are not available or if you are working in an area where the validity of the measurement criteria is not established.

In fact, to insist upon complete quantification in some cases may not be the most prudent action. To force numbers into an objective when it is unrealistic to do so will not result in a better objective. Although quantification is usually desirable, a number does not serve as a substitute for wisdom, judgment, or experience. For instance, in public relations there is no numerical substitute for sincerity, honesty, and fairness when dealing with clients or the mass media. Of course, that does not mean that the pursuit of such values prohibits quantification.

4 Guidelines for Nonquantitative Evaluation

The authors cannot point to a concrete rule that separates the quantitative from the qualitative objective. This is a task that each public relations practitioner must decide. We *can* offer this advice:

1. Determine what you are actually trying to achieve with this objective.

2. Assume you can quantify the objective.

3. Ask others to evaluate the objective to see if it is realistic. This is where judgment, wisdom, and experience count.

4. Apply the "rule of rigor" advocated by George S. Odiorne, leading MBO consultant, to "measure that which is measurable, describe that which is describable, and eliminate that which is neither."[11]

HOW TO IMPROVE WEAK OBJECTIVES

It may be helpful to examine some actual objectives the authors have collected from various public relations settings.

Meeting Employee-Employer Needs

"Develop good communication among company employees." The problem with this objective is that it is too general. It looks much more like a goal than an objective. It needs to be made more specific with some means of measuring its attainment.

It may be rewritten this way: *"By the end of the year, begin publication of a monthly newsletter distributed to all company employees."* Now you have a specific result—a newsletter—and a target date. If needed, you could write another objective telling how you are going to produce the newsletter.

That is fine as far as it goes, but it still lacks results clearly in the client's and public's interests.

A rich source for ideas for corporate publication objectives was published in 1981 as part of the Longman series on public communication. The objectives-oriented theme in *Inside Organizational Communication* was underscored by Roy G. Foltz, ABC, APR, 1981–82 president of the International Association of Business Communicators, and vice president of Towers, Perrin, Foster & Crosby. Foltz offered these policies leading to specific communications objectives:[12]

1. Better communication will encourage employees to make a greater contribution to organizational goals simply because employees will have a clearer understanding of the goals and what they mean to employees' well-being.

And, thus, they may be motivated to greater productivity, lower absenteeism, more years of service, higher participation in stock purchase or donor programs, and more, all measurable in terms of opinion, if not behavior.

2. More effective downward communication will stimulate increased ideas from employees, who will be encouraged to pass ideas upward without fear or concern that they will be considered dumb, stupid or beside the point.

So, instead of merely a mechanistic purpose of getting out 12 issues a year and monitoring effectiveness of circulation, this policy could lead to objectives measurable in terms of employee willingness to contribute ideas and of behavior in following through on modified attitudes.

3. Better communication will help secure wider support for the organization's stand on important national and local issues. And employees will be better prepared to explain the organization's position in contact with friends, neighbors, and government officials.[13]

And the actions and communications that flow from such objectives-oriented policy will bring results in the interests of employers and employees alike. These results can be projected. You need not be content with the mere initiation of *a* publication or program.

Media Relations and Publicity

Here is another objective statement in need of strengthening: *"Improve our organization's coverage in the local news media."* Again, this is the beginning of a good objective but, at the moment, it represents only an aim, not a result.

Here is an example of the way to begin improvement:

"Establish contact with reporters by meeting with them at the newspaper office by June 1." It is important that the media know who you are and that you serve as a spokesperson for your organization. Due to the frequent turnover among reporters, it is important to make sure a reporter knows whom to contact for news. This objective helps to ensure this personal contact. And you can complement it with objective statements such as these: *"Prepare news releases and hand deliver them to the news media"*; and *"Make videotapes for use on local television stations."*

Of course, both of these objectives could be improved by being more specific as to how many releases or videotapes and by what target dates.

Again, these might be sound as "production" objectives. But, unlike the production of goods and services for which an organization receives payment, the beneficial results to be secured for the client were not developed. Sophisticated public relations professionals and their executives and boards would demand more.

Even as far back as 1966, Edward G. Blinn recommended to those who handle media relations and publicity that they go beyond use of the tools of the trade in their objectives and suggested these examples of helping management "turn opportunities and problems into profits":[14]

Approach Number 1: Public relations can help to increase brand preference for a company's product by helping to build an understanding of "the company behind the product."

Approach Number 2: Turn public relations audiences into customers. . . . Consider shareowners for example.

Approach Number 3: Public relations can help a company establish an identity and leadership image in new or expanding markets.

Approach Number 4: Public relations can help develop or expand the total market for company products, particularly products where the public will have to foot the bill.

Approach Number 5: When public relations is building an understanding of the company's performance—as it must these days—it can simultaneously promote the company's products.

Of course, "promote" has turned into a cliché since the mid-1960s and the contemporary public relations professional would wish to be more precise here.

Approach Number 6: Public relations can sometimes help to overcome serious obstacles to sales and market growth, obstacles that are rooted in public misunderstanding.[15]

Objectives That Require Improvement

Another weak objective: *"Generate more effective communication with potential investors."* What is needed here is a way to keep the investment community informed of your company's activities. As a preliminary step, consider: *"Prepare a current mailing list of potential investors by July 1."* This can be refined so that it will be aimed at attitudinal and behavioral results beneficial to the client.

Here is another activity that does not qualify as an objective: *"Achieve greatest efficiency in dealing with customer complaints."* The problem is that there is no way for a public relations practitioner to plan for achieving "greatest." Here is one improvement: *"Investigate and answer customer complaints within seven days of receipt."*

Formulating Objectives

A well-written objective will cover only one end result and not a number of them. It will be written concisely and will avoid detailed descriptions of activities. And it will include a target date and be measurable.

The words in an objective must be carefully chosen so as to achieve understanding and clarity. Words can have complex and subjective meanings for different people. Precision provides a safety net. The more precise you make the objective, the less likely you allow a misunderstanding.

That is why phrases like "to achieve maximum input," "to the fullest extent possible," and "make a substantial improvement" should be avoided in writing objectives. They are subject to many interpretations.

FINDING OBJECTIVES

The typical public relations professional performs an exceedingly large number of tasks or duties. All of them could be described by objectives but that is neither practical nor desirable. PR-MBO should be a viable management tool with the purpose of helping you do your job better. Therefore, the number of objectives must be limited.

Because goals point to the future direction of your organization, department, or career, your objectives must support them. Goals and objectives do not exist as separate entities but are tied together to form a whole or system. So, begin your search for objectives by carefully reading the goal statements of your employer and your department and by examining your individual goals too.

As Frances A. Koestler wrote in a booklet on objectives published by the Foundation for Public Relations Research and Education, it is important to analyze which of your objectives require long-range campaigns and which can be handled in short-range projects.[16]

Improving Professional Effectiveness

Because PR-MBO is a futures-oriented philosophy, you could begin by looking toward areas of improvement. What can you do to improve your effectiveness? Some areas of improvement will relate to your department and others will reflect more personal aims. For instance:

1. Improve the organization's image.
2. Raise agency morale.
3. Provide better service to clients.
4. Acquire new technical expertness.
5. Capture more resources for the department.
6. Improve the quality of company publications.
7. Attend more professional meetings and conferences.
8. Increase the number of clients.
9. Investigate computer applications.
10. Strengthen planning efforts for dealing with crises.

Any of the suggested areas of improvement will guide you in the direction of future changes. And in so doing they will suggest areas in which to develop objectives.

While these examples are fresh, pause to note down others that you wish to pursue in your own organization.

Problem Areas as Cues

Look for objectives in that part of your job where problems frequently occur. Any professional can describe aspects of the job where problems either recur or have never really been solved. This is fertile ground for discovering objectives.

An investigation of organizational or departmental history should reveal previous problems. Other individuals or committees may have attempted to solve them with varying degrees of success. You may have an idea that can be turned into an objective for solving these problems.

But "old habits may be bad habits," Koestler cautioned in suggesting:

Unless yours is a newborn organization, your public relations program is part of a continuum. It has a past. It can be well worth your while to cast a critical eye at that past and its effect on the present. Ask yourself such questions as: What are we doing just because we've always done it? What activity may have outlived its usefulness? Do we still need it—and, if not, what do we need instead? Objective reconsideration of ongoing programs may well show the desirability of selective pruning.[17]

Causes and Solutions

Some problems recur due to special causes. Because they return or persist, they offer excellent targets for objectives. Optimally, your objective can remove such a problem completely. But even a partial solution is a step in the right direction.

Keep in mind the *concept of causality*. Something may be perceived as *the* cause of a problem. Actually, you are likely to find many causes of a single problem. But if you can find and eliminate some of them, then you have arrived at a solution. It may be a partial solution, but it is a solution nonetheless, because you have now decreased the probability of the problem's recurrence.

For instance, suppose through a community survey you discover that your organization does not really have a negative reputation but that it is unknown to many people. There may be many causes, or causal factors, related to this particular situation. But you have arrived at a solution if you discover that one of the causes may be that your organization does very little in the way of public relations to earn a good reputation.

Through additional research, you may discover other reasons for this particular image that will require *other* solutions. Each cause thus may suggest one or more solutions.

Although any public relations position has its unique problem areas, some are more common, such as:

Poor reputation
Bad press relations
Unhappy clients
Ineffective house publications
Lack of communication with top management
Unclear description of job
Inadequate budget
Lack of planning
Unexpected crises

No contingency planning
Emphasis on downward communication
Deficient product or service
Policies that discriminate
Lack of concern for important publics
Inability to show how PR contributes to profits
Poor management of time
Rumors that are partially or completely false
Interdepartmental disputes
Staff deficiencies
Techniques that do not solve problems
Lack of understanding of issues

Issues Identification

A productive area for discovering objectives lies in issues identification. The professional public relations literature has frequently suggested that the practitioner try to identify those issues that will have to be dealt with in the future.

An issue may be economic, demographic, sociological, technological, or political in origin, but it is of concern because it may affect the success or even the survival of an organization. In identifying issues so that you may write objectives for dealing with them, you need some strategies for classifying them.

A simple, but important, classification strategy assigns issues to a time frame. Those that will occur in the next year may be assigned to the immediate category. Those that occur in two to five years may be called intermediate, and those in the next decade, long-range.

Issues may also be classified according to expected impact. For instance, an issue expected to have major consequences for your organization could be labeled direct or primary. Issues affecting you, but not nearly so directly, could be called secondary.

Here is a beginning list of emerging issues affecting many public relations practitioners:

1. Identifying publics in an extremely mobile society
2. Negative attitudes toward large corporations
3. Lack of confidence in public institutions

4. Declining energy reserves
5. Pending state or federal legislation directly affecting the way your organization operates
6. Recent court decisions

Objectives may be written to help you clarify an issue or written so as to provide action guidelines for coping with it.

Charting a Personal Course

Your responsibilities provide a key to important objectives. So do your activities. One way to begin charting your objectives is to draw up a list reviewing what you do.

From this list, you should be able to categorize your duties under various headings: production or actual outputs (such as a publication), projects (special assignments) and growth (developing special skills or knowledge to do your job).

After this classification has been completed, ask yourself:

1. What could I do to improve my performance in each area?
2. If no one told me, how would I know I am effective?
3. What authority does my position have?
4. What can I most easily improve?
5. What will be the most difficult to improve?
6. On what do I spend most of my job time?
7. On what would I really like to be spending it?

Answers to these questions should enable you to write objectives for the results you wish to achieve in the directions in which you wish to move.

Remember that movement represents direction. By using goals and objectives effectively, as in PR-MBO, you can calculate and chart your direction. Through PR-MBO, you can make this process a deliberate one with specific outcomes in mind. And by guiding your route through goals and objectives, you help assure that you reach your destination rather than wander off course.

OBJECTIVES TREES

The authors recommend the objectives tree as another aid in writing goals and objectives. This is a technique used in research and development firms and departments. Usually, the objectives tree is illustrated as a graph with several levels of detail. A beginning point is to write down all objectives that come to mind. Figure 3.1, "Skeleton Objectives Tree," illustrates a basic framework of an objectives tree.

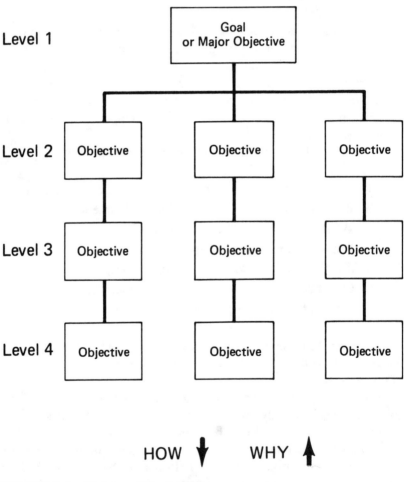

FIGURE 3.1   Skeleton Objectives Tree.

Branching Out with *How* and *How Else*

To proceed to the second level of objectives, you ask *how* after every objective. If an objective is a primary branch, the answers to the *how* may be envisioned as smaller branches growing out of it. So you work your way through the tree with your *how* questions.

After objective 1, ask yourself, How am I going to be able to meet this objective? The answer becomes your next objective. You will notice that after each *how* question, your answer adds greater and greater detail to your original objective. You also may wish to ask *how else*.

How many *hows* do you ask? That depends on the amount of detail you need to meet the objective. Or you may decide to add until you simply cannot answer the *how* question anymore. Usually, 5 to 10 *how* responses are enough to give you a guide for meeting an objective. More than that is unwieldy.

Root Goals: Objectives with *Why* and *Why Else*

Another way to approach an objectives tree—if you know what kinds of programs are important, but you need help in figuring out objectives—is to keep asking *why* and *why else*. The answers will suggest your objectives and goals. Figure 3.1 illustrates the direction of *why* and *how*. The figure shows a vertical, or hierarchical, tree. A tree also may be turned on its side and read left to right as a horizontal, or linear, model.

MODEL 1: NORTHWEST DISASTER

The use of an objectives tree can be illustrated with a disaster that turned into a public relations event.

When Mount St. Helens erupted, doomsday headlines appeared in the Portland press. W. W. Marsh, APR, senior counselor, Rockey/ Marsh Public Relations and past president of the Foundation for Public Relations Research and Education, noted a number of public relations problems that resulted from exaggeration by the news media.

In his *Public Relations Journal* article,[18] Marsh noted that *Time* newsmagazine reported Portland's harbor was choked with mud. Marsh wrote that what really happened was that mud temporarily blocked the

Columbia River near Longview, Washington. Longview is about 40 miles northwest of Portland.

Obviously, for *Time* readers unfamiliar with the geography of the Pacific Northwest, this suggested that Portland would be a poor place to visit or through which to ship goods.

Your goal, if you were working in the public relations department for the Port of Portland, would be to correct the misleading information appearing in the mass media. With such a goal, you need to ask *how* you are going to move toward it.

First, generate a set of objectives.

The objectives can be generated through an objectives tree format. Figure 3.2, "Disaster Objectives Tree," illustrates how the structure of an objectives tree for this situation would appear. All the objectives actually were actions taken by Marsh but adapted to the vertical objectives tree format by Allen.

In more detailed text format, the objectives tree in the Mount St. Helens case might start with:

1. Distribute to local community the actual facts concerning the harbor, pointing out that shipping was continuing.

Objective 1 can be labeled your first level or primary objective.

The next step is to ask how to accomplish objective 1. The numbering system used here can be adapted to public relations proposals or reports as a means of making clear steps and substeps. Including the first level, here are some of the actual steps taken as they would appear in an objectives tree:

1. Distribute to local community facts concerning the harbor, pointing out that shipping was continuing.
   1.1 Write and distribute daily news releases that contain factual information concerning the status of the harbor.
   1.2 Place advertisements in commercial publications stating that the harbor is open for business.
   1.3 Send reprints of these advertisements to shippers, steamship operators, and other important publics.
2. Develop and place advertisements in travel publications explaining that vacation areas are open to tourists.
   2.1 Buy advertising space in major newspapers.

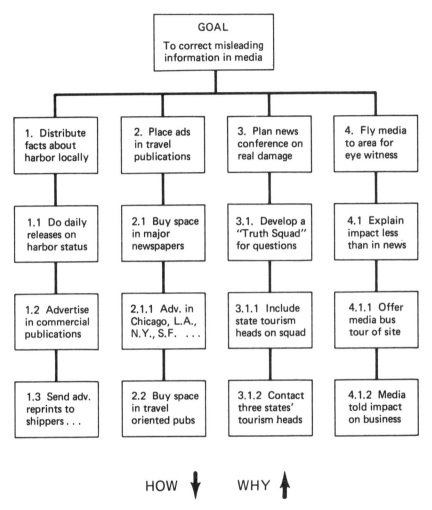

FIGURE 3.2   Disaster Objectives Tree.

> 2.1.1 Buy space in Chicago, Los Angeles, New York,
>   San Francisco, Salt Lake City newspapers.
> 2.2 Buy space in travel publications.
> 3. Plan news conferences to explain to the media the actual damage done in the region.
>   3.1 Develop a "truth squad" to answer questions at the news conferences.
>   3.1.1 Enlist as squad members the directors of tourism for Idaho, Washington, and Oregon.

      3.1.2 Contact the directors of tourism and prepare them for "Truth Squad" service.
4. Fly members of media into Washington and Oregon to get a firsthand look.
    4.1 Communicate to media that the eruption impact was not as substantial as reported in other parts of the country.
      4.1.1 Sponsor a bus tour to survey the region.
      4.1.2 Conduct news briefings to explain the eruption's impact on the local and regional businesses.

The careful reader will notice that these objectives could be more specific. But the important point to realize here is that the objectives tree format provides a structure for the writing of objectives.

By following the objectives, a structure of solutions emerges. By simply asking *how* after each objective, you are led to the next level of objectives, which offers more specific information.

An objectives tree also imposes a strict discipline on the user. The constant asking of *how* forces you to concentrate on the problem at hand. The asking of *why* makes you keep your client's purposes in mind. Figure 3.2 shows the direction of *how* and *why* questions and answers in the Mount St. Helens case. In dealing with a public relations problem as complex as Portland's without a tool such as an objectives tree, a tendency may be to lose focus. The sequential nature of the objectives tree structure forces a rigorous form of thinking.

The structure may impose rigor, but it also allows for creativity and flexibility for the adventurous public relations professional who wishes to experiment with adaptation of the objectives tree.

MODEL 2: THE C-R-E-A-T-E SYSTEM ADAPTED TO A JOB CAMPAIGN

It is a maxim of public relations veterans that a tool may be modified and adapted to fit the particular factors of the situation and the needs and style of the professional.

With this in mind, we take the liberty of illustrating a stylized objectives tree created by Nager.[19] Goals serve as roots, primary objectives as the main trunk, subobjectives as secondary trunks, and branches as means.

In this "Stylized Objectives Tree," illustrated in Figure 3.3, diamonds symbolize the rootlike goals; the larger rectangle represents the primary objective, squares serve as trunk subobjectives, and smaller rectangles graphically depict the branches of means to achieve the targeted results. With more space, one could leaf out the tree to show how the means break down into distinctive activities.

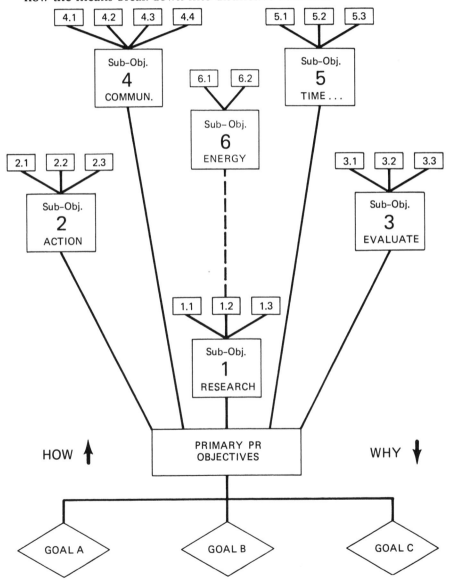

FIGURE 3.3 Stylized Objectives Tree.

The stylized objectives tree in Figure 3.3 examines goals, objectives, subobjectives, and means in dealing with the challenge of rising to a position in public relations. In one sense, the tree models professional growth. In another sense, and at the same time, it models the public relations C-R-E-A-T-E[20] system introduced in Chapter 2.

Figure 3.3, as a model of an objectives tree, depicts just the linear relationship of goals to objectives to subobjectives to means. It would complicate the graphics to the point of overshadowing the objectives tree concept, but one could also draw a web of loops connecting each part of the process with all others.

Communication
Research
Evaluation
Action
Time/resources planning
Energy

For purposes of limiting the graphic illustration to a page, we limit the number of goals. Nonetheless, keep in mind that a conventional or stylized objectives tree may extend as high, as wide, and in as much depth of detail as you choose to verbalize on paper or present on blackboards, rolls of butcher paper, or flip charts.

Goal A: Enhance your public relations professional capabilities.
Goal B: Secure position that fulfills your creative aspirations.
Goal C: Obtain work that surpasses your material expectations and needs.

PRIMARY OBJECTIVE: This hardened, near-term purpose could be to receive an offer for a public relations position:

- paying a specific salary of $??,000
- adding stock options (or other benefits you care to specify) at a minimum value of $?,000
- providing you direct access to CEO and board of directors
- working with a *Fortune* 500 corporation in a growth field such as computer technology
- starting within a time certain of six months (or by whatever date you feel is needed and feasible)

• assigning you responsibility for management counsel, issues analysis, opinion research contracting, governmental affairs, community relations, media relations (or whatever other specifications you may have)

• operating with a minimum budget of $?00,000 you set for the scale of program you determine as minimal

• managing the minimum number of creative and staff personnel you require

• other quantitative and qualitative criteria you feel are important and realistic

Again, you can move from goals through objectives to means by asking *how*. Or you can move from means to objectives and on to goals by asking *why*, as illustrated in Figure 3.3. As you move up the objectives tree from the primary objective, you arrive at subobjectives by asking *how* and go on to more and more specific means by continuing to ask *how*.

Here is how the tree could branch out from the primary objective:

SUBOBJECTIVE 1: RESEARCH—TO INVESTIGATE PROCESS,
JOBS, AND COMPANIES
    MEANS: 1.1 Literature
            1.1.1 PR journals and newsletters
            1.1.2 Corporate reports, periodicals
            1.1.3 Books on job campaigns
            1.1.4 Trade journals
    MEANS: 1.2 Interviews
            1.2.1 PRSA, IABC, WICI placement
            1.2.2 PR professionals in field
            1.2.3 Executive search consultants
            1.2.4 Educators who observe market
    MEANS: 1.3 Surveys
            1.3.1 Placement services
            1.3.2 Literature reports

SUBOBJECTIVE 2: ACTION—TO MAKE IMPROVEMENTS NEEDED TO
QUALIFY FOR POSITION
    MEANS: 2.1 Improve product
            2.1.1 Pursue advanced degree
            2.1.2 Take special studies

                    2.1.2.1 Marketing
                    2.1.2.2 Management
                    2.1.2.3 Computer science
                    2.1.2.4 Psychology
          2.1.3 Activate in professional groups
          2.1.4 Attend professional seminars
          2.1.5 Gain experience as volunteer
                    2.1.5.1 Civic-political service
                    2.1.5.2 United Way, A-I-D
                    2.1.5.3 Press club service
                    2.1.5.4 Submit articles

MEANS: 2.2 Improve style
          2.2.1 Join Toastmasters
          2.2.2 Engage in physical fitness
          2.2.3 Practice before video camera
          2.2.4 Display enthusiasm

MEANS: 2.3 Improve policy
          2.3.1 Listen more
          2.3.2 Avoid fault-finding
          2.3.3 Return dividends on favors

SUBOBJECTIVE 3: EVALUATION—TO ASSURE CAMPAIGN RUNS EFFECTIVELY AND ON COURSE
MEANS: 3.1 Field test with experts
          3.1.1 Resumé variations
          3.1.2 Cover letters
          3.1.3 Portfolio of samples
          3.1.4 Interview statements
          3.1.5 Anticipated question responses
          3.1.6 Follow-through communication

MEANS: 3.2 Outside audit
          3.2.1 Strengths and weaknesses
          3.2.2 Job level for qualifications
          3.2.3 Reasons given for "no"
          3.2.4 Entire campaign

MEANS: 3.3 Subjective audit
          3.3.1 Develop charts for analysis
                    3.3.1.1 Factors to emphasize
                    3.3.1.2 Interview observations
                    3.3.1.3 Responses to queries

SUBOBJECTIVE 4: COMMUNICATION—TO INFLUENCE BEHAVIOR OF
THE DECISION MAKERS
    MEANS: 4.1 Mass communication
        4.1.1 Listings in placement columns
    MEANS: 4.2 Interpersonal
        4.2.1 Phone calls
        4.2.2 Professional meetings
        4.2.3 Interview preparation
    MEANS: 4.3 Print, targeted to publics
        4.3.1 Resumé variations
    MEANS: 4.4 Letters, individualized
        4.4.1 Query
        4.4.2 Prepare for phone calls
        4.4.3 Application and cover letters
        4.4.4 Interview follow-through
        4.4.5 Maintain friendly contacts

SUBOBJECTIVE 5: TIME/RESOURCES PLANNING—TO ATTAIN OBJEC-
TIVES IN TIME AND WITHIN BUDGET
    MEANS: 5.1 Establish time line
        5.1.1 Include progress check points
        5.1.2 Build in periodic reassessment
        5.1.3 Flow chart for ease of review
        5.1.4 Build in attention to details
    MEANS: 5.2 Create contingency plans
        5.2.1 Create end-campaign "what if"
        5.2.2 Program lesser contingencies
    MEANS: 5.3 Budget resources
        5.3.1 Cost-out areas of expense
        5.3.2 Allocate own time as resource

SUBOBJECTIVE 6: ENERGY—TO FUEL CREATIVE PRODUCTIVITY
    MEANS: 6.1 Program time for gaining insights
        6.1.1 Set aside time for thinking
        6.1.2 Plan brainstorming sessions
        6.1.3 Budget time for reading, study
        6.1.4 Talk with fellow professionals
    MEANS: 6.2 Fuel the human systems
        6.2.1 Attend to nutritional needs

6.2.2 Program regular exercise
6.2.3 Provide for sufficient rest
6.2.4 Allow time for recreation

For references on additional perspectives and how-to instructions on objectives trees, please turn to the Notes at the end of this chapter.[21]

CREATING GOALS AND OBJECTIVES FOR TIME MANAGEMENT

In an eight-page paper filled with more than five dozen suggestions on time management, Dennis L. Wilcox, APR, head of the public relations degree program at San Jose State University, stressed the value of written goals and objectives and urged that they:

Provide substantial challenge and really give you a sense of accomplishment. On the other hand, a goal must be realistic. Unrealistic goals tend to depress us and give us a sense of futility. Set goals that can realistically be accomplished if you work at it.[22]

Although Wilcox, a former national agency account executive, wrote his paper for public relations educators, the questions he answered and the additional tips provided would prove beneficial to persons in practice.

Among the problems to which he responded:

Problem 1—Other people, with their priorities, make demands upon you and your sovereignty. You are asked to do things that have little or no relationship to the achievement of your goals and aspirations. . . .

Problem 2—Waiting for someone to approve your ideas or plans. You're blocked until the person gets around to it; and your plan or idea may not be high on his or her priority list. . . .

Problem 3—You assume new and increased responsibilities, but don't shed old duties. There is a tendency to continue doing what we have been doing because it is familiar and we do our best work. Our new duties are still uncomfortable to us, so we seek security and assurance. . . .

Problem 4—Long and tedious committee meetings [that] are not time efficient. . . .

Problem 5—The inability to say "no."[23]

For Wilcox, most of the solutions were grounded in priorities and strategies flowing from written goals and objectives.

An effective public relations program also requires systematic effort to develop objectives-based communication. Chapters 4 and 5 explore this by focusing on the PR-MBO writing system.

NOTES

1. Kalman B. Druck and Ray E. Hiebert, *Your Personal Guidebook: To Help You Chart a More Successful Career in Public Relations* (New York: Public Relations Society of America, 1979).
2. Richard W. Darrow and Dan J. Forrestal, *The Dartnell Public Relations Handbook*, 2nd ed. (Chicago: Dartnell, 1979), p. 806.
3. Ibid., pp. 1029–30.
4. Ibid.
5. Ibid., p. 91.
6. W. J. Reddin, *Effective Management By Objectives* (New York: McGraw-Hill, 1972), p. 93.
7. Robert J. Jameson, *The Professional Job Changing System* (Verona, N.J.: Performance Dynamics, 1977).
8. Ibid., pp. 180–87.
9. Ibid., p. 179.
10. James F. Tirone, "Measuring the Bell System's Public Relations," *Public Relations Review* 3 (Winter 1977): 21–28.
11. George S. Odiorne, "MBO in State Government," *Public Administration Review*, January/February 1976, p. 29.
12. Carol Reuss and Donn Silvis, eds., *Inside Organizational Communication*, (New York: Longman, 1981).
13. Roy G. Foltz, "Communication in Contemporary Organizations," in Reuss and Silvis, *Inside Organizational Communication*, p. 9.
14. Edward G. Blinn, "Learn How the Media Work," in *The Publicity Process*, ed. James W. Schwartz (Ames, Iowa: Iowa State University Press, 1966), pp. 123–57.
15. Ibid., pp. 140–42.
16. Frances A. Koestler, "Planning and Setting Objectives," as part of series of reports, *Managing Your Public Relations: Guidelines for Nonprofit Organizations* (New York: Foundation for Public Relations Research and Education, 1977).
17. Ibid., p. 16.
18. W. W. Marsh, "Public Relations and the 'Big Blow Up,'" *Public Relations Journal*, October 1980.
19. Norman R. Nager, "Project C" (set of four disks of planning system concepts programmed on *VisiDex* software, revised April 1983).
20. Ibid.
21. T. Harrell Allen, *New Methods in Social Science Research* (New York: Praeger,

1978), pp. 95–106. Also see J. Warfield, "Development of a Unified Systems Engineering Concept," (*Systems Engineering Workshop Notebook*, Seattle, 1971).

22. Dennis L. Wilcox, "Time Management in Academe" (paper Presented to Educators Section of Public Relations Society of America, National Conference, Atlanta, November 1980.

23. Ibid.

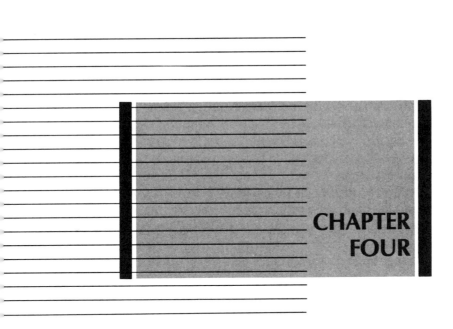

APPLYING PR-MBO AND SYSTEMS APPROACHES TO PR WRITING

PURPOSE OF PR-MBO WRITING SYSTEM

The objectives-based system refined and extended for *Public Relations Management by Objectives* was designed to aid veterans and newcomers alike in developing a patterned approach to public relations writing.[1] *This pattern involves systematic steps for analyzing, planning, researching, and executing public relations writing in situations with numerous and complex factors or variables.*

The system provides a patterned approach to help you develop and follow through in achieving the objectives of writer, employer, media gatekeeper, and targeted publics, even in situations in which you may have little experience.

Although the system requires painstaking effort at first, it becomes habitual over time. It fosters creativity and initiative through the stimulation of analytical thinking and questioning.

This chapter concentrates on giving you the rationale for the systematic, 10-step PR-MBO Writing System—the Communication in the C-R-E-A-T-E process. This information provides you with the logic to understand how to apply the steps. Chapter 5 discusses the actual application of the 10-step writing system.

After working with the "how-to" aspects of the PR-MBO Writing System, the next phase explores how to evaluate and measure the effectiveness of public relations campaigns, including written communication.

The 10 steps of the system were created and sequentially arranged for the convenience of the typical writer. But there is nothing sacred about the structure of a particular writing system. The order of the steps, although logical in sequence, may not necessarily have to be followed by each individual writer. As a matter of fact, the writing system works best when the person using it feels free to move out of sequence.

For instance, you may leap from idea to idea, each idea stimulating fresh thinking and modifying ideas that follow and precede it. A system should not be rigid. You may conceive of several ideas for different parts of the system simultaneously.

What the writing system does insist upon is a logical, systematic effort to answer a number of questions. Precision needs to be built into the way questions are asked and answered. You need to assure that key questions are raised and that you follow through in applying the answers.

If you wish, add to the system or rearrange it. Or consider combining parts of the system. In short, tailor the system to conform to your own approach to analytical thinking.

With that in mind, let's look at the 10 parts of the system, first in the form of an overview.

OVERVIEW OF PR WRITING SYSTEM

1. Client/employer objectives
2. Audiences/publics and why
3. Audience characteristics
4. Audience objectives
5. Media/channels and why

6. Media/channels objectives
7. Sources and questions
8. Communication strategies
9. Essence of message
10. Nonverbal support

The Structure of PR Writing

The first 10 steps of the analytical system provide a structure for public relations writing.

After completing the 10 steps, you outline the media backgrounder, news release, brochure, videotape script, speech, letter, proposal to management, or whatever else you are planning to write. Then you write the first draft of the message, not pausing to check grammar, look up spelling, correct typographical errors, or worry about vocabulary or syntax. That is what rough drafting means. Rough drafting on a typewriter or computer terminal saves precious hours of painstaking efforts of writing by hand or even typing first-and-last-draft material.

It may not seem like it to those who hate to rewrite and polish, but creativity tends to flow better when you are unimpeded by worry over fine details and not held back by the slowness of the pen or encumbered by the awkwardness of polishing every phrase before setting it down on paper.

Now go back and rewrite. And rewrite again. Polish it. Then give it one more reading to check for any errors you may have made while copyediting.

Between drafting and polishing stages, go back and review the creative written product against the guidelines you created in your analysis. How well does what you wrote meet your objectives? How well does it meet your specifications in the rest of the 10 steps? What is missing?

Of course, you may strengthen and refine your analysis at any time in the process and search for more information or build the new analytical points into the communication. That is the idea behind the system. And it is the idea behind an *11th step* of the process—measuring the drafted materials against the previous 10 steps and making adjustments as needed.

Chapter 5 gives you a chance to examine in full the basic 10 steps; Chapter 6 introduces you to several new adaptations of field research for evaluation of public relations communication.

Building Spiral Loops To Persuade

The basic 10-step analytical process may be seen as a helix. A helix is a spiral that looks like the spring that holds the batteries in a flashlight or portable radio. The spring is small at the bottom and large at the top, spiraling back, but never touching itself, and growing with each loop of the spiral. Social scientists use the helix as a model of the communication process. This is a process that is never static, but continuously growing and changing.

As a helixlike process, the public relations writing system grows with each loop (or step) of analysis you add, as illustrated in Figure 4.1, "Spiral Loops of PR Persuasion." But as you add to your analysis, as you develop new information or insights, the whole process changes.

So, as you add to client objectives, for instance, the spiral impact may demand changes in audiences, audience characteristics, and audience objectives.

The loops of the spiral grow and affect each other as you add media to reach your audiences, take into account special requirements of these media, and build these requirements into your strategies.

And the strategies for persuading your publics change with your conclusions based upon your analysis of the members of the audience and their perceived needs, aspirations, and relations with your client.

And with media and strategic change, the spiral process may suggest some modification of the essence of verbal communication and that which is communicated without words.

As in many systems, it is up to you where to enter this system. The authors recommend that you begin with client objectives. But if you believe that it is artificial to separate consideration of your client objectives from the audiences you target, for instance, tailor the system to work for you. *Just keep in mind that objectives form the core of the process.*

As you examine the various steps and the process as a whole, and then compare outline, drafts, and polished copy to the ever-changing analysis, a second helical structure grows springlike alongside the first

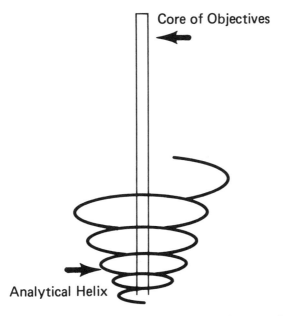

FIGURE 4.1   Spiral Loops of PR Persuasion. With client/employer objectives forming core of the PR-MBO writing process, each part of the 10-step system builds the springlike helix structure of analysis. As you add to the analytical helix, you continue to build a creative foundation for supporting the client's objectives.

helix. The second helix is the actuality of your communication. The pragmatics of applying and adapting the theoretical concepts in the analysis to the actual written product in turn has an impact on your analytical approach. The system demands flexibility.

To drive home the point of the relationship of objectives and analyses to public relations writing, consider that the model of the double helix for the writing system is patterned after the double-helix structure of DNA. And DNA is the basic life substance. *Communication is a living process.*

REALITIES OF PROFESSIONAL PRACTICE

The realities of professional practice might seem to make application of the public relations writing system a time-consuming effort, a luxury for the typical writer running to keep up with the demands of the job. Yet the system may be just what the harried practitioner needs to become more effective and to demonstrate to top management that investment in public relations writing may prove at least as profitable as investment in other corporate cost centers (departments that contribute to productivity and profitability).

Professionals have learned that some materials written in haste without doing a proper analysis have produced negligible returns or harm to the client. Answers developed through the public relations writing system may suggest that different channels of communication are warranted, that revised strategies need to be employed, that the essence of the message varies radically from what was first intended.

For instance, most employees and their families would be more receptive to newsletters with a human, interpretive style than the financial data prepared for analysts and investors in the annual report. That does not mean that employees are uninterested in the financial affairs of their companies; it only says that their focus of interest and background may demand different content and/or style of presentation.

Similarly, public relations writers have found it more productive to program interpersonal communication in certain situations than break the news through the media in a routine release. This may require you as an analytical public relations writer to draft statements for the client's experts or managers to deliver. It may demand that you anticipate questions that employees, shareowners, reporters, or others in the audience might ask. And with that responsibility usually goes the need to draft answers for anticipated questions. Moreover, you probably will want to observe a dry run (rehearsal under simulated live conditions) to evaluate nonverbals and suggest warranted changes in verbal content too.

For the newcomer to the system, the authors recommend that each of the steps be applied fully to each important area of writing. This could include, for example, reports to higher management, speeches, memos, news releases, audiovisual communication, newsletter features, background sheets, brochures, and correspondence to critical publics.

It takes practice to build the system into your approach to writing, just as it took practice to develop proficiency in touch typing. It takes experience to build the system, just as it took experience to apply lead writing principles to the production of readable articles that capture, focus, and guide attention. Practice takes time and work. You invest something to earn a profit. That is the reality of professional development and growth.

But you should not go to the extreme of spending so much time and effort on analysis and research that you have no time or energy left for doing. As John Hohenberg wrote in counseling *The Professional Journalist*, there comes a time when deadlines near and questioning and rewrite must be interrupted as the writer heeds the imperative to: "Go with what you've got!" . . . The finest reporting, the best writing, the most impressive segment of a TV news program are worthless if they are not ready in time."[2]

After you internalize—make the system an integral part of your thinking and writing—then you reserve the intensive, in-depth analysis for the more important writing jobs, such as proposals or reports to management and major projects or campaigns.

As veterans know from experience and as students of the profession learn, one speech, one media backgrounder, or one annual report, of and by itself, seldom yields important results. *The measurable impact of a particular statement, if isolated from all that precedes or follows, tends to be slight.*

It is when communications between organizations and their publics are planned and polished as pieces interacting with each other, building upon and from each other like so many building blocks, that the public relations writing system really works. A given piece of writing, then, should be viewed as part of a campaign.

Basically it is *the painstaking grounding of writing by objectives in precise results for clients* that characterizes the effective public relations writer.

For the public relations writer, then, "informing," "educating," and "entertaining" tend to be imprecise goals rather than results-oriented objectives.

Informing to what degree?

Educating how well?

Readers may be "educated" about fuel conservation methods, but fuel consumption may continue at the same level. And does "informing" or "educating" mean *persuading to act in a certain way, or preparing the persons to behave as the writer intends?*

The effective public relations writer aims for more precise behavioral changes to achieve results.

An important question arises: Is "informing" or "educating," per se, the end or a means to the end? The difference is major.

The "end" is the result you want, the WHY *with which you and your client are content as a reward, the profit upon your investment in writing and on your employer's investment in you. The "means" in "means to an end" is the way to get from here to there. The "means" is* HOW *you achieve something, not* WHAT *you achieve.*

MODELS FOR STRUCTURING PR WRITING

To grasp fully the concepts in the rationale behind the PR-MBO Writing System, let's look at several analogies or models from other professions.

Model 1: Learning from Architects

In your mind's eye, envision yourself as an architect. You would want a bedrock of analysis or the reinforced concrete of *systematic investigation of variables and options* as the foundation for your building.

You would sink shafts of the strongest steel into that foundation to provide the nucleus for the structure. In public relations writing, you might equate these steel cores with objectives.

Scrupulously consulting the findings of your *research and planning with in-depth analysis,* you would have the framework built before walls, floors, and ceilings were poured or windows installed. For the public relations writer, outline would serve as framework.

You would plan carefully, stage by stage, and not accept your first sketch as the ultimate. In the same way, a writer rewrites and polishes. But, as an architect, you would not stop there. You would want to *measure* your plans against safety standards and client needs.

So, too, does the professional writer check the outline and drafts against the analysis. This may include testing the writing on samples of targeted publics, as well as doing quality control to assure that the message will achieve most effectively what the client needs as results.

Of course, as an architect, you would be concerned that the engineers and construction supervisors would be able to work with your plans. So, too, the professional public relations writer develops materials that satisfy the *criteria of gatekeepers* such as editors and others who control information gates for the media and the publics.

But not all material written by public relations persons goes through gatekeepers. So you consider meeting the criteria for most effective use of other channels of communication, be they memos to the CEO, a speech for a board meeting, a script for a video report for investors or donors, or a brochure for customers.

Model 2: Learning from Surgeons

In your mind's eye, see yourself as a surgeon. Before piercing the patient's skin, you would call for the records. You would want to know the patient's history. You would want to review the findings of other specialists. Unless the patient were on the verge of a crisis, you would want to do a personal examination and interview to verify the findings of the referring physician and go beyond the patient's own self-diagnosis.

Similarly, as a public relations writer, you operate more effectively when you have the benefit of an in-depth view in the form of *an audit* of your client's history, publics, reputation, objectives, and resources. You need a history that includes how past situations were handled and with what results (and what has changed in the meantime). You would want to check how your employer has related to relevant publics and find out how publics have viewed your organization. And you would inquire how your predecessors and others in the organization have worked with news media or other channels of communication. You would audit much more about the client's business, products, personnel, problems, policies, and plans.

And, as a professional writer, you would go beyond that to interview experts within and outside the organization to develop a more comprehensive and up-to-date picture while taking advantage of the diversity of perspectives.

As a surgeon, you would wish to search the literature to determine what is known about the disease and to review what other surgeons have done with what effect. You might even want to consult with other medical specialists to confirm your findings. And you might want to call for follow-up testing of your patient's symptoms.

As a public relations writer, that would be like reviewing *Public Relations Journal, Public Relations Review, PR Reporter, Public Relations News, O'Dwyer's Newsletter, Ragan Report, Public Opinion Quarterly, Public Relations Research and Education*, and books and journals related to your field.

If you are a member of PRSA, you may start the search with a call or note to the PRSA Research Information Center in New York City. For the cost of a phone call or letter and a few dollars to photocopy and mail back original documents to the Center, you can have copies of articles, chapters, special reports, and brochures on a wide range of topics.

If you belong to the IABC, you can call or write the IABC Research Director in San Francisco.

The authors have monitored PRSA and IABC responsiveness to queries and found both to be prompt and helpful to professionals.

As do a growing number of public relations professionals, you may use an interactive computer search service of your trade association or a major campus or metropolitan library. Of course, some companies, not-for-profit institutions, and government agencies operate their own libraries or reference services.

And you may wish to consult other public relations specialists within the organization or with other companies or agencies.

In this surgeon's approach model, you would establish clearly in your own mind and that of the client exactly what range of results you should realistically expect to attain. If you follow the medical profession model, you determine—before sitting down at the computer keyboard or typewriter—the specifics of what you hope to attain with your written product.

Just as saving or prolonging the patient's life may be the ultimate objective of the physician, the writer is concerned with the survival of the client. Just as the surgeon may seek to restore partial function if full function is not attainable, so, too, does the writer aim at helping the client reach for whatever ends are needed *and* feasible.

Just as sharing objectives of surgery with others on the surgical team helps all work together more effectively, so, too, does it help assure cooperation for the writer to share objectives with others on the public relations team and in relevant divisions of the organization. And the CEO or other executive with whom you work on a particular project needs to understand your objectives (and the priorities, strategies, and resources for attaining them) if you wish maximum opportunities for support before and after the job is done.

Just as the surgeon must plan and work toward the specific objective of surgery, not just concentrate on the means, so, too, the writer looks beyond planting an article, arranging a television interview, or getting out an annual report.

As surgeon, you would plan for *follow-through* and check on how the patient progresses immediately after surgery and over time. You would probably order postoperative evaluation procedures.

Is surgery successful if the patient dies, suffers needless complications, or does not receive treatment warranted for full recovery? Of course not. This is why *building in evaluation and follow-through* is so important to the surgeon and to the public relations writer.

Model 3: Learning from Lawyers

In your mind's eye, picture yourself as a lawyer. Before determining your objectives, you would want to check out precedent. And you would want to investigate variables that make each case different. As a public relations writer, you do that too.

With a hardened objective for all your efforts as a lawyer, you would systematically build your case. But you would do that not just by applying rhetoric to points of the law; you would do that by analyzing your publics (jury, judge, witnesses, courtroom personnel, media, spectators, counsel for the other side). You would even analyze potential future publics, such as appeals judges.

As a public relations writer, you share the lawyer's orientation to finding out as much as possible about the persons with whom you communicate. Moreover, the lawyer provides the writer with a model of playing out *contingency scenarios*, preparing for the worst possibilities and opportune situations that may arise.

As a lawyer, you would have to understand the particular court's and judge's criteria for content and form of arguments you present, the public relations writer's equivalent of understanding the media's and editors' requirements for accepting and using information. As a lawyer, before you planned a sentence of argumentation, you would want to *analyze the attitudes* of individual jurors to you, your client, opposing counsel and their client, and relevant legal issues.

Would it be helpful to know how the publics dealt in previous situations—their past behavior? After all, as a lawyer or public relations writer *you want to influence their future behavior.*

As a lawyer, you would put rhetoric in its proper place as the finishing touches on the substance of your argumentation, rather than look upon the flow of verbiage and oratorical style as ends in themselves. This does not mean that the technique and style of the public relations writer is unimportant. To the contrary. What it does mean is that the public relations writer, like professionals in other fields, thinks in terms of the whole, that is, holistically.

Model 4: Learning from Executives

In your mind's eye, see yourself as the chief executive officer in the organization for which you will be working. Take a moment to note down all the research techniques, strategies, planning, analysis of individuals, and sources of data you would use in running your organization.

Based upon the previous models, see if you can develop this model by taking the role of your CEO and implementing the major points of this chapter. Do this by applying systems thinking to the role of the executive as it may be adapted to public relations writing.

Before moving ahead to the actual implementation of the 10-step process in Chapter 5, you may wish to review the systems concepts in Chapter 2 and basic definitions and format for goals and objectives in Chapter 3.

NOTES

1. Norman R. Nager, "A Professional Approach to Public Relations Writing" (paper presented to the Public Relations Division of the Association for Education in Journalism and Mass Communication, National Convention, Seattle, August 1978). Nager, "1-10 Writing System" (software feedback system on *VisiDex*, January 1983).
2. John Hohenberg, *The Professional Journalist*, 5th ed. (New York: Holt, Rinehart and Winston, 1983), pp. 29–30.

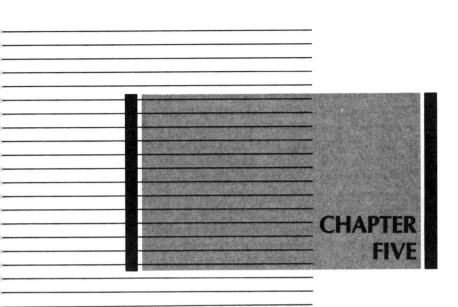

THE 10-STEP PR-MBO WRITING SYSTEM

TO HELP "FATHOM THE MYSTERIES"

Doug Newsom and Tom Siegfried introduced their public relations writing book by pointing out:

> Students taught that PR is a management function sometimes find that the realities of PR practice are dismaying. PR practitioners are expected to have a ready command of communication skills, and are expected to write, not just a little, but a lot—and do so effectively. As if this were not enough, they are also expected to fathom easily the mysteries of all media.[1]

There are far more mysteries to fathom than those of the media, the traditional orientation of public relations writers. For a number of useful public relations writing texts, please see Notes at the end of the

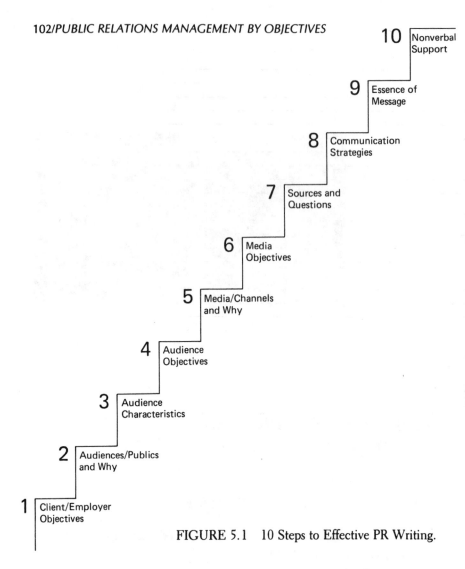

FIGURE 5.1   10 Steps to Effective PR Writing.

chapter. Two of the more promising newcomers to the literature are *The PR Writer,* a 1983 work by Frank Walsh, and the 1984 edition of *Effective Publicity* by Lawrence Nolte and Dennis Wilcox.[2]

But most books give little, if any, attention to the mysteries beyond those of the use of tactical techniques. To ease the fathoming of such mysteries and to provide a PR-MBO system that adds the dimension of placing the complex parts of public relations writing in an interactive perspective, we present the following 10 steps based upon "A Professional Approach to Public Relations Writing" and "The 1-10 Writing System."[3]

A graphic overview of the 10 steps in the Communication part of the C-R-E-A-T-E system is illustrated in Figure 5.1, "10 Steps to Effective PR Writing."

1. CLIENT/EMPLOYER OBJECTIVES

Ask yourself before you sit down to write a news release, speech, proposal to top management, policy statement, video script—anything: What are my client's (or employer's) objectives for this specific communication?

Aim for "hardened"—that is, realistic, measurable, attainable within a reasonable time frame—objectives. You are really spelling out *why* you are devoting organizational resources, including your valuable time and that of others who may become involved as you interview and prepare the communication, to this specific act of writing instead of meeting other important demands.

Why am I putting out this backgrounder to the media? Why am I writing copy for the quarterly report to stockholders or donors? Why am I ghosting comments for the CEO to present to the board of trustees?

Leading public relations educators have stressed the importance of asking why in their discussions at meetings of the PRSA, IABC, and Association for Education in Journalism and Mass Communication (AEJMC).[4] In this book and in this system, we raise that why to another level. You are trying to *affect the behavior of individuals in the interests of the organization you represent.* That is what you are paid to do. And, as a public relations officer, you are not only concerned about the interests of client or employer but also the larger interests of the publics and society.

Concentrate on Behavior and Motivation

Concentrate on behavioral objectives. Your focus here is on what behavior you wish and realistically may expect from persons to whom your communication will be directed. Envision what those persons will *do* if you are effective.

Sometimes in public relations campaigns that behavior may be needed months or years later, not on reading or hearing a message.

For instance, a manufacturer's communiqué to a new consumer may be directed at the purchase of the next home computer, automobile, or video recorder when replacement time comes. A politician may be concerned about behavior at the polls in November. A university may wish to influence still-young alumni to bestow endowments after they are successful. A hospital may want parents to request a pediatrician who can admit to several hospitals to treat their children in that institution. A bank's economic literacy campaign in elementary and secondary schools may seek to influence behavior when youngsters mature and become investors, homebuilders, or political activists.

So, sometimes you set objectives for your writing that concentrate on predisposition to behavior. A *synonym for predisposition to behavior is attitude*. And you can measure attitudes by analyzing opinion research survey findings.

Public relations professionals and researchers have found, however, not only that opinions and the attitudes they reflect are *subject to change over time* but also that *intentions are not necessarily the same as deeds*. For example, one may subscribe to such notions as buy American, practice preventive medicine, conserve energy, vote labor, support equal opportunity, and yet do the contrary when faced with the need to act. That is why behavior, rather than attitudes, may be the best objectives for your efforts.

But when it is not feasible to meet immediate behavioral objectives, predisposition to behavior offers a usable fallback position.

Think in terms of motivation, persuading individuals to act in a certain way, influencing predisposition to behavior, stimulating behavior, encouraging/discouraging action, and reinforcing tendencies to follow through with desired behavior.

As a case in point, public relations writers may help create the climate for sales or influence the potential customer to *want* to come to the showroom and listen to the sales person. Or public relations communication may follow up on the sales effort and bring the person back. Public relations writing may aid in marketing and sales, but as a general rule it neither markets nor sells.

As another case in point, you may intrigue potential employees to want to look into working for the organization you represent. But public relations writers do not hire for the rest of the company. You may attract candidates to write for materials, to call, or to meet with recruiters. Public relations writing may convince potential employees that yours could be a rewarding organization for which to work, a good citizen of the community, an employer that treats its employees well, an employer with a promising future for itself and those who work for it.

Similarly, you do not sell stocks and bonds. But you can contribute to investor confidence in your organization, arouse the interest of Wall Street and Main Street money managers and investment counselors. Conversely, you can have an impact on communication to avert panic dumping of stocks, intervene in the spreading of false rumors that erode faith in the company's fiscal management, and help put short-term setbacks in perspective. In long-range fund development for not-for-profit organizations, consultant Ray Gillingham pointed out that it is unrealistic to expect written materials to have a simple direct cause-and-effect relationship to the contribution of major gifts to your organization.[5] That is because other variables are involved, including the donor's experience with your institution, the personal relationship established with members of his or her peer group representing your agency, and the tax advantages your legal counsel explores.

But the campaign proposal you ghostwrite for the CEO, the film clip you develop, the letters and speeches you draft, the brochures you write, and even the interpersonal communication strategies you propose can be quite instrumental in helping bring in those large grants and bequests.

Cochrane Chase & Livingston's former vice president for public relations, Patrick Anderson, APR, who founded Anderson Communications in 1982, suggested:

> You do not sell groceries to distributors, let alone consumers. But you may help convince stores to stock your products on their shelves. And you may help persuade shoppers to try these products based upon the literature, posters, and presentations you prepare. That is because you, as a public relations professional, write to motivate sales personnel, dealers, and customers.
> Your vehicles may include:
> • The syndicated column item on your product
> • Recipes you plant in the food sections showing how your product is used
> • Nutritional public service information credited to your company in a half-hour cable television program
> • Articles published in specialized media for distributors[6]

Turning to public affairs or public relations aimed at affecting government actions: When State Treasurer Jesse M. Unruh was Speaker of the Lower House of the California State Legislature and president of the National Conference of State Legislative Leaders, he pointed out that what enters into inspiration or discouragement of the introduction of a legislative bill and passage, defeat, postponement, or modification in committee or on the floor included such factors or variables as legislative advocates (lobbyists) for your client; the long-range relationship between client and lawmakers and their *staffs*; activities of members of the executive and legislative branches, themselves, in creating bills or engaging in campaigns for passage, modification, or defeat; opinion surveys of constituencies; communication from respected individuals and organizational leaders; and research by staff.

But you can and do make powerful contributions to these results through public relations direct mail writing to influence the behavior of special-interest voter groups or organizations that may become allies; testimony you draft or edit for your executives and experts to have an impact on committee members or influential staffs; persuasive letters you draft to key elected persons or their staff, long before a bill is introduced or moved to committee; and backgrounders you supply editorial writers (whose comments are noted in local council chambers or field offices of legislators).[7]

Inform, Educate, Expose, Publicize: Writing Objectives?

The precision with which you define your targets—the client's objectives—may prove critical in how effectively you arm yourself with intelligence in the form of research data on markets, motivations, media, and relevant issues.

The precision with which you spell out clearly what you see as the exact parameters (the specific boundaries) of your objectives may prove critical in how effectively you position yourself in selecting communication strategies, messages, and media.

The detail you give to vital inner configuration or features of the target may prove critical in sharpening your aim and steadying your grip for follow-through in making sure that your communication efforts come close to doing what you intend. That is why an objective that merely proposes "to inform" people about the client's position, reputation, product, or even existence should be rejected.

Any message informs. All information, by definition, informs. Is your job done once you inform? If your client's employees are informed about management's offers to the union, but they go out on strike, is the "inform" target adequate? Will top management long remember originality of content, style, and design of the communication campaign as they observe traffic stopped by picket lines and production at a standstill?

By the same token, an objective that proposes "to educate" provides an elusive target. Workers may be educated by union "information and education" campaigns but refuse to sign petitions for union representation authorization. Consumers may be educated about solidarity with strikers and still cross picket lines or buy products or services from a boycotted company. Would union leaders who retained public relations counsel be satisfied with paperwork documenting that, indeed, their publics were educated, despite their anti-union behavior? Some public relations writing objectives may approach more precision by focusing on "exposure" of groups or persons. Yet, even when numbers of persons or percentages of populations are exposed, exposure still fails to serve as a viable public relations writing objective, although it may be an essential means to an end.

A political candidate does need to be known to stand a chance at election, but the voters' behavior relates to *what* they know and believe about the candidates. A president of the United States or a governor may have far more exposure than opponents but fail to win reelection.

Even in product advertising, exposure by itself serves only a limited function. Companies have found that exposure may not necessarily translate into consumer acceptance of a product, let alone recollection of positive traits and desire to purchase.

Exposing, as informing, showing, and educating, does not mean getting a public to act or understand, accept, or even pay attention to a message. Exposure does presume that a public has had the opportunity to see, hear, or read your message, but it does not indicate what you want the public to do.

There is a semantic trap in using such language as "the objective is to expose," "the objective is to publicize," or "the objective is to promote." For, even if you think in terms of affecting attitudes and behavior in the interests of client and publics, others in the organization may look upon proposals and progress reports that do not go beyond expose, publicize, or promote as reflective of what a *Wall Street Journal* (*WSJ*) interviewee called lack of awareness and concern for the impact of writing on the strategy and results of the company: "They [public relations persons] must have the characteristics of a businessman and be bottom-line oriented."[8]

Quaker Oats Board Chairman Robert Stuart told the *WSJ* that public relations professionals who progress and earn board and management respect are more apt to go beyond simple interest in the technical handling of the issues and the communication involved and are aware of the impact of what they do on strategy and objectives of the company.[9]

Although there are exceptions, effective public relations writers define their objectives precisely and in terms of the desired behaviors of members of publics that will benefit the client, rather than in terms of their own PR activities.

Awareness as a Writing Objective

For public relations writers, *increased* awareness may be suitable as a preliminary or secondary objective. But basic questions must be answered, such as:

• *Who* is to be made aware, preferably in terms of numbers as well as concrete specifications of publics and subpublics? For instance, who might be potential customers?

• Of precisely *what* should they be aware, beyond mere identification of a brand name? For instance, the kind of product and certain attributes such as economy, guarantee, durability, tamper resistance, attractiveness?

• What *level* of awareness should be attained for particular subpublics as well as the whole group? For instance, should engineering or computer science graduates be aware enough that they will write in for booklets on employment opportunities?

• For *how long a time* after exposure should awareness continue at the target level? (Awareness that fades quickly from memory and is not recalled at point of purchase or needed decision would have little value.) Should awareness last longer than the week in which the new computer hardware system models come out? How much longer?

Awareness does not necessarily equal patronage. The Ford Edsel, Freddie Laker's Sky Train, Pet Rocks, certain video games and TV series, and countless other products long gone from the marketplace stand in mute testimony.

Certainly, Presidents Lyndon B. Johnson, Richard M. Nixon, Gerald Ford, and Jimmy Carter had voter "awareness" as incumbents. So did California's Edmund G. (Jerry) Brown Jr. when the then-governor ran against a relatively little known opponent for the U.S. Senate. That they either were discouraged from running for reelection or were defeated by challengers indicated that far more than awareness was involved.

Awareness of "what is good" for individuals (be it responsibilities of citizenship, health practices, consumer protection, natural resources conservation, or driving under 55 mph on the open road) may earn relatively high marks for the public relations persons who wrote the materials for institutions, government agencies, corporations and associations. But when less than 20 percent vote in a school board election or one out of every 10 Americans suffers from alcoholism, it is suggested that more than surface awareness must be sought.

Certainly, McDonald's Corp. and Golin/Harris Communications sought more than awareness when they set out to create temporary residential facilities around the country "where families of children being treated for cancer, leukemia and other serious illnesses can reside while the child receives treatment at a nearby children's hospital."[10] Ronald McDonald House objectives went beyond mere exposure to win PRSA's national Silver Anvil for excellence in business community relations. The public relations team worked for awareness that led to fund raising and allowed McDonald's to grant more than $1 million toward local development of more than 30 of these special places for very sick children and their families.

Public relations programs were aimed at reinforcement of the perceptions and awareness of the client for "providing a unique and valuable service to local communities that would, in turn, further differentiate, by positive action, McDonald's from its competitors." The initial finding: "An unprecedented 80 per cent of all customers queried were aware of the Ronald McDonald House" in their own cities.[11] As an example of the news media feature backgrounders issued by a southern California agency for the Ronald McDonald House project, see the photo and release on Valerie Zucco, the young cancer patient who is "fighting back."

Southern California Ronald McDonald House™

a project of
Southern California Children's Cancer Services, Inc.
A Non-Profit Corporation

For Immediate Release

FIGHTING BACK - ONE DAY AT A TIME

"Am I going to die?"

The words spilled out impulsively after the physician announced the results of extensive hospital testing diagnosing acute myelogenous leukemia, a type of cancer affecting bone marrow and blood forming tissues.

The physician paused to eye his young, dark-haired patient cautiously after her first question, and then continued. Some do die, but not all, he said. With her cooperation, they would work together.

Valerie Zucco, a bright and bouncy 12-year-old, is willing to fight.

Despite the fact her young life has been turned upside down by an unwelcomed intruder, she's managed to maintain a positive attitude and sense of humor while being hospitalized.

Only weeks before she was squirting nurses with water syringes, the Southern California girl had been playing softball when a large suspicious looking bruise appeared on her forearm. A few days later, her grandmother noticed another bruise on her knee. Then a rash of smaller bruises surfaced.

-more-

Contact:
McDonald's Operators' Association of Southern California □ c/o Bob Thomas & Associates
835 Hopkins Way, Suite 505 □ Redondo Beach, California 90277 □ (213) 376-6978

Joan Zucco whisked her daughter into the hospital emergency room late one Saturday night with bruises, loss of appetite and eyes beginning to appear jaundiced.

Silently, the divorced mother of two girls suspected leukemia. She was familiar with the symptoms. Only three years before, she watched the disease claim the life of her aunt just six weeks after diagnosis.

Two days after Valerie checked into the hospital, a pediatrician and hematologist confirmed Joan's worst fears - leukemia - a kind of cancer where abnormal white cells in the blood crowd out healthy white cells on the front line of the body's immunity system.

Valerie was referred to Childrens Hospital in Los Angeles, specialists in treating childhood cancer, for a battery of bone marrow tests, spinal taps and blood transfusions.

"You just go along and wait," Joan says of the day-to-day ordeal. "Now we take it a day at a time. That's all we can do."

With her daughter confined to "Laminar flow," a sterile environment within the hospital to protect against infection, Joan Zucco faced a series of practical problems such as a place to stay.

She slept on a small cot in the hospital, avoiding costly hotel rooms, until a hospital physician told her about the Ronald McDonald House across the street. Arrangements were quickly made.

"It makes it so much easier for people who have to come a distance," Joan says. "To me it's a place to rest and leave the problems for a while. You can regroup your thoughts and return to the hospital ready for the next day."

-more-

111

With her mother as her closest trust, Valerie spends her days with Joan. They pass the time slowly, sharing new cards and letters from home, playing games, watching television and catching up on schoolwork.

Between times, there are new rounds of chemotherapy treatments, liver scans, x-rays and bone marrow tests that are physically painful and mentally punishing to both mother and daughter.

Evenings Joan retires to the Ronald House where other parents of hospitalized children gather to share information, commiserate or socialize over a glass of wine.

With a deep, unwavering religious commitment, the Zuccos are coping.

"Having faith doesn't mean that you don't cry and hurt, but it gives you what you need at that time," Joan says. "Valerie's attitude and cooperation with the nurses helps. If she can be brave, I can be brave. We help each other."

# # #

Contact: Rosalind Gray Smith, Bob Thomas & Associates, Inc. - 213/376-6978

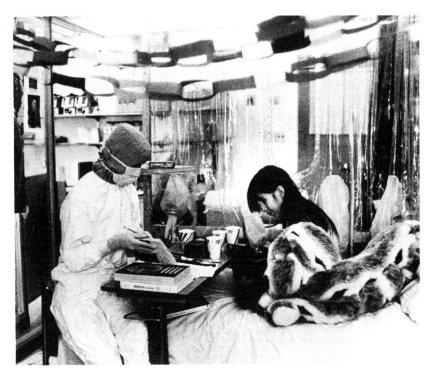

Coping with Cancer. Joan Zucco spends a quiet moment with her daughter Valerie, 12, in a laminar flow unit at Childrens Hospital of Los Angeles. The unit is designed to insure a sterile environment to protect against infection. Ms. Zucco has been a resident of the southern California Ronald McDonald House, sponsored as a public service by the international McDonald fast food chain. *(News media background material and photo courtesy of Bob Thomas & Associates.)*

Beyond Awareness

Some public relations writers think in terms of objectives that evoke or contribute to "favorable opinion" or "goodwill" for the organization. But you need to ask: How favorable? In relation to what specific criteria? Leading to what behavior? If people think well of your client, how do you want this opinion to be acted upon?

In the case of the Silver Anvil award-winning Monsanto campaign for Spray Guard Rain Flaps for trucks, Public Relations Manager Fred G. Marshall sought more than mere awareness.

PHOTO

Monsanto

C. Ann Wilkinson   (314) 694-3472
Fred G. Marshall   (314) 694-2915

FOR RELEASE   October 8, 1979

PUBLIC RELATIONS DEPARTMENT
Monsanto Company
800 N. Lindbergh Boulevard
St. Louis, Missouri 63166

The grassy surface of Spray Guard Rain Flaps by Monsanto catches water thrown off by a truck's tires and directs it back down onto the pavement, minimizing spray and keeping it primarily below the windshield level of passing cars.

-oOo-

NOTE TO EDITORS: Spray Guard is a trademark of Monsanto Company.

100879-23

114

Objectives met

- A study conducted in October 1980 demonstrated that Spray Guard Flaps as a mud flap had achieved an unaided awareness among decision makers of 21 percent, as compared to 8 percent awareness for the nearest competitor.
- As a splash and spray suppressant, the product gained 19 percent awareness, as compared to 1 percent for the nearest competitor.
- In roughly a one-year period, publicity gained more than 80 major trade stories and more than several hundred media articles.
- *Sales leads generated—3,286 through December 1980— were judged by sales force to be satisfactory to excellent in terms of volume . . . and quality. Over 50 percent generated were viable leads. Of the more than 3,000 inquiries, 40 percent were generated by publicity.*[12]

News materials generated were aimed at going beyond awareness to goodwill and from goodwill on to results even more meaningful to top management.

An example of the public relations communication is illustrated in the Monsanto photo-caption of a truck on a wet highway.

Measuring Opinions and Behavior

Opinions and behavior can be measured to determine the effectiveness of communication, as Monsanto did. You might launch your communication campaign in a test market, much as a marketing executive might evaluate a product's acceptance or an advertising director might compare a television commercial campaign's results in Peoria with findings in a city with similar variables but without that particular campaign.

You might correlate opinion survey results and actual behavior that follows from that opinion over set time intervals so that you can project public behavior to your CEO with at least fair accuracy.

To do this, you might ask help of your client's experts who work with marketing comparisons, opinion research, statistical analysis, and computer programming.

If opinion tends to be somewhat unreliable in predicting behavior, then you may profit by looking into how to measure the impact of communication on behavior as part of your writing process. Help is available in the literature of public relations, marketing, advertising, opinion, and behavioral research. You may profit less, but profit nevertheless, by pretesting the impact of your writing on a panel in which you try to include persons representative of the publics you are trying to influence.

With very small numbers involved in panels, it is unlikely that you will be able to assemble a scientifically reliable representative sample. But in the case of a panel, you look for insights and probe for depth of reactions to public relations communication before freezing them in finalized video, film, or print, according to Thomas Glenn, president of Telepoll and former chief research analyst for Decision Making Information.[13]

A small firm, institution, or government agency might be unable to afford the sophisticated services of a research organization that sets up panels or runs surveys. But some pretesting, even with margin-of-error risks, is better than investing a great deal in communication that may not prove efficacious or, worse, that may backfire.

Help may be available, even for those with a very modest budget, from universities or colleges: from professors, graduate students, or whole classes in departments of mass communication, psychology, sociology, speech communication, and business administration. But the writer must first answer, *whose* opinion, *whose* behavior, and *why* these persons instead of others?

2. AUDIENCES/PUBLICS AND WHY

One of the many meanings assigned to "audience" in the conventions of the English language defines the term as a group of persons gathered, tuned in, or paying attention to your communication as viewers, listeners, or readers. In *Mass Media III*, Ray Eldon Hiebert, Donald F. Ungurait, and Thomas W. Bohn made this distinction:

> Audience refers to the individuals who actually use the content produced by a basic media unit. For the mass communicator, the public is an abstraction; but the audience is a reality because audi-

ence members actually consume what the media produce. . . . The members of the audience are *active participants* in mass communication. They select, buy, consume, are affected by, and act on mass media content. Human beings are not vegetables in the media cooker. Audiences interact with the media, and the results are complex and powerful.[14]

Corollary questions may be suggested: Whom do I need to reach with my message? *Why* this group of individuals instead of assigning priority to others?

In public relations writing by objectives, the answer will relate to one or more of the client's objectives. The why may suggest different alternatives or priorities than the initial targeting of publics. In raising the question before, during, and after the initial selection of publics and subpublics, you cause yourself to pause and reflect. Is the why primarily related to ease of communication, tradition, or, best of all, solid rationale directly related to attaining client objectives?

Writing down answers to the *why* question helps you challenge weak selections or fill in gaps as you review your reasons.

The question also demands *pragmatic concern for who* CAN *be influenced,* not just who would be desirable to reach. Do the individuals you designate have the position, authority, influence, and power to help contribute to change?

It would be well to keep in mind that companies, service organizations, and bodies of government do not read, watch, listen. *Individuals within these entities do.* Public relations professionals think in terms of publics of individuals, not of nameless, faceless masses or composites. For it will be individual management personnel within organizations who may expose themselves to the public relations communication and who will choose how, if at all, to act upon it.

Can one communicate effectively with "the general public"? Does the general public vote? *Or is general public a term that is so all-inclusive that it defies analysis?* Certainly, the term could include babies, senile persons, nonreaders, and those too disinterested to expose themselves to television programs you might use.

Do you target "readers" of the *New York Times, Chicago Tribune, Los Angeles Times, Newsweek, Wall Street Journal, Philadelphia Inquirer, Fortune,* or other publications? Or might you sharpen your focus to investors, brokers, and analysts who specialize in given kinds of issues in certain areas and who are more likely to read the financial-business sections of those media?

Do you really want to reach employees of aerospace firms, *or* do you need to be more precise in tailoring your communication to aerospace board members, CEOs, financial officers, legal counselors, heads of research and development programs, or the like?

If your client is a U.S. senator from Michigan, does he need to reach *all* Michigan citizens, all eligible to vote, all registered to vote, all most likely to vote, those who are Republican and most likely to vote, those who are in that category but who are marginally supportive or marginally opposed, voters who gave funds or who are in the senator's correspondence files? Or do you even need to be more precise on variables involved in the specific issue at hand?

Untargeted Listeners

A few words of caution: Although you may target and prioritize audiences you need to reach, and you may tailor your communication and deeds in such ways as to achieve desired results, you need to keep in mind that untargeted individuals may have access to the communication.

Among the more common oversights are stockholder reports that assure investors of the financial strength of the organization and record earnings and dividends at the same time as employees are told that the company has recessionary problems that prohibit generous cost-of-living increases. Other problems may be generated by disseminating messages to proponents in media to which opponents are tuned. And consider the classic cases of politicians saying one thing to sectional interests and finding it picked up by media for other parts of the country in which they may have given somewhat different messages.

Perhaps in the instant global communication environment at the end of the twentieth century, the caution to public relations persons serves to *underline the value of consistency and ethics.*

3. AUDIENCE CHARACTERISTICS

For both intended and unintended audiences, the public relations person set on attaining objectives must ask, What can I find out about these persons relevant to my client's business and objectives and the communication needed? Thomas E. Eidson, senior vice president of Hill and Knowlton, one of the world's largest public relations agencies, stressed the importance of really knowing your audience:

> First, in all our communication—proposals to clients, media backgrounders, letters to senators—the foundation is a very common sense point of view. Is the individual who receives the message educated enough on the company, product, and issue to be able to understand? If not, the initial goal must be to bring the individual up to the level of education needed to understand. Second, does the audience have misperceptions about you, your organization, issue, and project? If there's a misperception, you better correct it.[15]

Audience Research for Strategic Communication

Audience characteristics dictate strategies of communication. For a company such as Hill and Knowlton, a great deal of data on the publics with which its clients must communicate can be carefully researched, continually updated, and stored for ready retrieval in computer information systems.

Some agencies and corporations on the cutting edge of public relations practice have developed computer capabilities for doing simulations with given public responses to actions and communication: "With these background variables, these situational aspects, and this message, the audience can be expected with X amount of reliability to respond in this way." Companies such as ARCO may subscribe to several professional research services to gain knowledge on how their publics think and behave, and, of critical import, what trends appear in the future. Others, such as Security Pacific National Bank, augment their corporate resources with futures research departments as well as gather relevant data on their publics.

The most relevant data may be an individual's *framework of reference*. This means the total structure of the individual's viewpoint as shaped by experience and other environmental factors. This is a systems orientation. Important framework of reference factors (audience characteristics) can include what you know about the media a person uses, schooling received, groups to which an individual belongs formally or with which he or she associates or identifies informally, group or societal standards important to the person, degree of commitment to those norms and values, family background, influence of significant others whose opinions the person respects in certain types of situations, and the complex of attitudes and behaviors that the individual has built up over the years. Such factors will guide you in effectively tailoring communication campaigns and strategies.

That is why companies such as Decision Making Information set up focus groups and do surveys for *Fortune* 1000 companies and such political clients as the President of the United States. (President Reagan contracted for surveys long before his election.) Clients want to measure the attitudinal and behavioral pulse and gauge the impact of particular messages under situational constraints.

Public relations researchers and writers share a common interest in the following:

• *Audience demographics*, descriptive information available from the U.S. Census and a diversity of sources and trend information as developed by such companies as Yankelovich, Skelly and White. (This firm conducts research for *Time* and a number of the country's largest corporations.) Examples of demographic information include where people live and work, size of household, family, age, sex, kind of work, level of income, organizational affiliations, consumer patterns, and other socioeconomic data.

• *Audience psychographics*, that which develops a psychological portrait of individuals who make up publics and which helps public relations persons understand more about how people may think and respond and what goes into their attitudes or perceptual processes.

• *Attitudinal and behavioral patterns*, what the persons you are targeting have expressed as opinions (or what similar persons probed in surveys or studied in experimental situations have said that might be representative of the audience with which you are dealing), and, most revealing, what they have actually done when confronted with similar situations.

General information, of course, may prove useful. But the public relations communicator looks for framework of reference factors as *relevant* as possible to the particular client's objectives, time, and situation in which the communication will take place.

Precision in analyzing an audience counts. Newcomers to audience analysis who define for themselves that an audience is "well edu-

cated, upper middle class, moderate, young, concerned about . . ."
are challenged by their seniors in public relations practice with such
questions as:

> How well educated is "well" educated? What range does that
> take in for the individuals in the public, what mode, mean, median?
> Educated in what, specifically, that is relevant to this particular sit-
> uation and communication? What does "upper middle class" mean?
> What does "moderate" or "liberal" mean? And how moderate, on
> what, under which circumstances, as related to the case at hand?
> How concerned? With what level of understanding? How young is
> young and is youth only chronological in this situation?

With intelligence on your audiences comes more than just a
foundation for the selection of style and logic with which to communicate. Knowledge of audience characteristics may suggest optimal media
or channels to use. Or it may dictate a change to a different set of client
objectives. And audience characteristics provide valuable clues as to
the needs, interests, desires—the objectives—of the persons you seek
to influence.

4. AUDIENCE OBJECTIVES

Today's most effective public relations offices develop profiles of what
the publics and subpublics perceive as their interests and needs. For
example, examine the case study at the end of this chapter and see
how the public relations department at the *Los Angeles Times* analyzed
its public in the Washington High School program.

In addition, for an investment in computer equipment costing
no more than a few standard typewriters, that information can be updated
easily, used to predict trends, and brought to bear in projecting how
publics may perceive client actions and communication. Bechtel Power
Corp. public relations staff in San Francisco uses several Apple computers, according to Jim Mackin, APR, who was requesting an additional one for headquarters for southern California.[16] Haley, Kiss and
Dowd were exploring in 1983 the setup of a network of computer
terminals for their principals in New York, Washington, and Los
Angeles.[17]

The authors of *Public Relations Management by Objectives* purchased matched microcomputer systems to store research data and process notes, drafts, rewrites, and copyediting. Both authors have found additional applications in their public relations counseling and teaching.

Even a student task force in California was given aid by Avco to purchase a computer system to help it analyze publics and individualize communication to donors, media, and potential program participants.[18]

Professionals have discovered a great deal of data now available from the federal government; registrars of voters who have precinct records on votes on propositions, as well as candidates; independent survey findings; Gallup, Harris, Roper, and university-based research organizations; and subscriptions to private data bases, such as Nexis, the Source, and the *New York Times* and Dow Jones services that feed their results over phone lines and directly into office or home computer systems.

All this strengthens public relations professionals for the exploration and understanding of the perceived objectives of publics so that they may design strategic programs.

In support of the fourth step of the informal public relations writing approach, Senior Vice President Eidson told an interviewer that Hill and Knowlton professionals ask:

> What are the self interests of the audience? What is the individual interested in? What does the individual want to hear?
> Finally, what do you want to achieve and how can you match up the interests of client and audience?[19]

In this part of the public relations writing by objectives system, you are essentially asking such questions as this: What might the audiences I have selected *want* from my client or employer and *look for* in my message if they are to be influenced along the lines I have specified in my client objectives statement?

Checklist of 10 Guidelines

Here are some suggested checklist items that may help:

1. Are objectives spelled out precisely for each relevant public and subpublic, particularly those to whom you attach the greatest priority?
2. Are nebulous and vague terms defined?

3. Have you considered all known audience characteristics and used this knowledge in developing audience objectives?

4. Are these objectives up-to-date or might the wants, needs, and desires have changed since the last research you consulted was done?

5. Have the hunches or hypotheses drawn from analysis of audience characteristics been subjected to a field test? (In other words, have they been tested by verifying with a representative sample or even a panel believed to represent important parts of the audience?)

6. Have you taken into consideration that old but true principle of public relations that publics judge an organization by its actions, not just its communication?

7. Have you included audience objectives directly related to behavior of the client?

8. Have you taken into account that individuals within publics may be torn between conflicting objectives? For instance, some persons may wish to see the government sharply reduce taxes but want it to increase spending on entitlements they perceive as important to their personal interests.

9. Have you balanced conflicting objectives among major publics or subpublics?

10. Do you keep in perspective that what an audience needs, as seen by relatively objective observers, may be different from what an audience *perceives* as its needs?

All this is *not* to suggest that a public relations writer will want to say whatever an audience wants to hear or read just to increase the chances that these individuals will be persuaded or prepared to act in certain ways.

Indicators of Change

Sometimes an analysis of audience objectives may lead to the conclusion that you face a no-win situation in which the potential damage may exceed the potential gains. Or analysis may suggest the need for a lengthy campaign to gradually shift opinion by helping members of the audience perceive their interests differently. Or you may become aware that the priority of publics and subpublics in a campaign may need to be changed.

Sometimes the communication may have to be preceded by a revision of policies or an improvement of products and services before you can develop messages that have an effective impact on the publics.

The strategist's understanding of the perceived realities of audience objectives will help in researching and designing messages that will gain and hold attention, influence perception, motivate retention, and build in the mechanism for recall and action. *But if the audience* PERCEIVES *manipulation or pandering, even if none was* INTENDED, *damage may be done.*

Public relations writers and their executives have become more sophisticated in analyzing audience characteristics and objectives. They have rejected as inadequate generalizations that "*the* public feels, believes, wants, expects. . . ." That is because publics, as the rational human beings of which are constituted, tend to be creatures of *varying degree* rather than simple either-or mechanisms.

With sophistication in the application of this system, professionals increasingly demand gauging the *strength* of commitment, the *degree* to which a perception is held. That is where computer scenarios may prove invaluable.

You may program in different conditions, as basic as timing of communication, if the client objective is to persuade donors to contribute more (for instance, at year-end with the Christmas spirit providing an audience with altruistic objectives and awareness of tax-bracket-change deadlines providing harder incentives).

Or you may program in such factors as the focus of the media spotlight on malpractice situations, not in your own company, but in the industry.

Or you may program in the contingencies of what competitors or detractors may say following an action or in the midst of a communication campaign. In a sense, this is similar to what the chess player does mentally in trying to reason several moves ahead: "If I move my knight to that space, she'll capture it with her queen. Then, I'll move my other knight in, and she'll. . . ." Poker players and bridge enthusiasts may see similar analogies in scenarios they create in their minds as they attempt to read the behavior and intentions of others.

The number of factors or variables that can come into play can tax the mind of a grand master or a public relations professional. There are more players on the board than the pieces being moved. And intricate combinations of actions and responses are possible. But there is more to chess than the pieces on the board, and there is more to public relations writing than the words in a message. Environmental conditions may affect the players.

In short, the audience may require more than the information in print or script to be persuaded in the direction the client wishes.

Among the questions the public relations writer may ask, consider:

1. What do members of the audience need or want to accept a speaker, article, brochure, or visual presentation as reliable and credible?

2. What do the individuals require to convince them, first, that points of the message are relevant to them and their situations and interests?

3. What do they have to see or understand to make the message— or series of messages and interaction with the client and the client's agents—so commanding as to motivate change or action?

4. What reputation does a company need to establish to predispose an elementary school youngster to think more seriously of conservation or be open to the company's side and pay attention to its communication later when it wants support in letters to regulatory commissions and legislators or when a proposition appears on the ballot?

Management Insulation

A large problem confronts public relations counselors who find top management people or themselves believing too much in the power of persuasion or the power of authority while dismissing the perceived interests of their publics.

Although business management authority Dale E. Zand found that businesses in the era of "the knowledge society" may exist as "caldrons of knowledge," the past New York University chair of management/organizational behavior warned in 1981 that the tantalizing promise of those caldrons still eludes, misguides, and overwhelms organizations:

Managers in business and government in the United States appear to be insulating themselves from views that differ from their own. Harmony and amiability are so highly valued that many organizations operate with ineffectual policies because managers are reluctant to risk unpleasantness by speaking up.[20]

So public relations professionals have learned that more is needed than antennae scanning the environment and computerized storage of data when dealing with audience objectives and trends in those objectives. Internal publics, starting with the CEO and board of directors, more and more frequently are being targeted first and their personal objectives and characteristics taken into account so that their defenses may be pierced.

Zand observed:

> The industrial citizen is faced with a dilemma. No single organization need account for its use of a public good, but the aggregate of all organizational use deteriorates the public environment [and, yet, each organization] will seek to minimize its costs, arguing it must do so to remain competitive. Ultimately, the accumulated deterioration is bound to reach catastrophic levels.[21]

Regardless of the sensitivity and responsiveness of public relations personnel, CEOs, and members of boards of directors and regardless of the strategic design of the content of the message, effectiveness of communication will depend upon the selection of means of communicating and, beyond that, anticipation of the objectives of the gatekeepers.

5. MEDIA/CHANNELS AND WHY

To introduce the incorporation of "channels" in this section, recall the interpretation of audience in the second part of this 10-step system with the concept of the individual as a public of one, and of small groups of individuals especially attentive to interpersonal communication.

For public relations writing, in its most complete and systemic sense, does not recognize any dividing line between mass and interpersonal communication as its boundary. Such public relations professional opinion leaders as the co-publishers of PR *Reporter*, Patrick Jackson, APR, past president of PRSA and head of the national agency bearing his name, and Otto Lerbinger, APR, Boston University persuasive communication authority, look upon one-on-one and small-group communication as the key to effective public relations, especially in this era of mass communication's greatest technological break-throughs and acceptance.

In asking you to think in terms of audiences as well as publics, we wish to reinforce consciousness of the value of employing *interpersonal channels and strategies* in addition to mass media for communication.

James E. Grunig, editor of the *Public Relations Research and Education* journal that began publication at the end of 1983, presented a theory earlier in *Public Relations Review* that targeted publics on the basis of similar communication behaviors:

> The internal communication professional must have both a means of identifying who the correct people are (to target his internal publics) and a means of determining what the correct information is (the information needs of these publics).[22]

For instance, in dealing with employee complaints, you could set up employee committees or T-groups (task groups) to discuss openly their complaints as they perceive them. At the same meeting, the public relations counselor or other management person not only would listen actively but also would interpret corporate policy and concern. This could be complemented by newsletter or video communication, but it would be hard to replace with either. Similarly, *quality circles*, which became popular in the early 1980s, also would provide for employee participation in problem solving.

And in dealing with external communication programs of the modern organization, you will want to make a mental note to consider when interpersonal channels should complement the use of mass media or be employed on a first-priority basis. A good example of this would be when management personnel discuss in an open forum concerns investors or financial analysts have about diversification into new product lines. Again, mass communication techniques could be helpful, but not as effective as the interpersonal channel with its opportunities for direct feedback and interaction.

Power in Interpersonal Roles

You may gain the most communicative power through interpersonal channels when you are involved in:

1. Researching and drafting briefing papers for CEOs, members of the board, and other organizational leaders

2. Preparing 3 by 5 cards or scripts for use by executives with such small but powerful groups as legislative committees, news conference attendees, boards of directors, the various levels of management, and shareowners or donors

3. Drafting speeches for trade associations, major community or regional organizations, and influential assemblages

4. Predicting the questions and writing, editing, and critiquing answers for delicate negotiations or interviews

5. Writing the scenarios in preparing yourself and others for potential crises

6. Developing the written proposals and sketching out the oral back-up you will use in addressing top management in securing support for future public relations programs or changes in corporate policies

The "Media/Channels and Why" step in the PR-MBO Writing System basically starts with a choice among print mass media, modern electronic and video communication vehicles, and interpersonal channels.

As a public relations strategist you are not limited to using one medium or channel, however. For purposes of employing the most effective means of communication with publics and subpublics under given conditions, you may wish to use a combination approach.

The value of redundancy across media and channels of communication is imbedded in the comprehensive public relations campaign. Unlike some practitioners in advertising, however, public relations professionals avoid repetition and provide a redundancy of theme, rather than slogan, a redundancy in which new aspects of the same theme are stressed to stimulate continued interest.

Moreover, when different aspects of a message are conveyed in newsmagazines, newspaper columns, television newscasts, radio reports, cable documentaries, luncheon speeches, trade publications, special circulation newsletters, and small-group sessions, they build a dynamic impact on the individual and the social entities exposed.

Exposure and the building of interest are only part of it. It is a truism that in many situations, most mediated forms of communication come in second to face-to-face or voice-to-voice contact. Such contact does not replace print communication but complements it with other forms of interpersonal and mass communication. The objectives no longer are to get a story in ink but to affect public opinion and behavior through any and all modes of communication that may prove efficacious.

Communicating Live and Electronically

For some veterans of the print media or long-time practitioners of public relations, the strong print orientation of yesterday was difficult to overcome, but overcome it they did. The discipline of public relations once favored the dissemination of information through newspapers followed by trade publications, general-interest magazines, and print materials published by companies and institutions for their internal and external publics.

But executives, who need preparing, if not scripting, now are experimenting with live video teleconferencing to link their far-flung offices and field operations. As ARCO Special Projects Manager Manuel Jimenez pointed out, when you have executives around the world listening in and entering into the conversation live, and being taped as well, what might be acceptable in conference room discussions may be inappropriate and ill received in teleconferencing.[23]

Several generations of citizens have been weaned away from print literacy to visual literacy. Commercial television, cable, videotape, videodisc, and other audiovisual channels have become increasingly dominant as credible, popular means of receiving communication for education and news, as well as entertainment.

New surges in the purchase of subscriptions to data bases that send information over phone lines to home and office computers and the mushrooming of cable television channels and programming further complicate *and* enrich the role of the public relations communicator.

Today and tomorrow, the public relations person, long frustrated with the limitations on interpersonal communication, will find that the state of the art of video and computer technology will make possible simulation of one-on-one and small-group communication. Moreover, public relations persons are exploring actively the increased application of electronic feedback loops, such as that provided by the Qube-type cable television in which viewers may communicate instantly to the stations.

With the trend toward electronic communication going beyond conventional television and video to computer transmission with offices and homes of members of influential publics come great new opportunities for public relations professionals. Innovators like Peter Dowd of American Medical International and Haley, Kiss and Dowd, the national consulting firm with such clients as AT&T, ARCO, and the U.S. Olympics Committee, have said that the computer-accessible, audiovisual, audience-interactive annual report will soon emerge.[24]

First, analysts and brokers will be able to review audiovisual and print-graphic annual reports on their computer screens and order those portions in which they wish more depth and documentation. Then, before the turn of the century, individual investors in the market will not only be able to tune in annual reports on cable stations or home computers, much as they now request printed reports, but also will be able to order that which meets their level of interest.

As Dowd noted, this will not replace printed annual reports, which probably will still be required by the SEC and will remain useful as back-up documentation or as primary communication for those who still prefer traditional print.[25]

Strategy of Choice

What the fifth step of the 10-step analytical system offers the strategist-writer is the challenge of choice that will prove most strategic. You look not only for exposure of messages but also for receptivity and the follow-through needed by your audiences after being exposed.

As in selection of publics and subpublics, the *why* part of this step represents the investment of analytical thought, preferably based on hard research data. The answers developed by the writer may look insufficient when set down on paper and examined again.

Or the answers may suggest turning to other communication vehicles. A novel example may be found in the Space Shuttle Columbia Coloring Book published for children by Rockwell International Rocketdyne Division.

Some individuals may have found themselves writing for the kinds of media for which they once worked or for which they were trained to write when in journalism school. There is nothing wrong with applying one's expertness, of course. But more may be needed than that

HITCH YOUR WAGON TO A STAR.

Space Shuttle Columbia Coloring Book

Rockwell International
Rocketdyne Division

Columbia and other space shuttles will make many trips into space carrying cargo. Now the cargo is Scientific Equipment to teach us more about our Earth and the space around it. One day the Shuttle will carry people to Space Stations far above the Earth . . .

A lot of work goes into a flight. Before a Launch, Scientists and Engineers make final preparations at Kennedy Space Center.

Then Columbia made 36 orbits around the Earth in two and a half days. While it's orbiting, the Columbia actually flies upside down.

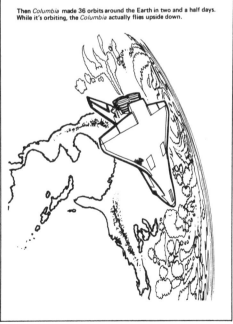

(Courtesy of Rockwell International Rocketdyne Division.)

brought to the job. Exploring the rationale for media and channels selection may suggest such needs to those who approach the question with relative objectivity. So it is the process of asking, not just the answers, that will benefit writers here.

The *why* questions and responses should relate to such concerns as characteristics of the audiences (what they read or watch, believe in, and prefer as sources, for instance); the criteria of the media (for example, is it feasible to satisfy them with the communication needed by the audience?); the strategies of persuasion (will appearance in a certain setting legitimatize a message?); and the relative advantages and disadvantages of the possible choices.

Targeting Media Components

The time may have passed for publicity barrages aimed at a class of media or channels, including some that may become inured to messages that fail to meet criteria and develop a systematic bias to future releases or phone calls, as University of Oklahoma's Bill Baxter reported in *Public Relations Review.* [26]

This step in the writing system calls for pinpointing specific organs of the media or channels of communication with the greatest applicability and value in a particular situation. [27] The fine tuning does not stop with selecting from among those that will do the most good for your client's objectives and at the same time be prone to use your material.

You gain power in developing persuasive communication and reaching highest priority individuals by selecting components of a medium.

By medium component, we mean a part, section, column, television segment, radio interview, beat, feature, byline article by a reporter with area of specialization, and so forth, that appears periodically. Normally, this implies that an idea or materials can be directed to a specific editor. It goes along with component selection to tailor materials for the medium to fit the peculiar, special criteria of each component.

For instance, a particular backgrounder on a merger in the offing might be directed to the business reporters for the local television channels, while a contribution to cultural enrichment of the community might be discussed with the media people who deal with the arts and entertainment.

6. MEDIA/CHANNELS OBJECTIVES

Thus far, it should be clear that the modern public relations writer serves as a student of business administration or public administration to analyze client objectives that require support and as a student of psychology and sociology to analyze audience objectives that demand client and writer attention.

To these roles, professionals have added that of student of mass and interpersonal communication to analyze the objectives of gatekeepers to the news media and the criteria of other media and channels.

Some basic texts, business and government executives, and folklore of public relations practice have lumped the mass media into a deceptive catchall term of "PR tools." The concept poses dangers to the newcomer to media relations who perceives of a newsmagazine, newspaper, wire service, television news department, or other independent medium as a "tool" of the public relations professional.

Gatekeeper Role Defined

Certainly the decision makers who govern the what, when, where, why, who, and how of treatment of information about public relations clients and employers do not look upon their media as tools of any special interests. These are the gatekeepers: news directors, editors, documentary executives, reporters, copyeditors, film editors, camera crews, sound technicians, photographers, even the telephone answerers and mail sorters who have the power to say what makes the news.

Will what you provide the gatekeepers be given in-depth or surface treatment? Will it be buried among the truss ads or on the rip-and-read news after "The Late, Late Show"? Will cynicism about its content be reflected in questions asked of interviewees, the single-word quotes that appear in print, the commentary, the choice of what information is included and what deleted?

Frankly, will the phone call message be left unanswered and will the envelope with the agency or employer name in the upper-left-hand corner be thrown in the trash unopened?

Will someone be assigned to call and get the client's side when potentially damaging news breaks elsewhere? Will background information from your client be used to put bad news in perspective?

If the media were tools in the sense that some employers seem to envision them, they would use what some gatekeepers would term garbage, stories for small-town papers without local angles; business items that do not meet the standards for the financial pages to where they were directed; news copy loaded with stereotypical adjectives, unsubstantiated claims, and too-obvious plugs; television coverage ideas with trite visual and audio angles; cliché photography possibilities; copy laced with spelling errors, typos, and poor syntax; stories on product publicity for trade publications that do not use product stories; and worse.

By and large, the gatekeepers of the media are very selective. That is why sharp public relations professionals invest so much effort in systematically reading, listening to, and watching media potentially important to their clients. And that is why public relations persons file away notes on what they learn about the media from firsthand observation, articles in the literature, seminars, and interviews with the gatekeepers themselves.

What Distinguishes Media Components?

General rules of writing or basic journalism are important but serve only as the beginning of your analysis of what specific news media components require.

You focus on both substance of content and stylistic criteria. You wish to focus on specifics of the situation at hand and analyze what is involved *now* in making the story attractive enough for the media and components selected to give your story or viewpoint prominent position.

That a columnist uses "human interest" material only scratches the surface. What *kinds* of human interest? Nostalgia? Controversy? Conflict? Irony? Satire? Empathy? Raw human emotion? Underdog vs. the establishment? "How-to" hints? Health and safety concerns?

That a family section prefers "features" tells the writer very little. Features on what? In what style? Features on the life styles of persons in a certain geographical area? Articles on unusual roles for women? Features written by certain byline writers with an empathetic style? Different media require different materials and styles of presentation. For instance, as the *Los Angeles Times* Theatre Trailer Continuity for the bicentennial series illustrates, the scripting provides for crisper, more direct verbal communication mated with music and filmed scenes.

LOS ANGELES TIMES THEATRE TRAILER CONTINUITY

BICENTENNIAL SERIES

#12 - THE FIRST ISSUE

- Run dates: November 9, 1981 to January 3, 1982 -

SCREEN	SOUND
The picture fades in on an elevated view of downtown Los Angeles, circa 1881. As the announcer begins to speak, the camera slowly zooms in towards one particular street corner. The picture dissolves to a close-up of a simple newsstand on the street corner (it is actually an original photograph that has been mocked-up to match the vintage shot). The camera continues to move in, and finds that the first issue of The Times is for sale at the newsstand. We are in a close-up of the newspaper when the announcer finishes speaking. The music comes up, and the picture dissolves to a title reading:	MUSIC CUE #1, UNDER FOR ANNOUNCER: It was the 4th of December in 1881. The population of Los Angeles was a meager 11,000. The city streets were made of dirt; buildings with more than three stories were rare. But on that morning, a very small newspaper published its very first issue.....and made a commitment to the community.....that lives on one hundred years later.

1881 Los Angeles Times 1981
 	
    A Century of Service
    to Southern California
	MUSIC UP TO FINISH

(Courtesy Los Angeles Times.*)*

135

Criteria for Client Media and Channels

Just because a company or institution publishes its own newspapers and magazines or produces its own video or slide presentations, professional public relations writers know that they are not relieved of the responsibilities of analyzing media criteria and tailoring materials accordingly.

Certainly, in-house editors and audiovisual producers have their own objectives for content and style factors in what they find acceptable. Public relations executives increasingly demand from their subordinates that they not only scrupulously analyze external media and gatekeepers' standards but also strive to operationalize like—or higher—standards of professionalism with internal channels of communication.

The viewers and readers of internal media still have a choice about whether to tune in to messages or discard something after a cursory once-over. These publics, as the publics of external media, demand more than the stereotypical puffery disclaimed by public relations and journalism professionals alike. Nor do these publics respond well to employer self-praise. If internal public relations objectives are to be met and if the channels of communication are to have credibility, internal criteria require attention.

If anything, your own media may need more rigorous criteria because they tend to be viewed sight unseen by some readers as management propaganda vehicles. You may have to work harder to earn the reputation for being a reliable, unexaggerated, germane source unless your client's media already have established that reputation.

Just as with external media, you will want to *earn* selection of your ideas and written materials. If you are the gatekeeper for your own medium, you will want to demand no less of your own submissions than you would of a stranger.

No gatekeeper may be involved in governing what gets through when you draft speeches, ghostwrite correspondence or statements, prepare a CEO for Q and A at a board meeting, provide briefing materials to department heads and supervisors, and prepare material for other interpersonal channels of communication.

In that case, the authors suggest that you research and analyze what may be required to provide for the most effective utilization of a given channel. A letter, for instance, should avoid bureaucratese and communicate to the individual with the eloquent direct simplicity and power counseled by Kenneth Roman and Joel Raphaelson in their 1981 book, *Writing that Works.*[28]

Should a speech be written in a different style than material for the eye? Public relations writers for the ear know that listeners cannot go back, pace their listening as they would their reading, glance ahead to find out where they are going, or stop to cogitate a point while nothing else gets thrown into the channel.[29]

And will both the style and content depend in good part on the factors of speaker, publics, timing, place in program, and other situational demands? *For even if there is no person occupying the role of editor or reporter gatekeeper, the members of the public have their own internal gatekeeper filters in their minds. And the mental and emotional controls of the individual are the most demanding gatekeepers of all.*

7. SOURCES AND QUESTIONS

The experienced professional writer and the newcomer to public relations will differ in their application of this most crucial part of the writing system.

For the professional, developing sources and getting answers to questions must be not only a necessary part of each writing exercise but also a continuing process in gaining analytical intelligence on a broad array of fronts related to effective public relations writing.

This seventh step of the system is most critical because the standard "do and don't rules" of public relations writing and "current" techniques tend to be temporal in nature. They are temporal because of the racing obsolescence of techniques and technologies; rapidly changing media, styles of communication, and media patterns of publics; the outmoding of long-accepted theories of communication; attitudinal shifts of publics; the increasing sophistication of publics; and a host of emerging changes.

This part of the system is most crucial because dependence on handout and dictated information to varying degrees may be born of too little practice and motivation for verification, challenge, interpretation, and development of additional facts and quotes.

Some introductory writing courses may have contributed to this dependence by having students work only with hypothetical handout materials. Supervisors may have contributed to this dependence by interns or newcomers on staff by asking them to rewrite handout information without urging them to go beyond the handout.

Whatever the complex of causal factors involved, the seventh step has helped the professional practitioner break the mold. And this step can be of value in providing clues to the rest of the 10-step system.

More than an analytical inclination is needed if the objectives-oriented writer is to support the right objectives, target the appropriate publics and subpublics, gain a grasp on their frameworks of reference and objectives, select the most efficacious media or channels of communication and meet their objectives or criteria, and develop strategies that will motivate and persuade as desired. The professional who graduated from college in the 1960s, for instance, and who has carefully read the *Public Relations Review, Public Relations Journal, Columbia Journalism Review, Journalism Quarterly, Public Opinion Quarterly, Journal of Communication, Journal of Organizational Communication*, and any number of other journals, texts, and newsletters, or who has participated in continuing education programs, has changed radically. So has the professional who entered the field in the 1970s. The increasing rate of change will make the 1985 graduate's training obsolete by 1990 *unless* continuing education is programmed.

8 Ways to Budget Time

Generally, and from the perspective of analyzing specific situational variables in each public relations campaign and writing assignment, as a strategist-writer you will budget in each month's or week's calendar the following:

1. A review of special-interest publications important to the top management of the organization and trade literature appropriate to your company or institution

2. A reading of journals and newsletters in public relations and allied areas for understanding of communication strategies and techniques

3. Attention to published reports (or your own subscription to private services) on trends in public opinion

4. A scanning of a wide range of literature that reports on the psychological and sociological bases of organizational, group, and individual behavior

5. A daily study of print and electronic media that have an impact on your organization and its publics

6. Interaction with specialists in areas other than public relations within your organization in a programmed manner to gain a stronger grasp on how public relations relates to marketing, advertising, sales, production, legal, industrial relations, and other areas

7. Interaction with public relations specialists in your field to share intelligence and to explore cooperative ventures

8. Interaction with public relations persons in other fields to gain fresh insights that may be applicable in your own field

Computerized and Human Searches

Some large corporations and institutions operate their own library services with computerized search capabilities. For public relations professionals without this resource, university and public libraries may be the place to turn. The so-called interactive computer searches allow a writer to submit combinations of coordinates to specify articles to be located; for example, public relations and nuclear plants—cover-ups and credibility. You may get more specific and call up additional coordinates, such as crisis public relations and explosions.

A reference librarian at a university or public library can help you cut through the mystique of how to use the *New York Times Index, Business Periodical Index*, other indices to available literature, media and marketing reference works, government and private data banks, and the like.

Some organizations have their own data available for analyses of audience frame of reference and objectives. For instance, investor relations may have access to a body of research on current stockholders and decision makers for brokerage houses and mutual funds. Or marketing and sales may yield a wealth of information on dealers, communities in which the organization seeks increased sales, and potential customers. Or the fund development arm of the institution may have detailed profile and pattern information on donors and prospects. Or industrial relations or the personnel office may be asked to share information on veteran employees, recruits, retirees, and persons in the marketplace they seek to recruit.

More than numerical data may be had for the questioning. Specialists in these and other areas also engage in continuing study of their fields of expertness.

The various line and staff officers of an organization may be queried to verify your hunches about organizational objectives, strategies that will work with certain publics, and problems that may arise. And sometimes the public relations person can turn to trade associations to which the company or institution belongs. Staff there have the full-time responsibilities for storing useful information for member organizations.

Colleagues in the field may share information if reciprocity is indicated. And, as mentioned earlier, professional organizations, such as PRSA and IABC, maintain library research services for members.

Persons in media or staff to government agencies and legislators may serve as vital links of intelligence in anticipating the informational needs and objectives of their colleagues.

Journalistic Questions and Sources Model

Even when writing materials for nonjournalistic media or channels, the strategist-writer will want to consider the journalistic model of asking questions of original and additional sources to verify, interpret, challenge, clear up, expand upon, complete, and test.

Books such as *Creative Interviewing* by Ken Metzler[30] will refresh the veteran professional's understanding of media questioning approaches and acquaint the newcomer with strategies and techniques you may be able to adapt. In addition, such books may yield valuable insights into the anticipation of questions that will be raised by the media. Other techniques found useful include analyzing questions in news conferences; studying articles in which interviewer questions appear, such as *Playboy* profiles; and while reading newsmagazines and newspapers or watching television news, asking, What question would I have raised to elicit that quote or point of information?

Building Patterns for Practice

Theory and practice tend to part ways when people develop early habit patterns of relying too heavily on handout information instead of exploring a multitude of sources and asking questions. Although what is desirable may not always be feasible, the PR-MBO and C-R-E-A-T-E processes move toward fulfillment when writers themselves program questions to be asked of their publics.

You may not have the time to do a scientifically reliable random survey before a given backgrounder or speech is drafted, but the possibility of doing so in the early stages of campaign preparation deserves consideration.

You may wish to program as part of the questioning phase a field testing of message components or build into the communication package a pretest of opinion before the message and a posttest following up on groups isolated from the communication as well as those directly exposed. Or you may wish to ensure that you receive feedback and monitor calls and correspondence to others in your organization. Questioning leads the way to communication strategies.

8. COMMUNICATION STRATEGIES

This eighth part of the system warrants a book by itself. As a matter of fact, libraries are filled with literature that would prove valuable to the public relations writer in developing strategies. We do not develop another persuasion or applied communication theory book here. Instead, we focus on the relationship of this step to others in the system and suggest a few guidelines.

Basically, the communication strategies step asks, How will what I write be designed to be most effective in supporting my client's objectives with the particular audiences I am trying to influence through the media or channels I am proposing?

Figure 5.2 illustrates how the first seven parts of the PR-MBO Writing System fit with communication strategies. Note how the arrows indicate the flow of steps into one another. Also note the broken line illustrating how the loop is completed by communication strategies supporting the attainment of Client/Employer Objectives to influence public behavior.

Answers to the question about using the system to build effective communication for your client may be found, in part, in your analysis of the characteristics of your publics. Those characteristics will dictate style and content and persuasion strategies that are capable of being understood and accepted by the publics and subpublics of priority choice.

Answers may be found, in part, in your analysis of what the

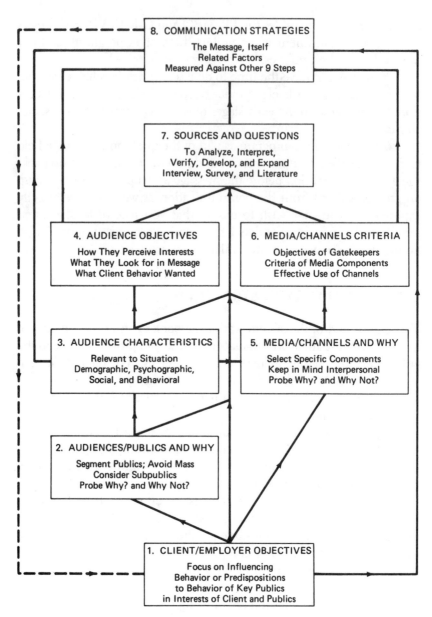

FIGURE 5.2   It All Fits Together in Strategy.

audience perceives as needs, wishes, desires—the objectives of the publics and individuals that comprise them. Unless necessary stimuli are taken into consideration for at least partially meeting public objectives, your communication may not even receive the attention of these individuals, let alone motivate them in any way.

Answers may be found, in part, in your analysis of the media and channels of communication and what the gatekeepers or channels themselves require of content and style.

Answers may be found, in part, in your in-depth questioning of data banks, literature, experts internal and external to the organization, and the members of the publics themselves.

Examination of what has worked here or elsewhere in similar situations may help. But note that even if the same individuals were involved, they and a lot of other situational variables have changed, and each case requires careful scrutiny.

26 Strategic Guideline Questions

In planning and reviewing strategies, you will want to develop your own checklists of general and specific situational reminders. Here are some to get the process started:

1. What are the obstacles to overcome with my key publics?

2. What obstacles may I anticipate with the media?

3. What is significant, special, even unique?

4. What are the strengths or strong points to emphasize for my client?

5. What weaknesses or weak points should I take into consideration?

6. What are the negative aspects of the situation?

7. Conversely, what are the positive aspects?

8. What needs must I satisfy in educating my publics—and my sources and media of choice?

9. What should be interpreted or explained for their level of background and understanding?

10. How can I plan my message to fit with other public relations and organizational communication—past, present, and future?

11. What (and how) should I anticipate and prevent in the way of negative interpretations, unfavorable effects, exposure to untargeted audiences, holes in logic, responses by competitors or critics, questionable actions or information presented to me, or other potential problems?

12. When is the most propitious time to communicate?

13. When and how will I want to follow through to reinforce or build upon this communication?

14. How do the situation and communication relate to other situations that affect publics and media?

15. What should I emphasize and how and why?

16. How should I target and tailor communication to meet differing characteristics and objectives of publics?

17. How have I taken into consideration the individual, group, and social values and norms of the members of the publics?

18. How have I taken into consideration the fact that certain individuals, media, and organizations may set the agenda for what members of the public will view as important and even serve as opinion leaders in the more classic sense?

19. How do I avoid overlooking individual variations within a subpublic or public?

20. Would *no* communication effort be more appropriate in this situation?

21. What contingencies have I anticipated?

22. What may I do to pretest or monitor the effectiveness and impact of the communication I plan?

23. Which internal publics, from the board and CEO on down, should be informed—and how—before I go public with the message?

24. Which internal publics need to have approval rights on policy implications, legal concerns, organizational security, technical accuracy, appropriate perspective, and other considerations?

25. How much are the biases of my sources and my subjectivity affecting my analysis and writing, why, and how should I control that?

26. What strategies should have greater priority in this particular situation?

This is a good time to pause for a moment to review the 26 guidelines and make marginal notes in which you write additional questions related to your needs.

These questions, in themselves, may suggest to some individuals a reason to explore the seminal literature on persuasion and gain exposure to recent findings of research (and proposals for filling in the gaps left by research).

Reframe Strategy. Sir Rodney's adroit briefing of the Little King illustrates the strategic principle that suggests the public relations professional writer search for and report positive aspects at the same time as releasing negative information the public has a right to know. (*Permission to reprint courtesy of Johnny Hart and Field Enterprises, Inc.*)

Mature public relations officers who return to campus to audit or take for credit a course in persuasion or communication theory discover and rediscover ideas they can apply to their programs and communication.

Strategic Communication leads to Essence of Message. Parker and Hart deftly illustrate how a communicator may take guidelines 6 and 7 into account to reframe strategy in the "battle report" cartoon episode of *The Wizard of Id* as Sir Rodney offers an unusual, but life-saving, essence of message.

9. THE ESSENCE OF MESSAGE

The professional may start with the essence of what is to be communicated following the conception of client objectives and may modify that essence as the rest of the analysis takes shape. That, too, is strategic.

Essence is neither the lead-in to a message nor necessarily a summary of the communication. Look upon this part of the system as a challenge to you to state tersely in a modest-sized paragraph the core, or bottom line, of what you are trying to get across to the members of your audience.

Essence will be defined here as the planned communication impact that may lead to the predisposition to behavior, or better than attitudes alone, to the behavior itself. Several questions help make this clear:

1. If I am to be most effective in this campaign, what concept should be clear in the minds of the individuals in my publics?

2. What is the major point (or points) I want them to process, understand, accept, remember, relate, and act on?

Before, during, and after developing this essence, review your client objectives and strategies of communication and ask these additional questions:

3. Does the essence support the client's objectives effectively?

4. Does it fit with the strategies developed, and are they adequate to earn acceptance of the intended message?

The essence will be developed and supported in the verbal body of communication *and* in the nonverbal context planned to create mental images of the realities you seek to modify or create.

10. NONVERBAL SUPPORT

In an increasingly audiovisual society, it is well to consider that much communication takes place or is conditioned by individuals' perceptions of what they see, hear, smell, touch and taste—what they sense—beyond the words used.

The public relations writer is challenged to plan for nonverbals in order to:

- Complement verbal points
- Make their own points
- Create audience confidence
- Provide a comfortable sensory setting
- Develop identification of client
- Depict what the client represents
- Attract interest to the verbal message
- Hold or build that interest
- Guide the reader or viewer sequentially to the next point
- Bridge parts of verbal communication
- Provide symbols that strike responsive chords

In some respects, the challenge to the writer is to meet the nonverbal criteria of media or channels. In another sense, it is to make optimal use of nonverbal possibilities through such communication vehicles as corporate symbols.

A public relations writer should not stop with "a photo of X" and leave the rest to the photographer, unless that person has been briefed on the objectives, strategies, and media criteria and can have a sense of the whole message. The writer also may suggest action, setting, foreground, background, color, focal point, and persons to be included.

Ford Aerospace and Communications Corp. and Rockwell International used two different visual approaches to illustrate their roles in America's space shuttle program. The Ford media kit included the photograph of Mission Control in operation while the Rockwell backgrounder materials provided both color and black-and-white copies of an artist's rendering to show the reentry of the *Columbia*. These pictures demonstrate how nonverbal materials communicate with publics.

In ordering or developing materials to be produced internally or vended, you as a public relations writer will not just request the design

Mission Control. Ford Aerospace and Communications Corp. provides a service to the media by furnishing this photograph of Mission Control operations to complement written materials in its media kit during a space shuttle mission. *(Courtesy of Ford Aerospace.)*

of a brochure, for instance. Instead you will find it advantageous to share your ideas with the artists. This includes thoughts about needs for nonverbal communication to contribute in certain ways. In the brochure example, this may involve suggesting graphics, photos, layout, color, and even paper texture that will convey part of the message to readers.

Elinor Selame, president of Selame Design, makes a similar point about the importance of nonverbal communication with this observation about corporate identity problems:

> Your visuals look old, tired and inflexible. Your image is faded and aged. Remember, in the beginning it was the innovation, daring, and flexibility that created your success and growth. If you cease to

project that dynamism, in time your position will be preempted by younger, more aggressive organizations. And it will be difficult to attract bright young employees.[31]

The writer who scripts a videotape, slide show, or live presentation will be concerned with the voices of speakers, sound effects, titles or graphics, visual illustrations of key points, and even the personality that will come across on the screen or in front of the microphone.

Most of all, the professional public relations writer will be concerned with the *substance* of the whole communication and its effects. Nonverbals that serve only as attractive packaging for weak communication may inadvertently do more damage than good by building expectations of executives and publics with first impressions and letting them down with the contents.

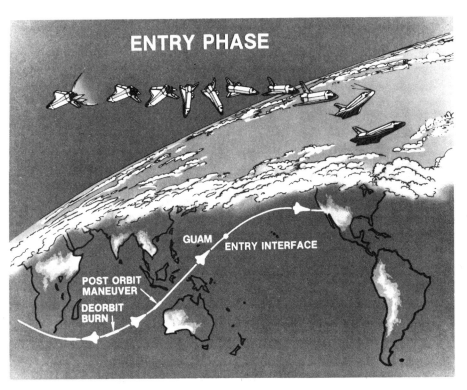

Graphic Nonverbal. Rockwell International media backgrounder materials included both color and black-and-white copies of an artist's rendering to show the reentry of the *Columbia* space vehicle. (*Courtesy Rockwell International.*)

PUTTING IT ALL TOGETHER

All the analyzing, strategy developing, planning, outlining, drafting, rewriting, polishing, field testing, and evaluating come down to a *unified systems approach to public relations writing to attain objectives.*

Consideration of all the analytical concerns will become part of your approach to public relations writing if given a chance to be operationalized on several projects. But even when you feel secure with this or a modified system that meets your individual client's needs and meshes with your personal style, it may be prudent to keep reminding yourself not to skip steps.

One of the most important steps in the system is holding up that tentative final draft against the evaluation criteria you established. And in holding it up to that creative yardstick and in finding areas that may not measure up, the challenge is to try to make adjustments as time permits and to do the research and planning next time that will assure greater conformity between analysis and communication.

Neither should be set in concrete. Unconsciously, you may improve upon the analysis in developing the actual message. Consciously, you may discover that the analysis has weaknesses or calls for an ideal out of your range at this time.

A Last Check for Fit

Formal evaluation procedures are required to put both the analysis and the written communication to the test of pragmatic effectiveness. But, in the meantime, ask yourself these questions about the last draft before accepting it as final:

1. How well does my creative product appear to support my client's objectives?

2. How well is it aimed at and tailored for the publics needed for support of client objectives?

3. Does it do well enough in taking into consideration their characteristics and objectives as publics and as individuals?

4. How did I do in selecting the most effective media and channels of communication for these client objectives, this selection of publics, and the situation in which we are involved?

5. What could be improved upon in assuring that the commu-

nication I have designed meets the objectives of media gatekeepers and makes the most effective use of nonmediated channels?

6. How realistic are my strategies? How comprehensive? How effective? And have I really followed them as well as I might?

7. Will the essence of what I wish to convey really come through? What may I do to increase its chances considering the constraints imposed by media, publics, and even my client organization?

8. How well have I mated verbal and nonverbal communication into a cohesive whole?

Professionals who have worked with such a systematic, analytical, objectives-based approach to communication have found that, ultimately, the test of effectiveness lies in the influencing of individuals within selected publics to act in ways that will be in the mutual interests of clients and publics.

LOS ANGELES TIMES PR-MBO CASE

The *Los Angeles Times* has established a number of records in its development as an international prestige publication, including its rise to the largest full-size metropolitan newspaper in America, its claim to the most advertising linage in any newspaper in the world (with the resultant greatest space for news and features of any newspaper in the country), the capture of 11 Pulitzer Prizes, and the distinction of becoming one of the first businesses to adopt a management by objectives system.

The *Times* also has invested in PR-MBO by charging Promotion and Public Relations Director Gordon Phillips and his staff of 40 with going "over and beyond good day-to-day objectives to a few very important ones, objectives that can be achieved over day-to-day necessities."[32]

The primary objectives of public relations writing, as of the rest of the department, relate to the publishing company's profit orientation and responsibility to shareholders. More precisely, these objectives support Board Chairman Otis Chandler's and Publisher Tom Johnson's interests in:

• Increasing advertising accounts and linage
• Strengthening circulation quantitatively and qualitatively (in areas advertisers and editorial staff appreciate)

• Enhancing attraction to its work force of applicants from the cream of the crop nationally

• Motivating increased productivity and incentive to improve the economic and qualitative aspects of the product

• Building on the reputation among its own employees, investors, advertisers, subscribers, and business and social communities as a "classy, exciting, modern, healthy" institution

• Increasing respect among elected and appointed officers of government at all levels and their trusted sources of counsel and inspiration (opinion leaders) that will contribute to support of editorial positions and causes supported by the publishing company.

And in recent years the newspaper has become increasingly concerned about its relations with the large black, Hispanic, and Asian communities of southern California. In parts of the black community, in particular, the newspaper has sought to reverse perceptions of the *Los Angeles Times* as a fortress of the establishment, hostile, cold, inaccessible, unconcerned with the problems and needs of blacks.

The public relations program started with actions to attract and develop more minority employees, investigate problems in black communities, place its editorial support behind business and government programs, and more.

"And more" included the investment of parent Times Mirror grant funds in special enrichment programs in Los Angeles communities, including a pilot study at the predominantly black Washington High School.

Public Relations Manager Carolyn J. Hom and two staff writers came out of a brainstorming session inspired by objectives to be achieved in challenges and opportunities posed at Washington High School.[33] The 10 steps of this chapter are illustrated in the text that follows.

Times Client/Employer Objectives

A not-so-hidden agenda item of the public relations staff was to involve the corporation's top executives and, through this involvement, reinforce them in funding such programs plus increased commitment of *Times* human resources in working with black students and their teachers.

Although the case study focuses on the PR-MBO Writing System as it related to black publics, this kind of *objective of influencing the thinking and behavior of top management is important to recognize by public relations writers who wish to assume more responsibility as change agents.*

Hom and her staff sought to develop among the black students:

1. Enthusiasm, as reflected by their participation in the project.

2. Feelings of being part of the newspaper publishing process, as indicated by their involvement and feedback during and after programmed activities.

3. Perception of the company as human and reachable, as indicated by observation of the students interacting with employees and in feedback from teachers.

4. Stimulation of communication of the experience to parents— "This is what the *Times* did for me. . . ."

5. Increased understanding of the process of putting out a newspaper, as operationalized by the students working with staff to put out a Washington High edition of the metropolitan newspaper.

6. Reduction in fears and frustrations with the job application process so that young black persons would feel more prepared to apply for jobs.

7. In the long run, encouragement of newspaper readership built on understanding and familiarity. (Hom said this was secondary to the above purposes.)

8. Indirectly, contribution to the affirmative action program of aggressively developing long-range programs for hiring qualified minority employees.

Times Audiences/Publics and Why

The *why* is imbedded in the objectives. The public relations staff recognized the persuasion principle that the best time to develop predispositions to behavior (attitudes) is while individuals are more malleable and adaptable, before opinions form or become hardened. Yet the students had to be at a mature enough stage to understand some of the complexities involved in the newspaper process and to be able to become involved in a hands-on sense.

Keep in mind that *Times* executives were a primary public targeted by the staff.

Secondary audiences included parents and teachers, who would serve as interpersonal channels of communication to other members of their communities and at the same time reinforce through questions and discussion the interest of the youngsters in their experience. Black media editors constituted another secondary public as a channel of communication to other opinion leaders and members of their communities.

Times Audience Characteristics

From on-site investigation by Hom at Washington High School, including observation of classes and interviews with teachers, and from her study of sociological literature, she developed a profile of the student audience that included such factors as:

1. Very shy, somewhat withdrawn
2. Ninth grade level with age mode of 13 to 14
3. Volunteers in year-long program sponsored by Times Mirror for 125 ninth graders in which classes of 10 to 15 students spent an hour a day working with the metropolitan newspaper as textbook and teachers as coaches on reading and communicating skills
4. Working from a base of extremely low reading skills
5. Difficulty in ability to communicate orally, as well as in writing
6. Intimidated by process of filling out paperwork for jobs
7. High dropout rate from school activities perceived as dull

Times Audience Objectives

The public relations manager's research indicated that these students respond to learning experiences when they are:

1. Fun
2. Doing/participatory, in which the youngster experiences by being as directly involved as possible
3. Activity, with enough diversity to hold attention

Interpersonal Communication. Here's how *Los Angeles Times* staffers Eliza-
beth Christian and John Oligny clear up the mysteries of paste-up and photo
development skills for visiting ninth grade students in an innovative communication program brainstormed and analytically planned by the manager
of public relations and professional writers on her staff. *(Photos by Ted Roberts,*
reprinted with Times *permission.)*

The youngsters are interested in and impressed by "important" people. Yet they need what Hom called "the warm, cuddly" kind of relations with adults whom they perceive as caring about them.

They are more comfortable with persons with whom they can identify (including others who are black); and they require communication that is direct, interpretive to their level of vocabulary and simplicity of syntax.

Times Media/Channels and Why

The public relations staff's primary channel involved interpersonal communication. As the highlight of the year-long program, the *Times* brought the youngsters directly on-site.

1. Hom and the Washington teachers prepared the students in their own classrooms for the visitation.

2. Chairman of the Board Otis Chandler and Publisher Tom Johnson conducted a question-and-answer session for the boys and girls.

3. A procession of executives and experts met, worked, and lunched with the students. The experts were selected (and prepared) by public relations staff for their ability to relate with warmth, enthusiasm, and a simplicity of communication. "We needed somebody who could cut through the shyness and the reserve real quickly," Hom explained.[34]

4. The students were given hands-on instruction in selecting stories for their own edition (budgeting), laying out the front page (dummying), writing their own stories (much as teams of journalists may be assigned to specific breaking stories, each contributing a portion), and pasting up their own stories as they had dummied them. They learned to develop pictures in the editorial photo lab. (Actually, the process started before the visitation, with the students given a list of subjects on which they were requested to write. Their stories were compiled and typeset by newspaper employees before the students came on-site.)

5. Public relations arranged for the communication of sight and sound, including tours of the three-story, block-long pressroom; editorial offices; and other facilities.

6. Management and personnel specialists oriented the students to job applications to prepare them for the time when they would enter the employment market.

The students saw a slide show with action simulated by the four-projector, multimedia process as part of the focus on activity, color, and fun in the making of a newspaper.

The print communication consisted of the earlier editions of the newspaper the boys and girls had studied before and during their visitation and the parts and whole of their own Washington High School edition of the *Times*. Their involvement and identification of the special edition with their own and classmates' efforts and photographs served as reinforcement and communication they could share with their parents and friends.

The *why* in each case flowed from the characteristics and objectives of the students as analyzed by the public relations staff.

Copies of the Washington High School edition and news releases on the program were given to editors of black media as backgrounders. And Times Mirror newspaper and foundation executives also received follow-through communication, including copies of letters from the students.

Times Media/Channels Objectives

Discussion of the criteria of the interpersonal, audiovisual, and print communication is imbedded in the section on selection of media and channels. In this instance, the students role-played gatekeepers, based upon their instruction by their professional coaches. All the media and channels required an underlying current of activity to hold and focus attention, a human style geared to their characteristics and objectives, and an interpersonal touch to break the ice.

Times Sources and Questions

Hom and her staff analyzed not just the Washington High School data but also notes based on their observations of school tour groups over the years, and their college and continuing education study of mass and interpersonal communication, sociology, and psychology.

They verified hunches with the Washington teachers, members of the newspaper staff, and the students.

During the Washington High day at the newspaper, the staff took notes on what they saw and heard of the communication and behavior. In addition, both newspaper staff and teachers provided feedback. The questions of the students and their letters provided additional information.

Times Communication Strategies

The strategies included:

1. Programming of hands-on experiential involvement
2. Programming of fun
3. Programming of action
4. Directing communication to the level of understanding of the public
5. Involving the public in the decision-making process
6. Providing authorities and experts they would respect
7. Preconditioning to the experience
8. Reinforcing, including recognition and identification
9. Providing role models
10. Establishing relevance to their lives

Times Essence of Message

The *Times* is approachable. It is human and is personified by people like paste-up expert Debra Washington, editorial cartoonist Paul Conrad, National Editor Dennis Britton, Publisher Tom Johnson, and Board Chairman Otis Chandler.

The *Times* cares about people, and that includes young blacks.

Newspapers are understandable and exciting. Reading and writing can be fun and valuable. Filling out a job application may not be exciting, but it is not frightening.

Times Nonverbal Support

Key nonverbals resided in the voices, facial expressions, body language, and touch of the newspaper persons who worked with the Washington High students.

The smells of ink, photo lab, and machinery; the sights and sounds of equipment and humans; the music, visuals, and vocal nonverbals of the slide show; the feel of the paste-up process and job application forms; the taste of the food at lunch; the warmth that came through in a sixth sense—all this combined to present a wealth of complementary

Washington High School Edition

Los Angeles Times

Wednesday, April 14, 1982

Punk-Funkers Head List of Music Groups

Washington High School students' choices in music ran a wide range—from punk-funk, to rhythm and blues, to mainstream pop. However, of the four students who chose to write about their favorite music groups, two mentioned punk-funk musicians, the Bar-Kays and Rick James.

"My favorite musical group is the Bar-Kays," wrote Willie Cater, "because I like their style of music. Two of their hit songs are 'Hit and Run' and 'Freaky Behavior.' I enjoy listening to their songs. Sometimes when I hear their songs on the radio, I record them on my cassette recorder.

"I listen to all of their new recordings and I also enjoy seeing the group perform. Their last appearance was on 'Soul Train.' They sounded great!"

This article was written by Willie Cater, Victor Edwards, Angela Jackson Sneed, and Tenita Sargent.

Victor Edwards wrote:

"My favorite kind of music is punk-funk, by Rick James and the Bar-Kays. I have an interest in other kinds of music but punk-funk has a beat with a slow natural rhythm. The rhythm that is used in punk-funk makes it very easy to do the latest dances such as the Pop-Lock, K-Swift, Gigolo and the Grapevine.

"Rick James' songs are great and a lot of the words have very good meanings if you listen. He talks about things that happen in the street such as hanging out and ghetto life. This comes from his album called 'Street Songs.' He tries to warn us that hanging out is not where it's at. He tries to tell you that you can't make it in life living on the street corners.

"Punk-funk is enjoyable and danceable music and a whole lot of fun."

Angela Jackson Sneed's favorite form of music, however, fell into the category of mainstream pop:

"My favorite entertainer is Olivia Newton-John. She was born in London, England. She lived in Australia ever since she was five. I like the rhythm she puts in her songs. Her songs have meaning. She has a unique style of singing popular tunes.

"Her record 'Physical,' is a record you can dance to or exercise by. Some of the records I like are 'Magic,' 'Suddenly,' 'Little More Loving,' 'Make a Move on Me.' She has sung with Cliff Richards, John Travolta and Andy Gibb. She also made two movies, 'Grease' and 'Xanadu,' and two television programs. Olivia Newton-John is a good performer."

Tenita Sargent, on the other hand, was attracted to the moving lyrics of rhythm and blues singer Richard "Dimples" Fields:

"My music group is 'Sky.' But I really like this person. It's not a musical group, it's Richard 'Dimples' Fields. I love his music. I like him. He's very mannerable. I love his records, 'Earth Angel,' and 'She Got Papers on Me.' My favorite is 'If It Ain't One Thing, It's Another.' I like the part when it says: 'Everybody shacking up, married folks are packing up. Country going up in smoke, where is Noah with his boat? Back matching on A.C 400 years and still not free. Martin pay all a man can pay, still we ain't got no holiday. Folks messing with my mind, make me a Frankenstein. This woman she by my side, she Dr. Jekyll, Mr. Hyde. Can't keep my head on right, *problems* day and night. It calms my nerves, I try to

Please see MUSIC, Page 2

TED ROBERTS Los Angeles Times

Washington High Students pose for a group picture after their day at The Times.

Washington Students Criticize Reaganomics

President Ronald Reagan came under sharp attack this month from students at George Washington High School. Students cited budget cuts and rising unemployment figures as two of the biggest reasons for their disillusionment with the President. Here, in detail, are their opinions.

Cassandra Rodney: I think President Reagan is an unfair man because he is making unnecessary budget cuts and forcing the unemployment rate to go up. Some of the programs being cut are strongly affecting minorities, like Social Security and welfare.

Sometimes I wonder if my mother and father are going to get laid off their jobs. I hope that doesn't happen, because my mother and father have been on their jobs for several years and need their incomes to survive. I feel President Reagan needs to be more considerate of minorities and shouldn't make budget cuts that strongly affect just minorities.

Michelle Alexander: I think President Ronald Reagan is not fit to be a President. He should have stayed an actor because that's the only thing I think he does half right.

The reason why I think this way is because it seems like everybody is becoming short on cash. He's even talking about cutting down on Social Security, welfare and retirement benefits. If he does, then how is everybody going to make it? I think that he thinks he's playing another role in Hollywood.

Renee Collins: President Reagan is messing up this country by cutting out jobs for the youth. He is also cutting out some of the Social Security checks and he is making it hard for the handicapped people to get jobs.

Today everything is not going all right for our country. But President Reagan has made it hard for the poor people to get jobs, pay rent and pay their car notes. So I feel that President Reagan should not cut out programs that are going to make it hard for people to survive.

Tyrone Boyle: I think President Ronald Reagan is a very good President but some of his so-called budget cuts are uncalled for because of the fact that some of the cuts are hurting other people. And budget cuts are not called for under Social Security, and the County of Los Angeles benefits and many, many more.

When President Ronald Reagan first began to run for President, I had a feeling he would be assassinated and someone else would be re-elected. Because he was hurting too, too many people. And I still feel that President Ronald Reagan will be assassinated.

Mother, Self Cited as Heroes at Washington

Students at Washington High School were asked who they considered to be heroes and why. The answers? One student listed her mother in recognition of a lifetime of work in raising her children and another student cited himself because he had saved someone's life.

"The person I consider a hero is my mother because when I need her, she's always there," said Norma Rodriguez. "I figure she's accomplished a lot in life by raising her kids up right and, to me, no one in this world can take her place."

"The things she's accomplished are that she raised her kids alone and now she owns a house front and back and a clothes factory and is getting to open another. To me, when I get older I have to accomplish more than she did, because I have more opportunities than she did."

"I consider myself a hero because I once saved a little girl from drowning in a swimming pool over at my cousin's house," Grant Williams said. "Her sister pushed her in. Soon she started to go under. At first I thought she was playing and her sisters were just watching. I saw her go under, waving her hands then. I said to myself, 'She's drowning,' so I dived in to pull her out. I grabbed her and took her to the edge of the pool so she could get air and she didn't even thank me. But I said that's okay, because I know I did something, too. I saved someone's life. That's why I consider myself a hero."

Trust, Respect Keys to Finding True Friends

Nearly everyone agrees that friendship is an important factor in our lives. In a recent survey, several students at Washington High School addressed themselves to the question of what friendship means to them and what they look for in a friend. Most agreed that friends respect, trust and truly care about each other. Here, in an exclusive feature report, are their opinions.

Tenita Sargent: Friendship means someone you know very closely and you trust and respect. Have manners, and you two will be friends for a very long time. For example, this is true. Jessica Singleton and Arleene Graves are very close friends. I mean both of them are my cousins, you know, and we share things. We are cool, close, you know. We do things for each other. If anyone messes with us we won't turn our backs and neither are we two-faced. Friendship is love, protection, trust in someone. Have respect, take up for someone, don't talk about them. And you shouldn't talk about anyone behind their back. Say it to their face.

Teresa Ward: Friendship is a word that is really important to me. The word friendship is a word relating to a friend. A friend to me is somebody or a person who's very related to you. It is a person who will always need you for something and you'll always need them for something. A friend to me, too, is a person who will call you and see how you are doing at times. A friend is someone who helps you, too. Like if you have a fight, they will help you and if someone talks about you they will tell you. If your friend talks about you, calling you names, that's not a friend for you.

What I look for in all my friends is love. I believe that you're supposed to love all your friends. What I look for in a friend is their personality, too, and how they look and how they dress. I like friends who share things with you and tell you about their personal problems. Friends are for talking things over and who answer your personal questions. Friends let you know what you want to know. Friends are people who you can really get together and talk things over and go places together. That's why I think friendships are for very important people, which I could consider as special people.

Andre Wright: Friendship means having friends you can trust, respect and depend on. My friends all respect me and I respect them. We don't fight, steal or distrust each other. We are not enemies, we are friends. I really care about my friends not getting hurt or in trouble. I choose my friends by the way they act. I enjoy being with people who have friendly personalities and can be trusted. My mother, sister and my three brothers, we all enjoy each other. My sister gives me money to take my little brother swimming. Friends are good to have and do things with you.

Tara Williams: Friendship means having someone to talk with and she will understand me and help me with my work. A friend is someone who tells you when you are doing wrong, someone who cares, someone who takes time to say, "Hey, I like you."

Please see FRIENDSHIP, Page 2

Drug Use Considered Dangerous But on Rise

Of the Washington High students answering a question about drug use in school, only one feels that it is declining. The consensus among the other students responding to the question is that the use of drugs, while extremely unhealthy, is on the rise.

Michelle Alexander: No, I don't think that drug usage has increased. It seems to me to be dropping somewhat.

The reason why I think so is because the students see drugs affecting many other people in so many ways and don't want it to happen to them.

Leslie Blair: I think drugs are our number one killer of all diseases. They tear up a person's mind. They put the body in addiction shock to always need drugs. And when they're not necessary, people use them anyway.

People abuse their bodies. I see them everywhere, shooting needles in their arms, popping pills in their mouths. It's getting bad. Little kids are being introduced to the drugs. They are being shown how to use them. What will the world be like 5, 10, 15, 20 years from now? How will everyone deal with it? Will it break up the family circles, or the world?

Lisa Boswell: I think more kids and teenagers use drugs because they think it's a fun thing to do. Drugs are not a good thing for you. They mess up your brain. They give you trouble. You waste your money on drugs. You could be saving for something you dream for.

They do things like that because they don't have anything or anyone who would probably listen to what he/she has to say. If they really wanted to stop it, they could. A friend would listen to what they have to say. All of the drugs are no good, even cigarettes are no good. If I could, or had a chance, I would stop it any way I could.

Chris Hereford: Well, I do think that drug usage has increased. Because when I was in the fifth grade, I was asked about three to four times a day, did I get high. My response was no. Now, when I was in the sixth grade, I didn't hear much about weed anymore. They were now popping pills.

I'm now in Washington High in the ninth grade. They have everything from booze to weed. Names of weed: Thai, sens, shernis, wetones. Names of booze: night train, a 99-cent wine. Everywhere you turn, it's booze or weed, mostly weed.

Wesley Randall: I think that drugs have increased among young teenagers over the years, because now more and more young people are killing themselves with drugs. Drugs are becoming a very serious problem in Los Angeles and other cities and states. Young people seem to think that drugs can cure all the problems and stress that they have. If a young man or woman has a problem with something in life, he or she should go to a parent or relative who may be able to help them, instead of taking drugs, making things worse than they already are.

Young people need to get together with the drug problems they are having. If more and more young people tried to talk to each other, instead of going to drugs, thinking that will make things better, more young people would be alive and well instead of walking around like little miniature time bombs about to explode and kill them. I, myself, feel that if young people stop using drugs and try to make something out of themselves, Los Angeles would be a better place to live.

Gary Robinson: Drugs have increased more than ever among young people in the '80s. But it's not just the young people any more, it's older people now, too. It seems like everybody's doing it—kids, young people, older people, sports players, movie stars.

It seems like drugs are just another thing that's there. When drug sellers and makers get put behind bars, they just get back out again. I think there should be a strong law! Put those drug sellers and makers away for good, because when they give drugs to kids, it puts them away for good. I think the bad part of this is people today just don't care, they just think about themselves. Maybe one day people will get hip with what's happening to the world. And maybe they won't.

Sitcoms Make Strong Showing in TV Survey

"Gimme a Break" and "Diff'rent Strokes" were the most popular television programs listed in a poll of students in the George Washington High School Reading Program. In the informal poll, 10 students replied to the queston, "What is your favorite television program and why?" Three students picked "Gimme a Break," two chose "Diff'rent Strokes" and the rest were scattered among several of television's most popular programs.

To Brenda Ramos, "Dynasty" is the best program on the air.

She said: "My favorite television show is 'Dynasty.' It comes on every Wednesday at 10 p.m. My favorite character is Fallon. I like her because she is very smart and sensitive.

"In 'Dynasty,' Fallon's brother got married to Sammy Jo and no one likes her because she lies all the time. She works on cars. She is not like everyone else.

"I watch this program every Wednesday because it has an interesting plot and good characters."

Brenda Youngblood went with the favored "Gimme a Break," however. She wrote:

"My favorite television show is 'Gimme a Break.' I watch the picture every Thursday at 9:30 p.m. on Channel 4. I like this picture because Nell plays a good part and the other girls are my age. Nell is always the funny one of the show. She enjoys making the other characters laugh at her. This program is funny to watch because I love to laugh along with all the characters.

"I can relate to the show because it deals with problems everyday people have. Nell sings the theme song 'Gimme a Break' at the beginning and end of the show. I liked one episode when the chief's oldest daughter formed a singing group with her friends. Nell helped them out."

"Dallas" has been a popular program for several years, and Angela Jackson Sneed explained why she is a loyal fan:

"My favorite televison show is 'Dallas.' I just love the big beautiful house the Ewing family lives in. My favorite character on 'Dallas' is J.R. He is always getting into trouble when he makes deals that cost him the Ewings' money. The good thing about J.R.'s that he is always trying to please his parents. No matter what it costs, he tries and tries.

"His brother, Bobby, is so different from J.R. Bobby tries to help everyone. He is very kind and understanding. He cares about his wife, Pam, and would do anything to please her. He tries hard to hold the family together. Bobby and J.R. make the show interesting."

Deborah Tucker placed her vote for "Diff'rent Strokes." She wrote:

"Todd Bridges on 'Diff'rent Strokes' is my favorite actor. He is very handsome, healthy and crazy.

This article was written by Brenda Ramos, Brenda Youngblood, Angela Jackson Sneed, Deborah Tucker, Arneise McGowan, Tonga Griffin, Stacey Tatum, Ben Littlejohn, Raymond Russell and Searcy Jackson.

I like him because he is a good actor and singer. He has one album, but I haven't bought it yet.

"Todd is actually Willis on 'Diff'rent Strokes.' He also likes to be on the show with Janet Jackson. They both have a good sense of humor, they make a cute couple and they are falling in love on their new TV series. She is a good actress who visits the show from time to time. Maybe one series will show both Todd and Janet getting together and living happily ever after."

Arneise McGowan's favorite show is the long-running "Jeffersons." She explains:

"My favorite television program is 'The Jeffersons.' I like George Jefferson because he is very mean to the others. George is about 5'5" tall, 50 years old, rich and owns a dry cleaners. George is always bossing the maid, Florence, and he calls his neighbors Zebras.

"'The Jeffersons' comes on Channel 11 at 6 p.m. every evening. I enjoy watching this program. George, Louise and Florence always make me laugh."

Please see TV, Page 2

Football Heads List of Students' Top Sports

Football and baseball are Washington High students' favorite sports, followed closely by basketball. Students also enjoy boxing, skating and weightlifting. Here are the responses to, "What's your favorite sport and why?"

Denise Allen: My favorite sport is skating. I like to skate because I enjoy dancing on skates and I also like to have a good time on skates. Skating is good for your health!

I go to Venice Beach and skate around and have lots of fun! This keeps me out of trouble. You don't have to know how to skate really good to really like skating. And, then you really don't have to like your skates to enjoy skating. You can skate just to exercise and still have fun.

Derrick Beck: My favorite sport is baseball. I like baseball because every baseball season I play on a team at Helen Keller Park. Once a week during the month of May, tryouts are held. The young men try out for their favorite team. Last year, I played right field for the Reds baseball team. I really enjoyed playing last year and I will try out again this year.

Playing baseball provides good exercise for you. When I warm up, I like to run, do jumping jacks, push-

Please see SPORTS, Page 2

Girl Meets Boy; Girl Loses Boy; All Ends Well

By **Cherlee Jamerson**

I will describe my boyfriend and me. When I was in the 7th grade, I had a crush on this guy who was in the 9th grade. When I was going home, he was walking my way. I said, "Why are you going my way?" He said that he lived on my street and we sat together and talked, and I introduced him to my mother and father and my sister and brother. January 6 of last year, it would be a year and a half, but he did not feel like I did. What I like most is that he is a nice guy. I love him and I know he loves me. He asked me to go back with him and I said yes. I think we make a good couple.

communication. The pictures of the boys and girls and the format of a newspaper *they* produced provided other experiences of nonverbal communication.

And from the Children

The feedback from black media, teachers, newspaper staff, and the children provided qualitative insight into the campaign's public relations impact. Particularly poignant feedback came to the board and staff in the glistening eyes, blurted out thanks, and hugs for some staffers.

Later, in painstakingly neat print and script on lined tablet pages came the notes, including these verbatim excerpts:

> I am proud that my picture appeared in the Washington High School's Edition of the *Los Angeles Times*. Thanks once again. Sincerely yours, Benjamin Littlejohn. P.S. Please tell Paul Conrad that Benjamin Littlejohn will come back to see him.

> I had a nice time & opened my eyes and saw just what I would like to be in my life. I think I would like to be a paster or a writer. I believe in myself. . . .Tell Pamela I read her story in the Business section and I liked it. Sincerely, Thurman Davis.

> The most interesting person I met was Paul Conrad because he cares about us the children. Having a good education and reading he said is very important in your life as you grow up. So learn as much as you can. In my opinion the trip was VALUABLE because it taught me a lot. Not only about newspapers but . . . without reading, you won't get anywhere. Grant Williams.

> Some day I hope to work for the *L.A. Times*. Thank you for a lovely day. . . . Sincerely yours, Victor Edwards.

The impact upon the Times Mirror Foundation resulted in extended funding of the program plus a decision to create a panel of experts to go beyond the Washington High School program in investigating means for improving reading and remedial reading programs, according to Foundation Secretary Stephen C. Meier.[35]

Meier, who also serves as director of public affairs for Times Mirror, said that reading improvement over the pretest was not as strong as expected. But while his foundation and the new panel experts figure out how to strengthen the program, they will continue involvement with Washington High School.

> School administrators face very difficult problems in moving quickly. The students come from appalling situations. Yet these kids don't want to miss school. We made some very poignant discoveries. A real side benefit: they got interested in professions. A lot of positive things happened. We will develop more and more ways not only to strengthen and test reading improvement, but also attitudes.[36]

TOWARD A BUSINESSLIKE APPROACH

From the journalistic roots of the public relations profession come new lessons in businesslike approaches to public relations including systematic analysis that has an impact on the behavior of publics, lessons that reflect that even newspapers go beyond mass and print communication to reach their objectives.

In a similar vein, Roy G. Foltz, ABC (Accredited Business Communicator), APR (Accredited Public Relations), stated in *Inside Organizational Communication*:[37]

> If nothing else, we are seeing a more businesslike, disciplined approach to communication activity than ever before. Articulating management *objectives* and getting at *audience* needs and interests are preceding *message* preparation and *media* selection. In fact, both message preparation and media selection are easier when communicators know where they're going. . . . And the importance of communication in organizations will continue to grow as it becomes apparent that communication activity has a real impact on overall organizational results. In truth, management itself is communication.[38]

That the concept of management as communication has been accepted as part of the substance of heading a corporation was indicated by an informal briefing given by the chairman of the board of a diversified company that is the world's largest in the field of LP-gas and related petroleum products and services.

R. J. Munzer, who served as CEO of Petrolane, Inc., from 1957 to 1983, pondered on the question of what public relations means to him. First to come to mind was his anguish at having to lay off employees during the height of the recession and the world petroleum glut. Concern for those employees and their families and the employees who remained on board and the company's actions and communication to hold human damage to a minimum—that was public relations.

But he didn't "really know much about public relations," he told a group of students visiting him in his office. A former practitioner who had studied Munzer's and Petrolane's record suggested that the board chairman epitomized by his own activities an understanding of public relations.

Munzer conceded that, "yes," he did serve as chairman of the board and director of a major nonprofit medical center and other voluntary organizations and encouraged members of his executive team to do likewise. And, "yes," he did believe in doing more than belong to his professional service organizations. And, "yes," he and his company supported college scholarships. And, "yes," involvement in civic and governmental affairs accounted for part of the time of his executive team. And, "yes," investor relations, as employee, community, and government relations, was an important part of his life. And it was "part of my job" to talk with five public relations students and a professor for an hour and a half while a foot-high stack of paper brought in by his secretary that morning and phone messages awaited his attention. "That's really not public relations; that's all part of doing my job," the board chairman said.[39]

Helping Rudy Munzer's counterparts in other organizations to view public relations as integral to their jobs remains one of the biggest communication challenges to the profession. But it takes more than well-turned phrases and good intentions.

Increasingly, professionals are turning to research-based development of measurable results and applying evaluation procedures borrowed and adapted from the social sciences, business administration, the hard sciences, and even sister fields of advertising and marketing. Chapter 6 thus takes the process of PR-MBO a step farther before we show how the system is applied to planning major programs, crisis management, and executive development. The authors of a 1984 text, *Managing Public Relations*, stressed not only objectives for public relations communication, but also "evaluative research" in their manuscript.

> Now, more and more managers are asking their public relations staff to add up the bottom line—the equivalent of profit or loss. What has public relations done to make the organization more effec-

tive? Of what value is the beautiful company magazine? Was that brochure really necessary?

The public relations practitioner must do some kind of evaluative research before he can answer those questions.[40]

Before you turn to the chapter on research and evaluation in this book, however, you may wish to check your understanding of the PR-MBO Writing System by working through an anticipated closing of one of your organization's plants or services. In the following "You Close a Plant or Service" table add your thoughts and suggestions to each step by filling in the last column. Check your answers by referring to appropriate parts of the chapter.

SELF-TEST: YOU CLOSE A PLANT OR SERVICE

The 10 Steps	Beyond This	To This
1. Client/ Employer Objectives	"Aware" of closing? Publicize "facts"? Discover rumors?	
2. Audiences/ Publics and Why	General public? "The" community? Employees as whole?	
3. Audience Characteristics	"Middle" class? "Educated"? "Conservative"?	
4. Audience Objectives	Want the "facts"? When? How? Who? Where? What?	
5. Media/ Channels and Why	Press release?	
6. Media/ Channels Objectives	"Newsworthy?" "Human interest"? Report the "facts"?	
7. Sources and Questions	Ask CEO when? Interview everyone?	
8. Communication Strategies	Tell it as it is? Everybody at once? News conference?	
9. Essence of Message	We are closing?	
10. Nonverbal Support	Some kind of art?	

NOTES

1. Doug Newsom and Tom Siegfried, *Writing in Public Relations Practice: Form and Style* (Belmont, California: Wadsworth, 1981), p. vi.

2. Frank Walsh, *The PR Writer* (Englewood Cliffs, N.J.: Prentice-Hall, 1983); Lawrence Nolte and Dennis Wilcox, *Effective Publicity* (Columbus: Grid Inc., 1984); David L. Lendt, ed., *The Publicity Process*, 2nd ed. (Ames, Iowa: Iowa State University Press, 1975); and Raymond Simon, *Publicity and Public Relations Worktext*, 5th ed. (Columbus: Grid Inc., 1983).

3. The 10 steps were first presented in outline form in Norman R. Nager's "A Professional Approach to Public Relations Writing" (paper for the Public Relations Division of the Association for Education in Journalism and Mass Communication, Seattle, August 1978). Norman R. Nager, "1-10 Writing System" (software feedback system on *VisiDex*, January 1983). Ideas from Nager lectures to public relations writing and persuasion classes at California State University, Fullerton, have been drawn upon.

4. In their participation in professional meetings, the following are among the educators who have advocated analytical public relations writing and inspired the development of this chapter: Otto Lerbinger, Boston University; Dennis Wilcox, San Jose State University; Don Wright, University of Calgary; Mike Hesse, University of Alabama; Bill Faith and Ken Smith, University of Southern California; Jim Anderson, Bob Kendall, Jack Detweiler, Frankie Hammond, and Mary Ann Ferguson, University of Florida, Gainesville; Doug Newsom, Texas Christian University; Bill Baxter, University of Oklahoma; Scott Cutlip, Robert Bishop, and Frank Kalupa, University of Georgia; Bob Blann, Western Kentucky University; George King, Bradley University; Bill Toran, Ohio State University; Bill Ehling and Judy Van Slyke Turk, Syracuse University; Jim Grunig, University of Maryland; Frank Walsh, University of Texas, Austin; Linda Scanlan, Norfolk State University; Al Walker, Northern Illinois University; Tony Fulginiti, Glassboro State College; Jim Van Leuven, Washington State University; Rulon Bradley, Brigham Young University; Dave Safer, California State University, Dominguez; Robert Rayfield and Ed Trotter, California State University, Fullerton; and Allen Center and Glen Broom, San Diego State University.

5. Ray Gillingham, interviews, Long Beach and Laguna Niguel, California, 1967-1981.

6. Patrick Anderson, interview, Anaheim, California, November 19, 1981.

7. Jesse M. Unruh, personal discussions, Los Angeles and Sacramento, 1963-1967.

8. Robert Stuart, quoted by Sue Shellenbarger, "Working in PR Now a Route to Top Jobs," *Wall Street Journal*, June 24, 1980, p. 31.

9. Ibid.

10. Silver Anvil Portfolio, Ronald McDonald House, 1981.

11. Ibid.

12. Silver Anvil Portfolio, Monsanto, 1981.

13. Thomas Glenn, interviews, Fullerton and Santa Ana, California, February-May, 1981.

14. Ray Eldon Hiebert, Donald F. Ungurait, and Thomas W. Bohn, *Mass Media III* (New York: Longman, 1982), p. 183.

15. Thomas E. Eidson, interview, Los Angeles, November 20, 1981.
16. Jim Mackin, interview, Norwalk, California, December 18, 1981.
17. Peter Dowd, interviews, Los Angeles, Fullerton, and Westminster, California, August-December 1981.
18. Student Task Force for Communications Week, California State University, Fullerton.
19. Eidson, interview.
20. Dale E. Zand, *Information, Organization, and Power: Effective Management in the Knowledge Society* (New York: McGraw-Hill, 1981), p. 175.
21. Ibid., p. 184.
22. James E. Grunig, "Some Consistent Types of Employee Publics," *Public Relations Review* 1 (Winter 1975): 17.
23. Manuel Jimenez, interview, Westminster, California, November 21, 1981.
24. Dowd, interviews.
25. Ibid.
26. Bill Baxter, "The News Release: An Idea Whose Time Has Gone?" *Public Relations Review* 7 (Spring 1981): 27–31.
27. This section is based on Norman R. Nager's public relations writing course materials and "Developing a Public Relations Eye for Television News" (paper presented to the Educators Section of the Public Relations Society of America National Conference, New Orleans, November 1978).
28. Kenneth Roman and Joel Raphaelson, *Writing that Works* (New York: Harper & Row, 1981).
29. From course materials sent to instructors with Doug Newsom and Alan Scott, *This Is PR: The Realities of Public Relations*, 1st ed. (Belmont, California: Wadsworth, 1976).
30. Ken Metzler, *Creative Interviewing* (Englewood Cliffs, N.J.: Prentice-Hall, 1977).
31. Elinor Selame, "Keeper of the Mark," *Public Relations Journal*, November 1981, p. 44.
32. Gordon Phillips, interviews, Los Angeles, June 9 and 18, 1982.
33. Carolyn J. Hom, interviews, Los Angeles, June 9 and 18, 1982.
34. Ibid.
35. Stephen C. Meier, interview, Los Angeles, October 29, 1982.
36. Ibid.
37. Roy G. Foltz, "Communication in Contemporary Organizations," in *Inside Organizational Communication*, ed. Carol Reuss and Donn E. Silvis (New York: Longman, 1981).
38. Ibid., p. 16.
39. R. J. Munzer, conversation with students and Norman R. Nager, Long Beach, California, April 6, 1983.
40. James E. Grunig and Todd Hunt, *Managing Public Relations* (New York: Holt, Rinehart and Winston, 1984), excerpted from authors' manuscript December 22, 1982, by Grunig for Nager and Allen.

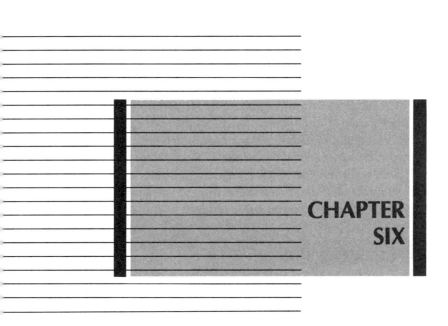

CHAPTER
SIX

PR-MBO RESEARCH-EVALUATION: FOLLOW-THROUGH FOR EFFECTIVENESS

NOTE: *To help the reader who may be somewhat unfamiliar with the language, we have included an extensive glossary of research and evaluation terms in the appendix. This is designed not only to provide a quick referral source for checking terms used in this chapter but also as a reference for your use in reading other books and articles in such journals as* Public Relations Review *and in examining proposals or reports from research consultants.*

EVALUATION FOR EFFECTIVENESS

As she planned for her 1984 term of office as national president of PRSA, Barbara W. Hunter, APR, called for structured objectives and research and evaluation "in such a way as to show results." She said PRSA's involvement of members and leaders in the review of priorities and direc-

tions of issues, goals, and objectives in 1983 epitomized a "planning process move by PRSA to MBO." The 1983 PRSA president, Judith S. Bogart, APR, noted that "the process is the important point in planning" and "it begins with basic research. From there we can build."[1]

A 1982 report on research on Silver Anvil judging identified the characteristics of the winners of the highest awards for excellence in public relations and those of the nonwinners and what distinguished the two at the beginning of the decade. Nearly three fourths of the judges for 1980 who responded, 73.5 percent, said that a Silver Anvil entry should have "an indication whether research preceded planning and was linked to evaluation by measurable results."[2]

MEASURABILITY TREND

The trend toward measurability and evaluation of public relations objectives continues to move rapidly, as indicated by criteria since 1982 that Silver Anvil entries must have measurable results and hardened modes of evaluation. Even as the May 1982 issue of *Public Relations Journal* went to press with the study, changes in the rules were reflecting the push toward measured results.[3]

This is interesting when it is noted that of the 1980 Silver Anvil Awards entries, 30 percent offered measures of results. And this was to change and continue improving in the 1980s.

Don Hill, APR, vice president, public relations, Federal Home Loan Mortgage Corp., and a veteran Silver Anvil Awards judge, has identified several characteristics that distinguished winners from nonwinners:

• Most winners (61.3 percent) included *desired behavior of audience among their objectives*. Most nonwinners (61.9 percent) did not. Disparity: 30.4 percentage points.

• Nearly three quarters of winners (74.2 percent) *cited results with some attempt to measure*. Slightly under two thirds of nonwinners (61.9 percent) did not. Disparity: 36.1 percentage points.

• Most nonwinners (73 percent) claimed media coverage as a favorable result. Most *winners* (67.8 percent) *did not*. Disparity: 40.8 percentage points.

• More than half the winners (58 percent) indicated *preprogram research*. An even greater number of nonwinners (67 percent) did not. Disparity: 25 percentage points.[4]

From this survey and the 1982 and 1983 changes in judging procedures, it is clear that the judges are looking for more objective evaluation as a necessary component in any public relations program. Sue Patterson, public information officer, City of Rockville, Maryland, and one of the researchers in the Hill survey, has *defined the measurement component of evaluation as quantifiable, time-bound, and cost-bound.* She added this is equivalent to saying, "Our target is to deliver X results by Y date at a cost of $Z."[5]

Because of the importance of evaluation to the practice of PR-MBO, this chapter explores the concept in depth and offers models and illustrative cases with techniques for evaluating your programs and results.

First, to indicate the progress of the profession and underline how today's leading professionals apply evaluation to practice, examine the following three cases of 1982 Silver Anvil winners.

CASE STUDY: NORTHEAST SAVES ENERGY

Northeast Utilities (NU) and its agency, Carl Byoir & Associates, researched consumer resentment to rising utility bills and attitudes toward conservation. Results of the research clearly showed that a substantial community-level energy conservation program was mandatory. NU decided to create a community relations program that would hold down public energy consumption, thus saving oil and laying the basis for renewed customer loyalty and support.

Objectives

The following were program objectives:

1. A massive public education campaign to inform customers *and motivate them to participate* in NU's energy conservation projects.

2. A net customer savings in energy costs in 1981 of 278,000 barrels of oil equivalent and a 1.5 percent ceiling on the annual growth of electricity consumption.

Results/evaluation

The program worked. Objectives were converted directly into results as follows:

1. Customer awareness of the company's energy conservation efforts increased dramatically as *demonstrated by the level of their participation* in energy saving projects.

   a. NU received 25,000 requests to insulate water heaters.

   b. NU installed 4,000 low-flow showerheads and 2,000 radio control switches.

   c. NU presented 1,100 energy efficiency awards.

   d. Additionally, 45,000 NU customers signed up for home energy audits.

2. The net *customer savings in energy costs, totaling 281,000 barrels of oil equivalent, surpassed* the first-year target by 1 percent. Practically *no demand growth* for electricity was experienced in 1981.[6]

CASE STUDY: DU PONT SOLAR CHALLENGER

In 1979, Du Pont sponsored with money, materials, and management a special event: the flight of the *Gossamer Albatross*, a human-powered aircraft that made aviation history with the first sustained, controlled, distance flight by man—under his own power—across the English Channel.

The media coverage generated by this event convinced Du Pont to sponsor an even bolder concept: to develop a piloted aircraft operated entirely by the direct conversion of the sun's rays to electric power without using batteries or energy storage devices. It would require unique, sophisticated applications of a variety of Du Pont ultra-lightweight engineering and plastic materials.

On July 7, 1981, the *Solar Challenger*, a 217-pound airplane constructed of Du Pont materials and guided by a 117-pound pilot, lifted off from a field near Paris by the power of the sun, rose to 11,700 feet, crossed the English Channel, flew 230 miles, and landed safely in England after a flight of nearly 5.5 hours.

Objectives

1. Associate Du Pont with a unique, historic event that would help dispel the concept that chemical companies befoul the air, pollute the waters, and produce dangerous products.

2. Focus public imagination and attention on an alternative energy source: solar power.

3. Generate massive international coverage of the France–England flight to identify the Du Pont name.

4. Produce a documentary film for worldwide distribution based on the flight.

Results/evaluation

1. Coverage was massive and international in scope.

2. Du Pont was associated with a major historical event.

3. It sparked interest in an alternative energy source.

4. The role of Du Pont materials in the successful flight was established.

5. Tour audiences exceeded 2 million.

6. The documentary film was produced and readied for worldwide distribution.

7. An effort was made to *quantify exposure by calculating costs on a paid advertising basis*. Du Pont halted calculations when estimated advertising costs of like exposure reached *half a billion dollars*. Even when Du Pont discounted the figure by 90 percent because no advertising was actually purchased, the estimated value of the exposure was at least $50 million.[7]

CASE STUDY: NEW YORK TRIPLES TEEN JOBS

Youth unemployment has persisted as one of the major problems confronting New York City and many other parts of the country. In 1980 fewer than 25 percent of the city's teenagers held jobs, compared with 50 percent nationally.

Objectives

The New York City Partnership, a nonprofit organization of more than 100 business and civic leaders, launched an effort to more than double the number of private-sector summer jobs for youths between the ages of 16 and 21. The private sector provided approximately 5,000 summer jobs in 1980; *the measurable 1981 objective called for 10,000 to 12,000 jobs.* The strategy was to develop and promote a "Summer Jobs for Youth/81" campaign.

Results/evaluation

1. The campaign found 14,000 private-sector jobs, *almost triple* the number employed in 1980.

2. A follow-up telephone survey showed that 87 percent of the CEOs said they would participate again in 1982.

3. And 84 percent of the workers said they would accept the same jobs in Summer 1982.

Support credited for helping surpass the objectives included backing from influential quarters: President Reagan, during two nationally televised speeches, praised the Partnership for finding 14,000 private-sector summer jobs. Two front-page stories on the program appeared in the *New York Times.*[8]

The Northeast Utilities, Du Pont, and New York City Partnership cases illustrate the importance of evaluating your program through hard, specific results. The three cases typify contemporary public relations practice in a growing number of corporations, public relations agencies, nonprofit institutions, and other organizations.

EVALUATION FLOWS FROM RESEARCH

If objectives flow from organizational policy, planning, problems, needs, and opportunities, then it may be seen that the measurable results are discovered through research. Evaluation depends on data or information gathered systematically. through various research modes. In a sense, evaluation serves the public relations professional as a strategy for demonstrating to higher management and boards of directors the ability of your public relations effort to have an impact on profitability, quality of service, and public acceptance in meaningful behavioral terms.

OVERVIEW OF REST OF CHAPTER

Because evaluation flows from research, this chapter helps the reader learn how to use several powerful research tools found effective by public relations agencies and departments to evaluate your programs and your techniques and strategies. We summarize 12 research designs:

1. Scientific surveys
2. Sampling procedures
3. Probability sampling
4. Nonprobability sampling
5. Tests to measure results
6. Computer-assisted analysis
7. Simplicity through Q-sort
8. Content analysis
9. Media tracking model
10. Participant observation
11. Unobtrusive measures
12. Futures research

We review several concepts of measuring and evaluation as a foundation for your examination of the 12 techniques.

MEASURING: THE REALITY TODAY

A misconception about public relations objectives used to be that they could not be measured. It was not unusual to hear some practitioners say years ago that "what we do in PR is intangible and therefore unmeasurable."

Donald K. Wright, APR, who was in charge of the November 1982 National PRSA Conference professional development seminars in San Francisco, and in Atlanta and Chicago in 1980 and 1981, placed this misconception in perspective in a *Public Relations Journal* report:

> Once it was possible to avoid public relations measurement on the grounds that the field was nebulous and had a nature that prohibited measurement. Communications measurement became more essential in helping to determine how much public relations programs were contributing to the attainment of overall goals. . . .
>
> Evaluation and measurement never supply all the answers in public relations, but they often provide enough information in planning for the future to make them *essential* functions in leading organizations.[9]

Under PR-MBO, public relations professionals strive to make all their objectives measurable. Most of these objectives can be quantified, and some may be measured in terms of quality too.

Yesterday's practitioner, who took the position "it can't be measured," was not unique in management history. Other managerial staff before him, such as those working in personnel, labor relations, law, research and development, and purchasing, plus chief executive officers themselves, had taken such a position. The majority of professionals, working in these areas and practicing MBO, have come to realize that what they do is clearly measurable.

Public relations professionals have increasingly taken the initiative in finding and adapting ways to measure effectiveness, as indicated by interviews with hundreds of professionals, observations at meetings and conventions of PRSA and IABC, a review of the literature, and correspondence and talks with practitioners and researchers.

Public relations officers seem to have found it productive to view the measurement of objectives as a positive step in the climb toward increased professionalism and personal achievement, as well as an opportunity to vividly demonstrate to executives and board members the contributions of public relations to organizational goals and objectives.

The founder of the Philip Lesly Co. and editor of the handbook bearing his name wrote in his second edition:

> With business and other organizations moving precipitately toward using computers and other quantifying techniques to "get answers" and "organize" efficiently, there has been growing pressure to apply the same methods to public relations.[10]

In 1983, Ketchum Public Relations, part of Ketchum Communications, Inc., began moving from its breakthrough in developing a then-revolutionary computer program for quantifying effectiveness of messages and media for product publicity campaigns to the next stage: developing systems for measuring communication effectiveness in public affairs.[11]

By following through with measurable objectives, public relations experts around the country have found that they, like other staff departments, have the chance to show concrete evidence of what they accomplish. The stakes have included capturing scarce budgetary and other resources of the employer. And at stake have been reliable means to get early warning of program defects and learn from both weaknesses and strengths indicated by measurement.

Although it once was tempting to look upon evaluation and measurement as academic exercises, analyses of the programs of General Electric, AT&T, ARCO, Hill and Knowlton, Burson-Marsteller, Ketchum, and so many other pacesetters of public relations practice have made it clear that this is the wave of the future—the near future—and part of the reality of the present.

James E. Grunig of the University of Maryland recognized both the importance of measurement and the problems encountered by some practitioners in stating objectives in measurable terms:

> There is no reason to expect every practitioner to be a researcher. I would recommend instead that public relations agencies or departments make research, planning, and evaluation a specialized role within the department, even if it is only a part-time role, just as they now make press relations, community relations, or government relations.[12]

The idea is to move as much as you can toward measurable objectives. Your research design may not be perfect. But as you progress along the continuum of measurability, you gain the advantages.

DEFINING PR-MBO EVALUATION

One of the most difficult things to do in any organization is to stop doing something. One of the purposes of operating under PR-MBO is to look at what you are doing now to meet future needs and gain a basis for deciding how much more you should be doing. Conversely, evaluation will prove valuable in suggesting where to cut losses—in valuable time and creative energy, as well as other resources.

Here is a formal definition of evaluation developed by John Van Maanen for *The Grantsmanship Center News*:

> To determine the operations and effects of a specified program—relative to the objectives it set out to reach—in order to contribute to the decision-making surrounding the program.[13]

Computer printouts may provide the numbers, but someone like the evaluator must assign meaning to them. Evaluation is designed to support decision making. *It is important to stress here that evaluation extends beyond the simple question, Was the program any good?*

Evaluation is much more than data collection and measurement. It is rapidly becoming a discipline with its own literature and methodology.[14]

A meaningful expansion of the definition has been offered by M. Scriven as "formative" and "summative" evaluations. *Formative evaluations* provide information for the development and implementation of a new program. *Summative evaluations* provide data on the overall effectiveness of an ongoing program.[15]

This is an important distinction for the public relations professional because the evaluation process usually has been seen as beginning after a program has been completed. However, formative evaluations may begin while a program is only in the planning stages.[16]

Being able to evaluate an activity while it is still on the drawing boards can save large amounts of time and money. For instance, the public relations professional who decides to survey attitudes of a particular public would *first evaluate the need for such an activity, costs, operational feasibility, organizational support*, and so on before deciding whether or not to implement such a program. In short, you are doing what J. H. Harless called "front-end analysis."[17]

It seems obvious that you will want to determine the needs, costs, and feasibility of a program before launching it, but public relations veterans tell of numerous "horror stories" in which this was not done. Often, an underlying cause is the focus on activities, rather than results.

The evaluation *process*, by definition, should *not* be divorced from the planning stage of PR-MBO. It is much more correct and useful to think of evaluation as occurring in several stages: a preliminary or planning stage, followed by a mid-course review stage and then an end-results or assessment stage. In other words, in addition to evaluating end results, it is necessary to evaluate the program design, implementation phases, and the program objectives.

THE CIPP EVALUATION MODEL

Perhaps the ongoing process of evaluation can best be illustrated by the CIPP Evaluation Model developed at Ohio State University by Daniel J. Stufflebeam.[18]

CIPP is an acronym standing for four essential kinds of evaluation: Context, Input, Process, and Product.

Context

Context evaluation forces the evaluator to consider the needs (goals) of the program and to answer such questions as: What is the scope of it? Who will be served by it? What problems need to be solved before it can be implemented? What are the costs in terms of scarce resources? When you are evaluating something, you need to consider the total environment of the organizational or business system in which you are operating. That is, does your proposed program support the goals of your client or employer?

Input

Input evaluation occurs after the objectives have been determined and alternative ways of achieving them are considered. Alternative routes (the means) for your end results need to be identified and assessed. Public relations professionals increasingly are required to build strong cases for itemized budgets, and this means comparing your actual costs against the expected benefits of the program. This is called the *cost-benefit ratio*.

Process

The focus of the CIPP Evaluation Model is on the program process rather than on the product per se. By focusing on the total process of creating the program with appropriate evaluation measures, program managers actually can influence the program as it goes along. For the pragmatist, this means you do not have to wait until a program is completed before you evaluate it.

The process focus is exemplified by the ongoing need to field test a public relations proposal from inception beyond completion of the program. Newcomers sometimes forget that research may start before the program but does not end when the proposal is accepted. And some neophytes have mistaken "mid-course" evaluation for testing or measuring only once although it refers to *ongoing* checking of progress and strategies.

Product

Product evaluation draws attention to the actual product the program was expected to yield. "Product" could well be reputation, attitude change, behavioral modification, or any number of other end results, not just the more tangible physical products produced in public relations programs. Of course, a videotape or a special event could be your final product, or you might look beyond such tools to the results they bring.

Because evaluation exists to serve decision making, the crucial decision to be served must be identified. That is what the CIPP model insists upon. Corresponding to the four kinds of decisions to be served are the four types of evaluation processes or steps represented in the CIPP model.

To show how CIPP can be of value, consider the decision making surrounding the writing of a news release on the promotion of a department head to vice president, as shown in Table 6.1.

Sources of Evaluation Information

In using the CIPP model, you will need data and may turn to some traditional sources used in public relations, marketing, and advertising. The listing that follows introduces several sources explored in this chapter's discussion of research techniques.

Questionnaires	Opinion surveys
Panel sessions	Statistical tests
Interviews	Physical evidence
Observation	Case studies
Records, documents	Ratings
Futures consensus	Scenario analysis

Whole special issues of *Public Relations Journal* and *Public Relations Review* have been dedicated to research and program evaluation.[19]

In-depth articles in these and other journals have examined specific applications. One of the interesting examples of using evaluation to measure a concept that seems evident to the profession but that is difficult to define with precision was reported by Byron Reeves and Mary Ann Ferguson-DeThorne in an article on evaluating corporate social responsibility.[20]

Table 6.1
CIPP In Action

Context	What is your purpose? How unusual is it for a person to reach VP rank (if you have five vice presidents in your organization or one)? What happened to the previous vice president? How will this report be perceived by other management and employee publics and by the financial community? How will it fit with other stories past and future on your client?
Input	What alternatives do you have for getting out the information? News conference (unlikely)? Phone it in? Mail release? Hand deliver to media? Input also includes development and verification of information, including background on the person, and ramifications of the change.
Process	You can approach this from two perspectives: 1. The mechanics of writing, checking style, and developing format. 2. The barriers to prevent or distort the way it is used: heavy news day, special gatekeeper criteria, such as one-sentence stories in major metropolitan newspaper business personnel columns.
Product	Again, you have two perspectives: 1. The release per se. For instance, has the release as a physical product been written and prepared for distribution? 2. The *effects* of the release. For instance, what will this announcement mean to the financial community of investors and analysts? How will it serve the interests of the client or employer?

The trend toward increased accountability also is evident in planning and program reviews of public communication in the federal government. Kenneth Rabin and Richard Franzen, researchers in government communication, suggested that planning here lags behind the private sector. And an overview of evaluation methods used by public information officers may be found in the same work, *Informing the People.*[21]

Thus, *evaluation procedures* are built into all phases of any public relations program; they are *not* appended as afterthoughts.

RESEARCH FOR RESULTS

It may be helpful to think of research and evaluation as inseparable concepts, as indicated earlier in the C-R-E-A-T-E model in which the *R-E* represents research-evaluation.

For the most part, it is almost impossible to tell where research begins and evaluation ends. Research and evaluation are intertwined. So, rather than divert yourself by considering at exactly what point each comes into play, view research-evaluation as one process.

Research in years past was surrounded by vague and sometimes erroneous perceptions. Even one-person public relations departments have learned that they not only can afford some forms of scientific research but also can have easy access to the resources for doing it. It is *not* true that you must have high quantitative skills and graduate work in research design in order to conduct public relations research.

Some concrete strategies for conducting research as it relates to the practice of public relations follow:

The editor of the *Public Relations Journal*, Leo J. Northart, concluded that the challenge to the profession is for "public relations results and effectiveness to measure up under searching examination by vigilant and cost-conscious managements."[22] The focus of this section is on research. More specifically, the aims are to brief you on when research is necessary and to offer in some detail major research design strategies of particular value to public relations professionals. Although a single chapter in a book cannot capture the complexity and fullness of research design, basic principles of research design and technique oriented to the public relations practitioner can be provided as a general guide. The research methods presented in this chapter do not represent every known research design but were chosen as among the most helpful to persons practicing public relations. Specific research sources are cited for those wanting additional information on a particular design.

RESEARCH DEFINED

Take a close look at the word *research*. Now take your pen and draw a line under "s-e-a-r-c-h." That is the key idea in research. The point in doing research is to take a good close look at what you are trying to discover.

Peeling Back Layers

You must make a close *observation* of your public relations efforts if you are going to be able to report to higher management on the effects. It is likely that you will have to look and look again over time to get some idea of the effects. Each time you look at your public relations efforts, you may discover glimpses of the effects of your work.

Actually, what you are doing is similar to the work of the archaeologist uncovering ancient relics by removing layer after layer of earth and sand. After the removal of each layer, the relic emerges in greater detail and clarity. Finally, with the object completely uncovered, some attempt can be made to classify it historically. So it is with your public relations campaign. After each observation, more and more of the actual effects can be determined. In a sense, you are "uncovering" the hard data that management wants. From a systems viewpoint, the pieces of your research come together to form the whole picture.

Here is a general definition of research: *Research is a strategy for gathering information that is based on systematic observation.*

Research is more than common sense, as valuable as that may be. Common-sense judgments are *sometimes* correct, but not always. The profession needs some strategy that reduces the error in its recommendations. If you make policy suggestions for your organization, seek to increase the odds of being right.

At issue here is, How do you know what you know? If you recommend a public relations action, How do you know it is the best one? Proof is needed. As the nineteenth-century American humorist Artemus Ward once said: "It ain't the things we don't know that get us in trouble. It's the things we know that ain't so."[23]

Scientific Method

At the heart of research is the scientific method. The scientific method can be viewed as a particular way of thinking. Generally, it is thinking about a problem based on reasoning and observation. (By "problem," we do not necessarily mean something that is negative. In fact, a problem can be a positive opportunity or challenge to bring about healthy change.)

Science deals in empirical, that is, real world, investigation. This means that there must be observable evidence before the scientist is prepared to say that something is "true."[24]

The work of the scientist is to describe reality based on data—facts—another word for evidence. The scientist is more confident that truth has been discovered if another scientist looks at the data and observes the same thing. When this happens, verification is based on empirical reality.

"Truth," of course, always is relative to the particular observation. It depends upon many factors that can change quickly, such as shifts in attitudes of publics as reflected in sudden turns against a political candidate or the gradual erosion of the reputation of a client.

Public relations professionals increasingly have discovered the value of "proof" to back up claims in proposals and reports to higher management.

The basic similarity between scientific investigation and public relations efforts is that both are *trying to describe reality*. The public relations professional who speculates that "our publics have a good image of us" may be describing *one* "reality." This view may be correct or incorrect. The crucial point is that you have no way of knowing if this is "reality" or mere conjecture.

The professional needs, as the scientific method would demand, proof based on empirical evidence, which ultimately means systematic observation. Examples of such proof would be scientifically conducted surveys of those publics. The responses on the questionnaire become the public relations professional's evidence.

In addition to observation, another important concept of the scientific method is *quantification—the use of numbers*. Although many persons who enter public relations have relatively little quantitative training, the same is not true of the business and public administration graduates to whom they report. They tend to subscribe to Lord Kelvin's notion that "if you cannot measure, your knowledge is meager and unsatisfactory."[25]

To facilitate measuring, or the use of quantification, professionals have found that expert assistance is easily obtained. This is similar to turning to experts in graphics, computer programming, photography, legislative relations, financial relations, law, or other areas of specialization.

You may find a resident expert in the information processing department, financial staff, marketing or advertising research arms of the company, or one of the executive officers. You may subcontract with a public relations or opinion research agency or hire your own specialists. Or you may secure training on campus or where you work from expert consultants.

Increasingly in public relations, the *degree* of effect of a particular effort must be stated. For example, it may not be enough to merely discover that a key public has changed its attitude toward your organization. The central issue is *how much*. The bottom-line manager who looks hard at profits and losses may say to you: "We spent this amount to change public opinion. Now, by what percentage did we actually do this?" You have to supply the figures to determine a cost-benefit ratio.

CASE STUDY: BLOOMING PRAIRIE

Scientific thinking won the Natural Gas Council of Minnesota and Wyman L. Spano Public Affairs, Inc., of Minneapolis a Silver Anvil for their gas conservation program in the town of Blooming Prairie. As Spano said in correspondence for this book:

> It is obviously possible to apply MBO better to much of the PR practitioner's tasks. Two things can be done: (1) establish a more systematic, formalized method of evaluating results, and (2) set goals and specific targets for results, which can be easily measurable according to the formalized standards set. . . .
>
> So, on one level of public relations practice—the support of sales, financial relations, etc., it is possible to have measurable objectives and to carry out a satisfactory MBO program. On another level of public relations—relating the organization to society's goals, the measurements are less well quantifiable.
>
> The extant Silver Anvil is an example. We can measure the energy saved, the publicity, the participation.[26]

The *cost-benefit ratio* is evident in the Blooming Prairie conservation program results.

Results/evaluation

1. There were substantial energy savings, 11.5 percent gas and 7.1 percent electricity.

2. Nearly every organization and most of the citizens of Blooming Prairie participated in the event.

3. Blooming Prairie won the President's Award for Energy Efficiency.[27]

In their strategic support of the conservation objectives, the Natural Gas Council and Spano generated considerable local and regional news coverage, but *the emphasis on measurement was on the actual conservation of energy,* not on the raw data of numbers or inches of clippings.

Quantification allows you to make much more precise statements concerning effects. In today's public relations departments and agencies, precision is becoming a significant part of hard data.

By measuring public relations programs, professionals can and do make comparisons. For instance, you may say public opinion toward your firm is becoming more positive. But the crucial question is, Compared to what? More positive than last week? Last month? Last year?

Comparison gives you a way to gauge the effectiveness of the total public relations program, as well as the various strategies, tools, and activities that make up the whole.

PROFESSIONALS AND COMPUTERS

Today's technology makes quantification easier for the public relations professional.

Peter Dowd, APR, vice president of American Medical International and a principal of the consulting firm of Haley, Kiss and Dowd, reported that his 1982 survey of *Fortune* companies revealed a strong trend toward increased utilization by public relations staff. Dowd, former senior vice president for the western United States for Hill and Knowlton, concluded:

> The computer is the single most important tool for public relations invented since the telephone. . . .
> Although more and more public relations departments are gaining internal proficiency in computer use, nearly a fifth of the respondents said they retained outside firms that use computers in opinion research and other monitoring. . . . To evaluate properly, we'll need to invest the dollars advertising professionals do in research.[28]

Betsy Ann Plank, APR, Illinois Bell's assistant vice president for corporate communication, said that computer technology is creating "new opportunities for the professional agenda of public relations people." Plank, past executive vice president of the Daniel J. Edelman, Inc., agency, previewed several major opportunities for research and evaluation in her report in the Spring 1983 *Public Relations Review.*

> *Improvements in our research capabilities.* We're already seeing how new technologies can be applied to issues scanning. We'll extend that to turn around research to narrow the frustrating time

gap between surveys and the delivery of results, which so often distorts our planning and responses.

Instant feedback from our audiences. Brace yourself for the mixed blessing of immediate reaction to our messages. Audiences will be able to "talk back" and the protective cover of one-way communication will be blown forever.

Improved opportunities for the measurement of the effectiveness of our performance. If the results justify the claims we've long asserted for our work, but have seldom been able to prove, then such new means for measurement can assure public relations a dedicated chair around the policy-making table of top management.[29]

Even though you may subcontract for computer analysis and opinion studies, you usually need to understand basic principles at work in the research. This is why Plank, Dowd, and others have found public relations veterans taking short courses, turning to experts within their own companies, or inviting in consultants on research design and computer analysis.

American society has become dominated by computers. But computers, if they are to compute, require data in a numerical form. A computer understands only two things: 0 and 1. To take advantage of this powerful tool, you or your consultants need findings that are machine-readable. Through the computer, you can analyze data by using complex, powerful statistical and mathematical techniques. Following statistical analysis, you may be able to ground your conclusions in observable data.

Ways of gathering information have increased dramatically. Scientific investigation, particularly in the social sciences, has the ability to provide answers to questions before unanswerable; perhaps not complete answers, but certainly more complete than before. It is possible with an overnight telephone survey to get an "answer" to what a particular public thinks of your organization.

On a more specific level, we turn now to the actual design of research projects.

RESEARCH DESIGN AND SETTING

Once the public relations professional has focused on the problem to be researched, the questions to be answered, or the hypotheses (hunches) to be investigated, the next step is to develop the research design. Here is a concise definition of research design: research design consists mainly of the procedures and conditions under which you collect data. There is no single research design for covering all public relations studies. Each is unique and requires different methods for collecting information. Nonetheless, there are some general principles or guidelines you may follow to assure reliable research. To follow them, you must think carefully about the purpose of the research. What do you want to know? And what do you want to do with the data you collect?

DESCRIBE OR EXPLAIN

A beginning point is to decide whether your main objective is to *describe* the phenomenon or to *explain* it. Actually these are *not* subtle differences. The first is an attempt to describe as completely as possible the subject you are examining, and the second is an attempt to explain the relationships that exist between elements in that subject.

Herbert H. Hyman said it this way: The descriptive study is concerned with "sheer description of some phenomenon or precise measurement of one or more dependent variables."[30] The explanatory study attempts to uncover the relationships between "one or more dependent variables . . . and one or more independent variables."[31]

Here is a brief definition of independent and dependent variables: Generally, an *independent variable* causes something to happen or has an effect of some kind. A *dependent variable* is the condition affected or influenced by the independent variable. This is not simple cause and effect. An example of independent variables could be a news release or brochure that may have some impact on one of your publics. And that public is your dependent variable.

For example, if the purpose of your research is to describe a particular public, then you are probably interested in making some declarative statements about that population. You may want to describe this public according to number of males, females, elderly, young adults, children, and so on. That kind of description of a public is called demographic.

Or, you may want to describe it according to particular attitudes. You can even describe it *behaviorally*, through buying habits.

If you are doing this, according to research authority Earl Babbie, "the researcher is not concerned with *why* the observed distribution exists, but merely *what* that distribution is."[32] ("Distribution," in this sense, means the statistical arrangement or profile of the measurements, such as range, mode, median, and mean.)

But if the purpose of your research is to go beyond description to *explanation* so as to explain the differences in this particular public, then you need a research design that is exploratory. For example, suppose you find differences in attitudes toward your organization among members of a particular public. If you want to explore why there are conflicting attitudes toward your company, then you need a research design that allows you to collect additional data.

A descriptive study can be a bit more general in its data collection. When describing, you want to be sure that your research design is large enough to capture the major nuances, or shades of difference. The research design should emphasize broadness of scope so that when you analyze the data, you can be fairly confident that your description is complete. For instance, if you assert that "our primary publics are . . ." you want to be sure none are missing. The same applies to "attitudes toward our organization can be classified as . . . ."

The explanatory research design, because of its emphasis, will require more precision in data collection. Another American research authority, Claire Selltiz, said that a major consideration must be accuracy.[33]

Therefore, a design is needed that will enhance the reliability of the data. If you are going to be successful in your attempt to explain why different attitudes exist or the nature of relationships among sub-publics and certain attitudes, then it is likely you need information of a *correlational* nature (the degree of interdependence among several factors). These are concepts that require precise numerical measures, and your design must allow for this.

Although a given research project may actually incorporate both description and explanation, and in practice projects often do, it is helpful to treat them as distinct when first contemplating your research.

Finally, do not fall into the trap of thinking research is something you do after launching a public relations campaign or project. It can be, but the proper time to begin thinking about research is before your efforts begin. This way, research can be a proactive or creative part of your overall public relations program and your subsequent evaluation.

As Kathleen Reardon observed in the *Public Relations Journal*:

> Unfortunately, most people think research is an after-the-fact activity. Actually, it is an unfolding process. It should not be used exclusively to assess the effects of a program, but also in the planning and development of that program.[34]

Pause for a moment to write down some of the areas of your public relations program that you would like to research.

Now, determine if your purpose with each is primarily to describe or to explain. For instance, do you wish to describe a public by listing its characteristics or explain its attitudes and behavior toward your organization? Or do you wish to describe the openings in the job market or explain the reasons for the current situation?

Now let's turn to the setting, the place where you will do your research.

Setting—In the Field

The advancement of science through rigorous research usually has been conducted in a controlled setting, such as the laboratory. The major advantage of the laboratory setting is that it allows the researcher to control the environment in which the research occurs. By exercising control over the research environment, the public relations experimenter is usually able to control important variables (factors) that account for final outcomes.

However, it is unlikely that the public relations professional on the job can conduct research in a laboratory setting. Public relations research generally takes place in the "field." Such research is generally referred to as a *field study*.

The distinguishing characteristic of field research is that it occurs in a natural setting. This is generally assumed to mean that such research occurs in empirical, or real-world, settings where people are observed or questioned in their everyday work or living environment. This means that the public relations program or project is researched where it naturally occurs.

Nonetheless, the power of control exerted over an experiment in a laboratory is too important to overlook completely. The idea for the public relations practitioner conducting research on the job is to try to approximate that experimental control.

Ultimately, if you want to state cause-and-effect relationships, you need to be able to manipulate variables. That is, you need to change some factor and see if it has any effect on other variables. As indicated, this requires a reasonable amount of control on the part of the researcher, and it is often unavailable in the natural setting of the field. However, through rigor and imagination, a close approximation, called a *field experiment*, can be conducted.

The field experiment for a public relations study would likely begin with two similar groups or test sites. For instance, the public relations campaign to get people to use seat belts is implemented with one group of individuals or at one location; another—comparison—group or locale receives *no* exposure to the campaign. The effect of the campaign is then measured by comparing the difference in attitude or behavior between the two groups or sites. In effect, one group, called *experimental*, is exposed to the campaign, referred to as *treatment*, while the other, termed the *control group*, is not. If differences are found in their subsequent behavior or expression of opinions, you may reasonably assume, if other things are equal, that the public relations campaign had an impact.

What is strongly suggested by the field experiment is a research strategy that focuses on a pre- and posttest design. *"Pretest" means to question or study before the treatment or campaign begins for any group. "Posttest" means to measure after the treatment or campaign.*

The idea is to measure before and after administering the public relations program. By gathering data before the public relations campaign goes into effect, you have what is often referred to as *baseline* or *benchmark* data.

You might think of this kind of data as the way things were before you began your public relations efforts.

Your "benchmark," or "baseline" data, then, serve as a starting point, and you will use them to help you determine if your public relations campaign has had an effect. You compare your new findings to those before you began your campaign.

This is such an important concept for public relations research, that we illustrate it in the following section through an actual case of a 1982 Silver Anvil winner.[35]

CASE STUDY: SCHOOLS IN CRISIS

Since 1976, the Columbus, Ohio, Public School District had been in a constant state of financial crisis. Voters had not approved additional operating millage (increased tax support) since 1968, despite raging inflation.

The public relations program used a pretest research design; *a focus group* (normally, a panel of up to a couple dozen persons who are fairly representative of the critical publics); and three formal scientific public opinion surveys. This combination of research tools revealed low support for the effort to levy taxes and a belief that such an effort would fail again.

A telephone survey showed support for the ballot measure slipping, with only 42 percent in favor and 46 percent opposed. Research also indicated the most likely sources of opposition and, most important, that the opposition voters were far more likely to vote.

Finally, during the three weeks of the active, visible public campaign, nightly tracking studies of key areas and constituencies were conducted. The nightly tracking studies were in the form of telephone surveys.

This is a vivid example of the process and systems concept in which research/evaluation is actually conducted *before, during,* AND *after the course of a campaign.* This ongoing research provided helpful direction for the targeting of messages toward particular audience segments.

What follows is the bottom line that won national recognition and a Silver Anvil.

Campaign Strategies

- 15-minute audiovisual presentation
- 50 volunteer speakers
- Direct mail campaigns to specific subpublics
- Targeted campaign to black community

Results/evaluation

1. The official vote tally was 64,814 "for" and 60,258 "against," a 51.8 percent victory.

2. Posttest precinct analysis provided a direct tie-in with the research and planning strategies.

3. Postcampaign research traced 3,990 votes of the 4,556-vote victory margin to the four audiences targeted in the campaign.

The case illustrates not only the use of pretest, posttest research design but also the conduct of research throughout a public relations campaign, from inception through execution, for ongoing evaluation of its effects and feedback for mid-course corrections.

RESEARCH METHODS FOR PR

With a basic understanding of research design and purpose, you can move to specific methods for collecting data. Start your examination of research methods with one of the most popular tools, not only in public relations, but also in the social sciences and such allied disciplines as marketing and advertising.

SCIENTIFIC SURVEYS

For the public relations professional interested in doing a survey of relevant publics, two basic designs can be considered. Even if you subcontract surveys or have them assigned to a resident specialist in your organization, it will be helpful for you to have a basic understanding of these designs. And after gaining a general understanding from this section, you will be prepared to advance to the more detailed treatment of survey methodology by Earl R. Babbie in his *Survey Research Methods.*[36]

Basically, you may choose a *cross-sectional* or *longitudinal* survey. Both kinds are interpreted and strengths and limitations are reviewed.

In selecting either survey design, time is a crucial variable. In the *cross-sectional* survey, you collect data from your sample at only one point in time. A survey of attitudes toward your organization will describe particular attitudes at the time of the study.

You may think of the cross-sectional survey as taking a single "photograph" of your key publics. This "snapshot" gives you a picture of their opinions and attitudes, but only on the day you took the photo. You may report what you found in reference to the time of the study.

Classic examples include the Gallup, Roper, Harris, Yankelovich, and other polls. This survey design is a good basic technique. The other major survey design, *longitudinal*, collects data at different time periods. It differs from the cross-sectional survey in that data are taken over time rather than only once. Babbie divided the longitudinal survey into three primary designs: trend, cohort, and panel.[37]

In the *trend study*, a particular public, for example, could be surveyed over different time periods. With this design, it is important to note that different members of your publics could be surveyed during the various time periods (every three months, for example) as long as this sample comes from the same population. You would *not* survey the same individuals each time.

A *major difference between trend and cohort studies* is that cohort research tends to focus on a more sharply defined population. Trend studies tend to be more general. You could do a trend study of Texans. You could do a cohort study of Texans in the oil producing industry.

An example of a project suggesting a cohort study follows. You launch a public relations campaign aimed at persuading an important public to move toward your client's viewpoint. This public has been rather neutral toward your organization. After the persons in this group have received your campaign materials, you then decide to survey a sample of this public for shifts in opinion. You do your first survey in January, and three months later you conduct another. Although the individuals differ, they are still drawn from the original neutral public population that received your campaign materials. You have done a cohort study.

Third, you may choose the *panel study*. It is like the other two longitudinal designs in that it collects data at different time periods, but it differs from them because it surveys the *same* individuals each time. Perhaps you are polling every month to detect subtle shifts in opinion. A good way to ensure a sensitive research survey is through a panel. When you have to get extremely close to the data, you have to talk to the same individuals. *If you have to be sensitive and quickly responsive to certain changes that might be crucial for your client in taking advantage of opportunities or preventing crises*, you will want to do this with some degree of frequency.

Survey Strengths and Limitations

There is no single best survey design because your decision depends on your particular research needs. Here is a review of some considerations on which your decision may depend. The examples help place these considerations in perspective.

If you only want to describe a particular public on a specific date, then the cross-sectional design is appropriate. For instance, if your organization has never done a formal survey of its publics, and you just want to describe "what is out there," the descriptive data collected scientifically in a cross-sectional survey can provide you and your management with a lot more information and solidly grounded insight than you have had.

Or perhaps your company has gained through merger very important new publics to target for communication. Of course, a one-time survey would give you valuable information for initial planning of your communication with such new publics as stockholders, customers, and employees of the firm with which your company merged.

Much of the time, of course, you need to explain differences in public attitude. Quite often, you need to know if your campaign is working. Is your project generating results? If you seek answers to such questions, then it is likely that you need a longitudinal study.

If your publics are rather general (such as food consumers versus customers for computer components), then a trend study is in order. If you need to narrow the focus to a more restricted population (such as employees who are stockholders rather than employees as a whole), then a cohort study is more appropriate.

If you need greater explanation or you suspect the effects of your campaign will be subtle but important change, then a panel study is the best design. For instance, assume your chief competitor continues to have a better reputation among potential customers, but you do not know why. In this case, the panel design is the best choice because it provides detailed data. Babbie observed that the panel most closely approximates the classic laboratory experiment. This ties into the earlier discussion of research setting in this chapter.

There are limitations associated with each design.

The cross-sectional design generates data only at one point in time. You can only say that "on such-and-such date, this is what people thought of us." It is quite possible that public opinion has shifted since your survey.

Longitudinal studies suffer from their size and complexity. They can be expensive; it costs money each time you go into the field. If you use a cohort study, you must be sure that the sample comes from the same population.

The panel study has a major limitation through the attrition of panel members. Individuals on your panel may move, die, or drop out, leaving you with an inadequate sample. One way to reduce this problem is to increase the size of the panel by about 20 percent more than you actually need. This gives you some extra members to cover for those that leave. Also, if you restrict the panel's lifetime to no longer than one year, you reduce attrition. If a study is going to take longer than one year, then a trend or cohort study may be more feasible.

Your decision on which kind of study to do depends on what kind of data you need and what kind of research you can afford to conduct with the money and time you can budget. Effective research often comes from careful compromises between what you would like versus what you actually need with your limited resources as the determinant of what you can afford.

SAMPLING PROCEDURES

Once the survey data have been collected, the researcher is largely at the mercy of the data. That may seem acceptable, except that there may have been elements of *bias* in how well the data was collected. That means data may be contaminated with false information or impressions. (Bias may be unintentional, stemming from problems in design or implementation of the survey.)

So, when you get to the analysis stage, you have lost most of your control over the research. The time to exert control is at the beginning of the research design. With proper controls, you have a reasonably good chance of collecting unbiased data.

One way to do this is to collect information based on *sampling*. As a concept, sampling is sometimes associated with statistical witchcraft. Some people simply do not believe that the views of 1,500 Americans can be representative of the entire nation. Mathematically, sampling theory can demonstrate the validity of selecting a representative few to describe the views of the many. Rather than get into complex statistics here, it may be noted that opinion researchers such as Gallup, Harris, Roper, and Yankelovich conduct many surveys based on a national sample of about 1,200 to 1,500 Americans each year with accurate findings.

Actually, most persons do sampling all the time without thinking that they are engaging in research methodology. You go to a restaurant and select lunch from the menu. And based upon your sampling on a given day or over a period of months, you may judge the quality of the restaurant.

The public relations professional is selecting a sample when a few opinions are gathered about the new annual report, shareowners meeting, or open house.

The sampling examples just cited actually could be classified as nonprobability samples. In sampling there are two major designs: *probability* and *nonprobability*.

The quality of data you collect and, ultimately, its reliability will depend to a large extent on the type of sampling design you (or you and your research subcontractor or staff specialist) select. Before you explore these two major designs, several important constructs or conceptual building blocks that make up sampling design need to be defined.

Population

A *population*, in survey terminology, refers to all the elements defined in a particular way. For example, one of your key publics might be defined as women over 55 years of age. The population would thus include all women over 55. You could amend this to include only those women over 55 who have an annual income greater than $60,000. Now your population would have three distinguishing characteristics— sex, age, and income.

It is important to note that despite the use of the word, "population," it does *not* refer only to people when you leave the conventional meaning and work with the word as a research term. Population could refer to all brochures your firm has produced in the past five years or all cable television channels in your region.

And consider that *element* in the definition of population simply means units of whatever you are interested in studying—people, attitudes, publications, media, governmental actions, behaviors, and so on.

Census

A *census* is an actual counting of all the elements in the population. In theory, an attempt is made to count or interview *all* of the elements that define or make up your research population. Keep in mind that you may specify a population as broad or as narrow as it suits your purposes.

Sample

A *sample* consists of a portion of those elements making up the population. Differing from a census, a sample represents only *some* percentage of the total population.

Reasons to Sample

The basic reasons for selecting a sample rather than a census are time and money. It is usually easier, faster, and less expensive to work with a sample. If your population is large, in the thousands or millions, then you are unlikely to have the resources to interview each element of your population. The prudent thing to do is to conduct a sample.

A respectable body of research reveals that for a large population, a sample is likely to be more accurate than a census. Consider the effort required to hire and train thousands of interviewers and the complexities involved in their collection and reporting of data from a vast population. Also, the quality of your data could be affected by the time each element could be interviewed. A sample, because it is smaller, would allow the interviewers to conduct more in-depth questioning than a huge census. It also would allow you or your research specialists more time to train interviewers and prepare the questionnaire.

PROBABILITY SAMPLING

Remember the purpose of sampling. You want to be able, on the basis of selecting some elements, to make *inferences about the population.* You want to be able to describe the population based on the information you collect from the sample elements. In public relations, this means that you want to describe a particular public accurately as a result of the information collected from some individuals making up that population.

An important concept in our discussion of probability sampling is *accuracy.* If you cannot describe the population accurately, then the sample and your study may give misleading conclusions. You want to be able to describe the sample elements in such a way (accurately) that you are actually describing the population. A sample may be thought of as a mirror image of the population.

There are two major ways of ensuring this accurate relationship between sample and population. One is the principle of *random selection* and the other is *sample size.*

Random Selection

A *random selection process* refers to how the sample elements are chosen. In a pure sense, if anything other than randomness is the final criterion in selecting an element to be part of the sample, bias or built-in error may be present. If you choose individual A rather than individual B to be part of your sample, you want to say that *only randomness* *("chance," in its scientific sense) determined the selection.*

A common way to assure this is through the use of a table of random numbers, such as you will find in various research and statistical texts and even generated by some home computers.

This is different from the way the word random *is used in everyday* *language.* If you need to count on the validity of a survey, you need to make sure that you and whoever conducted the survey share the same meaning for "random." Two examples may help explain the difference between the ways people use the term:

The interviewer who stands in the center of a university campus from 10 a.m. to 3 p.m. not only misses persons who are on campus in the early morning or evening hours or on other days but also persons who work or attend classes without walking past the interviewer's location. Even if the interviewer is careful to select persons in the area on a scientific basis (to be explained in a moment), this is *not* a random study of the university population. At best, it may be a random survey of persons who may be found on that given day of the week or month, during those specific hours, just in the center of the campus.

As another example, consider the survey that attempts to study the attitudes of a population of all employees of the home office of a company by conducting interviews in the employee cafeteria. Some persons may skip lunch. Others may bring their own food to work. Yet others may eat in nearby restaurants. Some employees may be away from the headquarters on travel, vacation, or sick leave. So this is *not* a random sample of employees of the corporate headquarters. At best, you have only a random survey of employees who happen to be eating in the cafeteria during the period of the interviews.

Sample Size

Sample size simply means that your sample must be of sufficient size (determined by mathematical formulas) to be scientifically valid. If your sample is too small, then you cannot, with any degree of confidence, infer characteristics about the parent population. We refer to this process later in the chapter.

Let's turn now to four major kinds of probability samples: Simple, systematic, stratified, and cluster.

Simple Random Samples

The most basic type of probability sample is the simple random design. *Accuracy is achieved because each element in the population has the same probability of being selected for the sample.*

Each element is assigned a random number. For example, if your focus of study is a population of 10,000, each and every person (or other element) is assigned a random number. Then a table of random numbers is used to select the actual elements for inclusion in the sample. This means that nothing but randomness (the unbiased table of random numbers) determines the final sample elements.

In theory, this design can be used for any population, but it is seldom used in actual practice. There are two reasons for this. First, if the population is huge, then a massive amount of work is required to assign each population element a number. Second, it may be impossible to get a complete list of all the population members so they can be assigned random numbers. Consider this: Could you produce a list containing the names of every person making up all your key publics? Even if you could, assigning each person a number might be an unwieldy task.

Systematic Samples

If you have a list of all or most of the population elements, then you can use a systematic sampling design. Using this procedure, every *n*th element is chosen for inclusion in the sample. The *n*th element refers to *the sampling interval.* ("*n*th" could mean 10th, 33rd, 2nd—any interval that is reasonable to accept. The important thing to keep in mind is that you stay with the sampling interval you set.)

For example, if your population is 2,000 and you want a sample of 200, then every 10th element would be chosen for the sample. The first element is chosen with a *random start* and then every 10th element following it will be the sample.

Usually, this procedure is preferred over the simple random design because it is easier to implement.

Stratified Samples

In the stratified sample, the population is divided into two or more strata and then separate samples are drawn from each stratum. (Think of stratification as classification and separation of a whole into sections or groups based on characteristics. In a sense, public relations persons who differentiate among publics and subpublics already practice a form of stratification.)

Stratified sampling is generally preferred by researchers because it offers greater accuracy than the simple random design. This is true because the sample is more likely to reflect actual population characteristics.

For instance, suppose the population has a ratio of two men for every woman. For the sample to be representative, it should reflect this ratio.

The actual division of the population into strata may depend on how much you know about the population. Sex, education, and geography are common variables for developing strata, but the researcher may use others if they are known sufficiently to stratify. For instance, a very large company might stratify employees by areas of work specialization, levels of supervisorial or managerial responsibility, or even seniority in years of service. Part of the decision is based on purpose of the study, part on practicality.

When selecting a sample design, if other considerations are equal, the stratified sample is generally considered to produce the most accurate data.

Cluster Samples

For large survey studies, the cluster sample is often used. This procedure begins with groups—clusters—of elements and then smaller samples are taken within each of these clusters.

For instance, suppose you are interested in measuring the statewide impact of your public relations campaign. You likely begin with a list of cities—your clusters in this particular case. These are selected by random or stratified design. Then from this list of cities another list (cluster) is drawn—probably the division of the cities into districts. Within these districts, a sample of households is selected by random or stratified design for the actual interviews. You arrive at your final sample elements by first sampling larger groups or clusters.

The biggest problem with this procedure is the chance of sampling error at each stage of the selection process. The general rule for lessening this error is to increase the number of clusters initially while decreasing the number of elements within each cluster.

This method primarily is used by state governments when they try to draw profiles of their populations, ranging from villages to vast urban areas.

Sampling Error

An important concept in sampling is *sampling error*. This refers to *the difference between the characteristics of the sample and those of the population.*

When you conduct a sample, there will be some differences between the values you find in the sample and those you would find in the population if you were to conduct an individual element-by-element census of that population. Statistically, this is called the sampling error. Any number of statistical books illustrate this. The intent here is simply to acquaint you with the concept so that if you use research experts or consulting firms or notice the term in an article in *Public Relations Review*, you will have some basis for understanding.

In a typical study, you will see something like "plus or minus 5 percent." This means that the actual population value may be 5 points more or less than what the sample revealed. For example, your survey might show that 45 percent of those sampled had a favorable attitude toward your organization. If the sampling error is calculated to be 5 percent, then the actual population value might be as low as 40 percent or as high as 50 percent.

Even the Gallup Poll normally warns the reader of a sampling error of plus or minus 3 percent. That means that if a survey shows the governor leading the challenger 51 to 48 percent with others undecided, the governor actually may have an edge with as much as 54 percent or might even be behind with 48 percent. And to complicate this, the challenger could have as much as 51 percent of the vote or as little as 45.

Graphically, this could be represented as follows:

Candidate	% Favoring on Date of Survey	+3% Sampling Error	−3% Sampling Error	Range of % on Date of Survey
Incumbent	51	54	48	48–54
Challenger	48	51	45	45–51

The astute user of survey data is sensitized to, and takes into account, sampling error.

Because accuracy is important to you, your executives, and others who depend on the conclusions drawn from the data, you want to keep sampling error small. This is generally done by increasing sample size. But this increase costs time and money, so accuracy has its price. For most public relations studies, a sampling error of plus or minus 5 percent is sufficiently accurate.

Confidence Level

One more important point about sampling design: Your sample should state something about the *level of confidence*. This also refers to the accuracy of your sample. Basically it is a measure of how confident you or your survey consultants may be that you have captured the range of the sampling error.

A confidence level of 95 percent says that you are confident that the sample statistic is within two standard levels of the population parameter (the numerical point of reference or limits for the population you selected to study). Again, for most public relations studies, a confidence level of 95 percent is acceptable.

So, when working with opinion researchers, it is a good idea not only to ask about the size of sampling error you can anticipate but also the level of confidence you and your executives may have in projections from the data.

NONPROBABILITY SAMPLING

Although normally you will want to use probability sampling for research, there are instances when a nonprobability sample may be preferable.

In contrast to a probability sample, it is impossible to estimate the probability or percentage of an element being included in your sample under the nonprobability design. This can mean that some elements are overrepresented because their chances are so high and others underrepresented because their chances are so low. It can mean that some elements have no chance of being included in your sample.

This has some serious implications for your research. Remember that your purpose is to make inferences about the population based on your sample. But if certain elements have no chance of being included, then the question of how representative your sample is of the population begs for an answer. This also implies that *if you do not know the probability of each element being included, then you cannot be sure of the actual nature of the population you are trying to describe.*

Our point is to urge *caution* before we further discuss nonprobability sampling because of its uncertainty in describing actual populations. Syracuse University's Maxwell McCombs pointed out: "There is little assurance that such a sample is representative. One's best bet, in fact, is that it is unrepresentative."[38]

Nevertheless, there are occasions when a nonprobability sample can be used despite the risks involved.

First, you may not be able to afford the costs of a probability sample because of the large number of elements required. A second reason you may choose to use a nonprobability sample may relate to time. Something may happen late in the day and there simply is not enough time to construct a probability sample before you have to give an answer. Veteran public relations professionals are familiar with the "I needed it yesterday" demand and the needs for expedient decision making. A third reason may be that you do not need the precision and reliable representation of a probability sample.

Kinds of Nonprobability Samples

You have three choices when using nonprobability samples:

1. A commonly used nonprobability sample is the *accidental* or *convenience* sample. Here you select what elements you can to form your sample. This could be five or six persons you can reach by phone, eight or more brochures, or 15 to 20 customer letters. *You really have no way of knowing if this sample actually represents the population.* Your assumption is that it is somewhat representative.

Although there may be a fair to large amount of risk involved in basing decisions and actions on such samples, the level of risk may be considerably lower than making an assumption without any effort to verify. It adds education to the so-called educated guess. Public relations veterans with a wealth of experience on which to base decisions still demand more than the lessons of the past because they are sensitive to the fact that *what worked under one set of conditions may not work under the same set of conditions today because of changes in people.*

2. A second kind of nonprobability sample is called *purposive.* The assumption is that, based on your judgment, you can pick the elements to form your sample and that sample will reflect the true population characteristics. There is nothing wrong with judgment; that *can* be an intelligent decision.

An example would be if you picked opinion leaders of one of your publics in a particular area of opinion and talked with them about the nature of the whole public. Based on your selection, you would assume that such elements would reflect the characteristics of the larger population.

There are risks that persons who purport to represent the thinking of others may be out of step to varying degrees or that they may be opinion leaders in several areas but not in the particular topic of concern to you. But several generations of public relations professionals have derived value from this method through painstakingly careful attention to continuing study of their key publics and the selection of representatives.

3. A third kind of nonprobability sample is the *quota* sample. With this type, you attempt to make sure that various subgroups are included in your sample. In essence, you attempt to fill a quota of various characteristics that you think are in the population.

For instance, suppose you knew that elderly singles made up 10 percent of one of your organization's publics. Then, if you were conducting interviews, you would attempt "to fill your quota" of elderly singles.

The problem with quota sampling is the difficulty in actually defining and filling quotas. It may be very difficult to divide a large diverse population into accurate quotas, and it may be next to impossible to actually find people who are willing to be interviewed or fill out your questionnaire. Because of such difficulties, few researchers use quota sampling.

Although there are problems, nonprobability sampling is often used in public relations for reasons such as those reviewed. However, use *caution* when considering nonprobability sampling. It is unlikely that a nonprobability sample will give you the precision and representation needed to actually describe the population. Increasingly, CEOs who demand "hard data" are asking for information gained only from probability sampling.

TESTS TO MEASURE RESULTS

A well-conceived research or evaluation project *anticipates* the analysis of your findings. Your analysis may require the use of *statistics*. Some of the more common statistical measures are discussed here with emphasis on providing a foundation for strengthening you for:

• Consultation with research experts in marketing, industrial relations, advertising, finance, or other departments in your own company; in research and public relations firms with whom you may contract for service; and in the ranks of university and free-lance consultants.

• Greater understanding of the reports in such publications as *Public Relations Review, Public Opinion Quarterly, Public Relations Research and Education, Journal of Communication,* and *Journalism Quarterly.* Even publications and research reports aimed at persons in practice tend to use some language and concepts that can distract from the meaning of the articles if you are unfamiliar with what appears as jargon.

• Further study in statistical reference works or even some postgraduate work in a professional society workshop or university program.

Here are five of the more common statistical measures that seem particularly relevant to public relations research:

Central Tendency

A key reason for using statistics is to allow you to rely on numbers to describe the information you have collected. This information may be in the form of attitudes, responses to a questionnaire, or check marks on a survey instrument called a Likert scale that provides built-in ways of measuring and ranking degree of intensity.

If you have a large amount of information, it is economical as well as sound communication to translate it into numbers. A single number or two may accurately describe or summarize what you find in your research. Such numbers can then provide the basis for forming policy.

A particular class or set of statistical measures is known as the *central tendency. These measures are the mean, median, and mode.*

In a group of data the *mean* tells you the "average" score or response. It is calculated: mean = sum of scores divided by the number of scores.

Like the mean, the *median* also can be a single value. It tells you the midpoint. The median is not a conventional "average," but instead is the figure above which you will find 50 percent of the scores and below which you will find the other half of the results. The median is sometimes more accurate than the mean in describing a set of scores or figures. Unlike the mean, the median is *not* influenced by extreme scores. For instance, an extremely high score may pull up the group mean, while a low score may pull it down. The median avoids this.

The *mode* is the most common score in your data set. You use this statistic when you want to determine the most frequent score or response.

All three measures of central tendency could be useful in an analysis of data from your research, such as your attitude survey of a key public. For example, your sample produced 400 respondents to the survey. The scores were calculated for the results on a question on how your customers rated your client's after-sales service. Then all 400 scores on that question were added. The number was divided by 400 to arrive at the *mean*. Based on this, you could say that the mean (or *conventional* "average") respondent gave your employer a 72.5 percent favorable rating on service, compared to 54.3 percent before your client's new service policies and communication program about them went into effect. You arrived at the mean by dividing as you were taught to do long ago when you calculated your first "average" of a set of figures.

An example of the *median* could be that your organization ranked 4th highest on a scale of 10 organizations concerning social responsibility. You were above the median, the point at which half were above the midpoint, half below.

To illustrate the concept of the *mode:* the most common score on the attitude survey was 65 percent concerning your reputation as an employer. Your mathematical average or mean may be quite different. But, of all the scores, 65 percent was the most frequently attained by your company.

t Test

The *t test* (the *t* is always lower case) is a statistical measure used to determine if there is a significant difference between two sample means; for instance, the difference between the means of scores of two groups— an experimental and a control. The *t* test is like other statistical tests of significance in that it should tell you how frequently your results would be expected to occur by chance alone, just as if there were no real differences between the two groups.

Consider this example: Suppose a representative sample of one of your publics is randomly divided into two groups. Group A is given one of two alternate sets of persuasive public relations campaign material concerning a particular topic. Group B is given the second set of campaign material. You give them a test to see what they recall about the topic. The test scores reveal that one group has a higher mean score than the other. But you cannot be sure this difference is not just due to chance. The groups recalled almost the same amount of material. Your task is to rule out chance. Only then can you consider that there really is a difference in the strength of the techniques used in the two sets of campaign materials. In short, is the difference you obtained greater than a difference that might occur due to sampling error? You can answer the question with a t test.

Some of this may seem rather difficult at first glance. Again, you do not have to master t test or other statistical techniques, no more than you have to be a master of all other skills in public relations. The important consideration to bear in mind is that you should expect that companies or experts that do research for you must do t tests or other statistical tests of significance so that you can be assured of reliable information.

Briefly, here is what you, your research firm, consultant, or sophisticated computer software programs would do:

You calculate your *obtained* t-*value* by inserting your data into the formula for the t and then compare your obtained t-value against a *tabled* t-*value* (from a table usually in the appendix of a statistics book). If your obtained t is larger than the tabled t the difference between the means of the two groups is statistically significant. Now, you can seriously consider whether there is a difference in the impact between the two sets of public relations campaign materials and determine if one is actually superior to the other.

The t test is useful for measuring differences between any two groups. For example, attitude differences between groups toward your organization could be compared. There is one more *caution* you should note before using the t test: the two groups should be about the same size. If one group is 15 to 25 percent larger than the other, the t test must be used carefully, if at all. You could use it if the *standard deviations* of each group's mean are similar. (Standard deviation is a measure of dispersion of scores in their range from the group mean. Remember teachers who graded on the basis of normal class curves?) If the standard deviations of each group's mean are different, then the Mann-Whitney U test should be used.

Mann-Whitney U Test

Similar to the *t* test, the *Mann-Whitney U test* is designed to help you tell if your program or project has produced a significant difference between two groups.

But, unlike the *t* test, the Mann-Whitney U test focuses on rankings of group members rather than means. Your outcomes are not numerical scores but qualitative judgments—such as opinions—that are rank-ordered according to some criteria.

The Mann-Whitney U test can be used if your two groups are different in size and the standard deviation scores also differ.

Again, a statistic, *U*, is calculated. This *obtained U value* is compared with a table value, and if it is smaller, then the two groups are statistically different.

Correlation

If you need to measure the relationship between two measures, the common technique is the correlation coefficient, usually referred to as *r*: the correlation between two measures is expressed as a decimal between -1 and $+1$. A perfect correlation would be expressed as $r = 1.00$. (*r* is a symbol for correlation.) If the two measures move in the same direction, it is considered to be a positive correlation.

For instance, if your client is a nonprofit organization, it may be important to evaluate the effectiveness of fund development letters. You would say the correlation is positive if people score highly on recall of advantages of making life income gifts *and* if predisposition to explore this form of giving is high. However, if recall of the letter goes up while predisposition to make donations goes down, then the correlation is said to be negative.

Note that if you or your research specialists find a correlation between two measures, this still does not tell you what caused it. As statisticians are fond of saying, "correlation is *not* causation." But by finding a correlation you may have a better chance of finding causality.

If you use a statistics book for calculating *r*, you will find that the most common coefficients include the Pearson product moment and Spearman rank order.

Chi Square

The *chi square test* is used when data are assigned to categories. It is noted by the symbol X^2. Usually the question you want answered is whether the frequencies observed in your sample deviate significantly from some theoretical or expected population frequencies. Chi square can be thought of as a discrepancy statistic.

Consider this example: Suppose you have a sample of 60 persons that you ask to read three different versions of an institutional advertisement you are developing. You ask them to tell you which version they consider the most persuasive. As they perform this task, their answers become your observed frequencies. Under the *null hypothesis*, each of the three versions will be chosen equally, or by 20 persons each. Your *research hypothesis* is that one or two versions of the advertisement will be selected by more of the individuals in your study. A *null hypothesis* means that there is *no* statistical difference, and a *research hypothesis* means that there is a significant difference. Public relations officers who commission chi square tests normally start out with an idea that the research specialist translates into a research hypothesis.

Of course, the research is commissioned in the first place because the public relations professionals and their executives are concerned about getting the most value out of their investment in tools and strategies and demand more than untested ideas as grounds for decision making.

The chi square test will measure your observed (empirical or actual) and expected (theoretical) frequencies. Following calculation based on the formula, if the obtained value is larger than the tabled chi square value, then your differences are statistically significant. This means you could reject the null hypothesis in favor of your research hypothesis that says there is a statistical difference in the persuasibility of institutional advertisement options.

Not long ago, the public relations professional who wanted do-it-yourself operation of research test procedures would have had to learn complex statistical formulas. *Computer software advances have come to the rescue by building the formulas into prepackaged, easy-to-use programs.* By the early '80s, persons with home computers could buy software at their neighborhood computer stores with built-in statistical tests.

At the level of professional use, however, as the next section reviews, one particular computer software program has incorporated a number of the more complex statistical procedures needed in research for public relations, advertising, and marketing, as well as for the social sciences.

COMPUTER ASSISTED ANALYSIS

One of the most popular computer software programs for doing more complex statistical analyses is the *Statistical Package for the Social Sciences*, commonly called, the SPSS.[39]

If your research involves more than 60 cases or if you are using three or more measurements of the data, then it is practical to process the data by computer rather than by hand.

In using the computer, you may consider two approaches: You, yourself, handle the entire data-analysis operation, from feeding the data into the computer to analyzing the printouts. A second approach is to ask someone with technical computer expertness to do most of the operation. However, with the second approach, somebody still has to provide the data in a form that is usable by the computer. The SPSS manual should tell you most of what you would need to analyze data with the computer.

In addition to handling the statistical techniques covered so far in this chapter, SPSS can provide more complex analyses. Here is a brief review of the more common complex analyses that may be important in public relations research:

Analysis of variance (shortened to ANOVA in the SPSS manual) allows you to examine the difference in means scores from three or more groups. One SPSS program, ONEWAY, allows you to compare three or more programs based on a single outcome measure.

Partial correlation (PARTIAL CORR in the SPSS manual) shows the correlation between two measures when a third factor believed to influence the correlation is controlled for. That means the effects of the third factor are manipulated to avoid confusion of the relationship between the two other measures.

For instance, suppose you want to know the correlation between frequency of news releases sent out and their use in area newspapers. A high correlation would suggest that high-frequency mailings are associated with high usage in the papers. However, you know that available news space varies from day to day (much less on Saturday than on Sunday, for instance) and that this has some bearing on use of releases; so, you would want to use a correlation that removes the effects of available news space. To do this, you or your research specialist are going to perform a "partial" correlation to measure the association between news release frequency and actual use in the paper.

Multiple regression (in SPSS, REGRESSION) allows you to correlate one characteristic with a set of others.

For instance, suppose you wanted to know if a certain positive rating of your organization is related to advertising, community activities, income, and educational level. Assuming you can get scores on these variables from a sample of your key public members, the REGRESSION procedure can tell you the extent to which ratings of your client's reputation can be predicted from other characteristics. One note of *caution*: The multiple regression procedure should be used only with large samples, 100 or more subjects.

Discriminant analysis (in SPSS, DISCRIMINANT) is a procedure whereby you can identify factors that distinguish one group from another. For example, stockholders who received your annual report could be classified as "satisfied" or "displeased" with it on the basis of a questionnaire. If you would like to know what distinguishes those who liked the annual report from those who did not, other questionnaire items such as income, age, number of shares held, and years as a stockholder could be examined under this procedure to look for differences in the two groups.

Factor analysis (in SPSS, FACTOR) is a complex procedure that, in essence, correlates every variable with every other variable. The procedure looks for patterns based on any intercorrelations. It can be very useful if you have a large number of cases (100 or more) and a large number of measures (at least seven) and you would like to know if there are a few factors that might account for or explain most of your findings.

In concluding this section on statistical procedures and a review of some of the rich possibilities for making meaningful interpretations of public relations research data, we would like to recommend that you reinforce what you have covered here by turning to a few issues of *Public Relations Review* and scanning the contents under the "methodology" subheadings in several reports on research. As you do so, you will become a more critical consumer of reports that may be of value to you in following through on your own public relations objectives. You will not be alone. The vast majority of subscribers to *Public Relations Review* are *not* academicians, but the professionals and executives with responsibility for the practice of public relations.

Now, shift your focus to a little-known but increasingly popular research method that comes to public relations from the discipline of organizational communication. By way of bridge to the next section, it may be pointed out that the Q-*sort* can be operationalized as *either a scientific methodology complete with statistical formulas and procedures or as an easy, hands-on tool that you can begin to use without further training to assist you in making decisions.* The Q-sort has become one of the favorite tools of such individuals as the 1982 national president of WICI—Women in Communications, Inc., Carolyn Johnson, in her work with publications produced by public relations agencies and departments.

SIMPLICITY THROUGH Q-SORT

The Q-sort procedure begins with a set of items to be sorted according to the sorter's attitude. The items to be sorted may be statements, slogans, pictures, advertisements, words, logos, or other choices.

You might have a Q-sort done on one particular kind of material that you want to rank order and even score on the basis of how sorters indicate their preferences.

Usually the items are reproduced on, or attached to, 3 by 5 or 5 by 8 index cards, but they do not have to be. Then the subject (a person who does the sorting) is asked to distribute them into piles according to some criteria.

The purpose is to get the individual to place the items in a series of numerically ranked piles so that you can get an idea of his or her attitude toward the topic under review. What is important to this technique is that individuals provide their own frames of reference toward the items. The sorter responds to criteria provided by the researcher.

For instance, the names of actual corporations could be provided and each subject asked to place them into piles according to the sorter's perception of organizational financial strength. The sorter would then place the cards with the names of the organizations in various piles with "strongest" in pile one and "weakest" in pile nine. The pattern into which the subject places the names becomes the data base for that person's attitude. In essence, the Q-sort is believed to give a reasonably objective measure of a person's attitude toward a subject.

When sorters, or *you yourself, in the ordinary course of decision making have difficulty* in rank ordering several or more items, be it optional themes for corporate magazines, pictures for the cover of an annual report, or slogans for a campaign, *here is a suggestion to make life easier*: Instead of trying to use nine or so piles initially, start with three. The first pile is the one you use for those you are positive you like to any degree. The second is for those about which you are undecided or neutral. And the third is the pile of material you dislike.

Then, go through the same process with each of these piles, again breaking them into those you tend to like more, are uncertain about, or like least.

Eventually, after you do this as often as you feel is needed, you will arrive at the seven to nine piles normally required for a Q-sort.

One of the strengths of the Q-sort technique is its ability to be used in a wide variety of research situations. For instance, statements concerning the civic responsibility of your organization toward the local community could be written by a public relations professional.

Each sorter from a panel of several or more persons fairly representative of a particular public could then be asked to provide his or her viewpoint on each item (statement) by sorting the cards along a continuum numbered from -4 ("I most disagree with the statement") to 0 (no opinion) to $+4$ ("I most agree with the statement"). Each of the items (statements) would be placed at some point on the continuum. In the end, each respondent would give a picture of his view toward the civic responsibility of your company.

Next, you could calculate the score for each option by multiplying the value of the piles ($+4$, $+3$, $+2$, $+1$, 0, -1, -2, -3, and -4) by the number of copies of that card placed there by the sorters. From this, a total picture of the attitudes of one of your key publics could be formed.

Q-sort data may be analyzed along several lines including factor analysis and item analysis. Please see the Glossary in the Appendix for factor analysis. If you wish to become expert, useful instruction for such analyses is provided by William D. Brooks.[40]

We have used Q-sort in public relations research and in actual decision making and have found it to be a reliable technique. It has several strengths applicable to public relations. It appears to be a technique with wide application for a number of research settings. In addition, it is fairly easy to use as an instrument.

The number of items to be sorted is usually small—50 to 100, with 60 or 80 the norm. The items themselves can be generated from a number of sources: the public relations professional, responses gathered from a questionnaire, ideas from a book, statements from speeches, and newspaper interviews, for example.

Persons who serve as subjects generally find the sorting fun and easy to comprehend. This usually leads to a higher response rate.

Carolyn Johnson, the 1982 national president of WICI and former chair of the communications department at California State University, Fullerton, said she has found corporate executives and veteran public relations professionals eager to participate in the research and to learn more about the technique for their own decision making processes.[41]

Before moving to the next section on content analysis, pause to try your hand at doing a basic Q-sort or two.

Just for fun, write the names of the prime television programs scheduled for this weekend on 3 by 5 cards. Then, sort them as suggested above until you feel comfortable in allocating them to a final set of nine piles, with "like most" on the left, "like least" on the right, and "don't know" or "uncertain" in the center. When you get through sorting, see if you can determine the characteristics that make you like or dislike a particular television program.

Breaking the items into several piles along the continuum is related to scoring. This is particularly valuable when a number of sorters have sharply (or even slightly) different opinions.

One note of *caution*: Some persons will not react favorably to making forced choices. Explain that the neutral category can be large, if you really cannot make a decision, but that it is helpful to try to make the like-dislike (or other) choice.

Professionally, you may wish to practice with the basics of Q-sort by having a friend (or do it yourself, if that feels more comfortable at this point) sort through, say, 60 articles used in your employee or customer publications. You can prepare for this by either pasting up the complete articles on card stock or just using the lead paragraphs or headlines on cards.

Again, the same procedure prescribed for the fun exercise in Q-sorting television programs can be applied here. If you wish, you can go a step further, by assigning values to each of the nine piles. ($+4$ to -4). This has particular value if you have more than one sorter. Then total the score for each option. If you wanted to go even further, you could follow with a probe interview in which you asked your sorter *why* for each choice made. This should give you a foundation for utilizing Q-sort in your everyday public relations practice and the research to back it up.

CONTENT ANALYSIS

The public relations professional works in a sea of words. The day is often filled with writing copy or editing what someone else has written.

Because of the size of the investment, content analysis may prove a valuable research tool. Consider the cost of creative energy and the stakes in results sought from targeted publics.

One of the better definitions of content analysis comes from an authoritative source you may wish to explore at a later date, *Handbook of Reporting Methods:*

> Content analysis is an observation technique designed to take a sample of language and analyze that language for the message it carries. The goal is to be able to infer from objective, hard evidence what the sender of the message really means or to obtain some idea of the effect the sender intends.[42]

The purpose of content analysis is to allow you to *systematically* describe communication or messages. As one of the leading authorities in this field of research, O. R. Holsti, wrote in *Content Analysis for the Social Sciences and Humanities*, it is "the application of scientific methods to documentary evidence."[43]

This ability to apply systematic analysis to communication is an important strength because it avoids the pitfalls of purely subjective, unstructured, unscientific evaluation in which a person may make conclusions just by looking at one or a few examples of something. Such an approach lacks the validity public relations communicators and executives demand.

Content analysis is used to examine public relations materials as objectively and systematically as possible.

In deciding to evaluate public relations publications or audiovisual productions, as two examples, the volume of material may be too large for a look at all editions or prints, so *probability sampling* procedures, discussed earlier in this chapter and briefly defined in the Glossary, have to be used. This can be incorporated in the content analysis procedure easily.

The population would include all the materials in a particular category (such as speeches, reports, proposals, slide shows, videotapes, films) under review with a sample selected from this list. The sample may be random, systematic, stratified, or even clustered. (See Glossary or the probability sampling section earlier in this chapter.) This sampling step helps ensure the systematic requirement of the method.

With the use of content analysis, the research effort is now placed under certain controls. The controls help protect the study from bias and give it validity. Claire Selltiz suggested assurance that these controls are operating:

1. The categories of analysis used to classify the content are clearly and explicitly defined.
2. Analysts must methodically classify all the relevant material in their samples.
3. Some quantitative measure is used to analyze the findings.[44]

The assignment of content to various categories is a crucial step in content analysis. Careful thinking is required here. *Operational definitions, which spell out each procedural step so clearly that there is no room for ambiguity*, will be helpful *so that the meaning of each category is clear to anyone reading your proposal or report.*

Typical categories might define various themes for analyzing public relations materials. The units of analysis, the things you actually count, could be words, sentences, or paragraphs, for example.

Objectivity is increased by measuring for intercoder reliability among those judging the material. That means that the several persons coding the content produce similar scores on comparable material.

To assure greater objectivity and increase the confidence of your executives in findings from your own analysis of content, you should have one or two others code the same material. If there is agreement on the assignment of the content to the same categories, then you can have greater confidence in your findings. Because human judgment is involved here, it is not unusual to get disagreements over the assignment of content. As long as this is not too great, your study results are valid.

Although there is no precise measure, most researchers expect an intercoder reliability score of .80 or higher to accept the results. Unless you assign the content analysis to a subcontractor or specialist, you may find it helpful to look up the actual formula for calculating inter-coder reliability. It is presented clearly in *Content Analysis of Communications* by Richard W. Budd, Robert K. Thorp, and Lewis Donohew. [45]

After conducting your analysis of the content, you will have data in various categories. Simple descriptive statistics can be revealing, such as how often various themes are expressed in the publications or audiovisuals. The percentage of units that appear in each category can be calculated.

Perhaps you are interested in content analyzing level of complexity and readability measures, such as length of sentences or use of clauses, active and passive verbs, direct and indirect quotations, vague pronouns, editorializing adjectives or adverbs, and mention of your organization's name in a favorable context. The patterns of content style, then, emerge.

Because your data usually take the form of frequencies of how often units of content occur, the chi square test statistic may be appropriate for additional analysis. And if your procedure allows you to assign scores to your units, then analysis of variance may be useful. Public relations persons with quantitative or research skills may want to consult additional analyses of data, such as those discussed in the Budd book. [46]

The relevance of content analysis to public relations is well established. It has been a standard research method in the study of mass communication for years. A great deal about the content, style, and effects of public relations and media materials can be gleaned with this tool.

MEDIA TRACKING MODEL

At the end of 1982, Ketchum Public Relations opened a new era of going beyond traditional content analysis of media coverage of a client to a unique computer-assisted *Publicity Tracking Model.* Before going public, the agency disclosed to its employees in November 1982 that more than a year of testing in the field had demonstrated the effectiveness of a comprehensive system for evaluating publicity campaigns in terms of:

- The amount of target audience exposure received
- The degree to which planned messages were delivered to the target audience

More to the point, the Ketchum Tracking Model helps a public relations professional define what results a cost-effective publicity campaign should achieve and then reports on how well the campaign performed.[47]

The agency media research specialists developed, and tested on select campaigns, two evaluative measures, the Publicity Exposure Index and Publicity Value Index that integrate audience statistics for media reach in given markets (exposure units) and numerical values set for quality of message delivered to the target audience (value units).

Ketchum's computer was programmed with audience statistics of particular relevance to CEOs, marketing executives, and public relations professionals from national and local television and radio stations, magazines, and daily newspapers in the top 120 markets in America.

Ketchum Chairman Paul H. Alvarez, APR, said that all the tests "proved over and over again that a carefully planned and executed PR program can produce measurable results." And he noted:

> Because the Ketchum Publicity Tracking Model requires program *performance objectives* stated and agreed to by the client *in advance* of a media campaign, the Tracking Model is as much a tool for *planning* media relations and publicity programs as it is for *evaluating* their effectiveness.
>
> Use of the model assures a more disciplined, client objectives-oriented approach to program development, execution, follow-through, midcourse corrections, and use of evaluation data.[48]

In establishing the effectiveness, for example, of an interview of a client representative on "Good Morning America" in the Chicago market, the media tracking specialists would program value numbers for message content points that were conveyed (a qualitative measure) and length of interview. They also would build into the computer analysis how many individuals are watching from the publics *the client needs to reach*, not just gross exposure in terms of the number of people watching at a given time.

The program is sophisticated enough to recognize the diminishing value of time on the airwaves for an interview. Ketchum researchers had found that clients do not get that much more value out of a 30-minute interview over a 10-minute interview. Similarly, print media coverage impact was established as not arithmetically increasing by sheer size of the space provided for an article.

A preview of materials prepared for CEOs and marketing and public relations executives was made available to us by Alvarez near the end of 1982. In it Ketchum sounded the theme of four primary strengths for management concerned with objectives and research-evaluation:

1. For the first time, you'll have measurable, objectives-oriented data at your fingertips to guide your expectations of media or publicity programs. And you'll have this *in advance.*

2. . . . You'll be armed with reliability-tested, quantitative data to project results and determine the relative cost effectiveness of proposals. And you'll have this *in advance.*

3. For the first time, you'll have a media placement tracking report of results that's easy to understand, presented in quantitative terms that chief executives increasingly demand, and that clearly evidences how effectively the program was executed.

4. . . . You and your organization may count on data for evaluation from *systematically refined* and *impartially measured* records of achieving impressions of key messages on target.[49]

With shadow tracking of media coverage during the research and development phase of the project, in which Ketchum computer programmers and media research specialists quietly tracked and analyzed efforts in a number of campaigns, it was possible to build a base for determining what might be the norm for a variety of media campaigns.

With 1.0 as the previously established standard performance index for an effective campaign, media coverage with a Publicity Value Index of 1.59 would be reported to the client as 1.59 times better than the normal plan. A campaign that achieves a .89 index would be said to be 89 percent effective in reaching the predetermined objective for the expected delivery of a standard hypothetical placement schedule.

PARTICIPANT OBSERVATION

Early in this chapter it was pointed out that observation is a primary tool of scientific inquiry. Because public relations does not take place in a vacuum, it is natural that any research involving the profession rely on observational techniques.

One such technique is participant observation. This is a method that allows the researcher to *personally participate* in the actual research setting, even in the activity or process being researched. This can also be thought of as research in a natural setting, one in which people live or work.

Quite often in public relations research, the only way the needed data can be collected is through direct observation. For example, if you need reactions to a specific public relations project, such as an exhibit, then you probably want to get the opinions of persons attending the exhibit. You can become a participant by going to the exhibit and recording what people say about it.

Participant observation allows you to record ongoing behavior in particular settings or situations. This is in contrast to survey research, in which data are collected through a questionnaire after the fact.

Because participant observation allows you to capture data continuously *at the same time something is happening*, it provides helpful mid-course evaluation for monitoring and adjustment of important activities.

This research tool allows you to observe a group in great detail. Through such concentration, you can see relationships, conflict, change, and other dynamics common to a special public. By observing all these interactions, you may gain increased understanding, and ultimately, may make better predictions about future behavior.

For instance, you could observe a committee of employees as they go about their particular task. Or you could observe customers who are upset with particular activities at your client's stores. And you could observe a group that is part of a new public that your organization has just begun to try to reach with a new product or service.

To gain greater strength in understanding and applying participant observation, we recommend several sources in the Notes to this chapter.[50]

Despite its strengths, there are difficulties in using the technique. One is that you or other persons you assign as participant observers have to decide whether your presence could distort the natural setting.

The mere presence of an officer of the company, such as the public relations professional or another observer, may cause people to react differently. If so, the data may be based on an artificial premise. This leads to questions about the role the observer plans to assume before entering the group.

1. Depending upon ethical and legal considerations, you must decide whether to reveal participant observer identity and role to the group. If you believe such an announcement will distort the setting, then, if there are no ethical or legal problems, the observer may go unannounced.

2. Once you or other observers are in the group or at the activity being researched, the issue becomes one of whether to take an active or passive role. As a passive participant, you will do little more than stand on the sidelines and record the group process. The active role allows the observer to become more involved in the group, even to the point of exerting leadership and making suggestions.

Another difficulty lies in the recording of data. It may be difficult to overcome selective perception and personal feelings once a group has been observed for very long. Some public relations persons may even find themselves identifying with the group. One strategy for remaining relatively objective, as suggested by Peter Johansen and David Grey, is for you to record your own behavior, thoughts, and conversation while observing. They suggested taking detailed notes and keeping a daily journal.[51]

John Bollens and Dale Marshall further advised:

> You can easily become deceived into thinking that you will remember such details without a journal. But, unfortunately, important facts fade from memory or are changed to fit with later perceptions.[52]

Taking detailed notes while something is happening not only minimizes these risks but also allows you to record your own feelings and later analyze how, if at all, they may have colored your observations.

It also is important to structure the procedures for recording, interpreting, and reporting observations.

Despite the difficulties in conducting a participant observation study, public relations professionals have been discovering for years that the potential reward of data gathered from a natural setting more than offsets such problems.

A useful checklist for doing participant observation is available in *The Human Perspective in Sociology: The Methodology of Participant Observation*. It requires very little adaptation for a public relations professional to apply this checklist.[53]

UNOBTRUSIVE MEASURES

An intriguing method known as *unobtrusive measures*, or *nonreactive research*, combines several strategies for observing data.

A concern behind selecting unobtrusive research is to avoid the "reactive" tainting of data-gathering techniques. There is a chance that any time you attempt to collect data, your presence may provoke a reaction from whomever or whatever you are observing.

For instance, if employees or customers know they are being observed, then they may act differently. The mere act of observing may change the research setting.

The development of unobtrusive measures has been concerned with how to avoid interfering with the data. If you wish to polish your skills in this kind of research, we recommend further reading in *Unobtrusive Measures: Nonreactive Research in the Social Sciences.*[54]

A beginning point for unobtrusive research is a search for physical evidence resulting from previous behavior. Eugene Webb, an expert in this area, distinguished between two broad kinds of physical evidence:

> On the one hand, there are erosion measures, where the degree of selective wear on some material yields the measure. On the other hand, there are accretion measures, where the research evidence is some deposit of materials.[55]

His examples include the *measure of erosion,* or wear and tear, such as when certain tiles have to be replaced more often than others in a museum, suggesting the most popular exhibits.

Another example is to look at the records on titles of books that are checked out most often to monitor trends among library users. You are using records that already exist. You do not have to survey library members to get this finding.

To explain *accretion measures,* Webb cited a Chicago automobile dealer who had his mechanics note the position of radio dials on all cars brought in for servicing. From these records, the dealer determined the most popular radio stations among his customers.

Counting the particular frequencies by which complaint letters may be categorized could serve as an early warning of trouble spots between the organization and its clients. Again, no survey is necessary unless you want to probe deeper; it is just an examination of physical evidence. Complaint or commendation letter documentation serves a useful purpose, but *caution* should be exercised in drawing conclusions about publics to which the letter writers belong. Persons motivated to write to a client tend to be atypical.

Archival records are excellent sources of data. Indications of attitudes, desires, hopes, and concerns among an organization's publics may be gleaned from actuarial records on birth, marriage, and death. City, state, and federal governments all accumulate massive amounts of statistical data. From these records, much can be learned about your publics. On a very simple level, you could learn if a particular public is growing or shrinking in size based on births and deaths and indicators of migration in or out of an area. Sales of particular automobiles might give an early indication of economic activity and well-being among various publics.

Voting records are easily obtained, and the public relations researcher may learn about the political attitudes of a particular public by examining past voting behavior. For instance, how liberal or conservative is the public—not in how they describe themselves but in how they behave in the voting booth? How have they voted on special issues such as school bonds?

And consider the intelligence to be gained from an analysis of ballot initiative and referendum voting: Have the voters recently passed an unusual proposition signaling a marked shift in public attitude, such as on ownership of guns, prohibition or limitation of certain kinds of taxes, school busing, making of deposits on disposable bottles and cans, or use of video game arcades by youngsters? How did publics or subpublics in which you have a special interest vote on such issues? You could check city or precinct tallies and published results of surveys conducted as voters exit polling places.

Other records might reveal some insights about the effects of a particular campaign. For instance, a campaign to crack down on speeding could be evaluated for its effectiveness by looking at the police reports on the number of accidents "due to excessive speed" that have occurred since the campaign began. The same could be done for campaigns involving seat belts and driving while intoxicated. Various ways of evaluating public relations messages for persuasive effects should be open to imaginative researchers using existing records.

Archival records offer rich amounts of data for the public relations researcher without the costs and expertness that may be required for survey and similar forms of research.

By using unobtrusive measures, the problem of those being studied "reacting" to the researcher is avoided.

Although there are limitations and dangers, such as other variables affecting the physical evidence and distorting it, this is an underdeveloped method for doing public relations research. As Webb suggested, such measures can be used with more traditional approaches to get a more complete finding. Webb said that the Chinese proverb still holds: "The palest ink is clearer than the best memory."[56]

As a last example in this section, consider checking the wastebaskets in your lobby where literature is available or at work stations where employee literature may be distributed. Note not only if the materials appear to have been discarded without the smudging and dogearing that would indicate readership but also what parts seem to have the most wear.

Most of what we have reviewed thus far has concentrated on past or present behavior or activities, which can be most valuable to the public relations professional. Of at least equal value is the capability to help your client project the future.

FUTURES RESEARCH

Because public relations is a profession associated with problem solving and anticipating future climate or environmental concerns for an organization, we review here the concept of *futures* research.

Notice that the word futures has an s in it. This is intended. Futures research is concerned with *alternative* futures. The central theme of futures research is to broaden the concept from a simple forecasting tool to one that attempts *to explain the effects of various actions so that effective policies can be generated, thereby creating the future conditions deemed desirable.*

As a public relations officer, you can affect future outcomes through the decisions and actions you take on behalf of your organization or the decisions and policies you counsel executives and board members to take.

You may think of creating future public relations climates and environments rather than merely responding to whatever the future may bring. Similar futures research already has been done in such organizations as Security Pacific National Bank, the National Aeronautics and Space Administration (NASA), Monsanto, Bank of America, TRW, and General Electric.

As the pioneers in public relations applications of futures research have discovered, several tools for predicting future climates can be adapted to your needs. These include *Delphi technique, scenario analysis,* and *cross-impact matrix analysis.*

Delphi Technique

This technique relies on a series of questionnaires (called rounds or waves) administered to a particular audience or public. The purpose is to elicit a consensus of attitudes from the group on a particular topic. Generally, three rounds or waves of questionnaires are administered to the group. Responses from the first questionnaire are fed back to the individuals in the group for additional comment and agreement. These responses, in turn, are sent back in a second round of the futures survey for comment and agreement as you continue to move the respondents toward a consensus.

Usually, consensus among the respondents is reached after the third questionnaire.

Normally, the panel or group contains 30 to 60 members. All of them are considered to have expertness or special knowledge about the topic you are surveying.

The surveys usually are administered by mail. Ideas are fed back to the members of the group without attribution so that anonymity is preserved. This prohibits dominance of the group by a very respected individual. It also keeps highly vocal, but not necessarily the best, persons from dominating the group. And it avoids anyone having the feeling of censure or ridicule of personal ideas and viewpoints that may be imaginative but on the verge of being considered "far out."

As an example of the application of the technique, the Foundation for Public Relations Research and Education commissioned a futures study on educational needs in public relations by Frank B. Kalupa and T. Harrell Allen.[57]

The research focused on future needs and goals in public relations education at the university level by seeking viewpoints from public relations professionals and educators. This national panel arrived at a consensus on issues concerning public relations curriculum, as reported in the Summer 1982 issue of *Public Relations Review*.[58]

Scenario Analysis

This technique is used primarily to measure the impact of policy decisions. The idea is to use a *what if* approach concerning public relations programs.

The scenario usually begins by looking at the givens (those aspects of the problem that cannot be changed). Then the analysis starts to concentrate on those parts or aspects of the problem that can be changed. In essence, the scenario has now defined the area in which you may work in order to affect change.

The next step is to consider a policy option in the light of its impact on those factors that can change. The scenario allows you to trace the impact of corporate policy or the public relations program on future climates or environments.

It is a rigorous way of thinking through an action before it is taken. It may be done by a single individual or by a panel representing certain areas of expertness. This person or panel, then, can develop the scenario in detail and explore alternate scenarios.

In a sense, a *scenario analysis explores the options open to a decision maker and the "what if " considerations* as the organization arrives at crossroads where multiple paths converge. This goes a level beyond brainstorming in its detail and rigor.[59]

Cross-Impact Matrix Analysis

Cross-impact matrix analysis is a methodology for revealing and examining the *impacts* (interactions) among future events.

Typically, when using this analysis, a *matrix* (a table consisting of rows and columns of events) is constructed. Then the matrix is examined to measure the impact of an event on another event.

For example, following the oil crises and soaring fuel costs of the past decade, Americans drive less. This affects U.S. imports of oil. So the impact of less driving eventually reveals itself in the matrix in the form of less imported oil for motorists.

A public relations campaign to persuade Americans to conserve gasoline similarly could be traced to its impact on the behavior of drivers.

Relatively simple impacts of the matrix can be measured by hand. More elaborate matrices call for computer calculations.

The following is an example of a cross-impact matrix analysis from *New Methods in Social Science Research: Policy Sciences and Futures Research:*[60]

> Assume that a set of events has been estimated to have occurred before some future time period with varying levels of probability (as indicated in the following table). If the first event ("E") has occurred,

generally we will see the individual event probabilities change either positively or negatively with the occurrence or nonoccurrence of other events. For example, assume the following events and probabilities were forecast for a given year:

Event	Probability
1. Reliable energy consumption estimates for all winter months. (Event "E1")	.50
2. New sources of natural gas discovered. (Event "E2")	.20
3. Energy usage levels cut by one-fourth. (Event "E3")	.30
4. Alternative form of energy developed. (Event "En"*)	.10

*En means any number of alternatives.

Under cross-impact analysis this can be put in matrix form (in which the plus sign indicates something becoming more probable, the minus sign symbolizes less probable, the letter X is the sign for no impact, and a blank space is left in the square for the event itself).

If this event were to occur:	then probability of			
	E1	E2	E3	En
E1		X	X	X
E2	X		−	X
E3	+	X		X
En	X	X	−	

(Reprinted with permission of Praeger)

The procedure involves several steps, including forecast by the public relations person or a panel of probabilities in which a subjective scale can be used, such as:

Very likely = 90 to 100
Likely = 70 to 90
Somewhat likely = 50 to 70
As likely as not = 50
Somewhat unlikely = 30 to 50
Unlikely = 10 to 30
Very unlikely = 0 to 10

Cross-impact matrix analysis, as any other research tool, can be useful in some situations and not in others and can be combined with other approaches for projecting alternatives for the future.

COMBINED APPROACH

From a philosophical and pragmatic viewpoint, leading public relations professionals and research firms do *not* advocate the use of any research method exclusively. They seek to avoid the so-called "law of the hammer: If the only tool you have is a hammer, then everything looks like a nail."

Public relations practice is too complex to be dominated by a single tool. Indeed, *the most fertile research comes from a combined approach of various methods.* This means that any single evaluation of a public relations effort may be dangerously misleading. The careful public relations researcher develops a pattern of multimethod testing. This means making many observations. A way to do this is through a repertoire of research methods. Webb has observed: "If no single measurement class is perfect, neither is any scientifically useless."[61]

But regardless of the potential utility of measurement to public relations research and evaluation, the methodology only is pragmatic if it is *programmed* as parts of the *PR-MBO and C-R-E-A-T-E planning system* that incorporates an *objectives-related* time line, contingency planning, budgeting of resources, and actions affecting products and services. Chapter 7 turns to the action and planning parts of the process.

First, however, please pause to check your familiarity with the evaluation and research terms in the Glossary in the Appendix. You also may wish to make marginal notes next to those that provoke questions and add other terms and interpretations that you encounter in professional seminars, books, journals, and consultation with experts.

NOTES

1. Barbara W. Hunter and Judith S. Bogart, interviews (1983 Spring Assembly, PRSA, Salt Lake City), May 13, 1983.
2. Don Hill, "In Search of Excellence," *Public Relations Journal*, May 1982, pp. 36–37.
3. Joseph F. Awad, 1982 president of Public Relations Society of America, interview, Westminster, California, April 30, 1982.
4. Hill, "In Search of Excellence," p. 36. Italics added.

5. Ibid., p. 37.
6. "1982 Silver Anvil Winners: Index and Summaries," p. 1. Public Relations Society of America, 845 Third Avenue, New York, NY 10022.
7. Ibid., p. 13.
8. Ibid., p. 21.
9. Donald K. Wright, "Some Ways to Measure Public Relations," *Public Relations Journal*, July 1979, pp. 17–18.
10. Philip Lesly, "Emerging Principles and Trends," in *Lesly's Public Relations Handbook*, ed. Philip Lesly, 2nd ed. (Englewood Cliffs, N.J.: Prentice-Hall, 1978), p. 611.
11. Jacob L. Engle, interview, Chicago, November 10, 1981; telephone interview, December 15, 1981. Paul Alvarez, telephone interview, April 18, 1983.
12. James E. Grunig, "The Status of Public Relations Research" (paper presented to the Public Relations Division of the Association for Education in Journalism and Mass Communication, Annual Convention, Seattle, August 1978), p. 6.
13. John Van Maanen, "The Process of Program Evaluation," *Grantsmanship Center News*, January/February 1979, p. 30.
14. For a more complete discussion, see Carol H. Weiss, *Evaluation Research: Methods for Assessing Program Effectiveness* (Englewood Cliffs, N.J.: Prentice-Hall, 1972).
15. M. Scriven, *The Methodology of Evaluation*, American Educational Research Association, monograph series on Curriculum Evaluation (Chicago: Rand McNally, 1967).
16. Ibid.
17. J. H. Harless, "An Analysis of Front-End Analysis," *Improving Human Performance: A Research Quarterly*, 1973, pp. 229–44.
18. Daniel J. Stufflebeam et al., *Educational Evaluation and Decision Making* (Itasca, Ill.: Peacock, 1971).
19. *Public Relations Journal*, May 1982, and *Public Relations Review* 3 (Winter 1977).
20. Byron Reeves and Mary Ann Ferguson–DeThorne, "Measuring the Effect of Messages About Social Responsibility," *Public Relations Review* 6 (Fall 1980): 40.
21. Kenneth Rabin and Richard Franzen, "Increasing the Role of Planning," in *Informing the People*, ed. Lewis M. Helm, Ray Eldon Hiebert, Michael R. Naver, and Kenneth Rabin (New York: Longman, 1981), p. 191.
22. Leo J. Northart, "Editor's Notebook: Measuring Public Relations Effectiveness," *Public Relations Journal*, July 1979, p. 8.
23. Artemus Ward, quoted by Claire Selltiz, Lawrence S. Wrightman, and Stuart W. Cook, *Research Methods in Social Relations* (New York: Holt, Rinehart and Winston, 1976), p. 2.
24. For a concise discussion of the scientific method, see James W. Tankard, Jr., "Reporting and Scientific Method," in Maxwell McCombs, Donald Lewis Shaw, and David Grey, *Handbook of Reporting Methods*, (Boston: Houghton Mifflin, 1976), pp. 42–77.
25. Ibid., p. 60.
26. Wyman L. Spano, correspondence to Norman R. Nager, August 4, 1981.
27. 1981 PRSA Silver Anvil Notebook, Wyman L. Spano Public Affairs, Inc., and Natural Gas Council of Minnesota.

28. Peter Dowd, "Public Relations in a Computer World" (presentation at Communications Week 1982, Fullerton, California, April 26, 1982).
29. Betsy Ann Plank, "The Revolution in Communication Technology for Public Relations," *Public Relations Review* 1 (Spring 1983): 3–10.
30. Herbert H. Hyman, quoted in Selltiz, *Research Methods in Social Relations*.
31. Ibid.
32. Earl R. Babbie, *Survey Research Methods* (Belmont, Calif.: Wadsworth, 1973), p. 58.
33. Selltiz, *Research Methods in Social Relations*.
34. Kathleen Kelley Reardon, "The ABC's of Research," *Public Relations Journal*, May 1981, p. 22.
35. "1982 Silver Anvil Winners," p. 25.
36. Babbie, *Survey Research Methods*, p. 57.
37. Ibid., p. 63.
38. Maxwell McCombs, "Sampling Opinions and Behaviors," in McCombs, Shaw, and Grey, *Handbook of Reporting Methods*, p. 126.
39. N. H. Nie, C. H. Hull, J. G. Jenkins, K. Steinbrenner and D. H. Bent, *Statistical Package for the Social Sciences*, 2nd ed. (New York: McGraw-Hill, 1975).
40. William D. Brooks, "Q-Sort Technique," in Philip Emmert and William D. Brooks, *Methods of Research in Communication* (Boston: Houghton Mifflin, 1970), pp. 165–180.
41. Carolyn Johnson, conversations, 1977–1983.
42. Donald Lewis Shaw and G. Cleveland Wilhoit, "Mining Community Records and Documents," in McCombs, *Handbook of Reporting Methods*, p. 141.
43. O. R. Holsti, *Content Analysis for the Social Sciences and Humanities* (Reading, Mass.: Addison-Wesley, 1969).
44. Selltiz, *Research Methods in Social Relations*, p. 392.
45. Richard W. Budd, Robert K. Thorp, and Lewis Donohew, *Content Analysis of Communications* (New York: Macmillan, 1967), p. 68.
46. Ibid., pp. 72–90.
47. Paul H. Alvarez, correspondence to Norman R. Nager, October 8, 1982.
48. Alvarez, interview, San Francisco, November 9, 1982.
49. Alvarez, correspondence, October 8, 1982.
50. See George J. McCall and J. L. Simmons, *Issues in Participant Observation* (Reading, Mass.: Addison–Wesley, 1969); John C. Bollens and Dale Rogers Marshall, *A Guide to Participant Observation* (Englewood Cliffs, N.J.: Prentice-Hall, 1973); and Severyn T. Bruyn, *The Human Perspective in Sociology: The Methodology of Participant Observation* (Englewood Cliffs, N.J.: Prentice-Hall, 1966).
51. Peter Johansen and David Grey, "Participant Observation," in McCombs, *Handbook of Reporting Methods*, pp. 230–233.
52. Bollens and Marshall, *A Guide to Participant Observation*, p. 57.
53. Bruyn, *The Human Perspective in Sociology*.
54. Eugene J. Webb, Donald T. Campbell, Richard D. Schwartz, and Lee Sechrest, *Unobtrusive Measures: Nonreactive Research in the Social Sciences* (Chicago: Rand McNally, 1966).
55. Ibid., p. 36.
56. Ibid., p. 111.

57. Frank B. Kalupa and T. Harrell Allen, "Future Directions in Public Relations Education," *Public Relations Review* 2 (Summer 1982): 31–45.
58. Ibid.
59. T. Harrell Allen, *New Methods in Social Science Research* (New York: Praeger, 1978), pp. 146–157.
60. Ibid., pp. 132–145.
61. Webb, *Unobtrusive Measures*, p. 174.

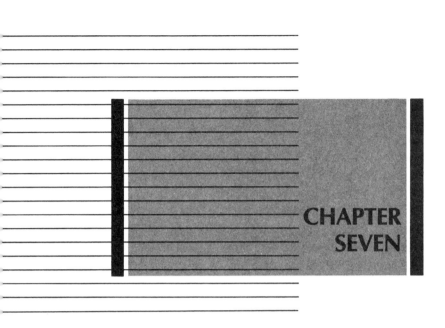

C-R-E-A-T-E SYSTEM'S ENERGY, ACTION, AND TIME/RESOURCES PLANNING

PUBLIC RELATIONS ENERGY

It may be helpful in understanding how to energize a company, public relations department, campaign, or individual public relations professional to return to the language and concepts of systems.

ENERGY AND ENTROPY

Entropy is a systems term borrowed from physics. Basically, it is a systems disorder in which the product is waste or even death of the system for lack of available energy.

When a distant star burns itself out or when an old-fashioned company that has retained the same ways of doing business is outstripped by its more modern competition and forced into bankruptcy, a similar phenomenon has occurred. The system has given off energy without the fresh inputs to keep it alive, let alone strengthen it. That is entropy. It is also a sign of what systems terminology refers to as *a closed system*.

A system energized by fresh sources of power would be termed an *open system*. (In this information era, such power would be communication/knowledge—the two are inseparable.) A public relations agency or department that continues to change, adapt its methods, grow in skills, and revitalize as it draws from resources outside of itself would be an open, or living, system.

The concept of entropy is useful to public relations professionals trying to energize their own profession, places of employment, departments, and individual capabilities. Rather than make a simple division between open and closed systems, you may wish to think in terms of *degree* of openness and *degree* of entropy.

When energy is expended with no return of capital to an organization, that could be equated to a form of entropy. That explains why business and public administrators concerned about the survival, financial health, and end products of their organizations look at the return on investments in salaries, fringe benefits, vended services, equipment, supplies, maintenance, and facilities in public relations and other areas.

RESEARCH PROVIDES THE FUEL

As the placement of Energy in the PR-MBO C-R-E-A-T-E planning system with Communication, Research, and Evaluation suggests, one way to provide energy to a client, its public relations system, or the individual professional is through research ranging from the informal kinds of fact-finding you can do in one-on-one conversations through the scientific procedures covered in Chapter 6.

Information serves as fuel for the human mind. Whether it is fuel that burns hot and clean and powers productive movement or the kind that burns unevenly and clogs the system is another question.

Program Continuing Education for Energy

Just as you program minute details and time periods for getting out materials to the news media or staging a presentation to the board, so, too, do you program energizing the system with useful information. This may include programming for yourself continuing education, such as time scheduled to:

1. Scan the news media at the national and regional levels on a daily basis.

2. Program reading of *Public Relations Review*, *Public Relations Journal*, *PR News*, *PR Reporter*, *O'Dwyer's Newsletter*, *Ragan Report*, and other periodicals in your field at least once a week.

3. Review financial, business, and trade publications for articles of interest to your client at least once a week.

4. Program time at least once a month to read books, such as those reviewed periodically in *Public Relations Review* and other journals or listed in the annual bibliography of books, journals, reference works, and newsletters you order from the PRSA research service in New York City.

5. Subscribe to one or more national research service public opinion reports. If your organization does not do this, you might want to develop a proposal recommending it and/or visit a college or city library reference librarian and ask for counsel on how to use the various public opinion studies.

6. Program at least one monthly meeting with fellow professionals in such organizations as PRSA, IABC, and WICI. Program enough time to get there early and talk with colleagues before the meeting.

7. Program at least one national conference or regional professional development series a year.

8. Program time for workshops and seminars sponsored by local campuses and professional societies once or twice a year.

9. Consider taking a university extension or regular course in management, basic computer, marketing, economics, public relations, psychology, sociology, television, journalism, speech communication, political science, or something else related to your work.

10. Conduct periodic surveys of your key publics, even if you have to "piggyback" (a term that means paying for one or a few questions to be added to another firm's ongoing survey).

11. Arrange for regular brainstorming sessions with your staff or a group of colleagues from other departments.

12. Arrange for weekly debriefing sessions from top management

on board and executive actions and what is being considered for change or might loom as a problem or target of opportunity for the organization as a whole as well as for public relations.

Keep in mind in selecting sources of information that systems tend to wither away when cut off from input from outside. A closed system is completely cut off. Burying yourself in routine tasks without programming input from outside your system may not cause you to wither away, but it may withhold from you an array of sources of creative, results-producing energy.

BURNOUT

Physical Burnout

The phenomenon of a system burning out is known to the college student and public relations practitioner as well as to the physicist and astronomer.

Physical burnout, which leads to mental and emotional entropy, can come from fatigue. Although fatigue normally may be seen as resulting from overwork and lack of sleep, it also can be related to emotional and mental drains on the system. Physical contributors to burnout can be remedied, depending upon the causal factors and the willingness of the individual to change.

One simple source of entropy is a lack of nutritional energy, which is common among compulsive dieters or persons so engrossed in their work that they forget to eat or subsist on junk food.

Another source is lack of sleep and rest to energize the system. The professional who works around the clock discovers the entropy principle at work around 4 a.m. or, if in stronger condition, the following afternoon, as mental processes slow and physical and mental slips occur.

Although many professionals have given up the old occupational addiction to nicotine, newcomers who have picked up the habit or who otherwise interfere with respiratory and circulatory systems by getting their tars from smoking other substances find that impairing breathing leads to smoking hangover and a degree of burnout. So, too, does ingestion of various drugs, including alcohol.

Burnout may be a more gradual physical phenomenon as the

person continues to focus on the same thing hour after hour, day after day, month after month, without a change of pace or adequate breaks for rest and relaxation. A professional who sits behind a desk and gets little opportunity to renew and build strength through systematic exercise engages in another form of entropy.

A growing number of senior executives in business have learned to pace themselves and to program as part of their daily regimen fueling of their physical systems with nutritional foods, sleep, rest, and exercise. They also have learned how to program vacation time, changes of pace, and even periodic medical examinations.

Nonphysical Burnout: PR Pressures and Workaholism

The so-called workaholics in public relations not only hurt themselves but others as well, according to Albert C. Smith, APR, executive vice president of Burson-Marsteller:

> Such persons may be extremely loyal, normally competent, hard working, and bright, but create total chaos in the system because nobody can work with them. Workaholics give impossible deadlines, don't anticipate problems people have, raise the stress level of the office over where it should be, and may even tend to be disorganized and miss deadlines themselves.[1]

Workaholism is a complex occupational disorder, normally not resolved by an executive or book giving advice to "take it easy." It may relate to insecurity on the part of the individual faced by a formidable amount of work and seeing no way out other than working himself and anybody who can be controlled past healthy limits.

In a sense, the workaholic may represent a system moving out of a healthy pattern of absorbing and giving off energy and changing into a system out of control. And part of that may stem from the particular demands of the profession.

But demonstrations of energy, short of destructive workaholism, appeal to executives with the power to hire and promote. Smith said that among the qualities he looks for in job candidates are service to a number of organizations plus work experience and extracurricular activity during college years.[2]

Another agency executive, Hill and Knowlton Senior Vice President Thomas Eidson, as many other professionals and educators before and since, said that he prefers to hire people "who like to work hard, are willing to tackle challenges, like variety, like multiple challenges, are willing to tackle problems. . . ."[3]

And Robert C. Will, APR, who was president of the western region of Harshe-Rotman & Druck before its merger with Ruder-Finn, noted that "some people find it hard to deal with the volatility in our industry, not job security, but the volatility of activity, such as working on three to five different programs."[4]

It is not uncommon to hear professionals recount pressures to work 12-hour and longer days, even round-the-clock marathons, to get out an annual report, work up a proposal, stage a series of special events, meet deadlines for their corporate publications, prepare a budget, handle crises, or just take care of daily activity—not to catch up, but just to keep from falling farther behind.

PROGRAMMING CREATIVE THOUGHT

HBO Vice President Roger B. Fransecky, formerly an executive with Westinghouse's cable systems, recommended that public relations professionals program specific time periods for reflection, restoration, and creative thought.[5]

So, even in the midst of harried work schedules, professionals who understand that energy loss can turn into entropy, that long hours and hard work do not necessarily equal results worth the time and intellectual sweat, may schedule the time to energize their creative processes.

Stanford University psychologist Paul Watzlawick and his fellow researchers noted that open systems "even evolve toward states of higher complexity by means of a constant exchange of both energy and information with their environment."[6]

A specialist in organizational psychology and sociology, Karl E. Weick, actually did experiments in which he found individuals gaining creativity by imagining that they already had accomplished their objectives and going backward from the point of achieving the results to how they got there.[7]

A number of practitioners have told us that they energize or revitalize their thinking by taking breaks to ride a bicycle, jog, play tennis or golf, swim, watch television, go to a movie, nap, read light fiction, or otherwise provide themselves with rewards for effort and time for the brain to subconsciously process all that has been fed into it before the programmed breaks.

Streamlining, Training, Delegating

Entropy can spring from the boredom of repetition and time-consuming routine labor. This can bring on creativity-robbing doldrums.

Professionals in public relations have learned that energy can be conserved through the investment of time and effort in streamlining a procedure, such as setting up a semiautomated reminder system, clearing the desk top of paperwork that stalls retrieval time of important work, or organizing a detailed system for handling special events once, rather than each time an event is held.

PR-MBO calls for working with people you supervise in developing their objectives, helping assure that they receive the training to do increasingly productive work, and delegating. This frees you for more responsible, creative activity.

Sometimes it costs more *initially* to spend time training, delegating, and providing follow-through oversight until you can have full confidence that the person will do as good a job as you would. And sometimes delegation does not work. But if there is a pattern, perhaps you may wish to obtain expert counsel within your own organization or at a management seminar.

It may help to consider incentives for persons to respond to training and delegation, including incentives of recognition, sense of achievement, and understanding of the whole to which they are contributing. That, too, can be programmed with built-in attention to detail and follow-through.

It may take some effort—on your part as well as others—to raise challenging questions, to overcome resistance to change. In *The Structure of Scientific Revolutions,* Thomas S. Kuhn observed that in science:

> Novelty emerges only with difficulty, manifested by resistance, against a background provided by expectation. . . . In the development of any science . . . professionalization leads, on the one hand, to an immense restriction of the scientist's vision and to a considerable resistance to paradigm change.[8]

But sciences and fields of professional practice, such as public relations, manage to nurture discovery and change through open exchange and seeking out of information and other sources of creative energy.

Perhaps the most powerful energizing force in public relations comes from becoming a change agent, a communicator of knowledge that leads to change.

That is where the action is, both figuratively and literally, in public relations.

FANTASYLAND CASE: CREATIVE ENERGY

As a bridge between Energy and Action, and as an illustration of how communication, research, energetic pursuit of creative ideas, and action can provide a promising program, we now present how brainstorming in troubled times led to an unusual 1980s investment in Walt Disney's West Coast Magic Kingdom.

The accompanying photograph of "The Mad Tea Party" ride from Disneyland's Fantasyland was part of a four-page media background release that announced a major 1983 renovation of the so-called heartland of the amusement park.

It came at an unusual time, even in the world of make-believe. The setting was post-oil-crisis southern California in the midst of the deep recession of the early 1980s, a period of declining air travel, and the beginning of the impact of declining population growth on the makeup of Disneyland's consumer public.

As case investigator Lawrence Berenato discovered, Disneyland *marketing, in teamwork with public relations, advertising*, designers, cost estimators from another division of the corporation, and others yielded an unusual target of opportunity.[9] The research director expressed interest in attracting more childless adults because of projections of a decline in the population of young people.

The Disneyland marketing people normally follow top management's decisions to develop promotional marketing for projects. On this occasion, at least, they and their colleagues *seized the initiative to explore various options available* for building new, or remodeling existing, customer attractions.

In view of the evidence that 90 percent of Disneyland's patrons were return visitors, the objective was related to a prevention of declin-

PHOTO FROM

Disneyland® PUBLICITY DEPT. • 1313 HARBOR BOULEVARD • ANAHEIM, CALIF. 92803 • (714) 999-4445 (213) 626-8605

CHANGING SCENE--Disneyland's Fantasyland, virtually untouched since the Park opened in 1955, is being renovated to create a bright, new world of make-believe. Construction has already started on the project, which will include a new Pinocchio attraction. Completion is slated for summer, 1983. In the meantime, much of Fantasyland will remain operational.

D-1123 R-4   Walt Disney Productions

ing patronage, if not bringing about an actual increase, in the mid-
1980s.

Construction began in 1982, and the word went forth to Disneyland employees and patrons. But the materials for the media announc-
ing the Fantasyland renovation actually were anticlimactic. For the
preliminary objective was to influence those with decision-making power
to fund the renovation of Fantasyland.

As in the *Los Angeles Times*–Washington High School case at
the end of Chapter 5, the first priority in identification of publics was
the selection of top management and board officers as the key individuals to influence. In addition, the 16 operating directors and vice president of operations were targeted as secondary but still important publics.

What Community Relations Manager Mary Jones later termed a
group action included a staff exploration of available options.[10]

Presenting Options to Executives

Four points are recommended here for giving management an appraisal
of options:

1. It is of value to anticipate other solutions that may occur to
management.

2. You or top management may find that one of the options is
better than the one you (or others) may have fostered originally. That
is similar to scenario research (covered in Chapter 6).

3. Flexibility in presenting options, rather than a single recom-
mendation, not only helps management in its decision-making process
but also increases its confidence in the professionalism of the staff.

4. Development of the pros and cons of all viable options is
important in earning management confidence and helping in the decision-making process.

Dividends on Disney Investment

The Disneyland case illustrates creative energy and serves as an example of action to improve a product for the consumer public. Disneyland's dividends may include not only a return of profit on the capital
but also the maintenance, if not increase, of jobs for the southern

California work force at the facility; continuation of support to the tax base of the host city of Anaheim; a draw of customers who also will patronize nearby motels, restaurants, and other businesses; and an enhancement of the entertainment value to those who ultimately pay the bills.

ACTION: TO CREATE CLIENT IMPROVEMENTS

The term public relations action is often confused by newcomers to the profession as descriptive of some event staged for media coverage or an activity such as an opening or exhibit. At other times it may be confused with such activities as producing a news release or videotape.

Public Relations Action Defined

The opinion leaders of the profession look upon public relations action as the essence of professional practice.

Public relations action may be defined as socially responsible acts taken by public relations departments or other parts of the organization with your counsel. The definition may be given more precision by specifying that the term refers to *actions in the sense of contributing to improvement in the organization's policies, products, services, and/or environment in such ways as to better meet the needs of the publics served by your client.*

What this means is that quality products and service and responsible treatment of employees and other publics, including those who share the physical, social, and economic environs, constitute the foundation of public relations practice.

Nevertheless, public relations actions do not take place in a vacuum. Nor are they done just for the sake of doing good, as noble an ideal as that would be. Add an important condition to the definition:

Public relations actions are directly related to public relations objectives that serve the client's interests while contributing to the well-being of publics.

That is not pure altruism, in the sense of complete selflessness of the client.

Of course, there are exceptions. Some corporation executives anonymously make generous gifts of service or resources without a thought for the dividends to be reaped, even in the sense of making the community a better environment in which to do business. Some would rather see the firm go out of business than produce defective products and would do what is right because of their personal code of ethics.

There is persuasive power in linking the public good to client interests. The public relations person acts as a change agent with research, communication, action, and evaluation woven into a backdrop for counsel to top management.

How Publics Perceive Action

This section does *not* view action in the sense that a former president of General Motors was understood when, as U.S. Secretary of Defense during the Eisenhower Administration, he said: "What's good for General Motors is good for America." Regardless of the meaning he intended, Secretary Charles Wilson was perceived as saying that whatever profited GM was in the public interest.

That a public relations action is in the public's interest does not necessarily mean that it is perceived by members of that public as such, or even that they have any awareness of the action. *Therein lies a two-pronged challenge to public relations to help both the organization's decision makers and publics go beyond mere awareness to an appreciation of actions as they benefit their respective interests.*

From a PR-MBO perspective, you can go a step *beyond appreciation* to motivation of, or predisposition to, behavior. In the case of management, that behavior could be to maintain existing actions in the public interest and to undertake new or improved actions as warranted. In the case of publics, the behavior flowing from the goodwill generated could relate to a number of causes ranging from influencing favorable legislative votes through increased productivity (including greater investment in the firm's stock or donations to the institution) to the purchase of more products or services.

Public relations professionals look at public relations action as a two-sided coin. And that means that prevention of harm to a public may be more important, if not equally as vital, as doing good deeds. Harm can come in endangering the health, safety, or sense of security of members of a public.

"Cheesecake," "beefcake," and ethnic "jokes"

Harm can come in giving offense, even unintentionally, to individuals.

"Cheesecake" or "beefcake" photos used to make up a fair amount of the publicity photos provided newspapers and magazines. Beauty contests were staged for television. Whether a public relations person or media gatekeeper thinks these things harmless or not, if the publics perceive exploitation and an unhealthy influence on the shaping of attitudes of the young, then there is ample reason for reconsideration.

One-liners poking "good-natured fun" at groups within society have tended to boomerang, perhaps leading to initial laughter in the audience but producing increasingly negative ripple effects as they have been picked up by media and passed from person to person.

In the 1970s, a U.S. secretary of agriculture and a U.S. president were brought before the court of public opinion for what were interpreted in the media and by publics as racial and ethnic slurs that inflamed public passions. In the 1980s, the lessons of the past were unlearned and electoral defeats, corporate strife, and social unrest continued to be harvested by those who sowed dissension with careless communication.

EXAMPLES OF PR ACTIONS

The following can serve as examples of public relations actions:

- Helping investors secure their funds when a company is threatened with bankruptcy.
- Increasing security for concert patrons.
- Minimizing traffic snarls and illegal parking near company facilities.
- Making an airline a better place to work by providing ear-safety equipment to ground crews.
- Developing nets for catching tuna that will allow dolphins to escape.
- Assigning executives on a lend-lease basis to United Way, A-I-D, or the Community Chest.
- Recalling a defective product *before* the government or consumer advocates discover it is defective, let alone demand its recall.

- Assuring that callers receive prompt, courteous treatment.
- Striking out at discriminatory practices such as unequal pay for equal work.
- Contributing to education and sophistication of publics as consumers.
- Operating disaster prevention and relief programs even when the client may not be perceived as responsible for potential crises.
- Retraining the chronically unemployed.
- Helping find jobs or homes for the displaced.
- Removing physical and social barriers to the disabled and elderly.
- Safeguarding the integrity of products by making them tamper resistant.
- Working for the improvement of the environment even if polluted by others.

Sense of Responsibility a Human Function

And public relations can do more. In the words of Lynn Bright, just before graduation and taking her first full-time position with an agency:

> Public relations can become so much more. Now there is technology to aid in [multiple-way] communication. Computers can help to pinpoint publics. . . . The only element that technology has not conquered is the human mind. Social responsibility is still a human function. Good character is not something that can be gained by reading a book or taking a course. Computers will never be able to instill social responsibility. So we, the students and practitioners, had better make good character something highly prized that we can continually strive for.[11]

The sense of responsibility is no less strong in those senior to Bright. Barbara Machado, community relations manager of St. Joseph's Hospital in southern California faced a crisis in public confidence when her medical facility accidentally dumped infectious waste at a county landfill.

The actions included sending hospital employees to the dump to sort through garbage to find bags that should have been sterilized; having maintenance employees take tests for color blindness (the infectious waste was in red bags); sponsoring refresher courses on disposal and other maintenance procedures; voluntarily reporting a repeat incident to the county, even when she and other executives knew doing so would result in punitive action; and offering to train county waste-disposal personnel on how to identify properly treated infectious waste.

The type of infectious waste was the less dangerous of two basic types processed at hospitals. Yet, as Machado said,

> This was not the time to educate the public that not all infectious waste was a serious health hazard. It was a time to take quick and responsible action. . . . In public relations, I think that we have a tendency to underestimate our power. . . .[12]

In sharing her professional introspection with an interviewer, Machado worried whether the temptation is "to delegate upward . . . responsibility for anything adverse" rather than come to grips with it in the public relations department. She, and a number of other professionals studied, *assumed responsibility and counseled remedial actions.*

One agency executive told of a client producing a product that killed several children after they had put it in their mouths:

> We don't pull off miracles. The first thing, everything was done to get [the product] out of kids' hands and off the market, no matter what cost to sales. We begged the media to cover the dangers.[13]

This section closes with two cases that illustrate the overlap of parts of the C-R-E-A-T-E process and the PR-MBO planning system.

In the first case, the evaluation component was intended to measure the behavioral results in a national public relations action program of the U.S. government. This case also underlines the capability of modern research to measure behavioral impact.

CASE STUDY: NUTRITION PROGRAM IMPACT

Dr. Thomas Glenn, president of Telepoll, reviewed the case with which he was involved before founding his own research organization.[14] A national evaluation of school nutrition programs was conducted to determine what impact, if any, the program had on nutritional status of the children.

Field research was done in 1980 and 1981 for the U.S. Senate, which sponsored it under Senate Resolution 90. Although the Senate did not wait for results of the research before acting (which is another public relations problem), the survey produced useful data.

The study probed who made decisions on where children eat, had subjects fill in diary logs and provided for in-home interviews. The researchers also had proposed direct observation in school cafeterias to determine how nutritional information disseminated in the schools and sent to parents influenced behavior in the home and in school eating locations.

One of the principle measures of behavior was recall (as well as observation). What did you eat in the last 24 hours? What did the school lunch give you? How many days this week? This month?

The eating behavior of children outside school was measured to serve as a control to determine if boys and girls who differed in their degree of participation in the school program had roughly the same behavior patterns at home. The theory was that involvement in the program should relate to better nutritional status.

Glenn said researchers wanted to know who was using the program, how often they were using it, why, and most important, how it was affecting the nutritional status of the child and the economic status of the family, especially if costs were increased for all but the lowest income groups.

The focus, then, was not on awareness or even understanding, but on what the U.S. Senate considered the bottom line of the program: the impact on nutritional and economic status of the child and the family. The battle continued in Washington well into the 1980s on the future of the school nutrition program.

The next case left no controversy in its wake, only evidence that promised further strengthening of a weakened national institution.

CASE STUDY: A GOOD DEED FOR SCOUTS

A 1982 PRSA Silver Anvil was awarded to the Boy Scouts of America and the Fleishman-Hillard agency for national excellence in institutional programs.

The public relations action plan was designed to revitalize a scouting movement that had plunged from a membership high of about 5 million to 3 million by 1978 with predictions that if something wasn't done, "the movement would be virtually extinct by 1990. Scouting needed to take a hard look at its program and develop fresh approaches and a more appealing image," the case summary reported.[15]

The initial part of the action plan was set in motion by a vice president of AT&T, who was credited with mobilizing several corporate leaders. They determined that "the Boy Scouts should *use a business approach: scientific research to get to the root of the problem, followed by an organized action plan.*"[16]

Private donors were organized and Fleishman-Hillard volunteered to contribute as much in volunteer hours as in paid time to coordinate the project.

Fleishman-Hillard's research division received 10,000 responses to a mail survey of several wide-ranging publics. They included persons who had never been in scouting or had dropped out, as well as several publics involved in the movement as members, parents, sponsors, and volunteers.

Based upon the research findings, the agency developed an action plan to design new programs and then did more research, interviewing several hundred key scouting leaders and volunteers. Next, materials for what were deemed the most crucial programs were field tested in eight midwestern cities.

After implementation of such programs as "Tiger Cubs," for younger boys and parents, and "Today's Family," a program to make scouting more attractive to single-parent and dual working-parent families by helping their children become more self-reliant, another wave of evaluation was conducted. This time, evaluation was in the form of personal interviewing in all eight test cities, and ·mail and telephone surveys of more than 500 persons.

Among the results: The area in which the eight test cities were located tallied the *first membership gain in the 10-year history* of that scouting region. And surveys indicated that "Tiger Cubs," "Today's Family," and other action programs were winning strong acceptance.

TIME/RESOURCES PLANNING

Even finding the time to put together the planning of scarce resources may prove difficult for the public relations professional under siege. This means having to get organized before you can organize.

PRIORITIES AND MANAGEABILITY

It may seem a luxury for some public relations persons to invest the time needed in effectively planning campaigns and the overall program. If that is a problem, you may have to make a hard choice among priorities for your time. Planning may have to take precedence over other priorities. This may be the moment to learn to say no to requests, to take a retreat for a day or so from day-to-day activities or even the work site to develop at least a preliminary strategy.

An integral part of the first phase of the planning process, whether it be to schedule research or an entire program, is to select a *manageable piece of the action*, to bring into sharp focus what may be accomplished with the limited time, manpower, and other resources at your disposal.

That is not an excuse for the newcomer to put off treatment of a larger problem. You have to begin somewhere. The point here is not to spread yourself so thin that you cannot give more than surface attention to priorities that warrant more.

TIME LINES

Flexibility and Systems Approach

A veteran professional's mental computer may be programmed so that he or she needs no written, formal *time line* with which to operate. *(Time line is a term public relations professionals use in reference to carefully laid out program or campaign schedules.)*

But for persons who need teamwork or who require higher management understanding, if not shielding, when executives try to load more tasks on an already overloaded public relations staff, a clearly laid out time line with a preface of hardened objectives and priorities may prove convincing.

And a time line may have to be written in sufficient detail so that others may write their adaptations if cooperation is needed in coordinating activities with other departments or other members of the public relations staff.

Circumstances demand written plans

As some professionals have discovered, the written time line is valuable on a number of occasions, even if the professional has a near-photographic memory and the ability to integrate effects of changes in an unwritten plan. Consider these circumstances:

1. The professional goes on vacation and is not available to handle a new or changed situation.

2. The professional is home ill. (One of the authors remembers when he was under a physician's order to remain home with flu and the President of the United States came by on three days' notice to visit Memorial Hospital Medical Center of Long Beach.) It is well to have written time lines and *what if* plans for oneself *and* for others to operationalize in a crisis.

3. The professional leaves for a better position or dies. The latter may seem macabre, but it is reality. And a mark of professionalism is a long-range concern for what happens to the public relations of an organization. The professional invests a great deal in a public relations position. The thought of years of work being undone has inspired some professionals to keep working plans in the files "just in case."

The flexibility of a time line means building into the instrument the freedom to take advantage of targets of opportunity that may not be on the horizon when the plan is written or to respond to crises that may emerge with little warning. This involves systems concepts.

In a systems approach, flexibility means leaving free time or at least constructing a plan that does not initially overtax the time of public relations staff and others. It also means *selecting in advance activities of lower priority that can be postponed or abandoned if targets of opportunity or crises demand finding additional time.*

Program into time lines specific intervals to pause periodically in the pursuit of multiple goals. During this pause, reassess goals and objectives based on the changes in your client, your publics, media, the social environment, your department, and yourself, to name just a few systems that affect goals and objectives.

Some professionals not only lay out a clear time line and allocation of resources, including their own time, for on-the-job responsibilities but also build a larger plan in which they consider what it takes for the survival of systems that are important beyond the job.

These include budgeting time and resources for maintenance of, at least:

- Family and friends systems
- Professional development
- Extracurricular activity
- Physical and mental health

A systems approach also suggests that because you and your client live in a world with conflicting demands upon resources and limited time, you will want to program time to *examine the systemic effects of diverting scarce resources from other client priorities.* This may be called *the robbing Peter to pay Paul syndrome.*

Equivocality Reduction

Equivocality poses one of the greatest challenges to public relations planning. Equivocality may be defined as the unknown or the uncertainty in any decision that has to be made.

Life is full of equivocality and multiple paths to follow, and there come times when we may indulge in too much time spent on worrying over a decision that has to be made by a deadline or delaying its implementation dangerously long. Meanwhile, the situation becomes more complex and approaches crisis stage.

One of the greatest roles of communicators in our society is the reduction of equivocality—the reduction of needless ambiguity and uncertainties. And one of the greatest roles of public relations persons is doing the preliminary and ongoing research and providing for *monitoring and evaluation to assure that you are on course and minimizing the risks for client and publics.*

16 STEPS TO PROGRAM

Basically, you want to implement the following 16 steps whenever you develop a workable time line for a public relations program:[17]

1. Write hardened, time-certain, precise, attainable, measurable objectives with built-in guides to evaluation.

2. Program research (primary and secondary) as a continuing process and in form of steps for follow-through.

3. Program public relations actions to improve substance of client policies, services, and products, as well as ways client is perceived.

4. Program steps for public relations communication for your client.

5. Program evaluation of tools, strategies, tactics, progress, and overall results.

6. Program contingencies (plural)—the *what if* planning—based on scenarios you can envision for problems emerging or options needed.

7. Develop time lines with specific dates or programmed intervals of time to start and follow up on specifics of the above components—research, communication, evaluation, public relations actions, contingencies. And make sure that your program has both the depth and quality of organization to make it work for you and your client.

8. Carefully review entire plan for clarity and results in meeting your and your client's specifications.

9. Base your project on your own research. Check reference books for relevant ideas or techniques. And do whatever other research is needed, from informal one-on-one interviewing to structured surveying to build a solid foundation for the feasibility of your time line.

10. Limit the narrative or essay portions of your plan, keeping in mind that neither your executives nor you will be able to reread long passages of text while trying to follow through on a time line.

11. Use keys if you develop graphic charts that allow only for symbols or a few short words to label activities. You want to make clear what symbols or labels signify.

12. Start planning and working on any plan long before you need it, and allow it to germinate so you can come back refreshed and review its pros and cons before hardening it.

13. Share your plan with top management, and, if you are willing to use them, invite their ideas for incorporation into the final product.

14. Do the same with colleagues in other departments that will be asked for cooperation.

15. Do the same with other members of the public relations staff.

16. Program the next review and updating before you put the last draft down.

Because these 16 steps are so important, you may wish to pause, review them, and make marginal notes on how you may incorporate them in your planning. Think what you could add, based on your own experience, to strengthen the process.

You may wish to apply the 16 steps to your own career development program as a means of testing their utility and gaining proficiency in making them part of your approach to planning.

As you do, you will want to place increased emphasis on building in follow-through and attention to detail in your time lines.

BUILT-IN FOLLOW-THROUGH

Consider that your time line, whatever form it takes, will serve as a detailed road map with accompanying *step-by-step procedures on how you get to your destination on course and on time.*

Interviewers for public relations positions tend to include in their checklists of most important skills follow-through and attention to detail. Heading their lists usually are copyediting and proofing skills.

Follow-through is illustrated in plans that call for rehearsing a banquet program, previewing an audiovisual showing, or *dry-running* (similar to rehearsing, but in the sense of making it as realistic as possible) a whole program.

Here is an example of public relations research follow-through: The early returns on your questionnaire indicate shifts in attitude among key publics, but you follow through by looking for *actual behavioral changes* in the next three months or year. The point is *not* to be misled by some early results of your public relations program. It is such follow-through that may give you the only way of detecting any real changes in the public. You do not want premature shifting of priorities or closing of a program because of deceptive first returns.

(Remember last election night when you watched the early returns on television and learned of the reverses that took place after the counting of the first handful of precincts?)

Follow-through and attention to detail can include such activities as writing thank-you letters in which the person to whom you are writing sees enough substance to feel that this is more than a form letter.

And you might thank persons who contributed to your research by answering surveys or engaging in one-on-one interviews. Or you might thank other departments for their assistance. And you might thank professional colleagues for their counsel.

Sweden's Axel Johnson Group time management system

Göran Sjöberg, public relations vice president of Scandinavia's third largest corporation, his executives, and his staff use a specially designed time management notebook to assure that Axel Johnson Group managerial personnel follow through in a number of important areas. Each person carries an identically indexed, purse-size binder with removable pages plus a vestpocket-size note holder.

Sjöberg, 1983 president of the International Public Relations Association (IPRA) and co-author of several Swedish books on management, travels more than 100 days a year on business. For him, the leather-bound, black planning book serves many of the time management functions that would be available on a computer at his Stockholm home office:[18]

• Numerically coded sections to enter or check a diversity of follow-through reminders and notes for action and file.

• A section for items to be discussed in person with the chair of the Axel Johnson Group.

• Individual sections for each member of the public relations staff on two-way and one-way communications to be conveyed at non-scheduled times, such as on Sjöberg's return from a trip or through telex or telephone communications.

• Printed (and indexed for quick checking) corporate and public relations policies and procedures.

• Detailed printouts of itineraries, including phone numbers of contacts en route. (Duplicate of records kept in Sweden.)

• Important office and home numbers and addresses of Axel Johnson Group subsidiary and corporate officers and staff, IPRA and other organizational colleagues, and government and media persons. (As other parts of the notebook, this is checked periodically and on trip returns by Stockholm staff to duplicate items entered by Sjöberg.)

• A time management section dealing with family and other personal matters.

• Conventional annual and monthly celendars for entering important events.

• A split page for each day of the week in which items on the left side are entered next to scheduled times; and things to do without concern for exact schedule are written on the right side of the foldout calendar pages. Both are checked off as done and transcribed periodically by his secretary.

• Boxes next to scheduled times for checking whether meetings should be interrupted for incoming calls or problems of less-than-crisis proportions.

• A separate mini-pad for taking notes to enter into the notebook. This keeps him from having to pull out the more cumbersome notebook from his briefcase when it would be inconvenient to do so.

Follow-through and attention to detail are exemplified when you plan to do the following:

• Keep computer or conventional files with quickly retrievable notes on the implementation of public relations programs.
• Maintain records on attitudinal and behavioral patterns of publics.
• Provide detailed reports on successful public service announcements (PSAs) and other approaches that worked plus your notations on why and how.
• Give advance copies of speeches and even video and audio tapes to media.
• Preview major public announcements for your executives and board officers.
• Write commendatory or informational notes to legislators and their staff members at a time when you have no immediate or apparent special interest.
• Update your brochures, biographical materials on executives, and slide shows.
• Program periodic review of your contingency plans for dealing with potential crises in the light of changing environmental conditions.

Programming Approvals

As part of your follow-through, you may have to program approvals in certain companies and government agencies, from authorization of your basic plan through clearance of potentially confidential information to be disseminated to media or external publics. This is not unusual in the aerospace industry or in companies with contracts with the Department of Defense, for instance. In other cases, it may be standard operating procedure in a given organization to submit materials to the legal department and one or more designated executives with clearance authority.

In PR-MBO time-line planning, you may wish to incorporate follow-through planning for submitting both program plans and project materials for approval *even if this is not normal procedure.* There are several reasons for this.

First, both traditional public relations practice and PR-MBO are based on the concept that public relations is a management process.

Thus there is a certain amount of logic in keeping management informed of what you are doing even if no formal authorization is requested or needed.

PR-MBO, *moreover, stresses the mutuality of decision-making on objectives.* At least that part of program development, plus the parts that relate to reporting progress and results and a reassessment of objectives, should be shared with your executives.

Beyond that, you may wish to program clearance procedures. These may range from a casual "thought you might like to see this before it goes out" to formal program approval.

One reason professionals submit programs and informational materials to executives is to assure that there is no conflict with existing policy or any potential change in policy that may be under consideration by the board or management. One such case involved the creation and launching of an intensive one-year research and informational campaign on a customer service. It had high priority at the inception of the service but was to be phased out by the board of directors in the first month of the program.

Public relations persons who lack expertness and authority in such areas as law or finance may voluntarily program a review of materials that may be sensitive or tend to be misinterpreted. And even professionals who follow the latest SEC regulations on financial disclosure may appreciate the need for a second opinion.

In technical areas, be they scientific, medical, engineering, or anything else with its own body of literature, concepts, and jargon, there is reason to program approvals by technical experts in the organization. Although an encyclopedia or other desk reference may be useful in helping a writer interpret technical concepts and terms, even plain English can be deceptive and have multiple meanings. The intent is to assure that information given to media or directly to certain publics be technically accurate and in proper perspective.

And, in times of crisis, as we develop in Chapter 8, or the heat of conflict or numbness of fatigue, it is sound practice to backstop the public relations professional by having a set procedure for securing approvals.

Basically, this means spelling out who receives approval copies, under what circumstances, when, with what time budgeted for turnaround, with what strategies set for resolving differences among experts, and with checks to make sure that executives or others have a chance to respond.

HOW TO FIND THE TIME

Ironically, one of the scarcest resources for many a public relations professional striving to become more organized to achieve objectives is the time to develop and devote to time lines.

Part of the function of time planning relates to conserving that scarce resource and getting more out of it. This may be compared to investing part of your income in the stock market, in government Treasury bills, and in money markets. It takes money to build financial reserves, and it takes time to gain time.

One way is to *learn to train others and delegate authority in order to free your hands for the more creative energies needed to devote to the overview and planning of programs and campaigns.*

Another way calls for *drawing priorities and setting aside less important activities.* A certain comfort may be found in doing that which is repetitive and familiar, such as personally becoming enmeshed in routine information development that could be assigned to a college intern or part-timer, writing basic news releases that require little creativity past the neophyte stage and that might be set aside or done by an aide.

Still another way to invest in time planning is to have other public relations staff members, or yourself if you are in a one-person operation, *log records of activities and things to do, by whom, and when in a journal or an electronic filing system, such as the VisiDex computer software* Nager used for filing, sorting, and retrieving his notes for this chapter. [19]

Ideas come flowing into public relations staff in the midst of conducting a public relations program. If those ideas and observations of what is working (and not working) and what else could be done and in how long a time were to be noted on 3 by 5 cards and sorted at the end or beginning of each day, soon the nucleus of flexible, situational variable-sensitive time lines would be at hand. Basically, computer software programs such as *VisiDex* and *PFS* create electronic memories that are the equivalent of 3 by 5 cards that can be stored, cross-referenced, modified, rearranged, retrieved, and printed out in a fraction of the time it takes to type up a plan from conventional 3 by 5 cards and provide for necessary variations.

A classroom cliché may drive home another point often overlooked by newcomers to public relations (and sometimes not observed by the veteran professional). With apologies to the reader, we take it from the business management, sciences, and public relations class-rooms and set it down in print: *Don't reinvent the wheel.*

Just as it may seem faster to do it yourself instead of investing time in training and delegating to others to do more routine activities, so it may seem more expedient to sketch out public relations time lines and all the collateral program elements that accompany them rather than invest time in using the telephone and library to find out what is already available.

So-called canned planning systems developed by others may come short of your needs and situations. But they may provide enough of the basic framework and details to save a considerable amount of time and free you for adaptation and building on ideas, instead of covering the same ground others have.

A phone call, or a conversation with a colleague at a meeting, may yield the loan of a planning system complete in some instances with detailed time line and budget. As professionals have discovered, an atmosphere of reciprocity and mutual assistance normally facilitates the exchange of such materials.

Even if written materials are unavailable because parts of plans existed only in the heads of public relations staff, or because of pro-prietary considerations, *the chance of exchanging and testing ideas makes mutual assistance efforts of value as a time saver, if not as a source of more creative and efficient programming.*

Newcomers to the profession have learned that their new col-leagues carry their own time-consuming burdens and need as much advance warning as possible to provide help.

Similarly, trade associations of which your CEO or organization may be a member, such as the American Management Association, National Association of Manufacturers, and American Hospital Soci-ety, may send literature, tape cassettes, and other materials to aid you in planning time and budgeting resources.

Such professional organizations as PRSA and IABC maintain reference services for members, primarily consisting of copies of articles and chapters, but also including some copies of detailed plans and procedures donated by members and their firms and tapes of seminars on public relations management and audits.

Public relations handbooks on the shelves of university and public libraries may prove helpful. These include *Dartnell Public Relations Handbook, Lesly's Public Relations Handbook, Nonprofit Organiza-tion Handbook, Public Relations Guides for Nonprofit Organizations,*

Stephenson Handbook of Public Relations, PAC Handbook, and *Manager's Public Relations Handbook.*[20]

For a current year's bibliography of books and periodicals on public relations subjects, a professional need only place an order with the PRSA Information Center. Traditionally, such bibliographies have been provided as a public service. The 10-page-plus listings come complete with prices and publisher addresses.[21]

Public Relations Review not only provides a book review section and articles aimed at the professional in practice but also an annual bibliography.

The Winter 1982 edition, for instance, presented 127 pages of an *annotated bibliography* with approximately 50 headings and titles collected from more than 200 periodicals, books, abstracts, and book review digests by a team headed by Albert Walker of Northern Illinois University. Editor Ray E. Hiebert also presented an index of *Public Relations Review* articles published in 1982. (An index of 1975–1981 issues appeared in the Winter 1981 issue.)[22]

BUDGETING RESOURCES

Experience, even the vicarious experience gained from books and interviews, intelligence drawn from a wide array of informal and formal research, and analyses of research and evaluation are among the more valuable resources to program.

Your preliminary programming of research for the entire public relations program or a campaign normally *incorporates a public relations audit,* if none has been done recently, or an evaluation and update of a relatively current audit, on relevant client interests, strengths, ongoing public relations programs, resources, and previous and current related efforts within the organization, industry, and operating region.

An important concept to bear in mind: It is not merely a matter of planning a particular campaign or part of a project; it is working out the timing so as to *integrate with other activities and needs of the organization, publics, and, perhaps, such entities as the media* and even the competition. The whole of a program and its parts should be *planned in systemic relationship with other systems.*

You *assign individual and team responsibilities* as part of the resources programmed in your time line.

Frequently, conflicting demands for scarce resources and problems that arise are not simple black-and-white situations in which a mere *no* will suffice. With top management and other parts of the organization on a need-to-know basis cued to program objectives and priorities, the public relations person may not even have to be put in the position of having to say no to the assignment of a secondary task.

Saul Warshaw, who became president of Ruder Finn & Rotman of California after the 1982 merger of Ruder & Finn and Harshe-Rotman & Druck, said:

> You're really after control of the entire situation. That means everything is committed to paper. . . . Who has the decision making power? Who is responsible for what? If coordination is missing, what are the parameters for making decisions? Prepare conference reports to make sure your client understands what has been done at meetings and what has to be done next.[23]

And Bob Gold, Ruder Finn & Rotman executive responsible for public relations development and follow-through for the Academy Awards (Oscar) production, added that one lesson veterans of complex, multifaceted, major programs can share is that if responsibilities are not spelled out precisely in time plans, "everybody thinks somebody else is doing it."[24]

When a student public relations leader who was present at the interviews with the Ruder Finn & Rotman executives sounded a note of frustration from her own experience in organizing a program and asked what she should do when she found herself spending all her time writing lists and watching others achieve, Warshaw asked: "Well, what's your job?" She responded: "Coordinating." "Well, be a manager this time," the agency executive counseled. "Your job is to listen and control."[25]

He recommended that anyone operating public relations campaigns *develop standardized forms for reports on objectives and results, monthly activities and progress, and problems solved*, even if nobody requires such reports.[26]

Budgeting Internal Teamwork, External Cooperation

Many public relations agencies program creative brainstorming sessions daily or weekly of account teams together with experts drawn in from various divisions of the company. And periodic meetings are scheduled to share information, provide opportunity for questioning and additional contribution of ideas, and work out details of coordination of efforts.

This concept can work, but it seems to be used less in public relations departments of corporations and institutions.

Internal teams or task forces are formed within organizations to bring together a diversity of expertness and the resources the individuals represent. The team can build on existing strengths and cover (not cover up) for any weaknesses through complementary skills and insights in a spirit of mutual assistance.

Even at the college level, more and more emphasis has been placed in recent years on team building to deal with public relations cases and tackle campaigns. Students, as their seniors in practice have learned, discover how to painstakingly audit their collective and individual strengths and weaknesses, divide and spell out responsibilities, provide for delegation of authority, program conferences with prearranged action agendas (with flexibility to add items), and consciously make an effort to evidence their respect for the ideas and feelings of others.

And professionals and students alike have passed from an earlier era in which many a public relations person operated alone, relying only on himself, for the most part, and worked apart from colleagues in marketing, advertising, industrial relations, and other parts of the organization in problem diagnosis and program planning and execution.

They have learned that communication professionals may at times want to talk more than listen. They have learned that ideas not written down can be of negligible value. They have learned that some ideas require the homework of research or the trial of field testing before they can be proposed beyond a brainstorming session. They have learned not to discard unusual ideas without hearing them out or doing more investigation.

And they have learned the systems notion that creative, highly motivated individuals can work together with greater productivity than when each of them is working apart. A key word here is *can*.

They have learned that to build a team, it helps to *start with objectives for the team process itself and agree upon a protocol of working together,* from reaching consensus on the *selection of a manageable portion* of the problem, through working out how to handle conflict, through following up on the completion of the mission.

Similar lessons may be seen to apply to *cooperative public relations*, in which professionals, even from competing organizations, arrange to work together in the mutual interests of all, to pool certain resources to buy research and communication capabilities on a *scale of economy* that they might not be able to afford without their joint purchasing power.

Organizations may share objectives in the passage or defeat of legislation, in creating a labor pool in talent-short areas (nursing and high technology, for instance), in establishing greater patronage of their kinds of enterprise, in gaining the confidence of investors or donors in their particular fields, and in fostering the kind of employee pride in the industry that leads to increased productivity and lower accident or defect rates.

Models from health and high tech industries

In one city, for instance, four competing nonprofit medical centers, at first tentatively and then with greater and greater commitment, launched cooperative public relations ventures. It started by having gestures of cooperation among the public relations departments displayed to their respective governing boards and management teams, as well as the media and external and employee publics.[27]

A start was made by the exchange of information on possible dangers to security. It then moved to the stage of sponsorship of a public service supplement to the daily newspaper in which citizens were given information on how to use emergency room facilities and even non-hospital emergency services. It was nurtured by joint exhibits at health fairs and joint advertising to recruit allied health specialists to the city's hospitals, and by joint news releases on precautions parents could take when traveling. It progressed to a higher level when two of the hospitals joined forces with government and private facilities in contracting for joint public opinion research projects. And it rose to an even higher level when executives and boards took actions to avoid or reduce the costly duplication of medical facilities and services. The cooperative pattern led to a joint program in which medical facilities in 12 states pooled their resources to take advantage of economy of scale in purchasing paper stock and printing for special annual report publications.[28]

Similarly, public relations executives for ITT Cannon, Du Pont, and Honeywell developed a cooperative program for trade shows, media kits, magazine backgrounders, and news conferences on behalf of their corporations' teamwork in the development of fiberoptic systems. Their joint objectives related to influencing the behavior of potential purchasers, venders, dealers, contractors, and the investment community, according to Richard Harmon, APR, who directed ITT Cannon North American public relations before his move to Hewlett-Packard in 1982.[29]

Rock concert confusion and chaos

Again, whether the cooperative effort is within the organization or with outside systems, the planning of agreement on protocol of working arrangements and exchange of information may be crucial.

For instance, a lack of protocol for coordination, including exchange of information, was revealed in a situation involving public relations personnel for a talent agency, a rock group, and a theater where all three were involved in a rock concert. Dissemination of information included contradictions as well as timing conflicts, media relations arrangements slipped through the cracks in the public relations structure, and unanticipated security and VIP problems arose.[30]

Space missions illustrate teamwork

On the other hand, one of the better examples of cooperative public relations can be observed during the missions of American astronauts.

Here you find teamwork among government agencies, such as the National Aeronautics and Space Administration, and branches of the military services from which some of the astronauts and experiments come; universities and institutes of technology; and a wide range of contractors and subcontractors, from those who build the primary space vehicle to those who prepare on-board space medical experiments or supply ground support.

Objectives may relate to influencing the opinion and behavior of:

• Congress and the administration when it comes to appropriations for the space program

• Taxpayers and voters in communication with their representatives or influencing the opinions of others by their turnout at launch and landing sites or responses to national polls

• Financial analysts of aerospace issues and persons who might be potential investors as individuals or decision makers on institutional trading of stocks and bonds

• Youngsters considering careers, as well as those who will grow up as investors and opinion leaders or decision makers in government involvement in space

• Officers of various agencies and corporations in their joint interests to strengthen mutually supportive relationships[31]

Such efforts are reflected in the accompanying reproductions of the beginning of a McDonnell Douglas media backgrounder on a teenager's experiment aboard *Columbia* and the cover of Ford Aerospace's interpretive media kit about Mission Control and the company's role in the space flight.

BUDGETING FUNDS CREATIVELY

Budgeting funds in the PR-MBO process is tightly *linked to objectives and the research-evaluation that says it is feasible to attain them and make corrections along the way.*

Not too many years ago, public relations budgeting for the most part was related to calculating amounts for starting up new programs, adding quantities to press runs or other increments related to growing size and number of publics, figuring costs for modifications, and, after consulting printers and other venders, writing in an inflation factor to account for projected cost increases.

With the help of the organization's accountants or financial officer, these budgets mostly tended to use the previous year's authorized expenditures as a guaranteed base and to introduce several additions for approval by higher management (and, in some cases, boards of directors).

Sometimes these additions were approved in entirety because of the prosperity of the organization and a benign management with confidence in its public relations arm. Sometimes arbitrary percentages were cut from public relations budgets, much in the way that management and labor tend to negotiate, each asking for more than it really believes the other side will give. That produced a quasi-creative budgeting by public relations persons in which more than inflation was built into the budget, as a means of providing some excess fat for cost-

Mission Control: where
excellence is tradition

STS 4

(Courtesy Ford Aerospace.)

News from MCDONNELL DOUGLAS CORPORATION

St. Louis, Missouri 63166   (314) 232 5911

FOR IMMEDIATE RELEASE

82-77

KENNEDY SPACE CENTER, Florida, June 25, 1982 -- The scheduled Sunday launch of the space shuttle Columbia on its fourth mission will bring the realization of a year-long dream for 16-year old Amy Kusske.

The Long Beach, California, sophomore is the youngest person to have an experiment flown aboard the shuttle. She was selected by NASA as one of 10 student finalists in the first Space Shuttle Student Involvement Program one day before her 15th birthday -- and notified that her experiment would be assigned to the STS-4 mission the day before her 16th birthday.

Since her initial selection, Amy has worked closely with Dr. William K. Douglas, the advisor assigned to her by her industrial sponsor, McDonnell Douglas Astronautics Company, a division of McDonnell Douglas Corporation.

Douglas, director of life sciences program engineering in the company's design and technology subdivision, served as a personal physician and flight surgeon for the Project Mercury astronauts during a 30-year Air Force medical career. He joined McDonnell Douglas in 1977.

(more)

(Courtesy McDonnell Douglas.)

265

conscious management to cut. Sometimes the additions were refused out of hand except for cost-of-living adjustments because decision makers felt there was too little justification for expenditures or because they saw higher priorities than what was perceived as the "luxury" of public relations.

With the move to management by results, management by evaluation, management by returns on investment—MBO, in short—came new perspectives for both proposers of public relations budgets and those empowered to approve or reject. The concept grew for public relations budgets to include reasons for future investments, inflationary costs, and additional expenditures.

Zero-Based Budgeting

Companies such as Coca-Cola and Texas Instruments started a business trend toward what has become known as zero-based budgeting. Georgia Governor Jimmy Carter picked up the idea from the Atlanta-based soft drink-entertainment-winery conglomerate and field tested it in his home state before taking the concept and a Coca-Cola executive to Washington when he was elected President of the United States.

President Carter had more problems than overhauling the bureaucracy, but the zero-based budgeting concept became solidly entrenched in business administration, if not in the majority of government agencies. Zero-based budgeting did not reach staff departments such as public relations initially. But the trend moved from line departments to staff.

Essentially, zero-based budgeting requires the department head to justify from scratch the investment of each dollar, based on projections of its return on the other side of the ledger. That means that even something budgeted annually since the organization's founding no longer will be accepted as a "given" by executives and boards.

Thus, the department head starts with a base of nothing—as if he or she were starting the department and function on the day the budget goes into effect. This base of "zero" means that as companies, institutions, or government agencies adapt the trend and require staff departments to adhere to it, the only "given" becomes the need to relate reliably expected results to dollars requested in the budget. For some public relations persons, this means having to struggle with reasons for continuing long-time traditional practices and pegging their proposals to hardened objectives.

Pragmatic strategy: variable budgets

One of the more pragmatic strategies discovered in interviews for this book was that of the public relations department of a major Midwest industrial organization that uses a modified zero-based budget approach. Monsanto Plastics & Resins Co. of St. Louis puts together communication programs in which marketing and public relations team up and develop *variable budgets.*

As Fred G. Marshall, who was in charge of public relations before moving on to Exxon Research and Engineering Co., described it, the approach is to specify what will be the givens and say:

> For X [X equals lowest possible cost] dollars, we will do this; if Y [Y equals whatever additional amount public relations and marketing judge to buy optimal program as needed by the company] dollars are added, we will achieve this much more.[32]

For example, for $5,500 you could produce a month-long campaign that research indicates should help reduce absenteeism by 5 percent the first three months following the campaign and by declining amounts for each month until the effect is negligible within a year. For $25,000 more, you could add opinion research and monthly video productions for a year that would be expected to reduce absenteeism by 10 percent for the last 10 months of the year and increase productivity by an additional 3 percent.

At Monsanto, public relations programs and budgeting are integrated with those of marketing and advertising. Public relations requests and results sought (objectives) are weighed against those proposed by the other divisions.

What is most important is that the first budget building block is considered basic and the absolute minimum required. *Then increments of funds—and the results they are expected to buy—are added.*

Limited resources; flexible approach

Judith Bogart, public relations vice president of Jewish Hospital of Cincinnati and 1983 national president of PRSA, noted that zero-based budgeting and increasing uncertainty about financial resources contributed to the climate for MBO in the not-for-profit sphere. But she stressed that the import of flexibility knew no distinction on orientation to profit:

In not-for-profit public relations, MBO has been used with PR for a long time, due in part to the need for zero-based budgeting in our activities and frequent uncertainty about resources. MBO works for PR in that sector *when and only when* other management understands the need for flexibility in public relations plans. In this respect, I don't see any difference between not-for-profit and other public relations management. By our ability to explain and demonstrate how we must be able to react as well as to plan, perhaps our examples will be of value to [other parts of management] in their own style.[33]

Building Foundation for Budget

Another approach is to present the case for a company's investment, much as Hill and Knowlton did in its May 1981 proposal to a manufacturer of carburetion systems that use liquefied propane gas.

The table of contents of the 39-page proposal indicates part of the strategy.[34]

D. Positioning
E. Themes
F. Elements

Note the *prominence of research* in the proposal and the *lead position of objectives* in the presentation of each of the primary proposals.

One strategy, then, is the presentation of the budget after you have built a solid foundation of research, objectives, strategies, communication, and other program components. The potential *returns on investment* and the research-based strategies for attaining objectives are carefully laid out first.

Propose Feasible Mini-maxi Range

The Hill and Knowlton budget proposal reflects another creative strategy of public relations agencies and departments: In the itemization of staff time, supplies, vended services, and other costs for research and the program that would accompany it, the agency gave a *mini-maxi range*, stating the minimum and maximum costs for each item, $3,500 to $6,000 for the market research subtotal, for instance.[35]

You want to be as confident as you can when predicting, for example, a 10 percent return on direct mail appeals for donations. This means making sure that such projections are rooted in research, not just assumption.

In one nonprofit organization's major fund-raising campaign in 1982, it was projected—without any research to back up the projection—that at least 1,000 persons would pay $25 each to attend a special function. On that basis, the organization felt that it could pay $10 per person for food and $8,500 for entertainment. In addition came costs of producing and mailing an invitation to several thousand individuals, running a supportive communication campaign of news releases, public service announcements, and media invitations. The revenue from the persons who did buy tickets yielded *less than $3,000*, a disgruntled new board member complained.[36]

If your research data do not allow you to be so confident as to offer an exact figure, then *present a range for the results*. And if the data base is weak or inconclusive, it is *better to be conservative and better yet to field test the drawing power of a campaign*.

Joe Cerrell, president of the Cerrell Associates political public relations and campaign agency, warned of another danger in budgeting when he spoke of the temptation clients have to spend money impulsively on a particularly attractive mode of communication, such as a television spot in prime time or a glossy, four-color-process mailing. "You can even burn up your budget on a full-page advertisement in a prestige publication."[37]

That burning up of available resources can take place unless there is both a *detailed time line and itemized budget with which both client and public relations staff agree*. The function of budgeting money, time, or any resource is to buy results, attain objectives.

Most public relations agencies calculate budget by charging for time of personnel, from lowest clerical worker to president of the agency. They include overhead factors in the variable hourly rate for different classes of service. Public relations agency personnel carefully log the time spent on activities for each account they service.

Even for the person not in a public relations agency, this might provide a method of establishing the real costs of public relations efforts in terms of your time and that of others in the organization. It certainly would be helpful in budgeting staff time for future projects. That, too, can be built into your time lines.

PLANNING TECHNIQUES

The rest of this chapter offers some actual examples of a diversity of techniques from which you may choose and adapt one or a combination of methods to fit your particular needs and style.

We start with the traditional checklist and then move to a higher level of sophistication. This is followed by a simple but pragmatic one-page form that can provide *structure* to your time-line planning program. Then more complex examples through PERT and DELTA flow charts are reviewed.

Checklists

The checklist system tells you what has to be done by a critical date or time certain. Its strength is that it provides sufficient detail plus a time period overview of the tasks at hand.

The most important point of focus is what has to be done by a particular date.

You start out with a total list of all activities that have to be accomplished. Next, determine the dates by which these various activities have to be completed. You may break up activities into component parts and show in your checklist when these events have to be started and completed. Then you review the list, making sure that you have assigned priorities and developed a realistic schedule.

You will want to program relatively frequent periodic reviews and maintain the flexibility to delete, add, or modify. Many professionals find it helpful to invite others with different perspectives, inside their organizations as well as in spheres with different frameworks of reference, to examine checklists for possible improvements.

An example from Memorial Hospital Medical Center of Long Beach illustrates this. In planning for medical special events, such as national seminars of the American College of Cardiology, American Academy of Pediatrics, or its annual symposium for physicians, the public relations department used a checklist that started a half year before the event and went several weeks beyond to follow up activities. In addition, the checklist incorporated overview lists of arrangements for other medical center departments as well as public relations staff.[38]

SIX MONTHS BEFORE EVENT

Liaison

_____ Medical specialist in charge of hosting event and making policy decisions contacts medical leaders of co-hosting organization for arrangements, resources, and names of medical persons with whom liaison to be maintained.

_____ PR event chair contacts administrative officers of co-sponsoring medical organizations for preliminary discussion of services and resources needed.

_____ Arrange for schedule of reviews of objectives, priorities, budget, plans, and progress reports with own administrative executive and medical officers.

_____ With national liaison person, if any, and executive and medical event officers, agree upon:

    _____ Quantitative objectives for paid attendance, broken down by types of groups to be invited.

    _____ Qualitative objectives for program and modes of evaluation for effectiveness.

    _____ Qualitative objectives for arrangements to be made and modes of evaluation for effectiveness.

    _____ Numbers of invitations and accompanying literature to be sent and mailing lists to order.

Agenda Determination

_____ Medical event committee and PR director to determine:

    _____ Rough time schedule for parts of events

    _____ Participants by type sought for speakers, panels

    _____ Criteria for such participants

    _____ Known individuals to invite as participants

    _____ Persons likely to have contact with such participants

    _____ Plans for invitations and telephone follow-through

    _____ Types of persons to be invited to attend

    _____ Known and projected interests of targeted audience

    _____ Topics to be covered

    _____ Rough time schedule for parts of event

    _____ Facilities needed for parts of event

Medical Publication Notices

_____ Help medical officer submit articles on event and on any calls for medical papers for presentation to following:

    _____ Hospital medical staff newsletter

    _____ City medical society newsletter

    _____ County medical society newsletter

    _____ Other medical publications as follows:

    _____

    _____

Professional and Community Calendars

_____ PR secretary to check dates with medical societies, hospitals, and Community Calendar for any conflict.

_____ PR director to advise other agencies of dates.

_____ Secretary to enter date on Community Calendar.

Academy Credits

_____ Check with medical chief which medical society credits are warranted for #___ hours and if General Practice Academy may be asked to give #___ hours of continuing education credits.

_____ Have medical chair secure approval of credits.

_____ Program PR to verify status on _____date.

Hotel Reservations

_____ If national, assure #___ rooms reserved at area hotels within a price range of $___ and $___ .

Hotel Name: _____#___ of rooms, $___ guarantee

Hotel Name: _____#___ of rooms, $___ guarantee

_____ If local, make #___ tentative reservations, $___ each, for out-of-town guests at Hotel _____ .

_____ Reserve facilities as follows for banquets, programs, media interview room, VIP reception suite:

_____

_____

_____ Query out-of-town speakers and guests on whether or not they wish accommodations and, if so, what kind, for how many persons, and for what dates.

Financial

_____ Foundation, medical, and PR officers review fund needs.

_____ Foundation director to determine financial sponsors.

_____ With medical chairman, administrative executive, and finance staff executive determine:

_____ Projected itemized breakout of income and revenue.

_____ What, if any, costs absorbed by PR or admin. budget.

_____ Contingency funding sources if shortfall on revenue.

_____ Price of tickets for our own medical staff $___ ; intern and resident physicians $___ ; physicians not affiliated with Medical Center $___ ; nurses $___ ;

_____ How many complimentary admissions may be provided for which portions of program for:

    _____ News media and medical media_____

    _____ Interns and residents here_____

    _____ Spouses of residents, interns_____

    _____ Persons who will be on program_____

    _____ Management committee and/or spouses_____

    _____ Other mgmt. personnel and/or spouses_____

_____ Set up account number, procedures with business office

Alert Memos and Checklists

_____ Send introductory memos on the event, its purposes, the role of the medical center, and basic information with specialized checklists on arrangements envisioned to:

_____ Management Committee	_____ Medical Education
_____ In-service Training	_____ Business Office
_____ Security	_____ Food Service
_____ Housekeeping	_____ Maintenance
_____ Audio Visual	_____ Volunteer Services
_____ PBX	_____ Members PR Staff
_____ Other____	

Literature Needed

_____ If out-of-area persons invited:

    _____ Chamber of Commerce/Convention Bureau materials

    _____ Medical Center literature

_____ Determine needs with national liaison and medical, executive, and financial officers and bid and schedule production and distribution as desired and feasible of:

    _____ 1st wave mailing of advance notices 3 months before

    _____ 2nd wave mailing of invitations 1 month before event

    _____ Program for entire event

    _____ Programs for banquets, special events named

    _____ Bound sets of papers, speeches, and/or abstracts

    _____ Media kit covers and/or materials

Checklists plus daily action folders

A variation of the checklist technique incorporates a system of folders for every month and every day of each month in which heavily detailed procedures are spelled out. The idea in both cases is to keep from just looking at a simple calendar that does not tell you more than a few *when* details and to clear your desk of excess paper reminders that may be lost or overlooked in the daily follow-through in your handling of multiple programs.

Copies of checklists with specific details for given departments that work with you are provided to the appropriate management persons and liaison is maintained to assure compliance.

Objectives program sheets

A checklist offering considerably more information is illustrated in the objectives program sheets technique adapted by Roger L. Burgess, vice president of the public relations division of the Nashville-based United Methodist Publishing House from a form originally developed by Planning Dynamics, Inc., of Pittsburgh.[39]

This technique goes beyond the kind of checklist used by a number of other organizations. As adapted by Burgess and his staff, this form presents an objective, supporting activities *and a priority scale and current status rating,* along with a projected completion date and monetary and human resources required.

The *name of the responsible staff person appears* at the top of each objectives program sheet.

In looking at the example, note the key on nine levels of priority and four levels of status and consider how this may be adapted for your purposes.

Flow Charts

For a graphic overview of a very complex set of activities, flow charts have been developed for controlling and monitoring public relations projects.

This technique allows a professional the option of laying out the entire public relations operation or the parts of a single campaign in chart format.

OBJECTIVES PROGRAM SHEET

	THIS	REPLACES
ORIGINATOR: Martha S. Pilcher	FILE:	IN-4
DISTRIBUTION: W	DATE: 9/16/79	4/30/79
SUBJECT: PR DIVISION	PAGE: 1 OF 1	2
Information Services Program		

Obj. # IN-2	Develop more adequate contacts with local and national secular media, particularly religion editors.

Program No.	Priority Status	Description	Comp. Date	Resources	
				$	Man/Days
1	U	Prepare list of UMPH persons and expertise of those persons to send to local and national media. Include information sheet on UMPH.	8/79		
2	A	Consult with Southern Baptist Public Relations contact person and other RPRC members about personnel related to local media.	8/79		
3	U	Develop list of specific programs and people working at local media.	9/79		
4	A	Local media--set up meetings (i.e., luncheon, tours, etc.) with the following:			
		W. A. Reed, The Tennessean	8/79		
		Frances Meeker, Nashville Banner	8/79		
		Editor, Advantage Magazine	9/79		
		Editor, Nashville Magazine	9/79		
		News editor, WNGE	10/79		
		News editor, WSM	10/79		
		News editor, WTVF	11/79		
		News editor, WLAC	11/79		
5	U	Educate Louise Gray, United Methodist Communications, of UMPH programs, products, etc., by sending periodic mailings.	2/80		
6	A	Schedule visits with national media persons in New York in connection with other trips.	6/80		
		Kenneth Briggs, The New York Times James Head, Parade Publications, Inc. Margorie Hyer, The Washington Post H. L. Stevenson, United Press Internat'l Richard Ostling, Time Magazine Louis Boccardi, The Associated Press Lillian Block, Religious News Service			

Priority: 1-3 Urgent/Essential   Status: A- Authorized
          4-6 Important   P- Proposed
          7-9 Desirable   U- Underway
                                                    C- Completed

Objectives Program Sheet. Form developed by Planning Dynamics, Inc., and adapted by United Methodist Publishing House public relations division illustrates a sophisticated model of checklists.

The most simple variation depicts several activities or projects as horizontal bars that start and stop at differential times. Symbols can be used to represent various activities, and time is generally represented by a straight line or horizontal bar.

That chart can be a single page, a foldout, or as long as several feet of wall chart mounted for public relations staff to check frequently and follow as a guide to make sure that all activities are being met. This keeps you from having to consult several different checklists and memorize what is supposed to be done on each day and where to find it among the checklists. This is particularly valuable when the public relations campaign (or entire program) has *important concurrent activities requiring careful coordination* and timing. In essence, these parts have to be conducted as a whole, in a team effort. Again, this gets back to systems concepts.

More sophisticated time-line charts should contain your programmed objectives and the subsequent support activities.

Symbols may be conventional for the particular type of flow chart or may be created to suit your needs, as long as you provide a key that identifies symbols clearly and explains their usage to you or anyone else who consults the charts.

In certain computer programs, such as those developed for PERT and DELTA charts, the software dictates symbols you must use. In this case, although a computer programmer may be able to create or change symbols, you are probably safer using the original program without modification. Opportunities to be creative exist when you wish to do such charting by hand.

However, software for flow charting even has been developed now for the home computer market. It normally is accompanied by manuals that explain exactly the steps to take. This may take time to learn, but in the long run it saves time.

The PERT chart

PERT is an acronym for **P**rogram **E**valuation **R**eview Technique. PERT was initiated in 1958 by the U.S. Navy to improve the planning evaluation of the *Polaris* missile program.

Through the success of PERT, the time needed for the development of the *Polaris* missile was reduced. As a result, PERT has been widely used in business, as well as government, as a planning technique.

PERT allows the public relations planner to determine if the time for completing a project could be varied. In view of the need for public relations staff to respond to both targets of opportunity and early warning signs of potential crises, this built-in flexibility feature of PERT has proven particularly attractive in practice.

A pragmatic value of PERT is that it allows you to compute the elapsed time in which a project can be completed and to identify *the critical path*. A critical path may be defined as a series of related activities that, added together, will tell you the earliest date by which the project can be completed.

The critical path is the designation for *the longest time sequence* of activities in the flow chart. This means the critical path tells you *the minimum time* for project completion.

If any activity along the critical path is delayed, then the entire project's completion will be delayed by the same amount of time. If you miss a printer's deadline by two days, for instance, the entire publication schedule is thrown off.

If you want to reduce the minimum time needed in which to complete your project, one or more activities along the critical path have to be shortened or eliminated, if that is practical. That is the only leverage you have in the critical path.

You can reduce an activity, but if it is not on the critical path, it will not help you in lessening the time to complete the project (although this may save time for other projects).

The chronological order of steps varies with each project. Each project you do has a different critical path.

PERT involves starting at the end, the date by which you must complete the project, and working your way back along the critical path. You can determine your probabilities of completing a project by a particular date.

For example, if your executive asks you if it is possible to prepare for a grand opening of a new outlet in 21 days, by using PERT you can determine the mathematical probability of holding that event in 21 days, how good a chance you have of completing it by that date. Depending upon other ongoing projects and what is required in this particular one, PERT may help you decide that it is not feasible to stage the grand opening by then or that you will have to sacrifice certain activities to meet that schedule.

Normally you turn to a planning specialist within your organization, perhaps a person in the financial, computer information processing, engineering, or other specialized area, for help in developing PERT charts. You also may learn how to do it yourself by following step-by-step instructions in the Summer 1980 *Public Relations Review* report on "PERT: a Technique for Public Relations Management."[40]

The PERT chart with an identifiable critical path is illustrated in Figure 7.1. The circles are PERT symbols for events or activities of a project.

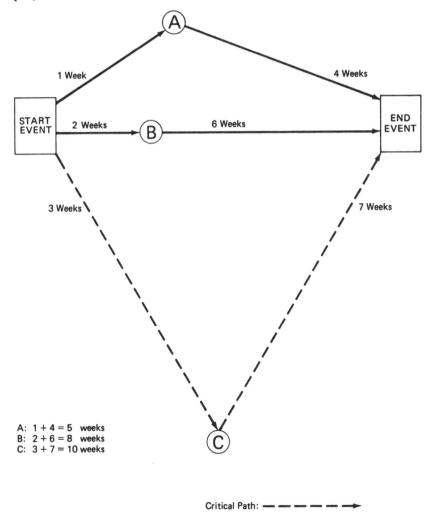

A: 1 + 4 = 5 weeks
B: 2 + 6 = 8 weeks
C: 3 + 7 = 10 weeks

Critical Path: — — — — — ➤

FIGURE 7.1   PERT Diagram.
(Permission to reprint courtesy of Public Relations Review.)

The chart could illustrate a data gathering project in which A represents a personal interview with your CEO, B a focus group session with a panel of employees, and C a survey sampling opinion of 1,200 employees. The critical path, the longest time, would be the sampling of the 1,200 employees.

Actually, all three data-gathering methods take place simultaneously, but as the chart indicates, the minimum time to complete the project is the 10 weeks it takes for C to be done.

The DELTA chart

A second type of flow chart in common use in industry and government is DELTA.

The name is formed from the five types of graphic symbols used in the flow chart: Decision, Event, Logic, Time, and Activity.

Figure 7.2 shows the symbols used in DELTA:

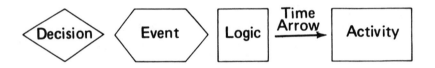

FIGURE 7.2   DELTA Chart Symbols. *(Permission to reprint courtesy of Praeger.)*

The Decision diamond indicates when you, as project director, must select among alternatives. The Event point in the chart represents something that happened at a particular time. The Logic square represents the logical functions of the event and activity boxes. Time is represented by the arrow symbol leading to the next activity. The Activity rectangle represents a specific task that must be completed.

DELTA allows more flexibility and control for monitoring a project than PERT. In a sense, DELTA is more of a decision-making tool, which allows for the uncertainties of real-world contingencies and exigencies to be programmed. PERT, on the other hand, tends to be more rigid as a tool and is less sensitive to environmental change. Typical examples of PERT's insensitivity to outside influences are found in the cost overruns and missed deadlines in government contracts.

DELTA's key feature and strength lie in its built-in decision points throughout the flow chart. The public relations program manager is given a choice of which set of activities to pursue. That is like coming to a fork in the road. Your choice: right or left fork.

To envision DELTA, see Figure 7.3. This chart, reproduced from *New Methods in Social Science Research*, depicts a project that operationalizes graphically techniques and decisions covered in Chapter 6 on research and evaluation.[41]

You may wish to pause here to practice with the symbols freehand (or pick up a plastic template at a bookstore or a software package at a computer store and develop a rough DELTA chart of a project on which you are working). See if you can determine where the critical decisions concerning the project already have been—or need to be—made. This is where *you control the project*, where *you make the decision*.

A concluding note of expert advice on the selection of the particular adaptation or combination of time line systems comes from Thomas Nunan, APR, former Burson-Marsteller southern California executive and now national communication vice president for the Dallas-based Mostek Corporation:

> Although you should select from the smorgasbord of planning systems available and fear not to combine and adapt, you should make sure that the system upon which you ultimately rely is not so complex as to become unwieldy. . . . A certain amount of simplicity, at least enough so that you will feel comfortable in using the plan and living with it, is necessary.[42]

C-R-E-A-T-E CASE STUDY: S & L MERGER

When Santa Fe Federal Savings and Loan Association, a client of California's Cochrane Chase & Livingston agency, prepared to merge with Pacific Federal Savings and Loan, both opportunities and dangers loomed.

That is the kind of public relations project that ideally calls for a year of research, planning, and implementation. In the actual situation, however, the agency had *less than two months* to do the whole thing.

Yet the case illustrates many of the C-R-E-A-T-E components at their best. And where it does not, the case investigator, Ingrid Andrews, and her professor fill in the gaps.[43]

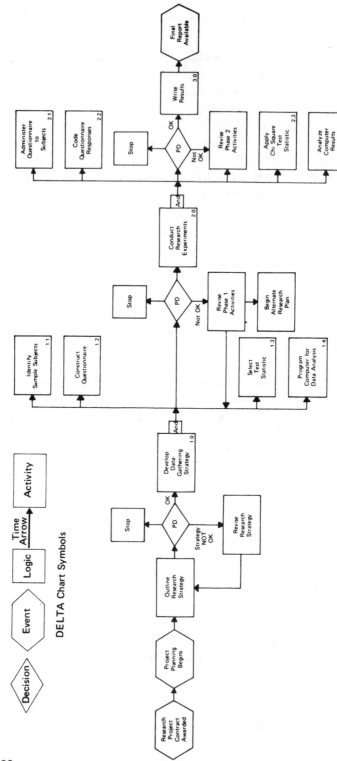

FIGURE 7.3 DELTA Chart Example. *(Permission to reprint courtesy of Praeger.)*

282

Cochrane Chase Account Supervisor Dan Pittman stopped short of reporting precise, measurable objectives for the merger campaign. But objectives definitely were related to interests of the client and were based on the opportunities and potential problems anticipated. For example, with the client and partner to the merger agreeing to call the merged association Pacific Federal and to move the corporate headquarters to the coast from the inland base of operations, an important objectives challenge presented itself. (Name changes create identity problems for some employees, customers, and investors. So does the move of a base of operations to a city that is as different in life style as it is distant in miles.)

> In order to keep as many present customers as possible from leaving either association, particularly Santa Fe Federal customers concentrated in the inland San Bernardino area, and making up the majority of savings dollars, extra efforts for maintaining these publics were required.[44]

Another objective related to keeping up the productivity of employees of both associations; attracting them to remain, despite changes and the headquarters move; and motivating them to help persuade customers to continue doing their business with the two associations before and after merger. To complicate matters, much of the planning had to take place in the midst of equivocality, uncertainty related to whether banking industry regulators would approve the merger.

Communication actually had been in process for more than the five years Santa Fe Federal had been a client of Cochrane Chase. For this case, however, the *first phase began with intensive debriefing of management personnel on their knowledge, insight, and concerns.* This was followed by consultation within the agency among personnel on this particular situation and similar kinds of merger experiences. Communication with top management continued throughout the campaign to assure that executives knew what was intended next as well as what had been implemented already with what effect.

Within the agency, the modus operandi of Cochrane Chase has included brainstorming in which ideas and problems are proposed and built upon in sessions ranging up to several hours. The participants are fueled by the creative energy of preliminary research and the interaction of ideas. Wine, soft drinks, and crackers help provide a casual atmosphere.

Former Cochrane Chase Vice President Patrick Anderson, APR,

who founded Anderson Communications in mid-1982, later told one of the authors that during the course of preliminary communication with any client, "we need to probe for *why* they want a particular program. Sometimes, what clients want to accomplish is *not* possible."[45]

And he offered a *strategic model for client-agency assurance of shared interpretation* of communication:

> Objectives need to be very clear in the minds of the agency and the client. It's important for us to sit down together and make sure we understand each other totally. [And, to refresh client memories and keep the record straight], after any decisions are made, we write a report for those who met summarizing the topics discussed, the points made, the budget agreed upon, and the actions planned. We ask that anyone who finds a problem in this get back to us in 48 hours.[46]

Cochrane Chase staff initiated research on several fronts: At the local level, *research started with the development of intelligence on the customer and employee publics.* Research followed on the perceived problems and needs of the associations individually and collectively. The agency looked for variables that distinguished this merger situation from others. Publics were identified and assigned priorities by the degree to which groups are stakeholders (have stakes in the situation). The agency also sought to project the potential effects of the merger on these publics. Then the projected effects on key publics were traced through to possible impact on the client's interests.

Even before the merger was filed, Cochrane Chase staff contacted the PRSA Research Center in New York City, used library resources in the area, conducted a telephonic marketing survey with 200 respondents who held accounts at *a third, uninvolved* savings and loan association (to avoid premature disclosure to publics of the two associations that would merge) and planned a program to monitor feedback from employees and customers.

In reviewing past cases, Cochrane Chase staff focused not so much on what others had done *but with what results.* Public relations specialists explored such areas as name change and customer perceptions of financial health of savings and loan associations.

The research-evaluation process was exemplified in this case by *monitoring of the actual behavior of key publics during the campaign.* This behavioral monitoring included: *Patterns of deposits and with-*

drawals, opening and closing of accounts, employee resignations, and other measurable actions.

In addition, a hotline provided for monitoring of expressed employee and customer opinion as questions were answered or complaints reported. And another barometer, at least of information passed on through mass communication channels, involved monitoring of media coverage of the merger.

Resources not only included the specialists within Cochrane Chase and venders to the agency but also top management teams from both savings and loan associations and the client's own marketing, public relations, and advertising staffs. Cost of the program was budgeted at $197,725 for the agency's part, plus existing internal marketing budgetary expenditures from the client.

The agency *planned the program with a PERT chart, with very detailed planning leading up to and following the actual point of merger.* In addition, the agency developed a tightly organized 15-page written plan that incorporated an overview of its assessment of the problem, a definition of strategy, and an itemized budget.

Also included in the plan was a consideration for *contingencies,* such as what if news leaked before the actual filing date. The agency provided two scenarios and drafted proposed responses for both.

Communication was programmed in the time line through a variety of modes aimed at the different publics.

One of the agency's strategies centered on the concept that *credibility tends to go to whoever initiates communication first (and well). This avoids being put in the defensive position of responding to rumors or defending against charges.* Such strategic communication anticipates rumors and fears.

Newsletters were planned for employees of the merging associations immediately after every board meeting between client management and the agency. Interpersonal and small-group communication was programmed in the form of regular meetings and the hotline. News media backgrounders and releases targeted customers and other external publics. Brochures with a question-and-answer approach were distributed at both savings and loan associations right after the filing date of the merger. Videotapes of presidents of the two merging associations were prepared but targeted primarily at the San Bernardino area. Direct mail was a tool of communication to members of the loan market public.

The Parts Interact

As case investigator Andrews observed from her training in application of systems thinking to public relations and marketing: "The interactive effect of the individual parts of the communication program contributed to the effectiveness of the whole being greater than the sum of the parts."[47]

That, too, is the basic concept of the PR-MBO C-R-E-A-T-E system as it is operationalized in planning public relations campaigns and programs.

Among the more formidable challenges in applying PR-MBO, Time/resources planning, and other parts of the C-R-E-A-T-E system are those related to one of the oldest, most crucial roles of public relations professionals—crisis management and prevention. That is the topic of Chapter 8.

NOTES

1. Albert C. Smith, class discussion, California State University, Fullerton, May 23, 1982.
2. Ibid.
3. Thomas Eidson, interview, Los Angeles, November 21, 1981.
4. Robert C. Will, interview, Los Angeles, March 20, 1981.
5. Roger B. Fransecky, interview, at Communications Week 1981, Fullerton, California, April 28, 1981.
6. Paul Watzlawick, Janet H. Beavin, and Don D. Jackson, *Pragmatics of Human Communication* (New York: Norton, 1967), p. 238.
7. Karl E. Weick, presentation, University of Southern California Summer Seminar on Organizational Communication, Los Angeles, June 27, 1975. Also see Karl E. Weick, *The Social Psychology of Organizing* (Reading, Mass.: Addison-Wesley, 1969).
8. Thomas S. Kuhn, *The Structure of Scientific Revolutions*, 2nd ed. enlarged (Chicago: University of Chicago Press, 1970), pp. 64–65.
9. Lawrence Berenato, "Selling Top Management on the Remodeling of Fantasyland" (term project, California State University, Fullerton, May 27, 1982.)
10. Mary Jones, telephone conversations, June 1982.
11. Lynn Bright, term project, California State University, Fullerton, December 17, 1981.
12. Barbara Machado, quoted by Lisa Parks, term project, California State University, Fullerton, May 27, 1982.
13. Interview conducted by Norman R. Nager, March 1982. Identification of interviewee, agency, and client withheld by interviewer.
14. Thomas Glenn, interviews, Fullerton, May 18, 1982, and February 24, 1983.

15. "1982 Silver Anvil Winners: Index and Summaries" is available from Public Relations Society of America, 845 Third Avenue, New York, NY, 10022. Quotation is from pp. 11–12.

16. Ibid.

17. Norman R. Nager, "Project C," computer data programmed on *VisiDex* software, updated April 1983.

18. Göran Sjöberg, interviews, April 27–30 1983, Westminster, California.

19. "Project C," "Project B," "Project A," "Problem Process," and "MBO" (computer data programmed on *VisiDex* software, updated April 1983).

20. Richard W. Darrow and Dan J. Forrestal, *Dartnell Public Relations Handbook*, 2nd ed., (Chicago: Dartnell, 1979); Philip Lesly, ed., *Lesly's Public Relations Handbook*, 3rd ed. (Englewood Cliffs, N.J.: Prentice-Hall, 1983); Tracy D. Connors, *Nonprofit Organization Handbook* (New York: McGraw-Hill, 1980); *Public Relations Guides for Nonprofit Organizations* (New York: Foundation for Public Relations Research and Education, 1977); Howard Stephenson, ed., *Stephenson Handbook of Public Relations*, 2nd ed. (New York: McGraw-Hill, 1971); *PAC Handbook* (Washington, D.C.: Fraser Associates, 1981); and *Manager's PR Handbook*, N. H. Sperber and Otto Lerbinger (Reading: Addison-Wesley, 1982).

21. "Bibliography 1984" (or current year) is available from PRSA Information Center, 845 Third Avenue, New York, NY, 10022.

22. Albert Walker, "Public Relations Bibliography: 10th Edition, 1981," *Public Relations Review* 4 (Winter 1982): 1–127; Ray E. Hiebert, "Public Relations Review Index, Volume VIII, 1982," *Public Relations Review* 4 (Winter 1982): 150–152; and Hiebert, "Public Relations Review Index, Volumes I-VII, 1975–1981," *Public Relations Review* 4 (Winter 1981): 115–130.

23. Saul Warshaw, interview, Fullerton, California, April 20, 1982.

24. Bob Gold, interview, Fullerton, California, April 20, 1982.

25. Warshaw, interview.

26. Ibid.

27. Based on participant observation by Norman R. Nager as director of public relations for Memorial Hospital Medical Center of Long Beach, California, from 1967 through 1974, and as president of the Southern California Society of Hospital Public Relations Directors.

28. Ibid.

29. Richard Harmon, interview, Westminster, California, February 12, 1981.

30. Identification of organizations and individuals withheld by interviewer, Norman R. Nager, to protect confidentiality of sources.

31. Based on packages of government and corporate public relations materials provided to the authors by Don Flamm, APR, West Coast director of public affairs for Ford Aerospace and Communications, from Houston Mission Control and Florida's Kennedy Space Center for the shuttle mission that concluded July 4, 1982.

32. Fred G. Marshall, correspondence to Norman R. Nager and telephone interviews, June-July 1981, and telephone interview December 28, 1982.

33. Judith Bogart, interview, Salt Lake City, May 13, 1983.

34. "An Introductory Communications Program for Vialle U.S.A." (proposal submitted by Hill and Knowlton, Inc., Los Angeles, May 11, 1981). Italics added.

35. Ibid.

36. Identification of interviewees and organization withheld by interviewer, Norman R. Nager.
37. Joseph Cerrell (presentation, Public Relations Society of America, Los Angeles chapter, June 19, 1981).
38. Norman R. Nager, "Memorial Hospital Medical Center of Long Beach Medical Special Events Checklist," (planning tool created 1967, modified after each event with last modification—for this book—April 17, 1983).
39. Roger L. Burgess, correspondence to Norman R. Nager, November 10, 1981.
40. T. Harrell Allen, "PERT: a Technique for Public Relations Management," *Public Relations Review* 2 (Summer 1980): 38–49.
41. T. Harrell Allen, *New Methods in Social Science Research* (New York: Praeger, 1978), Chap. 7.
42. Thomas Nunan, interview, Los Angeles, March 20, 1981.
43. Ingrid Andrews, "Financial Merger Between Pacific Federal and Santa Fe Federal" (term project, California State University, Fullerton, May 25, 1982); and Nager, "Project A," "Project B," and "Project C."
44. Ibid.
45. Patrick Anderson, interview, Fullerton, California, March 4, 1982.
46. Ibid.
47. Andrews, "Financial Merger."

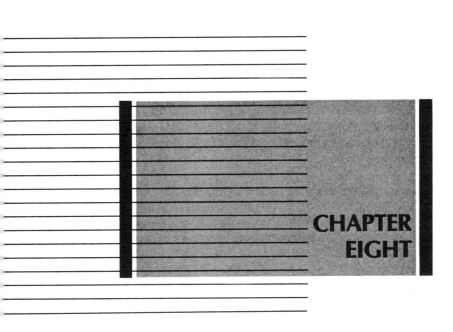

CHAPTER
EIGHT

CRISIS MANAGEMENT BY OBJECTIVES

FIGHT-FLIGHT SYNDROME

Danger lurks. And the primitive programming of humans for survival takes over.

PROGRAMMED FOR SURVIVAL

Adrenalin pumps into the bloodstream, placing all the body's survival systems in a state of alert and building for a jolt of speed or power.

Nostrils flare and lungs suck in more air and enrich the blood with a high mixture of oxygen fuel. The heart muscle pounds the oxygenated blood to where the system needs it most as the body prepares for danger.

Efficient body air conditioning takes over with increased perspiration to dissipate excess heat.

Senses of smell, sight, hearing, touch, taste, and maybe even a sixth sense come into sharper focus.

Electrical and chemical stimuli throughout the complex human nervous system are sent through the skeletal-muscular-sensory systems.

The physical and emotional systems fire up as they did eons ago when danger lurked in the dark recesses of the primeval forests.

And as the founding president of the American Neurochemical Society said:

> A million years ago, a certain signal would cause a primitive man to experience anxiety and scan the horizon for a real or imagined enemy. Mankind survived and so did the receptiveness to stimuli, the emotions these stimuli aroused and the behavior patterns that followed.[1]

This theory of Eugene Roberts fits with his research of the brain substance GABA and genetically preprogrammed nervous system circuits that give inhibitory-disinhibitory or "go–no go" signals to release specific functions that allow an organism to make adaptive responses to environment.[2]

Roberts, a City of Hope neurochemist who wrote more than 300 scientific papers, devoted a lifetime of research to developing his model of the nervous system. One of the authors of this book was prompted by the interview to extend the theory to better understanding of how CEOs, public relations officers, and others may respond in times to what they perceive as danger to their employers or themselves.[3]

PR AND SURVIVAL CUES

By extension, the quick movement of a shadowy form in the primitive jungle, the tremor of earth, the fire burning closer, the scent of predatory beast, and many other survival-threatening cues that mobilized early physical and emotional defenses may be seen in modern corporate or institutional environment counterparts, such as:

- Threat of labor strife
- Ensnarement in a government investigation
- Looming of restrictive legislation
- Attempt of hostile takeover of a corporation through buy-up of its stocks by a raiding company

- New thrusts by the competition that endanger profitability
- Request for an interview by television's "60 Minutes," "20/20," or any investigative and sensational team
- Product failure leading to injury or death to consumers
- Naming of the client in a multimillion-dollar lawsuit
- Plans for picketing or other demonstrations
- Extortion threats ranging from product tampering to bombs
- Disability or death of a key executive
- Hostile media queries
- Upheaval in the social environment
- Accidental contamination of places where people live and work
- Investigation by an agency of the government
- Mobilization of an adversary consumer group
- Rumors that send stock prices plummeting
- Conflict in the board room
- Fire, earthquake, storm

At the individual level, the primitive being within the contemporary CEO, public relations person, or other member of the organization may sense a potential loss of position as predecessors sensed the saber-toothed tiger; a potential damage to the organization as primitive ancestors responded to perceived danger to the tribe and self; and even negative coverage in the media as early humans responded to snarls from predators.[4]

The stimuli may cause the same set of physical and emotional responses to gird the modern professional for the primitive human's *fight or flight* reaction.

Fight Instinct Can Harm Client

But in the realm of professional public relations, *fight may lead to escalation, rather than resolution, of conflict.* The use of verbal weapons and attacks through news media and other channels of communication may provoke prolonged, increased attacks and shifting of targets to do more damage by both sides—or by other forces that become engaged.

Fight may lead to the so-called *public relations offensive*, a term used in the Nixon Administration to describe the response to media and public criticism, perceived as threats to survival in the aftermath of the Watergate burglary. The offensive actually fueled the resulting scandal and contributed to bringing down the Nixon Administration.

The fight instinct may lead to management and/or labor losing sight of survival objectives and engaging in no-win, prolonged mortal combat, first with words and then with actions, in which both sides lose.

And the primitive fight response to perceived danger may see government agency and regulated business narrow their options to attacks and counterattacks, rather than allow processes of negotiated settlement in the interests of both sides and the publics affected.

Flight Instinct Can Endanger Client

In the realm of public relations practice, *flight may yield to cover-up activities that tend to incite* media, other powers, and publics to greater investigative heights and even vindictiveness. *Flight also may take the form of ostrichlike hiding* from the realities of the environment, of evading an issue or a reporter's question or consumer's complaint.

The *combination of fight and flight responses* that helped primitive humans survive more complicated threats may become manifest in organizational and individual paranoia. And this persecution complex may be evidenced by some CEOs' anticipation that most media are "out to get them" or that all consumer organization initiatives have to be repelled.

All this does not deny that standing up to fight *certain* battles or withdrawing from dangers *under certain sets of conditions* may prove the most effective and successful strategies. But the physical-emotional, fight-flight response of primitive humans may fail to consider variable factors and nuances, logic and evidence, strategies and tactics, research and evaluation, consultation and investment of thought, development of alternatives and playing out of scenarios.

Actions (and inaction) and statements (and silence that may communicate the unintended) may flow from the less prepared, defensive CEO and other executives. Even sophisticated, seasoned professionals have found themselves responding emotionally under the psychological equivalents of primitive human's physical fears for survival.

As conflict scholar-researcher Morton Deutsch has found:

In addition to the distortions arising from the pressures for self-consistency and social conformity, the intensification of conflict may induce stress and tension beyond a moderate optimal level and this overactivation, in turn, may lead to an impairment of perceptual and cognitive processes in certain ways.[5]

CEOs, staff legal counsel, directors of industrial relations, production heads, security officers, engineers—all kinds of persons in organizations—can build up within themselves fear, anger, suspicion, frustration, insecurity, and all the other response sets that interfere with clear judgment and careful reasoning. And public relations persons are not immune.

SYSTEMS OUT OF CONTROL

A systems concept may be seen to be operative in certain stress situations involving unusual inputs from the environment. Systems that normally have well-organized patterns of motion may go out of control. It happens in astronomy, in chemistry, and in human reactions to crises.

Counseling an executive to calm down and not get upset may have an *opposite effect* in time of duress.

The most skilled of communicators can succumb to illogic and emotionalism when nature brings tears to the eyes, a sharp edge to the voice, a pounding in the chest, a dryness to the mouth, aching throbs in the head, constriction of the muscles, and the instincts of fight or flight assume ascendancy. Some manage to restrain the outward symptoms and signals of the fight-flight syndrome without controlling the inner effects upon judgment.

Optimal Solution: Prevention

Ideally, the optimal solution lies in preventing the development of crises. Realistically, despite tremendous gains that can and are being made through public relations and management preventive action, crises will continue to plague an imperfect world.

Prevention—with early, planned, effective detection and intervention as a second line of defense—suggests coping mechanisms.

It may be argued that *the less prepared* your organization and critical internal and external publics are for anticipating potential and developing flash points of danger and disaster, *the greater the risk* that they will move to crisis proportions and the greater the probability of shock and surprise feeding physical and passionate forces that may tend to do even more harm. And the less prepared, the more likely public relations persons and those they counsel may be to say and do the wrong things (again, keeping in mind that silence and inaction can reduce, as well as heighten, explosive situations).

First Objective in Crisis: Self-Management

Although anticipation, prevention, and self-disciplined calling forth of logic and reason seem ideal prescriptions for dealing with the physical-emotional aspects of the fight-flight syndrome, more may be needed to release and dissipate the primitive urges and symptoms.

So, your first objective as a public relations person faced with crisis may relate to the management of your own physical and emotional responses. This means assuring that your professional training and experience and your faculties for reason dominate your thinking and actions.

Controlled release of tension

Anger, fear, and other emotional stresses can be reduced by a controlled release of the buildup of tension. In noncrisis times, logic says that self-restraint and introspection work. In crisis times, physical and emotional release, be it yelling in a soundproofed room or taking a moment to do vigorous exercise, tend to be effective.

Deep breathing, isometric exercise, and even creating in your mind sensory images of physical activities and relaxation may work for the public relations person who does not have the luxury of privacy or the time to do push-ups or such equivalents as jogging, bicycling, racquetball, golf, mountain climbing, gym exercise routines, or aerobic dancing.

Programming exercises and relaxation as part of the regular routine, and especially as part of the regimen in times of crisis, should prove valuable. So may the self-hypnosis-like visualizing of yourself in favorite leisure activities and settings that recall pleasant sensory perceptions, such as the feeling of cool sand on the feet and warming sun on the back, the scent of sea and suntan lotion, the sound of surf pounding and gulls crying, the sight of cresting blue-green waves and birds wheeling overhead, the taste of salt on the lips, and the inner feelings of motion in strolling along the shore.[6]

OBJECTIVES TO MINIMIZE DAMAGE

Despite preventive efforts, crises can and will occur. Just as there are principles involved in prediction, detection, and prevention of crises, so, too, there are principles for minimizing damage once a critical situation faces you. To begin a review of some of the more salient principles for operating in the midst of crises, consider what may be learned from the cases that follow.

CASE STUDY: LLOYDS BANK ROBBERY

Media coverage of a bank robbery and the success of a several-thousand-dollar holdup might just plant or feed the idea in the minds of others. So the public relations staff of Lloyds Bank saw no value in having such a story appear.

But February 18, 1982, was what Lloyds Vice President Margaret A. Merrett termed "a light news day in San Francisco." And the *San Francisco Chronicle* found out about the "routine holdup" and wanted more information. Even with Lloyds protocol for early alert of public relations staff, the newspaper knew about the Bay Area robbery six minutes before the public relations staff did.

Public disclosure of some details could impair police work or give away confidential bank procedures. "You can't give information detrimental to your own company," Merrett noted.[7]

Yet Lloyds needed good relations with the *Chronicle*. This situation, as so many confronting public relations officers, was fraught with *conflicting needs of different publics.*

Merrett invested time and effort to help the reporter understand "what it was like to be in my shoes." She wished to respond "as quickly and openly as possible" but "hold the line" when information could not be divulged.

In another situation, one that involved a complicated legal suit in which giving out information would have been "like slapping the competition," a reporter had kept asking questions. "He didn't get much out of me, but he did develop understanding." As the public relations vice president pointed out, working with the media is "a very subtle thing—you know what they can do to you." The strategy is to be sensitive to deadlines and "as honest and up-front as you can be with the press."

Media understanding, however, is a secondary objective in the aftermath of a robbery. "Our first concern is if anyone is injured." After assuring that anyone injured is aided and the trauma of family and co-workers is eased, the concern turns to reduction of the inconvenience to customers and return to normalcy.

Merrett said she believed that with the customer public, it was not the reporting of a robbery that counted, "but how well we responded."

First and most important, she said, it is her company's objective to prevent harm to customers and employees in a robbery. That means "discouraging heroics and getting the robbers out as fast as you can." Taking note of descriptions and other information to help the police is important, but not at the risk of running out after the robbers.

The objective of retaining confidence of customers and employees in Lloyds measures and policies to safeguard them goes along with prevention of injury.

It is not possible to entirely prevent crimes, but it is feasible to reduce the number of incidents through strategic communication and action. To deter crime, Vice President Merrett and her counterparts from other companies serve with the California Bankers Association Public Relations Committee and engage in cooperative projects such as the distribution of posters of "the 20 most wanteds" to member banks. One technique that seemed persuasive as a deterrent was to have slashes marked across the pictures of those who were arrested. But the program was not publicized to the media.

In banking, as in other areas of enterprise, *compromises are made.* Merrett recalled that in her native England, tellers operate behind bulletproof windows and that the plants, chairs, and friendly atmosphere of American banks tend to be missing. But the tradeoff provides a more open environment in America with friendliness and the sense of human contact between employees and customers.

CASE STUDY: DISNEYLAND SAFETY FUROR

Lives Are at Stake, the *Los Angeles Times* headlined a 1981 editorial critical of Disneyland's emergency medical procedures.[8]

The editorial followed the death of a teenage stabbing victim and came in the midst of a furor in the southern California print and electronic media. Some health and community leaders charged that the amusement park sacrificed the public's right to the fastest, most expert medical assistance available to procedures they perceived as primarily designed to maintain the wholesome, safe, family image of Disneyland. As the *Times* summarized the issue:

> The young man had been taken to the hospital in a Disneyland vehicle accompanied by a Disneyland registered nurse and two security guards.
> Health officials were disturbed that paramedics weren't called and that the patient wasn't taken to a trauma center. . . . Disneyland's infrequent use of the Anaheim Fire Department paramedics, who are only minutes away, has been a longstanding irritant to emergency service officials. They believe that Disneyland's failure to summon the paramedics on a regular basis denies the public the highest standard of emergency medical care now available.
> Disneyland officials, however, insist that they don't have a policy against calling paramedics or using trauma centers. That decision, they explain, is best left to the registered nurse who handles medical emergencies.
> The recent tragedy requires another look at the system. . . . The guests of such public establishments have every right to assume that speedy and skilled medical help will be there should they ever need it. The proprietors have the obligation to be sure that their guests receive nothing less. [9]

Whether or not Disneyland's procedures in such cases as the stabbing of the teenager were medically sound, it is apparent that:

1. If publics with access to media *perceive* (and, of course, perceptions and realities may be at opposite poles) that a so-called low media profile psychology, rather than the protection of individual life and limb, dominates organization policies, an "incident" may be blown up to crisis proportions. And the somewhat higher negative profile of news coverage of an injury or death may turn into an excessively high-level profile in which the focus is not so much upon the incident but the client's policies and actions.

2. Repeated incidents and charges may lend themselves to perceptions of callous disregard for the public interest.

3. Even organizations with a strong tradition of excellent customer relations and positive media relations may be summoned before the court of public opinion (as well as the law courts) when it is per-

ceived that damage has been done just to protect so-called image. (Some persons assign a cosmetic meaning to "image," even though a number of public relations professionals use the term to refer to *earned* reputation.)

DILEMMA: PUBLIC PANIC OR MEDIA WRATH?

In an era when it is not uncommon for institutions, government agencies, and corporations to receive bomb threats might not public disclosure in some situations create panic as much as the cry of "Fire!" in a crowded theater? And might you do unnecessary harm to your organization and its publics, including investors, employees, suppliers, customers, and neighbors, by rushing to the media with stories of threats?

But do you handle such threats internally in the hope that they will prove to be false alarms? Or do you risk a police reporter tuning into the radio calls or noting the daily logs of law enforcement and firefighting agencies?

Each situation is different. There are no simple rules with universal application.

Paul Etter, who was a Los Angeles newspaper reporter before beginning his quarter-century career with Fluor Corp., mused that the journalistic instincts bred into public relations professionals through media experience or training in college journalism courses may subconsciously influence behavior that leads to leaking stories to the media or building stories out of proportion to their merit.[10] The Fluor vice president for public relations said he had asked himself the question introspectively in handling potential crisis situations involving media.

Etter also challenged a colleague to consider how much of his efforts to open up to publics and media news of post-Watergate hospitalizations of former President Richard M. Nixon were dictated by public relations concerns for the Memorial Hospital Medical Center of Long Beach client and how much influenced by the excitement of working with the media on a breaking story.[11]

PROCEDURES FOR DISCLOSURE

Written guidelines that have been carefully reviewed and approved may help avoid compounding a crisis.

An example of written procedures based on research of how others prepare for crises comes from Pacific Mutual's "Public Relations Plan for Emergencies." Here are a few of the procedures presented in the 39-page manual.[12]

> ACTION: (To be taken as soon as situation is brought to senior public relations coordinator's attention.)

> • Contact SPOKESPERSON and . . . other appropriate company OFFICIALS.
> • Notify proper PUBLIC AUTHORITIES (fire, police, etc.).
> • Collect all available information—WHO, WHAT, WHEN, WHERE, WHY, HOW. . . .
> • Contact appropriate media representatives as soon as information is VERIFIED and cleared for release.
> • Determine if CRISIS COMMUNICATION CENTER should be activated. Notify necessary personnel.
> • Determine if PRESS HEADQUARTERS should be established. Notify media.
> • Notify switchboard to DIRECT CALLS appropriately.
> • Determine advisability of keeping offices open; NOTIFY EMPLOYEES of status.
> • Contact key COMMUNITY LEADERS if necessary and keep them informed of potential impact.[13]

To strengthen your own procedures for action, pause and analyze the protocol established by Pacific Mutual. Consider the questions that follow.

1. Would you change the order in which the steps are prescribed?
2. Which and *why?*
3. What would you add to your employer's action plan?
4. Does your organization have a written emergency or disaster plan?
5. Do members of the public relations staff have their own procedures spelled out?
6. When does the plan need to be updated?
7. Who would you consult in checking on how complete and appropriate the procedures are?
8. To whom should the plan be disseminated?

The questions provoked by even looking at a small portion of another client's crisis plan point to the value of requesting copies of materials from a diversity of companies, including some outside your own field.

The Pacific Mutual plan went on to itemize responsibilities and include an exhaustive listing of addenda instructions in support of objectives to minimize damage during an emergency.

OBJECTIVES TO MINIMIZE COVERAGE

Sometimes the objectives are not only to minimize damage but also to minimize media coverage.

CASE STUDY: NIXON AFTER WATERGATE

One of the authors of this book was a participant observer in a case that attracted international media attention and provided data that led to the creation of projections on the processes and effects involved in the aftermath of media exposé of a cover-up.

A conflict in public relations crisis management philosophies was illustrated in the first contact between Norman Nager, public relations consultant to Memorial Hospital Medical Center of Long Beach, and Ronald Ziegler, press secretary to President Richard M. Nixon when he was scheduled for hospitalization immediately following his resignation from the presidency:

> In telephone conversations before the first admission of Mr. Nixon and in person the day of his arrival, Ziegler warned Nager that "we'll pull the President out of there" and blame it on the hospital if his wishes were violated. He also emphasized legal restriction on disclosing information against a patient's or his agent's (Ziegler's) wishes.
>
> When Nager cited hospital needs as indicated in its public information objectives, Ziegler used an expletive in discussing the hospital. . . . He used an expletive before the words "the press" when Nager suggested that Mr. Nixon would benefit in his own media relations from an open information policy. . . . Ziegler wanted

to maintain what he called "a low profile on his illness" at a time when the former President was being subpoenaed to testify in the trials of subsequently convicted former chief aides.[14]

The "low profile," despite some successes by the medical center and physicians to open up to the media, resulted in such conclusions as this from *Time* correspondents and editors:

> That waspish cynicism greeted the news this week the ex-president will finally enter a hospital. . . . Health grounds could possibly help Nixon escape taking the stand as a witness. . . . [15]

"Waspish cynicism," born of Nixon Administration handling of the Watergate crisis, a crisis that forced him to resign the presidency, continued to haunt him even when he was genuinely ill, as this excerpt from the transcript of a press conference on his hospital discharge indicated:

> REPORTER: A lot of people are going to be viewing the fact that the President now is unhealthy after a certain number of years, relatively healthy in life, and the fact that now he can't travel and the fact that there is also a court case coming up, that people [are] going to be rather skeptical that the President is actually sick. I wonder what you can say that might stem the tide of this rising skepticism?[16]

The lessons of Watergate apparently were not learned. When he had to be rehospitalized a few weeks after his first hospitalization, Nixon and Ziegler ordered physicians and staff to keep the admission a secret from the public relations consultant to the medical center and, especially, from the media.

Former President Nixon cited California law that prohibited disclosure of information on a nonemergency private patient without express consent from the patient.

But orders to keep something hidden from the media and reality may be two different things. A garbage collector spotted Nixon being spirited into the delivery dock at the rear entrance of the hospital and called a reporter.

With reporters beginning to overload hospital telephone circuits and fill a hastily arranged press room, the public relations consultant was retained by the medical center to cope with the latest problem. In the presence of Secret Service agents and physicians, Nixon asked the consultant how many reporters were downstairs.

> His facial features sagging and pale under a stubble of beard, the former President seemed to smile. Then he asked Nager if the *Los Angeles Times* were among them. He was assured that a reporter from the *Times* was there.[17]

The former President of the United States issued a direct order forbidding release of any information to the press if the "damned *Los Angeles Times* is here." He refused to explain. The man who had been one of the most powerful CEOs in the world illustrated his understanding of media relations by trying to get even with a newspaper and then, when pressed, by asking that all information be given exclusively to the *New York Times* even though he was hospitalized 3,000 miles from New York and less than 10 miles from Los Angeles. Other media could get the story from the *New York Times*, he insisted.[18]

The medical center gave the information simultaneously to Associated Press and United Press International and immediately followed with a briefing to assembled reporters, including Jerry Ruhlow of the *Los Angeles Times*. Media interest was so high that John Brewer, news editor for the Los Angeles office of the Associated Press, said that the photo-cutline (reproduced here) and an accompanying story went out "to something like 80 countries."[19]

COVER-UP CRISIS GUIDELINES

A number of lessons may be derived from the Nixon case. And we can reach the following conclusions—stated as axioms—on how to handle similar crises. These axioms were developed in an analysis of Watergate and other cover-ups.[20]

1. *The greater the aura of apparent secrecy* the media perceive, the greater, longer, and more innovative will be the efforts to break through to what is concealed. (This is aided by internal pressures that may result in unlikely leaks.)

2. *Lies, or perceived lies,* once they become apparent to representatives of the media, will relate to cynicism on the part of journalists

Long Beach, Calif.—NIXON RETURNS TO HOSPITAL—Long Beach Memorial Hospital spokesman Norm Nager reads a statement from Richard Nixon's doctor to newsmen Wednesday night after the former president was admitted for further tests and treatment of phlebitis. Nixon was reported to have walked into the hospital with a slight limp after the 50-mile drive from his San Clemente estate. (APWirephoto)

and public, even to accepting as truthful normally unquestioned information relating to the perpetrator.

3. *Discovered or perceived efforts to thwart,* by honest means, as well as trickery, the media's pursuit of a story . . . may increase the intensity, duration, and innovativeness of the pursuit and even lead to attacks on third parties seen as getting in the way.

4. *The more information the media perceive is being held back* . . . the greater will be the intensity, duration, and innovativeness in attempting to gain information and the more likely that the search will spread to other sources.

5. *The more new angles* the media are able to extract on successive days of a breaking story, and this includes information in response to questions as well as investigative reporting, the more likely that the story will grow in terms of space/time allotted by the media and prominence of display in a particular format.

6. A curvilinear (U-shaped) *relationship may be expected between the competitive situations provided for media access to information and the intensity, duration, and quantity of coverage given a breaking story.* It is suggested that the least coverage generally will be given in situations providing for little intramedium competition and the greatest in situations providing for exclusive coverage by one organ or mass coverage by all principal media.

7. *The greater the competition among the media,* the more prone they will be to accepting unverified information, making mistakes, and expanding the base of information to be explored.

8. The greater the competition among the media *and between the media and source* of information, the more the opportunity for tempers to flare and for conflict to escalate with the possibilities of increased errors and biases building on both sides.

9. *That although a source with a reason to cover up may take some bruises away from first-day media coverage following prompt, full, and open disclosure of painful information, the in-and-out story will appear more attractive than the protracted and increasing beating one can take in the public eye day after day, week after week [in a protracted, building, long-run exposé series].*

MANAGING "ROUTINE" CRISES

Not every crisis involves something as unusual as the hospitalization of President Nixon after he was forced to resign, the furor in the wake of a stabbing death at an amusement park with the reputation of Disneyland, or the robbery of a bank. Public relations staffs must prepare for a diversity of contingencies, including "routine" crises. The challenges to most public relations officers in crisis management arise long before "situations" reach the proportions of Watergates, breakdowns at nuclear power plants, spills of dangerous pollutants into a city's water supply, crashes of jumbo jets, poisonings of medications and food products at point of sale, collapses of balconies loaded with hundreds of partygoers

*onto crowded dance floors, failures of alarm devices or protective sprin-
kler systems in skyscraper hotel fires, or discoveries that hundreds of
thousands of motorists are driving cars with dangerously defective parts.*

CHECK OF YOUR ORGANIZATION'S PLANS

Let's review some of the "routine" crises that can happen and examine
your organization's procedures. After you have done this, you may
wish to make marginal notes on additional kinds of crises and how
your client is prepared for them.

What is your company's policy (and how does it follow through
on that policy) when a "small" fire breaks out in a wastebasket, when
traces of smoke are detected in the air-conditioning system, when strangers
are reported lurking in your parking lots or buildings, when "low level"
mechanics or members of engineering staff question building or product safety, and when "crank" calls or letters of a threatening nature
come in?

Does a fire spread to the conflagration stage while an employee
is sent to investigate before the fire department is called?

Do claims of illness of an initial handful of consumers of your
company's products result in recall of the product and alerts to consumers while investigation of causal relationships begins? Or does it
take verified reports of an epidemic nature?

Does your organization evacuate employees and customers in an
orderly, prearranged manner when the threat of a bomb is reported to
internal security after several previous false alarms?

The answers are not easy. If you work for a hospital, for instance,
do you stop lifesaving operations and move patients in critical or painful
conditions on the basis of a phone call that may turn out to be a prank?

If an employee observes incompetence in the practice of a part of
the organization, do procedures encourage voicing concern and a follow-up investigation? Or is public relations staff limited to dealing with
the media, special events, and publications and avoiding concern with
product defects, employee safety, or environmental dangers?

How many wildcat labor walkouts or strike actions have followed
upon less-than-strategic procedures for handling employee grievances?

The lesson to be derived: A public relations professional should
get to *know the policies* AND *the realities* of the procedures. This means
that you must go beyond examining the procedures as they are written

up in the organization's manual or passed on in oral instructions to employees. (Procedures *not* in writing are subject to greater misinterpretation or memory lapses.)

EARLY WARNING ROLE

The management of crises, regardless of how rare or routine, tends to be enhanced by early warning. And the concept of public relations staff developing an early warning system for potential crises has gained in popularity over the years.

The PRSA Research and Information Center in New York City offers its 11,000 members a valuable package of crisis public relations reprints and brochures, including detailed steps to take. Yet the emphasis in the package, as in many journals, newsletters, and handbooks of public relations, tends to focus on crisis management rather than *prevention and early intervention.*

Syracuse University's William P. Ehling said the place of public relations in crisis management has been unclear and at times dangerously confused and misinterpreted. Some fresh concepts for approaching the management of public relations in conflict situations may be found in Ehling's written report to the Public Relations Division of the Association for Education in Journalism and Mass Communication.[21]

The problem may reside in part in a lack of communication, let alone agreement, among professionals *and* the executives to whom they report on the appropriate roles and scope of involvement in investigating trends, policies, plans, and activities that may not be seen as within the purview of public relations. Not every executive understands the place of public relations in crisis prevention, intervention, and management.

For instance: "Ridiculous. Here's PR coming around sticking its nose in my responsibilities again. If—and when—a disaster happens, I'll take care of it."[22]

This is what a public relations person may anticipate from some other managers, counseled Robert Slater, vice president of the public relations firm of Manning, Selvage & Lee, as he urged colleagues to budget and plan for known *and* unknown crises:

> To anticipate crises and to arm against them, *know your organization down to every division and location.* How each operates. If a corporation, know how it buys, manufactures, prices its prod-

ucts, distributes them. If a nonprofit, know how services are rendered, to whom, the training of staff, who donates. You must be *knowledgeable* if you are to be sensitive to potential problems.[23]

PLACE TO START: PROPOSE PR CHARTER

It may not be easy to find the time or gain the cooperation of managers of some divisions as you try to really get to know your organization. We recommend that *the place to start may lie in proposing a charter for public relations to top management.*

This is not to be confused with a disaster plan in which the roles of public relations and other parts of the organization focus on responding to crises.

Your charter could include written goals and objectives related to the role of public relations staff in studying parts of the organization that represent potential problem areas. Such a charter could also seek to define the precise role of public relations in the organization, including what you would like to see top management accept as the research, problem-prevention, and problem-intervention aspects of public relations. And a charter proposal could incorporate definitions of factors of potential problem or crisis areas that justify public relations involvement.

Beware of creating a charter that may seem threatening, rather than supportive, to other members of management. And lest public relations resources be spread so thin as to make them ineffective in this and more traditional roles, consideration should be given to:

1. Limiting to feasible proportions the scope of responsibilities

2. Securing the funding, staffing, and concurrence of top management on priorities and resources

By synthesizing—bringing together—and *adapting to the specific variables in your own client organization* earlier lessons on systems management and PR-MBO, goals and objectives, strategic communication, research and evaluation, and planning of time and resources, you will be in position to create a system to help alert you and other members of the management team to potential internal and external environmental dangers before they reach crisis proportions.

Study of history indicates that *crises happen in cycles and build over time.* As a public relations professional, you can use examples from the past to offer guidance on some factors in the early development of crises that may be repeated or follow a basic pattern.

(Can you call to mind how a relatively isolated demonstration or incident of violence at one site spread through a city or a nation? Recall all the incidents of tampering with food and drug products that came in the wake of the late 1982 discovery of cyanide poisoning of *Tylenol* capsules in the Chicago area?)

One of the authors recalled a newspaper column by the late Matt Weinstock in which the humorist spoke of "the perversity of inanimate objects . . . or why the toast always falls butter-side down."[24] Seasoned professionals cite similar "laws" or "principles" (Parkinson, Murphy, and Peter, for instance), but the concept goes beyond humor toward quasi laws of nature in suggesting that the more unsuspecting or unprepared, the greater the chance of something turning into a crisis. It goes beyond humor when you or your CEO realize that a costly, damaging crisis could have been prevented or its impact lessened if effective early warning procedures had been in operation.

10 SOURCES FOR DETECTING POTENTIAL CRISES

Sources for projecting potential crises are similar to sources for developing other client public relations goals and objectives:

1. Check historical records of your organization including files of news conference transcripts, clippings, news releases, memoranda exchanged with management, minutes of board and executive meetings, and publications.

2. Interview management personnel (and board members, if feasible) on their experiences with other employers, as well as with your client. Find out about concerns and expectations they base on conversations with current contacts outside the organization, review of literature, and attendance at conferences in their spheres of expertness.

3. Interview staff experts such as legal, quality control, training, safety, governmental affairs, medical, industrial relations, marketing, computer resources, and security.

4. Network, that is, keep in touch with public relations colleagues in your industry so that you can exchange observations and brainstorm on potential problems. *Propose a pact to alert each other at the earliest stages of problem situations that could spread.*

5. Gain perspectives on potential crises by networking and attending meetings with persons *outside* your employer's system. A brewing problem in another field could presage one in your area. The value of

stepping outside your system also lies in gaining a fresh perspective on how other organizations operate their crisis intervention systems.

6. Carefully monitor journals, newsletters, books, and newsletter reports on speeches in your client's and other industries.

7. Have your name placed on the mailing lists of public relations staffs in and outside your field and carefully analyze annual and quarterly reports and external and internal publications. You may want to develop fresh insights by asking yourself: Why was that action taken? Why was that information communicated?

8. Subscribe to one or more of the "insider" newsletters in your client's field or area of business.

9. Pay attention to daily media reports around the country where trends in development of crisis situations may emerge. As part of this alert to media, a growing number of professionals monitor financial media, as well as weekly newsmagazines, general-interest magazines, and special-interest publications.

10. Apply research methodologies cited in Chapter 6 from unobtrusive research and participant observation to control-group/experimental-group, pretest/posttest studies; from content analysis of media reports to content analysis of correspondence from consumers; from scientific sampling of opinion commissioned by your client to subscription to reports of opinion research and trend projection services; from futures research to analysis of past cases.

TIMING CRISIS PREPARATION

If you are preparing your operation and your client for early or mid-course intervention in a crisis, timing is of the essence. Some veterans say crisis prevention and intervention planning should begin at the moment you accept a position or even as you are researching an organization in preparation for a hiring interview. Crisis preparation is best begun when not even a hint of a critical situation looms on the horizon.

CASE STUDY: THREE MILE ISLAND

At the top of the priority list is the establishment of a reputation for credibility and concern for the interests of the publics of your client. *Perspectives*, in its introduction to an examination by Edward L. Bernays of the Three Mile Island nuclear accident, warned, however, that "credibility built during several years of effective communication can be destroyed by one bad experience of crisis communication."[25] It should be pointed out that *this may be so to varying degrees, depending upon a host of factors specific to the organization's established relations and the realities and perceptions of what happens.*

At the heart of PR-MBO lie objectives and programs for building the strength of organizational reputation. *And the strength* AND *duration achieved may mitigate the impact of the one bad experience.*

11th Hour Initiatives vs. Goodwill Reservoir

Certainly, professionals in a number of organizations have demonstrated over the years that public relations remedying of wrongs, initiatives to open up communication, and concern over quality of products and services do *not* have to await the eve or midst of crisis.

The development of small-group communication programs, letters to employees at their homes, and the announcement of new benefits *after* notice of intent to organize a union or strike is given obviously do not have the same impact as long-range efforts begun in times of peaceful labor relations. *The 11th hour initiatives to improve communication may even lead to cynicism and suspicion. It takes time to build a reservoir of good will deep enough to sustain an organization in bad times. It takes time to cultivate with publics and media a reputation not only as an honest, concerned source but also as a good citizen of the community who deserves a hearing, if not understanding, when things go wrong.*

CASE STUDY: ST. JOSEPH'S DAILY PATTERN

For example, the community service department of St. Joseph Hospital of Orange, California, had a pattern of daily communication in place for years when it had to explain to its employees negative news about a crisis involving improper disposal of infectious waste. In addition to regular meetings, special telephonic communication, and an open-door policy by management, the institution had a five-day-a-week newsletter that had developed credibility with employees.

So, as southern California media turned to St. Joseph's accidental disposal of infectious waste in a county landfill after a buildup of worse incidents in Los Angeles County, the story was quickly told to—and accepted by—employees in their regular channels of communication. Note the reproduction here of the front-page report of *Another Day.*[26]

Tuesday, Jan. 19, 1982

Another Day

THOUGHT FOR THE DAY:

*It is one of the most beautiful
compensations of this life that
no man can sincerely try to help
another without helping himself.*
(Emerson)

Census at midnight, House: 319 (77.6% occupancy)
Census at midnight, med/surg: 173 (79.7% occupancy)
Census at midnight, critical care: 44 (67.7% occupancy)
Babies born yesterday; 12
Emergency visits yesterday: 89
Surgeries yesterday: 35
Outpatient surgeries yesterday: 19

UPDATE ON INFECTIOUS WASTE FOUND AT DUMP SITE:
Approximately 50 bags of infectious waste materials were discovered last Friday at the
Santiago Canyon landfill and traced back to
St. Joseph Hospital. According to our policy
and procedures manual, this practice is in
violation of the hospital procedures for disposal of these waste products.

Although the risk of infection due to the
disposal is minimal, according to epidemiolo-
gist Marya Grier, the reason many are fearful
of infectious wastes is that if you are
susceptible to disease, have an open wound,
have dry mucus membranes, or a chronic skin
disease, you could possible pick up an infection. Even healthy people, if they come in
contact with infectious materials, could con-
ceivably pass along an infection to a person
with the aforementioned problems.

However, Grier feels the problem is being
blown out of proportion.

"I would be more concerned with picking up
an infectious disease in a restaurant than I
would in a hospital," she said. "Restaurant
personnel usually don't have to take hepatitis
tests or tests for mononucleosis, and these
are highly contagious organisms. I don't understand all the publicity about infectious wastes
being dropped off at the dump site. Most doc-
tors and veterinarians work with the same kind
of infections and they aren't required to perform any special procedures with their infectious waste products.

"Actually, about 90 percent of the contents
of those bags are very similar to organisms
found in the environment," she continued. The
bags at the dump site did not contain any bio-
logical waste, such as tissue. They contained

such items as masks, dressings and paper
supplies. So how did the bags end up at the dump?

One of the EVS staff members, it seems, took
the bags of material from 2-North to our steri-
lizing area, but discovered it was locked, said
Jody Winder, director of environmental services.
Instead of trying to find a key, he simply left
the bags out in the open, hoping when someone
with a key came along, they would put the bags
in the sterilizer. Instead, the bags were put
into our trash compactor, where they were mixed
in with office waste, and delivered to the dump.

This waste has been retrieved and properly
disposed of. The employee responsible for leaving the bags out has been suspended for three
days without pay.

Our waste products are classified into three
categories, says Grier: regular, contaminated,
and infectious. Regular trash includes all
office waste; contaminated material includes
such items as IV bottles, tubings and other items
not necessarily infectious; infectious waste
includes all waste that comes from people with
"communicable diseases," which includes people
with wound infections.

When properly implemented, our system is one
of the best in the area since we have our own
"retort" or sterilization facility on site. A
good system, however, is only as good as the
people who work with it.

On learning there was a breakdown in the
disposal of the infectious waste material, Jody
Winder called meetings with all EVS janitors,
stressing the importance of following procedure.
Meetings were also held with all members of the
EVS management staff.
(Continued on back)

Published Monday through Friday by the
Community Services Department of St. Joseph Hospital
For additional copies call extension 7475

(Page 1 Courtesy of St. Joseph Hospital.)

INVEST IN "UNTAPPED RESERVOIR"

When proposing objectives in periods of relative normalcy, *it may prove helpful in winning over top management if you can project specific potential dividends on your company's investment in crisis prevention and strengthening of relations with important publics.*

George Hammond, APR, retired chief executive of Carl Byoir & Associates, Inc., and past national president of PRSA, supported this point in a speech to the Center for Strategic and International Studies, Georgetown University.[27]

> The major undertaking needed now, to demonstrate the mutuality of interest between business and the other segments of society, is a major challenge. . . .
> Yet, its success may hinge on another undertaking that business must shoulder: recapturing its acceptability as a full member of the American Society.
> Those who have the stomach for this fight will find that . . . there is a great reservoir of support, untapped, once the millions of men and women—in their many interest groupings—have been convinced of mutuality of interest with business.[28]

When crises are developing, it becomes increasingly important to educate executives on program costs as investments and *reinforce their convictions that public relations objectives are integral to bottom-line corporate interests.*

Patrick Jackson, APR, co-publisher of *PR Reporter*, head of Jackson, Jackson & Wagner, and past national president of PRSA, put it this way in a letter to one of the authors.[29]

> It doesn't hurt any to have clearly in mind a concrete definition of public relations. . . .
> In sum, if you don't know what public relations can accomplish . . . and aren't clear on the activities properly assumed by practitioners . . . and haven't got a definition of the field which justifies both of these . . . how can one apply public relations to a set of organizational objectives, or evaluate public relations activities in a total context?[30]

Jackson's thinking can be incorporated in your development of the charter we recommend to strengthen public relations and top management understanding of how public relations supports organizational objectives. This is important in times of both crisis and normalcy. R. Seymour Smith counseled in his *Public Relations Journal* report on planning for crisis communication: "Crisis communication programs must be planned in periods of noncrisis. Failure to do so can produce a crisis in itself."[31] Smith predicated this on the importance of public relations staff and others in the organization to *be prepared in advance to work together without duplication or neglect of functions.*

And, as indicated earlier, public relations persons, the CEO, board members, and employees throughout an organization may be disoriented by the physical-emotional complex of reactions to crisis.

For similar reasons, you may also want to *budget resources, financial and human, in anticipation of crises* rather than in the midst of turmoil.

CASE STUDY: MOSCOW OLYMPICS BOYCOTT

As Peter Dowd, vice president of American Medical International and principal of Haley, Kiss & Dowd, Inc., pointed out, if you wait for a crisis to come upon you before planning, there will be *no* time to budget in advance and little time for the research and strategy upon which to base programs and budget. "But you have to make the time and make do with what you are able to do."[32]

Dowd, former senior vice president for the western United States for Hill and Knowlton, recalled being asked for counsel by the U.S. Olympics Committee after President Jimmy Carter started talk of boycotting the Moscow Olympics in 1980.

Under critical pressure of time, a meeting was arranged with Mr. Carter and 11th hour research was initiated to project public reactions to the boycott. Public relations counsel needed to have reliable data for projections on what to expect from traditional sponsors of the U.S. Olympics Committee, advertisers, members of Congress, Olympics committees around the world, sports enthusiasts, and the media.

The Roper organization was retained to do a survey of several publics. Roper did a phone survey of key members of the U.S. Senate and House of Representatives. The polling organization also conducted one-on-one structured interviews with business leaders.

And the surveys confirmed our worst fears: The President believed the boycott was the centerpiece of his foreign policy. Athletes were willing to go along. Business executives realized the [potential] backlash if they didn't go along with it. National Olympics committees in other countries were mixed. The larger American population surveyed favored boycott by more than 70 percent.

The U.S. Olympics Committee had moral leverage but no economic leverage, no leverage on the International Olympics Committee . . . and the moral leverage vanishes when athletes back the President.[33]

The counsel at this point shifted to going for reparations to the economically damaged American Olympics movement. The U.S. Olympics Committee achieved its fallback position of gaining federal and private financial support.

It remains questionable whether the actions that led to the crisis achieved anything toward the objectives of the Carter Administration.

Even as the United States was taking its turn in sponsoring the 1984 Olympics, and backers of the worldwide competition were looking beyond that and puzzling over the very future of the Summer Games, the systemic effects of the American boycott of Moscow in 1980 could not be projected. The answer may never be known, but if more time had been invested and more brainpower enlisted, would the forces behind the boycott have found it advantageous to go ahead?

Publicly announced objectives of the Carter Administration had included influencing the Soviet Union to withdraw troops from Afghanistan and deter future Russian military intervention in countries in the eastern bloc. The Soviet fighting in Afghanistan was to last for years and Poland was to continue to experience intense intervention long after the boycott.

Among the lessons to be derived from the Moscow boycott case:

1. Emotions, even of the people and governments of nations, may rise once crises are allowed to build up; they may be heated to the boiling point in which the *focus shifts* from dispassionate analysis of long-range options and cost-return ratios to the fervor to strike out now.

2. Once the opinions of publics have been allowed to crystallize and harden on a particular issue, public relations *strategic options* are limited.

3. Even research conducted in limited time under crisis pressure can be of significant value in presenting a clearer picture of present options.

4. But more time to research long-range implications is preferable.

5. Contingency planning for any organization, be it the U.S. Olympics Committee, the American government, or a business enterprise, would call for *budgeting of reserve resources*.

6. *Fallback objectives* should be considered when it appears that it is not feasible to attain initially sought results.

HOW TO BUILD PR STAFF RESERVES

Some professionals include in their annual plans time to investigate environmental conditions and develop strategic campaigns for probable scenarios.

That is why you should avoid stretching your resources so thin that you do not have the *elasticity to get basic jobs done and still divert fresh, capable persons to do the research, planning, and follow-through that may be warranted when problems arise*.

That is also why organizations with normally ample public relations staffs of their own in noncrisis times:

1. Keep agencies on retainer so that special experts or additional manpower may be mobilized quickly.

2. Build staff reserves so that if a crisis arises during a vacation, a sickleave, or on a weekend when staffers may be unavailable, or when crises reach disaster proportions, they have experts and even unskilled labor as needed.

3. Train higher management, as well as support personnel, to take specific public relations roles as needed during crises to augment limited staff.

4. Establish mutual assistance pacts with other public relations professionals to come to each other's aid when a call goes out for help.

5. Clear with executives first-, second-, and third-priority drafting of personnel from other departments for specific missions during crises. (Can your limited staff handle dozens of phones, scores of media people, relations with critical publics, internal brushfires, preparation of statements, fact finding, security problems, thoughtful counseling to higher management, and liaison with critical internal publics, by itself?)

6. Make sure that such arrangements do not come as a surprise to middle management or that those to be drafted or assigned will not be in the dark on where to report and what to do.

HOW TO ADAPT DEADLINE TECHNIQUES

Public relations professionals, including persons who deal with problems not related to the media, may find journalistic techniques in anticipating deadlines of help in preparing for potential crises.

Perversely, even when contingency plans are in place, crises seem to happen at the wrong time: when you are understaffed, ill, near fatigue, on vacation, in transit, or when people you need to reach (important executives or legal counsel) are away from phones. Sometimes crises happen in the midst of the most hectic schedules or in the middle of the night. And you or your sources of information, the persons who check legal and technical considerations for you, may be caught up in the physical-emotional effects of the fight-flight syndrome.

In drawing up overall objectives and strategies for coping with crises, how conducive will such conditions be to remembering everything that needs remembering?

Might the pressure of the moment and lack of sleep send your (or another's) eye flying over a mistake? Or lead to a Freudian slip when written protocol or statements are missing or sketchy? "What he really meant to say . . ." starts out many an attempt to retract what was already reported by the media. Even veterans have encountered temporary stalls in writing when no deadline pressures or crises were upon them.

But even if all your sources and consulting experts are available instantly, even if all your minds are alert and relatively free of the negative effects of stress, and even if your thoughts flow quickly, effectively, and clearly, time may still be so short as to run out before you are ready.

A colleague of one of the authors once told of racing from a labor-management negotiation session and within 45 minutes having a bulletin circulated to every employee within the plant, only to learn that the grapevine had gotten out the other side's story while he was still at the typewriter.

To top off a number of other problems, particularly for the relative newcomer who is not yet up to speed, but also for the veteran who has become somewhat rusty in handling critical deadline situations or in using skills that were once part of the daily routine, the speed in writing a plan or a statement may be slow in coming.

Similarly, pilots who do not get in so much airtime a month under day and night conditions, police officers who neglect to qualify periodically on the firing range, heart surgery teams that operate less than five times a week, runners or tennis players who get out of training, and editors who only rarely have to write copy, find their reaction time slowed and their effectiveness handicapped.

Media Models for Making Deadlines

From their journalistic roots, some public relations professionals have borrowed and adapted techniques they found of value in racing from breaking, complex, in-depth stories to print or on the air in seconds and minutes. One of the better explanations of these techniques, as applied by journalists, may be found in John Hohenberg's *The Professional Journalist*.[34]

How does television come on the air with an hour-long documentary on the death, moments earlier, of a national celebrity? How does a newspaper reach the street so quickly with a lead story on a jury's verdict in a controversial case? How does an executive face the electronic and print media with strategic statement and responses to questions minutes after the media arrive at the scene of a disaster?

In the case of the death documentary, most media have files (including film and videotape for television) on prominent individuals. Moreover, they may have the productions or stories already prepared, lacking only footage or information on the circumstances of death, reactions to death (although previous testimonials already may be on file), and update details.

In the case of a controversial trial, the landing of a manned spaceship, an election, or other breaking story in which no medium wishes to be far behind, let alone behind at all, the entire story may be on videotape or in the computer ready for printout with only filling in of the final details needed.

When there is no pressure on television crews or newspaper reporters, all the *background material may be gathered and organized in anticipation* so that when the news angle does develop, there is relatively little to be written, edited, or filmed.

Hohenberg referred to similar processes as "writing the story backward," "piecing the story together," preparing "A copy or A matter" and "B copy or B matter."[35]

Even journalists differ about the terminology and some disagree about the value of including material that may have to be rewritten or severely edited depending on situational variables. *But the technique that works so well for television, wire service, radio, and newspaper people under deadline pressure also works well for public relations persons preparing for crisis.*

It also offers the advantage of providing the luxury of *time to analyze, reconsider, and rewrite;* to put down the material and have the opportunity to collect thoughts; to attempt to read between the lines and consider how others may perceive something; and to show more sensitive plans or statements to policy makers, legal counsel, technical experts, and those who may have to act as on-camera representatives long before anyone experiences traumatic crisis pressures.

HOW TO USE SCENARIO PLAYING

Hohenberg referred to "dummy leads" as another technique.[36] Some public relations persons call it "playing out scenarios."

You could start by considering all the probable (and even less probable, if time permits) alternatives that can occur in a given crisis situation. The journalist then would write out several alternative leads. And with a minimum of time and effort he could select the most appropriate, add necessary details, attend to changes necessitated in the body of the story, and look at the whole for validity in a fraction of the time it may otherwise take.

Scenario playing is *not* confined to anticipating possible leads for statements to the media. As public relations experts use the approach, it *may include pretesting several options* the client may have *for actions or interpretation* of a given situation with panels somewhat representative of important publics.

Scenario playing also may prove useful in *preparing for and testing milestone actions and communications,* including those that may be the critical pivotal points at which problems may become crises.

Scenario playing suggests *anticipating all questions to be posed by members of boards of directors, legislators, media representatives, and investigative agencies.* This means working on potential questions and challenges over a period when thoughts have time to germinate and when the mere looking at a question can stimulate ideas for more. And it may mean asking others within or outside the organization what they think may happen if something develops to crisis stage.

Of course, *by anticipating questions and challenges in preparing information for publics or media, you may actually head off a crisis based upon misunderstanding or lack of information.*

The questions and challenges may suggest more than verbal answers. Public relations counselors and their executives may look beyond dissemination of information to *changes in policies and procedures or preventive actions.*

Similarly, although experts may have the answers and be able to field questions on their feet before a worried, hostile, skeptical, or otherwise emotional audience, such scenario playing frequently is augmented by *drafting alternative responses* that may be required by variables that arise.

And by preparing answers and subjecting them to scrutiny by internal experts and external friends before the questions, let alone full crisis conditions, arise, you may find inaccuracies, language or concepts prone to misinterpretation, or information that could violate legal statutes or subject the organization to unnecessary conflict with other institutions.

Computer and Video Technology

With the aid of computer programming, your organization may be able to quickly project almost infinite combinations of variables that might arise, not only in responding to questions but also in dealing with entire crisis situations.

With the aid of video equipment, persons selected to deal with media and critical publics and experts who coach these spokespersons may have the vantage point of critiquing and improving upon how they would come across in verbal and nonverbal communication.

With the aid of both computer and video technology, public relations counselors, other staff experts, and executives may be helped to rise above the limitations of individual perspectives and passions of the moment and *examine options before positions are frozen* and *review communication while there remains the opportunity to strengthen it.*

But all the strategies, techniques, computer software, video playback capabilities, legal consultation, disaster plan procedures, and literature "rules" cannot operate in the limbo of reaction to crises and performance of duties. What counts in public relations counseling and activities in crisis prevention and management is *not* so much style, technique, actions, and proposals, no matter how streamlined or sophisticated, but the achievement of objectives in the best interests of the client organization and its publics.

TURNING CRISIS INTO OPPORTUNITY

So far, this chapter has discussed objectives to prevent crises, reduce potential damages to the lowest possible level, and minimize negative media coverage. In some cases, however, as Michael Cooper suggested in the Public Relations Journal, *"a crisis can display an organization's conscientiousness. Some crises even have happy endings."[37] Changing the language from "crisis" to "challenge" does not turn crisis situations into opportunities. But it is profitable to explore the concept that crises may present within themselves possibilities of creating new initiatives, of improving an organization's substance (as well as its reputation), and of strengthening a client for achievement of ultimate objectives.*

CASE STUDY: FORD, UAW CREATE NEW AGENDA

The rank and file of the United Auto Workers voted in 1982 for a historic first in the nontraditional settlement of traditional conflict with one of the "Big Three" American automakers.

In the midst of a complex of crises beyond the "normal" strike-shutdown posturing, both labor and management veered from their past demand-threat-counterdemand negotiations over wages and fringe benefits to the consideration of a revolutionary pact between Ford and unionized auto workers.

As UAW and Ford entered negotiations, a combination of forces threatened labor and management alike: recessionary forces in the marketplace; increased competition from Japan; downward spiraling car sales and upward spiraling layoffs of skilled workers; a declining confidence on the part of investors; economic experiments at the federal level causing increased insecurity on Wall Street and Main Street; and near-disaster situations looming over the nation's auto capital, Detroit, neighboring cities, states of the region, and even remote locales with auto assembly plants.

Automakers and some economists predicted that greater wage and benefit concessions by Ford would contribute to increased auto costs and decreased sales, which in turn would lead to layoffs of more workers in a worsening economy ill prepared to cope with greater unemployment.

Strikes and shutout actions—or worse, a prolonged closing of assembly lines and reduction of income for workers and company alike—were possible. But in 1982, Ford and UAW leaders took their historic initiative to break past cycles in which declining sales led to the layoff of thousands of workers and in which even the prospects of layoffs might have influenced people to invest or buy less.

The Japanese, together with American observers of Japan's auto industry, had earlier concluded that one contributor to a higher productivity of workers in Japan was the identification of employees as involved, secure, loyal participants whose jobs were safeguarded by companies loyal to their interests.

The Ford-UAW 1982 bargaining and settlement turned on contractual *safeguards to keep employees on the job good times and bad, rather than continue the unsettling, crisis-prone cycles of automaker scrabbling to build up the labor force to meet demand peaks and to lay off as demand slackens.*

CASE STUDY: DISNEYLAND REVISITED

Lightning struck again at Disneyland. Six weeks after the death of a stabbed teenager led to public and media furor over the park's policies and procedures in responding to medical emergencies, a 34-year-old woman collapsed near Sleeping Beauty's Castle and went into convulsions.

And just a little over a month after the *Los Angeles Times* editorially questioned Disneyland's use of its own nurses and vans (rather than calling in of paramedics, ambulances, and other nonpark emergency resources) and of taking some patients to smaller nearby hospitals (rather than trauma centers) the park was back on the evening newscasts and in the headlines in the aftermath of the woman's death.

Although Disneyland sources cited in the *Times* said that the public relations actions that followed were not linked to the two deaths but had been in the works longer, the newspaper reported park officials taking the following action:

1. Disneyland was looking into installing sirens and other emergency equipment in their own vans.

2. In the meantime, the park had contracted for full-time, on-the-scene coverage of an ambulance service and driver.

3. And Disneyland had started setting up meetings with county officials "on the best policy for handling medical emergencies."[38]

County officials, the medical establishment, and the media welcomed the steps taken by the park as *socially responsible actions in the interests of future ill and injured guests*. If not a happy ending, the crisis at least moved toward a *positive new beginning*.

CASE STUDY: DIALOGUE WITH JEWISH LEADERS

From across the country, the *New York Times* inadvertently set in motion an initiative by Fluor Corporation's J. R. Fluor in opening up a dialogue with Jewish community leaders to aid in mutual understanding.

The international corporation's ties with Arab countries in which it served as prime contractor on a number of construction projects, its role in the production of a film on Arabian culture, and its involvement in two controversial situations in which anti-Israeli overtones were perceived led to a buildup in negative media coverage. Fluor, personally, had been blamed for his role in helping establish a mideastern studies chair at the University of Southern California under conditions alleged to violate academic integrity and contribute to a pro-Arab bias. (Fluor was chairman of the USC board at the time.)

When a national foundation, backed by Fluor contributions, reversed the action of a staffer in inviting two controversial Israelis to an American seminar on Arab cultural issues, charges were made in some media that Fluor had been involved behind the scenes. This time, the negative coverage was compounded by media reports including background material on the previous Fluor-USC furor.

As Fluor's public relations vice president, Paul Etter, explained: The Aspen Institute had been inviting influential leaders and scholars from Arab countries to a series of seminars. The Arabs realized that in attending the Aspen Institute, they would be confronting a fairly significant number of Jewish participants from among the business executives and intellectuals invited. Despite initial reluctance by the Arabs to participate, the program was perceived as a worthwhile undertaking, and so they came, Etter said.[39]

Although there were arguments as well as discussion in the seminars on the Arab world, he said it was generally concluded that there was a fruitful exchange of views. The East/West Foundation sponsored the seminars with Fluor serving as the largest contributor among the corporate backers.

When the program was announced, the Aspen Institute director found that one of the participants was a former West Bank special administrator for the Israeli government, who was perceived by the Palestinians and a large portion of the Arab world as an enforcer of strict discipline on Palestinian cities. As Etter recalled, program planners worried "that if this fellow was invited to attend as a part of the faculty on the culture of the Arab world, this would be perceived by Arab participants as a slap in the face."

The director of the East/West Foundation secured an agreement from the director of the Aspen Institute that the controversial Israeli would have his invitation withdrawn. This led to heated allegations of tampering with the integrity of the program. Although the vice president for public relations felt that Fluor would face a hostile reporter in granting an interview with the *New York Times*, he counseled acceptance in the belief that the CEO's candor in laying out the facts from his side would mitigate some of the damage already done, contribute to understanding, and minimize the risks of a biased report that might result from lack of cooperation with the media.[40]

The front-page news feature, however, was interpreted by Fluor executives as distortion, a biased selection of interview fragments, and the solicitation of anti-Fluor quotes from Jewish leaders, including a legislator who complained to Etter of biased questioning. But, in retrospect, the public relations executive said that Fluor probably would have been hurt more by a refusal to cooperate.[41]

(For other industry perspectives on media coverage perceived as biased and hostile, readers are referred to Kaiser Aluminum, Illinois Power, Hooker Chemical, and Dow Chemical U.S.A., who have made available packages of materials to professional practitioners and educators.)[42]

In the wake of a round of negative stories in the media that followed the *New York Times* story, Fluor, with Etter's counsel, started an initiative to open a dialogue with Jewish community leaders, including executives of the B'nai B'rith Anti-Defamation League. Although the press coverage of the favorable quotes on the results of such meetings did not receive the front-page attention of earlier, anti-Fluor stories, progress was made toward the goal of increasing understanding of Fluor's policies and the objective of establishing open channels of communication with American Jewish organization leaders.[43]

CASE STUDY: KAISER VS. ABC'S "20/20"

The bad news for Kaiser Aluminum, at least on ABC-TV's "20/20," started with the opening of the "Hot Wire" segment April 3, 1980. What follows are excerpts we made from a transcript of that broadcast.[44]

Audio	*Visual*
ANNOUNCER: Tonight you may have a time bomb in the walls of your home that you may not even know about. If it hasn't already burned your home down. Aluminum wiring. Was the danger covered up for 10 years? Or was it just good business? Geraldo Rivera with a special report—"Hot Wire."	Burned wire. Seared socket. Socket erupting in flames. Home in flames. Face of plug. 2 shots of gov't reports. Exterior shot Kaiser plant. Rivera standing with wire in hand. Rivera, with "Hot Wire" LOGO behind him.
RIVERA: We're talking about aluminum wiring. Despite 5 years of bad news and despite the fact that the Consumer Product Safety Commission made it their number one priority, it's still installed in two million American homes and house trailers. This is a report about how and why and, most importantly, about who is responsible for putting aluminum wiring on the market in the first place. Here is "Hot Wire." One hundred and sixty-five people died two and a half years ago when fire destroyed the Beverly Hills Supper Club near Cincinnati, Ohio. On February 20th a jury ruled that aluminum wiring was not the cause of the blaze. The decision was cer-	Beverly Hills Supper Club file footage. Bodies laid out on gym floor. Black/white stills of victims, onlookers.

Audio	Visual
tainly a major victory for the aluminum industry. And clearly it was a decision some of the companies involved had not expected. By the time the jury handed down its verdict, these nine companies had already settled out of court with the families of the dead and injured. Kaiser Aluminum, one of the major defendants, settled for $1.2 million just two weeks before the jury verdict. We have been unable to determine whether or not Kaiser and the eight other companies felt something was wrong with their aluminum wiring. But the evidence uncovered by this seven-month investigation supports the conclusion that something may be wrong. . . .	Courtroom sketches. Court exterior w/ graphics listing the nine companies. Kaiser Gramercy plant exterior, two other plant shots. Face of plug. Seared test socket. Socket bursts into flames. Kaiser Aluminum electrical product brochure cover, fading back to a montage of brochures.
RIVERA: What government investigator Kelly called a time bomb was marketed to the unsuspecting American public as a safe, inexpensive alternative to traditional copper wiring. . . .	
We know now that Kaiser Aluminum at least knew their product needed special handling. These confidential documents, for example, were obtained by 20/20. They show that way back in the 1950s, Kaiser Aluminum conducted extensive lab tests on aluminum wire. Their own scientific evidence warned that aluminum wire was very hazardous unless certain procedures were taken to prevent oxidation. . . .	Shot of report cover page. Camera zooms in and holds on CONFIDENTIAL stamp [not placed there by Kaiser].

Audio	*Visual*
We asked Kaiser Aluminum at least to make someone available for an interview. They also refused. Although Kaiser did say they would make a televised statement five minutes in length if 20/20 agreed both to air the entire statement and then not ask the person making the statement any questions. That, of course, would have been a violation of ABC News policy. . . .	

The transcript included interviews with the mother of a 15-month-old baby killed in a fire and a fire official who described the scene graphically while visuals showed the body being removed and the parents on a couch with a photo of the baby.

A critic from the Consumer Products Safety Commission was interviewed, as was the mother of a 16-year-old and a 9-year-old killed in a trailer fire. Accompanying visuals included "fireman carrying shrouded body" and mother "breaking into tears."

A builder, a housing authority representative, and a spokesperson for the National Fire Protection Association were interviewed for quotes building the case against Kaiser.

The two Kaiser institutional advertisements reproduced here summarize the bad news–good news story of the metal company's battle for what it considered a fair hearing.

Whether the "good news" compensated for all the damage done is another question. But Kaiser got out part of its story, not only through ABC-TV's airing of a short response at a later time, but also through its own national campaign involving a number of different forms of media, including a series of institutional advertisements.

HOW TO COME OUT POSITIVE

Crisis perception by publics and coverage by media may focus on all the negative aspects. The public relations staff and those authorized to speak for the organization may be constantly on the defensive, providing infor-

mation in response to questions and reacting to charges or rumors. But objectives may be pursued by demonstrating the quality of the organization's overall record, the strengths of its employees, and the policies and deeds that evidence responsible citizenship.

PREPARATIONS TO BRING OUT STRENGTHS

Several areas of preparation are recommended for public relations professionals who prefer positive communication to defensiveness. These preparations require effort *before* crises.

1. Prepare and keep updated background materials on your client:

a. General profile as provider of services or products with sufficient data so that a relatively small aspect of the organization, a defect in one product of many, an incident involving a few of numerous employees, or other detail *may be seen by media and opinion leaders in perspective.* Corporate brochures, annual reports, and specially prepared background sheets or kits may be used for this purpose.

b. Profiles of key executives, including *background facts that might inspire confidence and credibility.*

c. Glossary of jargon or terms used *to prevent or clear up* misinterpretation or confusion, which would lead to more negative perceptions.

d. Contributions to the economic, social, cultural, and civic health of community, region, and/or nation. *Document your client's social responsibility as a good citizen.*

e. Records of innovations in the field, *recognition for achievement,* indicators by trade organizations and others of client reputation in its industry.

f. Data on quantities of products or services provided, *data on defect/accident/incident-free performance* (so many hundreds of thousands of miles driven by company personnel without an injury accident; so many million cans of tuna sold without contamination).

g. Film footage and stock photos with *positive scenes incorporating focus on human competence, warmth, concern.*

Trial by Television

The American system of justice is founded on a simple principle: The accused has the right to be fairly heard in his own defense, and to confront and cross examine his accuser.

This principle, more than any other, defines the difference between freedom and tyranny.

Yet today, here in America, charges are aired before tens of millions of people without fair opportunity for the accused to respond.

They call it "investigative" television journalism. We call it "Trial by Television."

Much of investigative television journalism is solid and responsible reporting—but much is not. Many producers of "news magazine" programs too frequently select story segments with their minds already made up about the points they want to make. Then they proceed to select the facts and quotes which support their case. "Interview" opportunities are sometimes provided the "accused." But the edited "interview" format puts the producer (i.e. the accuser) in full control of deciding what portions, and how much of, the accused's defense the public will be allowed to see.

Rarely does this result in balanced and objective coverage.

The television production team becomes the accuser, judge, and jury. With no real recourse for the accused to get a fair hearing in the court of public opinion. Yet the viewing public is led to believe that the coverage is balanced and objective. This is a deceptive and very dangerous practice.

"Trial by Television," like the kangaroo courts and star chambers of old, needs to be examined. If we decide, as a society, that we are going to try issues, individuals, and institutions on television, then some way must be found to introduce fairness and balance.

Here's what we're doing about it.

Recently, Kaiser Aluminum was the victim of grossly misleading and inaccurate statements on a segment of ABC's "20/20" program. On its "20/20" segment of Thursday, April 3, the announcer accused aluminum house wiring of being unsafe, and Kaiser Aluminum of intentionally marketing an unsafe product. These accusations are blatantly wrong.

Although we were offered an opportunity to be "interviewed," "20/20" reserved the privilege of editing any part of our statement. Any defense we might have made would be subject to their sophisticated editing techniques, and to their commentary. Since it was evident to us that the producers had already formed their opinions, we declined their offer. How can a defense be fair if it is subject to censorship by the accuser?

We have been advised by many to ignore the "20/20" attack on the basis that you can't fight the network, and to prevent further harassment. We will not allow ourselves to be maligned or misrepresented by any group—even television.

Here is what we are doing:
1. We have demanded a satisfactory retraction from ABC-TV.
2. We are asking the Federal Communications Commission, under their "Personal Attack" doctrine, to order ABC-TV to provide us with time and facilities to present our side of the story to the same size audience in a prime time segment.
3. We have asked Congressman Lionel Van Deerlin (D-California), Chairman of the House Sub-Committee on Communications to consider Congressional hearings to examine the implications of this increasingly insidious and dangerous practice.

Here's what you can do about it.

Unfortunately, not all victims of "Trial by Television" have the resources to defend themselves, as we are trying to do. Their only defense is you.

If you believe the rights of the accused to fairly defend themselves are more important than sensational attempts to increase TV ratings; if you believe the right of the public to get balanced and objective information on issues of importance is as important as it has ever been, please speak out and let your elected representatives know.

America was conceived to prevent tyranny by providing checks on the power of any institution. Today, a new power is dispensing its own brand of justice—television. There's only one check against it. You.

If you are upset by the unfairness of "Trial by Television," write your elected representatives, or us at Kaiser Aluminum, Room 1137KB, Lakeside Drive, Oakland, CA 94643.

One person can make a difference

KAISER ALUMINUM
& CHEMICAL CORPORATION

over

GOOD NEWS

ABC News has taken a bold step toward fairness and balance in TV reporting.

For over a year, Kaiser Aluminum has been focusing as much attention as we could on an issue we call "Trial By Television."

"Trial By Television" occurs when a TV production team does an unbalanced investigative report. The production team becomes the accuser, the judge, and the jury of people or institutions. By controlling the editing of pre-taped interviews, they even control what the accused can say in his own behalf. This isn't necessarily conducive to fair or balanced reporting.

Most of our argument has been directed at ABC-TV who we believe badly abused us

in a segment of their "20/20" show. Understand, we are not arguing with anyone's right to criticize. We just believe that the other side ought to have a fair opportunity to present its case.

Well, fair is fair. ABC-TV in what we considered to be a milestone of responsible broadcast journalism, has developed an innovative technique to allow the other side to be heard in a balanced and fair way. They call it "Viewpoint." It premiered July 24. We were pleased to be a part of that program and to have the opportunity to present in our own way our response to the charges made against us by "20/20"

before a prime time audience.

ABC is to be congratulated and applauded for its leadership in addressing one of the most perplexing problems in television. We sincerely hope their example will encourage other broadcasters at both the local and national level to undertake similar experiments in responsible broadcast journalism.

We think it will lead to better TV news. And better TV news is good news for all of us.

ONE PERSON CAN MAKE A DIFFERENCE

KAISER ALUMINUM & CHEMICAL CORPORATION

300 LAKESIDE DRIVE, 1137KB
OAKLAND, CA 94643

2. Have on hand, or at least know how to obtain, even on weekends or when least convenient, *industry-wide data that might help place in perspective your crisis.*

3. Give instructions to field representatives or officers at the scene or in other locations to search out and report back specifics to public relations headquarters:

a. Acts of heroism by the organization's employees.

b. Acts of heroism by police, fire, medical, or other emergency personnel; customers; bystanders.

c. Services to contribute to the health, safety, comfort, security, and general well-being of victims.

d. Actions taken to prevent more damage than occurred or prevent harm to more individuals.

e. Names and locations of persons, including employees, customers, emergency personnel, family members, witnesses, or others *who observed efforts in the interests of the publics* and who might agree to being interviewed.

4. Have on hand *interpretive* information on policies, quality-control procedures, safety equipment, specialized personnel, and other material that may help media and publics understand and respect your client's posture in:

a. Preventing crises.

b. Responding to crises.

5. Have handy at home, office, or on the road, telephone numbers to reach your client's experts and authorities at any hour of day or night for *providing, updating, or verifying* information. This minimizes risk of inaccurate rumors spreading or of media and publics perceiving they are being stalled because the client has something to hide.

6. Develop with appropriate executives statements on:

a. What *investigative actions* the organization will take.

b. What *preventive actions* the organization will take to avoid additional incidents or worsening of a situation.

c. Meaningful expressions of concern for those affected.

7. Be sure that as much as possible executive statements are *not* released merely to appease media and publics with no intent for follow-through. ("You may be sure we will have a thorough investigation," when none is planned.) Modern journalists, like modern public rela-

tions officers, maintain calendars and follow-up files for checking on progress in delivering on corporate promises during crises. And be sure that legal staff is consulted.

HOW TO MOBILIZE PUBLICS

That crises—and sound public relations programs—may help mobilize publics was indicated in studies by two researchers. George W. Corrick, University of North Florida and John S. Detweiler, APR, University of Florida, Gainesville, found that crises may have value in mobilization of community forces.

> Often citizen action is crisis-oriented. A nonprofit organization or community group springs into life as a result of a tragic event. A publicized instance of child abuse or the slaying of a runaway may spur the community to initiate a number of child welfare activities. A crippling illness, receiving publicity locally in the case of a particularly brave and appealing individual, may stimulate new initiatives in the health field. Press exposure of inadequate housing conditions may stimulate the formation of a group seeking housing reform. Many movements associated with crime or criminal justice reform are started this way. Many environmental groups have either started or grown rapidly during a time when a controversy raged over a proposed threat to a community's natural resources or natural beauty.[45]

We can extend the Corrick-Detweiler principle beyond the boundaries of the not-for-profit sphere. *Objectives may be developed to mobilize the internal publics of a company or institution to work for greater productivity, feel increased identification with the organization, and want to communicate more positively for their employer in crisis.*

CASE STUDY: CONTINENTAL TAKEOVER FIGHT

Continental Airlines pilots, flight attendants, ground crews, and ticket agents rallied around management when it tried to resist the early 1980s takeover of the airline by Texas International. They not only rallied to bring public pressure to bear on government agencies but also almost managed to block the takeover by offering to buy up a controlling portion of the stock.

Even while Continental was trying to merge with another airline and persuade stockholders that this option would be in their interests (despite the added several dollars a share to be made by accepting the tender offer from TI) and even before employees seemed to be in position to block the takeover and buy up their own airline, *a pragmatic public relations professional was preparing to take the most positive stance if worse came to worse.* Publicity Director Jack Gregory confided to a colleague: "I would be disappointed. But then I would take a look for bright spots. You know, an airline like Continental and TI could control the Southwest."[46]

Reversals of hearing decisions finally authorized the takeover. Gregory set out to motivate employees, investors, and customers to join forces in making the best of the new opportunities.

CASE STUDY: TYLENOL'S COMEBACK

The legend on the cover of the March 1983 issue of the *Public Relations Journal* termed the rebound of the brand name and product "Tylenol's remarkable comeback" and the article credited the manufacturer's public relations action and communication for mobilizing support.

> Johnson & Johnson handled the "cyanide crisis" with quick action in the public interest and a marketing and promotion plan that won the support of the media—and the confidence of consumers. . . . J & J clearly positioned itself as a champion of the consumer, gave meaning to the concept of corporate social responsibility, and demonstrated communication expertise that will be hard to equal for years to come. In fact, the handling of the crisis already serves as an excellent public relations case study of how to make the best of a terrible situation. . . .
>
> According to James H. Dowling, president of Burson-Marsteller [public relations counsel to the manufacturer of Tylenol], "The great lesson here is that you can overcome bad news. You can win. You can come back."
>
> [According to Lawrence G. Foster, J & J public relations vice president,] "The poisonings called for immediate action to protect the consumer, and there wasn't the slightest hesitation about being completely open with the news media. . . . During the crisis phase of the Tylenol tragedy, virtually every public relations decision was

based on sound, socially responsible business principles, which is when public relations is most effective. Almost immediately planning began for phase two, the comeback, and this involved a more detailed and extensive public relations effort that closely followed important marketing decisions and reached out to many audiences."[47]

The expensive national recall of all Tylenol capsules was followed by a teleconference that linked 30 major U.S. markets by satellite in which the company showed and explained its new triple safeguard packaging to deter tampering and to help consumers understand the *how* and *why* aspects.

As Blair Jackson, vice president, Burson-Marsteller, explained in a background briefing, *a key strategy was to place the emphasis on concern for consumers, not Tylenol or manufacturer concerns.* Video technology made it possible for journalists in New York, Chicago, Los Angeles, Philadelphia, and Washington to ask the J & J chair questions. The satellite transmission combined with expert representatives of J & J at each of the 30 locations provided a sense of involvement for local reporters and contributed to the intensive and supportive coverage—and making—of the Tylenol comeback.[48]

CASE STUDY: MCDONNELL DOUGLAS DC-10 STIRS LOYALTY

Following the May 25, 1979, crash of a McDonnell Douglas DC-10 in Chicago, the FAA grounded 275 of the jetliners for 38 days. Media and public attention increased "and all manner of speculation arose . . . and we seemed to make the headlines every day," recalled Ray Towne, who headed public relations during the long-drawn-out crisis for the company.

The crisis in confidence in DC-10 safety formally ended in January 1980 when the FAA issued a report Towne said "proved DC-10s meet the toughest standard of airlines safety, and the grounding had been unnecessary." But that was eight months later, and some publics and media related the crash to two other DC-10 accidents in the same year, even though the accidents were not caused by the plane's design or production. *"Our objective was to restore confidence in the DC-10 by the traveling public,"* Towne said.[49]

Such confidence had to be evidenced in the behavior of travel agents and airline crews and passengers if McDonnell Douglas customers—the airlines—were to continue to contract for purchase of DC-10s.

Employees' personal cars with bumper stickers expressing pride in the DC-10 began to become commonplace in towns where the 80,000-employee firm had aircraft facilities. But they were not the only public to rally to the company's side in the crisis.

An intermediary public of opinion leaders—travel agents—responded affirmatively to the company's campaign. As Towne pointed out, travel agents sold approximately three fourths of all airline tickets. Another important public in a role of channel of communications was constituted of the employees of customer airlines. *"You have to give ammunition to your friends,"* Towne said.

Such ammunition was passed to employees, investors, travel agents, customers, the media, and anyone who asked through a variety of interpersonal, print, and electronic channels of communication.

One of the more effective was a terse, candid brochure (reproduced in part here). The question-and-answer format brochure material was prefaced by a statement to "Set the Record Straight." Public relations staff stressed the expert data foundation for the answers and sought to explain why it was necessary to raise the questions once again:

> These are facts, not opinions. They have been established by teams of experienced, respected, independent technical experts using rigorous objective methods. . . .
>
> But good news often doesn't travel as far or as fast as bad. The vindication of an airplane, especially when it's based on thousands of pages of mathematically precise data, isn't as dramatic a story as a calamity. It lacks the human interest appeal of a grounding that disrupts the whole world's air travel system.[50]

WHEN <u>NOT</u> TO PUBLICIZE GOOD DEEDS

Although public relations programs may result in positive actions in the aftermath of crises, and although the temptation to "set things straight" with the media or impress important publics may be strong, some situations demand that the good deeds be done without giving due credit to the client. As Towne reflected on the aftermath of the DC-10 crisis: "Follow-up stories may lead to rehashing of previous accidents. And you don't want to keep reminding people."[51]

CASE STUDY: WOMAN'S NEXT-TO-LAST DEATH

When a patient was declared dead on arrival at a medical center and later showed signs of life at a mortuary, media coverage of the hospital's role in the incident and in the nearly two months the patient survived in a coma was generally favorable.[52] But two opportunities for positive follow-up stories were discarded.

The media were kept informed of changes in the woman's condition in deference to their requests. And within 10 minutes of the second declaration of death, public relations staff issued a one-paragraph statement. More than 20 pages of anticipated question-and-answer material had been developed and reviewed with several medical and legal experts within days of the woman's return to the hospital and when it became apparent from test data that there was no brain activity. Blanks had been left for inclusion of last-minute details. But only one question was asked by members of the media and that question had been anticipated: "How are you sure she's really dead this time?"

The first opportunity for positive follow-through came a few weeks later on the initiative of members of the woman's family. They had developed strong ties with the medical center and its physicians and nursing staff before the incident, when she was under care for severe heart disease and previously had been resuscitated from clinical death and returned home to a normal life. A member of the immediate family, who had previously visited the public relations office to express gratitude for the director's protection of the family's privacy and for the concern evidenced by several nurses, returned to the office several weeks after the funeral.

She expressed concern that some persons in the community might have interpreted the coverage of the story as reflecting negatively on the medical center and asked how she could go about getting a letter commending the hospital staff placed on the front page of the local daily newspaper. She wanted to make it clear that the family disavowed any perception left by media that everything possible had not been done before, during, and after the crisis.

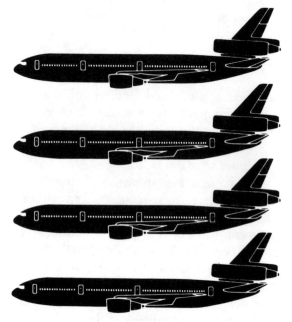

The DC·10

A Special Report

(Cover and beginning of basic questions from DC-10 Special Report courtesy of McDonnell Douglas.)

The
Basic
Questions

Why did a DC-10's pylon and engine separate from the wing at Chicago?

The accident investigating team, including representatives of government agencies and independent outside experts, established that the pylon and engine separated from the airplane's wing because of a very large crack in what is called the horizontal flange of the pylon's aft bulkhead.

What was the origin of this crack?

The investigators found that the pylon could not have been damaged in this way while attached to the wing. It could not, in other words, have been damaged in flight. Rather, as the National Transportation Safety Board stated, it was "damaged by improper maintenance procedures." The maintenance procedures that caused the crack were of course banned by law as soon as the problem was identified.

Have changes in the pylon's structural design been ordered?

No. As the FAA stated, "there are no fundamental shortcomings in the design of the DC-10 wing pylon." In the six months after the Chicago accident, the DC-10 underwent a relatively new and highly sophisticated structural examination called Damage Tolerance Analysis. This examination, in which the

She was warmly thanked, but it was recommended that the idea be dropped to spare family and friends, as well as the medical center and physicians, a renewal of media coverage and, to use Towne's term, a rehashing.

The second opportunity came later when, in direct response to the "dead on arrival" crisis, a new portable piece of equipment sensitive to the slightest life signs was ordered to hospital specifications. This equipment was designed to be rushed into action even as ambulances with patients believed to be dead drove up to the emergency entrance. No statement or release about the equipment was issued to the media, although the staff was prepared to answer questions if any arose. News of the availability of the equipment was passed to other hospitals without credit to the medical center.

CASE STUDY: SURGICAL GAS MIXUP

Only a few individuals on the staff of a hospital knew that a patient who died in surgery succumbed not to trauma of the operation—as had been initially concluded—but as a result of being given the wrong gas after workers accidentally mixed up two wall outlets in performing normal maintenance.[53]

The risks of disclosure of the findings were obviously great. But there was no hesitation in immediately communicating what happened to the coroner's office, where the case would be a matter of public record, and in telling the family, who had accepted an earlier conclusion. Executive, public relations, and legal staff agreed that there was no way to compensate the family for their loss, but a seven-figure out-of-court settlement was made.

There was no media coverage. Nevertheless, the possibility of coverage was considered so great that detailed statements and responses to anticipated questions were prepared. Public relations counsel developed a procedural document with precise instructions on how to service the media in the event the story broke.

When an engineer retained by the hospital came up with a life-saving preventive step, to color-code the in-wall gas lines and outlets, the information was disseminated nationally through hospital channels so that others in the country could protect their patients from similar accidents. No identification of the source hospital appeared. In this situation, the public relations objective was simply to mobilize other hospitals to take actions to protect their patients.

PREPARING FOR THE IMPOSSIBLE

The mixing up of gas tubes was one of those "impossible" situations. But, increasingly, public relations professionals have found themselves having to write contingency plans to prepare for the impossible, even terrorism. By any code of government or civilization, the first case in this section should never have happened. But a trend had been in the making around the world.

CASE STUDY: HOSTAGES IN EL SALVADOR

On September 21, 1979, a Beckman Instruments plant in El Salvador was attacked, a guard was killed, and the American resident manager and visiting engineer were kidnapped.

The 47-day ordeal for the two Beckman hostages (and public relations and other staff around the world) ended with their safe return after the company met demands to place propaganda advertisements in 25 newspapers for the Revolutionary Party of Central American Workers and paid an undisclosed but substantial ransom.

The situation posed a severe dilemma not only for Beckman but also for potential victims whose kidnappers might be influenced to follow the model of taking hostages and making similar demands. Willard B. Gregory, APR, public relations manager, briefed other professionals on the objectives his company adopted as hard choices were made:

> First, we wanted the safe return of our people; second, aid and comfort to their families; third, to portray Beckman as a company concerned about its people, which it was; and fourth, to elicit the fullest possible support from the media.[54]

Among the lessons learned by Gregory: "Companies definitely need to draw up a formal crisis procedure."[55]

CASE STUDY: ENSURING INSURANCE FIRM

A veteran public relations officer in Willard Gregory's audience, Pacific Mutual Life Insurance Second Vice President Thomas S. Santley, APR, took the counsel seriously. Santley interviewed other veteran practitioners, consulted public relations professors (including one of the authors), hired a student researcher, and set out to create the national corporation's first comprehensive public relations plan for emergencies. [56] And in subsequent overall annual corporate responsibility plans, Santley has included a *continuing review and refinement of the organizational response to emergencies.*

Like a growing number of companies, Pacific Mutual has begun to anticipate—with objectives of prevention and optimal management of incidents that cannot be prevented—a number of emergencies that could befall the modern organization. [57]

• *Deaths or injuries* of top executives, employees or visitors, and deaths by suicide, by shooting, or during building construction

• *Terrorist acts* such as militant actions, bomb threats, letter bombs, explosions, snipers, and robberies

• *Government and legal matters,* under which Santley listed legal actions, government policy changes, suits, unlawful activity involving Pacific Mutual personnel, confrontation, hostile takeover, merger attempts or failures, building code changes, loss of major contract, and company interests in building on controversial sites

• *Disasters:* flood, earthquake, hurricane, fire, false alarm, and water cutoff

• *Financial problems such as proxy fights, tender offers, or disruptions of annual meetings*

• *Emergencies* such as labor union trouble, serious accidents involving company personnel or vehicles, systems malfunctions, scandals, embezzlement, computer sabotage, mass electrocution, and food poisoning

Santley did not calculate probabilities, but his fact-finding effort was national in scope as he took advantage of the combined experiences and thinking of organizations outside his company's field, as well as that of others in the insurance industry. Among the lists of guidelines drawn upon by Pacific Mutual were those published by *PR Reporter*[58] and several sections of *Lesly's Public Relations Handbook.* [59]

Pacific Mutual's document built upon a foundation of disaster plans from other companies, including: Atlantic Richfield; Bankers Life; Clorox; Cyanamid; Eaton, Yale & Towne; First Colony Life; Ford Motor Co.; Gulf Oil; Hunt Wesson Foods; Jim Walter Corp.; Manufacturers Life Insurance; Monsanto; Owens-Illinois; Southern California Gas Co.; and Tenneco Oil.

A number of others have been known to share copies of plans or tips with other firms, including National Gypsum Co., Raytheon, Marathon, and Bronson Methodist Hospital, 1981 winner of the highest award in public relations, a PRSA Silver Anvil.

CASE STUDY: TORNADO HITS KALAMAZOO

Year after year, Bronson Methodist Hospital planned, rehearsed, tested, and revised its plans in community-wide disaster drills. Kalamazoo, Michigan, lies in the tornado zone and had previously responded to a range of disasters including an airliner crash and savage storms.

Veteran public relations director Paul T. Clark, APR, had even worked at another hospital in Ohio when 413 cancer patients were involved in a radiation accident.

Aside from the diversion of manpower resources, which must be considered a major expense, the total preparedness cost relatively little, $100 for printed materials and $564 a year for telephone lines.

For the public relations operations alone—Clark said he drew upon people and services from such divisions as personnel, human resources, business office, library services, chaplains, physical facilities, educational services, food service, and school of nursing, *all placed under his direction* when the real test of preparedness came.[60]

The concept behind the hospital-wide annual preparedness drills and ongoing planning process was to train the staff so that "before a disaster, it is ready to act instinctively."[61]

1. Give care promptly to all people who needed it.
2. Allay fears of patients, families, and others in the community.
3. Service the media with current, accurate information so they, in turn, could do their job.

Most important, it's everybody's job in crises and normal times to take care of people. And this department is here to support that care.[62]

There was ample opportunity for panic, helter-skelter emergency operations, the proliferation of false rumors, and even more injury, psychic as well as physical, when the real thing happened and a series of tornadoes blackened the late afternoon sky over Kalamazoo. Clark recalled:

> They carved a path of destruction down the main street and devastated the central business district located just two blocks from Bronson Hospital. Within minutes . . . five people were killed, more than 80 were injured, and property damage exceeded $50 million.
>
> Within minutes after the touchdown, hundreds of telephone calls from relatives and media began pouring into Bronson's Emergency Communication Center.[63]

The efforts of Clark and his task force freed the hands of medical and paramedical personnel for their primary mission of care. And efforts started even before the casualties were brought into the hospital, as illustrated by the photograph of the triage area—the place where the injured were assigned priorities of medical treatment and dispatched to surgery, intensive care unit, radiology, and other areas, and where medics already started giving emergency aid.

As he reflected later about how the hospital achieved several of its objectives through the command organization, Clark offered this counsel to other professionals:

> The key element here that may be of most value . . . is that I, as director of public affairs, was located in the Disaster Control Center with the vice president of nursing, chief of medical staff, and administrative disaster chief.
>
> That core group was in charge of making the major decisions and allocating resources during the disaster period. . . . I believe my presence there aided in the entire process, whether information gathering, disseminating, or making those decisions on how to take care of the discharged patients, families, and friends. . . .
>
> I think our experience here proved something that all of us in communication believe, at least in theory; that is, beyond the physical care of the injured, current, accurate information is the most important commodity and the one most valued by all involved.[64]

Public relations activities, including the more traditional role of servicing the media and publics that require information are important in virtually any crisis situation. Bronson's basic disaster plan, although it incorporates this, places the primary focus on patient care.

Yet, as veterans of disaster operations have learned, the pressure on phone lines may overload circuits and prevent important calls from coming in. Media personnel and curious citizens drawn by live media coverage may create traffic blockages that delay emergency vehicles and employees.

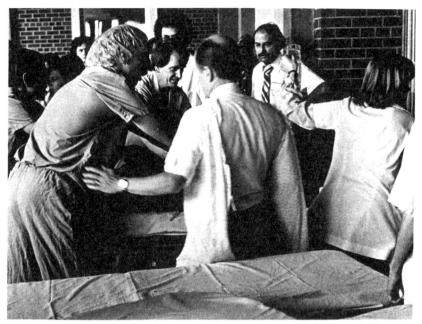

Care for Victims. Medical and paramedical personnel check patients and begin emergency care in Bronson Triage. (*Courtesy of Bronson Methodist Hospital*)

Part of any disaster plan should include *anticipation of disruptions*. Prompt and accurate servicing of the media, including earning editors' and reporters' trust that they can count on quick, accurate telephonic reports, may not keep away all the camera crews and other journalists who need to get firsthand views, but it can help.

Bronson's basic disaster plan specified that "it is anticipated that . . . response to any type or magnitude of disaster . . . would minimize the disruption of the normal hospital operation."[65]

The creation of a press room that is not in the midst of critical disaster operations, a checking of credentials, prearrangements with the media to come to a specified location, and posting security personnel may be helpful.

While taking care of acutely ill patients who were in the hospital before the tornado touched down, Bronson credited the well-rehearsed and carefully laid out plans for allowing staff to:

1. Treat and release 75 percent of all victims needing emergency care (even though it was not the only hospital available near the disaster site).

2. Admit five victims who required continued care.

3. Process other persons killed by the tornado.

4. Service hundreds of relatives and friends who called in about people who were hurt or temporarily missing.

5. Transport victims out of the cordoned-off disaster area.

6. Set up an emergency aid station right at the heaviest hit area of the tornado and treat people on the scene for injuries from flying glass and debris.

7. Aid Red Cross nursing staff and volunteers in that agency's disaster relief operation.

8. Share the experiences gained and lessons derived with other sectors of the medical community.

9. Calm the population through media reports, its own special print editions, and telephonic and in-person communication during and after the tornado.

10. Provide recognition to internal and external publics involved in the tornado crisis response for past efforts and incentives to rise to future incidents through a diversity of ways, including special publications, board resolutions, advertisements, and other means of action and communication.[66]

In turn, the hospital and its public relations staff were given widespread recognition in the media and by community and professional organizations. The 1981 PRSA Silver Anvil paid tribute nationally to this public relations program.

In so doing, the PRSA worked toward its own objectives, including the creation of role models for other professionals and their clients who may be *motivated to anticipate and manage crises with objectives-based research, priorities, strategies, time and resources planning, and energetic follow-through with action, communication, evaluation, and incorporation of findings.*

That is what PR-MBO is all about, in crisis management as well as in the attainment of other organizational objectives.

"THE BEGINNING OF THE ANSWER"

President Ronald Reagan's Export Council chair, J. Paul Lyet, asked more than 1,500 public relations professionals and 600 educators, students, and guests at the November 1982 PRSA National Conference:

"How do we continue to enhance the benefits of technology and offset human costs at the same time?"[67]

And Lyet, former board chair and CEO of Sperry Corp., sounded the theme of PR-MBO when he told the public relations audience: *"The beginning of the answer requires the setting of objectives."*[68]

The next challenge, as reviewed in the concluding chapter of this book, is to select from the options for implementation and refinement of a PR-MBO system the approaches and strategies that will work best for you, your executives, your publics, and your organization as a whole.

NOTES

1. Eugene Roberts, interviews, City of Hope, Duarte, California, March 1975.
2. Ibid.
3. Norman R. Nager, "Anatomy of the Aftermath of Cover-Ups" (Ph.D. dissertation, University of Southern California, 1978), pp. 86–90.
4. Inspired by Desmond Morris, *The Naked Ape* (New York: McGraw-Hill, 1967).
5. Morton Deutsch, *The Resolution of Conflict: Constructive and Destructive Processes* (New Haven: Yale University Press, 1973), p. 355.
6. Inspired by William S. Kroger, M.D., *Clinical and Experimental Hypnosis in Medicine, Dentistry, and Psychology* (Philadelphia: Lippincott, 1963).
7. Margaret A. Merrett, interview, Los Angeles, February 19, 1982.
8. *Los Angeles Times*, "Lives Are at Stake," March 15, 1981.
9. Ibid.
10. Paul Etter, interviews, Westminster, Irvine, Long Beach, and Fullerton, California, 1979–83.
11. Ibid.
12. Lynda Schmoll and Thomas S. Santley, "Public Relations Plan for Emergencies" (Newport Beach, California: Pacific Mutual, 1980).
13. Ibid.
14. Nager, "Anatomy of the Aftermath of Cover-Ups," pp. 198–99.
15. "Nixon Depressed and Ill," *Time*, September 23, 1974, p. 17.
16. Transcript of press conference at Memorial Hospital Medical Center of Long Beach, Long Beach, California, October 4, 1974.
17. Nager, "Anatomy of Aftermath of Cover-Ups," p. 217.
18. Ibid., pp. 218–219.
19. John Brewer, correspondence to Norman R. Nager, October 29, 1974.
20. Nager, "Anatomy of Aftermath of Cover-Ups," pp. 34–37.
21. William P. Ehling, "Toward a Theory of Public Relations Management: Applications of Purposive and Conflict Theories to Communication Management" (paper presented to Public Relations Division of the Association for Education in Journalism and Mass Communication, East Lansing, Michigan, August 1981).
22. Robert Slater, "Two Types of Public Relations Crises: Known-Unknowns & Unknown-Unknowns," *PR Reporter* Tips & Tactics Supplement, October 26, 1981.

23. Ibid.
24. Matt Weinstock, column published in *Los Angeles Daily News* in 1953. Cited here from memory.
25. Introduction to Edward L. Bernays, "Crisis Communications Failure—Three Mile Island," *Perspectives*, May 1979, p. 5.
26. Valerie Orleans, "Update on Infectious Waste Found at Dump Site," *Another Day* (daily newsletter), Community Services Department, St. Joseph Hospital, Orange, California, January 19, 1981, p. 1.
27. George Hammond, "Business Has Failed to Explain Itself," (speech reprint, the Center for Strategic and International Studies, Georgetown University, 1979).
28. Ibid., pp. 32–33.
29. Patrick Jackson, correspondence to Norman R. Nager, February 5, 1982.
30. Ibid.
31. R. Seymour Smith, "How To Plan for Crisis Communication," *Public Relations Journal*, March 1979, pp. 17–18.
32. Peter J. Dowd, interviews, Los Angeles, Fullerton, and Westminster, California, February–June 1980.
33. Ibid.
34. John Hohenberg, *The Professional Journalist*, 5th ed. (New York: Holt, Rinehart and Winston, 1983), pp. 173–176.
35. Ibid.
36. Ibid.
37. Michael Cooper, "Crisis Public Relations," *Public Relations Journal*, November 1981, p. 52.
38. "Park Hires Full-Time Ambulance; Disneyland Aide Says Action Long in Works, Not Linked to Deaths," *Los Angeles Times*, March 20, 1981, pt. 2, p. 1.
39. Paul Etter, telephone interview, March 7, 1982; and conversations, 1979–1983.
40. Ibid.
41. Ibid.
42. Kaiser Aluminum, "Trial by Television" and "Television Audio Transcript—Aluminum Wiring/Trial by Television Segment," ABC-TV's "Viewpoint," July 24, 1981; Illinois Power Co., "60 Minutes-Our Reply" videotape and associated materials; Dow Chemical U.S.A., "Who's Watching the Watchdog" (videotape and print attachments); Hooker Chemical Co., "Hooker Fact Lines" 10, 11, and 12 on Love Canal.
43. Etter, conversations.
44. Transcript of "Hot Wire" segment, ABC-TV "20/20," April 3, 1980, provided courtesy of Kaiser Aluminum.
45. George W. Corrick and John S. Detweiler, "Involving Community Leadership and Citizens," in *The Nonprofit Organization Handbook*, ed. Tracy D. Connors (New York: McGraw-Hill, 1980), pt. 5, pp. 23–37.
46. Jack Gregory, interview, Fullerton, California, March 1981.
47. Mitchell Leon, "Tylenol Fights Back," *Public Relations Journal*, March 1983, pp. 10–14.
48. Blair Jackson, briefing of Norman R. Nager, Los Angeles, March 4, 1983.
49. Ray Towne, seminar workshop, Anaheim, California, October 1980.
50. McDonnell Douglas External Relations, "The DC-10: A Special Report" (St. Louis, Missouri, and Long Beach, California, 1980).

51. Towne, seminar workshop.
52. Nager, "Anatomy of the Aftermath of Cover-Ups," pp. 28–31.
53. Nager, recollections of a case that involved him as a consultant.
54. Willard B. Gregory, in a speech to the Orange County Chapter, Public Relations Society of America, January 1980.
55. Ibid.
56. Schmoll and Santley, "Public Relations Plan for Emergencies."
57. Ibid., pp. 20–23.
58. Robert L. Barbour, "Guidelines for Drawing Up Public Relations Emergency Disaster Plans" and "Who Does What in Emergency Public Relations," in Tips and Tactics Supplement to PR Reporter, November 28 and December 12, 1977, respectively.
59. Philip Lesly, ed., Lesly's Public Relations Handbook, 2nd ed. (Englewood Cliffs, N.J.: Prentice-Hall, 1978) chaps. 23, 24, and 39.
60. Paul T. Clark, correspondence to Norman R. Nager, July 28, 1981.
61. Bronson Methodist Hospital, 1981 Silver Anvil Notebook.
62. Clark, correspondence, combined with quotes from telephone conversations, July 1981.
63. Bronson 1981 Silver Anvil Notebook.
64. Clark, correspondence.
65. Bronson 1981 Silver Anvil Notebook.
66. Ibid.
67. J. Paul Lyet, "The Environment of the '80s" (tape of panel remarks, 35th PRSA National Conference, San Francisco, November 8, 1982).
68. Ibid.

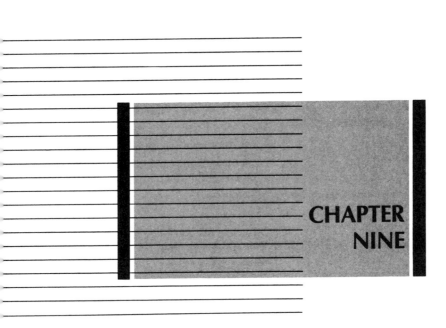

IMPLEMENTING A PR-MBO SYSTEM

On October 25, 1983, the elected leaders of the more than 2,500 public relations professionals in the Corporate Section of the Public Relations Society of America scheduled a National Conference review of "The State of the Art of MBO Applied to PR." Corporate Chair W. Thomas Duke, APR, said that the choice fit well with the transition theme of the New York convention: "We feel that the state of the art of management by objectives as applied to public relations is one of the hottest topics being discussed in the profession today, both pro and con. . . . We have to learn that we're business people and organizational people and that whatever we do fits in with the goals and objectives of our companies."

Duke said that as director of community relations for BF Goodrich, he has worked with PR-MBO in different forms, including more recently as "our own system with some of the same techniques of MBO but adapted as guidelines with more flexibility. . . . You can apply MBO to public relations just as to any other system."[1]

A TIME FOR DECISION

The time has come for decision on applying MBO to PR and *implementing PR-MBO as your system* where you work.

A natural question to ask is: How do I begin? The best counsel we can give is to advise you to explore several questions suggested by the literature of business management and grounded in experience in implementing MBO and its public relations equivalent, PR-MBO. The first question relates to the strength of your personal decision to work with an MBO system: *How committed are you to PR-MBO?*

Degree of Commitment Predicts Success

The MBO literature, actual cases, and work with PR-MBO in the field support the stand of business executives who say that the single best predictor of success in implementing PR-MBO is the *degree of commitment* you bring to it. To practice public relations under a management system of objectives is hard work. PR-MBO cannot be decided upon in a Monday afternoon meeting and be in place by Friday. Recall from Chapters 2 and 3 that PR-MBO is a complete management system and that it takes a lot of time and energy to ensure its success. The success of organizations and departments that have implemented MBO seems to be in direct proportion to the effort they put into it.

In making your decision and gauging the depth of your commitment to determine the value of your investment in PR-MBO, consider the counsel of opinion leaders in the public relations profession and the changing expectations of chief executive officers. Then weigh the potential benefits and the costs of investing the capital of your time and energies into implementing such a system.

A MANAGERIAL CHALLENGE FROM WITHIN

One of the greatest forces for change comes from within the profession itself. Delegates to the National Assembly of the Public Relations Society of America broke 35 years of tradition to adopt a statement that makes clear the trend toward management by results, management by evaluation, management by action, management by planning—in short, public relations management by objective.

PRSA's Statement on Public Relations

The preamble to the November 1982 position paper that won the unanimous endorsement of the elected leaders of 11,000 professionals reiterates the ideals, mission, and role expressed in so many earlier attempts to define the place of public relations persons in society and business.

The body of the statement, which follows, goes *beyond traditional visions to prescriptions for rising to the demands of hardening public relations practice as objectives-oriented, research-based, evaluation-responsive, planned management.*

The national assembly adopted the statement with emphasis on the management function. Note particularly the references to goals, objectives, ongoing research and evaluation, actions supportive of employers and their publics, and all the planning, budgeting, analytical work, and follow-through.

Public relations helps our complex, pluralistic society to reach decisions and function more effectively by contributing to mutual understanding among groups and institutions. It serves to bring private and public policies into harmony.

Public relations serves a wide variety of institutions in society such as business, trade unions, government agencies, voluntary associations, foundations, hospitals and educational and religious institutions. To achieve their goals, these institutions must develop effective relationships with many different audiences or publics such as employees, members, customers, local communities, shareholders and other institutions, and with society at large.

The managements of institutions need to understand the attitudes and values of their publics in order to achieve institutional goals. The goals themselves are shaped by the external environment. The public relations practitioner acts as a counselor to management, and as a mediator, helping to translate private aims into reasonable, publicly acceptable policy and action.

As a management function, public relations encompasses the following:

• Anticipating, analyzing and interpreting public opinion, attitudes and issues which impact, for good or ill, on the operations and plans of the organization.

• Counseling management at all levels in the organization with regard to policy decisions, courses of action and communication, taking into account their public ramifications and the organization's social or citizenship responsibilities.

• Researching, conducting and evaluating, on a continuing basis, programs of action and communication to achieve informed public understanding necessary to the success of an organization's aims. These may include marketing, financial, fund raising, employee, community or government relations and other programs.

• Planning and implementing the organization's efforts to influence or change public policy.

• Setting objectives, planning, budgeting, recruiting and training staff, developing facilities—in short, *managing* the resources needed to perform all of the above.

Examples of the knowledge that may be required in the professional practice of public relations include communication arts, psychology, social psychology, sociology, political science, economics and the principles of management and ethics. Technical knowledge and skills are required for opinion research, public issues analysis, media relations, direct mail, institutional advertising, publications, movie/video productions, special events, speeches and presentations.

In helping to define and implement policy, the public relations practitioner utilizes a variety of professional communication skills and plays an integrative role both within the organization and between the organization and the external environment.[2]

A MANAGERIAL CHALLENGE FROM THE TOP

Samuel Armacost, an international trendsetter in management style as the 43-year-old head of the world's largest banking institution, sounded a similar theme in his challenge at the opening plenary session of the November 1982 PRSA National Conference.

Armacost, Bank of America chief executive officer, said that he and his colleagues "fully acknowledge and expect managerial competence" from public relations officers and "depend upon your advice."[3]

Moreover, the CEO told nearly 2,000 professionals, educators, and students that financial executives now have higher expectations of public relations officers:

They can and they do expect you to find *objective measures* to help them allocate finite resources and precious financial and human resources across your activities and other required corporate activities in a meaningful and constructive way. This is management indeed![4]

And the Bank of America CEO appealed for efforts toward greater mutual understanding and cooperation: "You and I are going to have to cooperate and we're going to have to understand each other a lot better than we have in the past if we are going to go forward."

As you make your decision on whether and how to begin, keep in mind the value of PR-MBO as a system that earns respect for public relations officers and places them in position to work more closely and effectively with other members of the management team.

"Imperfect Alignment" Challenge

Craig E. Aronoff of Georgia State University and Otis W. Baskin of the University of Houston stressed the importance of the pragmatics of planning for public relations effectiveness in their 1983 *Public Relations* book.

> Public relations efforts often fail because of communication breakdowns, occurring not between the organization and its publics, but between public relations practitioners and other managers within the organization. The cause of these breakdowns can frequently be traced to an imperfect alignment between the public relations planning process and the planning done in the rest of the organization. These misunderstandings can usually be prevented if public relations practitioners analyze their organization's management as carefully as they do any other audience. Planning documents are messages prepared to communicate the needs and potential contributions of the public relations unit to other segments of the organization. Therefore, when we plan we must learn to do so using the terms and methods common to organizational management.[5]

PR-MBO BENEFITS

Even if your organization is not using management by objectives, you may find it of value in your professional development to learn, practice, and advocate the adoption of PR-MBO. The personal benefits can con-

tribute to your professional growth. The challenge, however, will be to involve others in PR-MBO. The process really works most effectively when objectives are mutually established and pursued by public relations and top management and when it gains widespread participation and support. Four of the most important benefits follow. They appeal particularly to members of management with responsibility for public relations.

BETTER MANAGEMENT OF TIME

One of the most pressing needs of any professional is to find the time "to do everything that needs to be done." Actually, PR-MBO *would help you to find the time to do only what is important*, because, as Robert R. Updegraff pointed out: "Time has three dimensions—hours, energy, and money. If we waste one, we waste others."[6]

PR-MBO means, then, that *every effort is directed toward results* and that before any activity is begun, the objective is clearly stated. This helps you avoid time-consuming activity that yields relatively little while making prohibitive the investment of time in researching, planning, developing, evaluating, and improving upon what you find to be more important.

FEWER UNEXPECTED CRISES

By detecting a potential problem early, you have a chance to direct resources and energy to divert it or lessen its impact and thus *avoid operating in a "management by crisis" mode.*

Because of its futures orientation, PR-MBO helps you anticipate events. PR-MBO's heavy emphasis on feedback also gives you a better chance to get the information early and take action.

NO DILUTION OF EFFORT

Because of the nature of the job, it is easy to become burdened with so many activities that your effectiveness and creativity may be impaired. Typically, when others are unaware of your precise role and priority of objectives, new task after new task is assigned or requested. And few of the more routine, demanding tasks seem to go away.

Nevertheless, with a clear set of objectives for a specific time period, it is easier for you to show that you do not have the resources to take on any more assignments. If you are told that the latest assignment is "highest priority," then you can show written or graphic evidence of other mutually agreed upon high priorities and either make a case for investment of more resources or redistribution of activities.

BETTER JOB DESCRIPTION

Often the role of the public relations department is unclear to top management. Too often, as indicated by reports in such business publications as *Management Review, Business Week, Wall Street Journal,* and *Fortune,* it is viewed by those unfamiliar with the profession as a publicity factory with a firehouse attached.

When goals and objectives are written jointly by you and your executives, you have an opportunity to direct your energies toward work you—and they—believe important. At the same time, this allows you to educate others about the realities of your public relations practice and what you contribute to the organization. The result is greater job satisfaction and a chance to become a more integral part of the management team.

INTRODUCING PR-MBO

With a strong commitment to investing in PR-MBO and a firm grasp on the principles, you should proceed with the implementation phase and ask another important question: Will PR-MBO be introduced properly?

TIMING AND CLIMATE FOR CHANGE

Your answer to the question on introduction first needs to address the issue of timing. Any organization will have particular times of turmoil and instability. Some of this may be seasonal and recurring. If so, you would pick the most appropriate time possible for beginning PR-MBO.

If other persons or departments will be involved with the implementation of PR-MBO, it is important that they are fully aware of what you are doing. This is particularly true in the case of executives to whom you report and people in your own department.

It is not unusual for an objectives-type system to be viewed with a degree of uncertainty or even anxiety by persons who feel reluctant about any major change in managerial operation. Some individuals may worry about the *change of emphasis from working hard to working for achievement of results.* This can bring out feelings of insecurity. You will want to stress that PR-MBO is designed to help all persons in the organization get the most out of their own efforts individually and as part of the greater whole. You must reduce, if not eliminate, fears so your efforts to implement PR-MBO do not meet heavy resistance.

This means that the proper climate must be established in the introductory phase:

1. Plan (more than in the sense of just scheduling time) *face-to-face* discussions with those who will operate under a set of objectives.

2. Furnish participants with *background reading* materials. You may wish to have portions marked by a highlighter or accompanied by marginal notes to make them more relevant and useful to the readers.

3. During the introductory phase, conduct several informal workshops on the principles of PR-MBO. This is where *you function as change agent or trainer in helping others.*

4. *Focus on how to build trust.* In the successful implementation of PR-MBO, trust is a necessary ingredient. If your organization or department has a high degree of trust among employees, then your job as trainer is easier. But if trust is low, then the workshop atmosphere is even more critical.

5. Motivate (and that includes helping others to motivate themselves) *active participation* in the PR-MBO process by as many persons as possible in whatever nucleus you establish for implementing the system.

6. Begin the process of motivation of internal publics with analysis of their characteristics (or frameworks of reference) and their objectives (their perceptions of what they need from their employer and communication). Part of the strategy in motivating active participation lies in *communicating what PR-MBO will do for them as individuals,* as well as for their department and the organization as a whole.

7. If you think the introductory phase is too complex for one public relations professional to handle alone, consider bringing in an outside expert in PR-MBO. A consultant can offer guidelines, suggestions, and support for preparing the climate for PR-MBO.

8. During the introduction, anticipate the concern that PR-MBO may mean more paperwork for everybody. Done properly, PR-MBO will actually serve as a stimulus for face-to-face communication among peers. Stress to participants that PR-MBO *generates dialogue among people and paperwork arises only to verify what was spoken. The emphasis on oral communication could reduce paperwork and red tape in the long run.*

The introduction phase is critical for a successful implementation of PR-MBO. Active participation among all those involved should generate a climate of trust. This leads to the next question: *Where do I begin the implementation?*

WHERE TO BEGIN PR-MBO

It is important to understand that your organization does not have to have a formal PR-MBO system in place or even another department operating under MBO. You, as an individual, can be the actual beginning point or, just as easily, so can your public relations department. Our beginning point in this book was the individual public relations professional. Throughout this book, the system was designed to begin with you as change agent. Obviously, if your organization operates under some form of MBO, then you will start at a different point in the implementation cycle. If so, chances are you have already had the opportunity to write objectives and present them to management. If you are not operating in such an organization, then PR-MBO will begin with you.

FORTIFYING YOURSELF

If you would like to fortify yourself with additional background reading on MBO implementation as a general management system for business, government, or nonprofit organizations, then you should place at the top of your list the names George L. Morrisey and Dale D. McConkey. Both have written excellent books on this subject.[7]

You also may wish to check for articles on implementation strategies in the *Business Periodicals Index, F & S Index of Corporations and Industries*, and a microfiche listing called the *Business Index*.

Consider reviewing the Notes at the ends of chapters in this book to study the sources named. Also explore such bibliographies as the several annotated *Public Relations Bibliography* editions available from *Public Relations Review*, through Communication Research Associates, 7100 Baltimore Boulevard, Suite 500, College Park, Maryland 20740.

3 BEGINNING POINTS

When you initiate the implementation of PR-MBO, you may select from three common options for beginning points:

1. You may begin with the entire public relations department. Under this approach, all public relations employees operate under objectives. This applies to everyone from the vice president through clerical staff.

2. You may have the option to start with one section or level of the public relations department. The focus is on one unit or section, such as professionals and support staff working with specific publics. For example, PR-MBO may begin with specialists who work in governmental affairs.

3. You may begin with staff members working on a specific project or with a particular client. This is a good place to start, provided the project or account is large enough to require a significant amount of staff, planning, resources, and complexity.

Advantages and disadvantages are associated with each beginning point. If you wish to go further than the discussion in the rest of this section, you will find an expanded treatment of this topic by McConkey.[8]

Beginning with the Department

Experience cited in the literature and reported in field research indicates that successful implementation is usually related to the speed with which it was completed. Many implementation case reports suggest that haste indeed makes waste. *It appears to be far better to go slowly with the implementation, making sure everyone understands PR-MBO as a complete management system.*

This suggests that the beginning point of the entire department is the most difficult and has the least probability of success. This tends to be so because it takes much more effort to persuade and teach PR-MBO to the many employees involved in a large department than to the relative few in a section. Some individuals may find operating under objectives difficult and confusing and therefore may require more time to digest it. Remember that *PR-MBO is an action-oriented way of managing, and you do not want action until all participants understand what is expected of them.*

You do find some advantages to implementing PR-MBO all at once. If successful, you can be operating under the objectives approach much sooner. Also, you achieve *more immediate involvement of all employees* and can *reduce your training time through less duplication of training sessions.* There is a possibility of a visibly large impact on attainment of results because the entire public relations department operates under PR-MBO.

Not only is beginning with the entire department the most difficult starting point because it requires more time, but it also requires more resources in terms of energy, materials, and consultant services.

Attitudes of employees toward objectives (are they eager to try the system?) *and the degree of previous participative management style leading to a climate of trust directly influence your success rate.*

Beginning with One Section

The primary advantage of beginning with only one section in the public relations department is that the implementation can be *focused more sharply.*

In essence, one section of the public relations department serves as a model or prototype for implementing PR-MBO. The idea is to *make it successful there and then move on to other sections* in the department. This is a useful approach for a good-sized agency or large public relations department with diverse operations. For example, if PR-MBO is effective for the section dealing with governmental affairs, then the next step is to try it in another section.

Other advantages include the opportunity to demonstrate the feasibility and advantages of the objectives approach to other sections. This beginning point also provides a chance to involve the generation of professionals who have experience with PR-MBO. *This group can then teach others in the department.*

Disadvantages include the possibility of selecting an inappropriate section to begin the implementation. It is important to *select the section that has the best possible chance for success.* Certainly you will *not* want to begin with a section that looks doubtful under the premise that "if I can get it to work here, it will work everywhere else with ease."

Consider the danger that the objectives created for such a section may be unique and not mesh with those of the other parts of your department later. Ultimately, the entire department must adopt PR-MBO, and thus *all objectives must support one another.* There may be a tendency when working with only one section to lose sight of this systems concept.

Beginning with a Specific Project

This beginning point usually involves the least number of participants. You limit it to persons working with a specific project or particular client. Normally, such a beginning implementation point involves at least three other practitioners. *The small group allows for a healthy exchange of goals and objectives.* However, it is *not* a requirement. Actually, you can begin with only yourself, and one project or one client.

Public relations professionals who have begun at the specific project level have concluded that a major advantage of this approach is that the implementation can proceed on a carefully managed narrow front. There are fewer peers to train and coordinate and the *chances for error are minimized.* In addition, the opportunity for extensive in-depth participant understanding is maximized. A more gradual, step-by-step process may be preferable to some individuals.

Should errors arise (and they always do to some extent), they are limited to a small area of the total public relations department. This means that *mistakes are not multiplied* by others, and rumors of problems in implementation are not so likely to spread to other sections. Such rumors, whether correct or partly so, can spoil the climate for implementing PR-MBO beyond your project.

Disadvantages to this approach include that it will consume more time and require duplicate training in other sections. And in weighing the pros and cons for the selection of a beginning point, you should include the disadvantage that what is learned in one area may be too limited and not easily applied to other projects or clients.

Related to this disadvantage is the *possible lack of communication between the implementation group (or individual) and other levels of management.* Sooner or later, more narrow objectives developed at the project level have to *integrate with the broader objectives of the department, as well as other parts of the organization.*

POINT OF ORIGIN: 3 OPTIONS

Regardless of which beginning point you choose, another basic decision must flow from your analysis of the next question: *Who writes the first objective?*

After much thought, you decide on the beginning point for your PR-MBO implementation. Then you have to decide who will actually begin writing goals and objectives. Should you initiate the process or should someone else?

Generally, three options are open to you. Goals and objectives may originate at the top, bottom, or middle.

If the *top approach* is used, goals and objectives are written first by the person in charge (of the department, section, or particular project) and passed down to other employees. The direction is set by the manager in charge. Other persons are expected to use this as a guide when writing their own goals and objectives.

In the *bottom approach,* goals and objectives are written first by staff persons without supervisory responsibility and then passed *up* the chain of command to the highest manager. The expectation is that persons at each level will use the objectives passed up to enhance their own objectives. The writing process here is just the opposite from the top approach, in which goals and objectives move from the general (broad) to the specific (narrow). In the bottom approach, they move from the specific to the general.

As a third option, you may choose the so-called *middle approach.* Actually, goals and objectives do *not* begin in the middle but are written by both managerial and nonsupervisory employees (top and bottom) *simultaneously* and then spread to the middle of the system. "Middle" is used here to indicate the rest of the entire department or section.

Considerations in Choosing Among Options

As you discern, all three options for the actual writing of goals and objectives present advantages and disadvantages.

Top approach advantages and disadvantages

In the top approach, a major advantage is found in the broad, futuristic perspective of the goals and objectives. Top managers tend to be positioned well by their experience and access to privileged information.

Another advantage is that the goals and objectives have authority behind them and suggest a serious tone to the PR-MBO effort. In other words, *if top management is willing to get involved from the beginning, then the department can expect to operate under PR-MBO.*

Disadvantages to beginning at the top include the possibility that staff members may feel that something has been imposed on them, and this can decrease enthusiasm for PR-MBO. Second, some employees may try to guess what top management wants to hear and then feed back objectives that look like mere copies of the original. What is missing here is open, honest dialogue between manager and staff member.

Bottom approach advantages and disadvantages

Several advantages may be found in beginning the writing of objectives at the nonsupervisory level. For instance, the goals and objectives may reflect the realism of day-to-day operations in getting the job done. Although these objectives may not be broad, they should reflect the necessary details of completing a task. A second advantage comes from the *feeling of individuals at this level of actually participating in the PR-MBO program rather than having it imposed on them by top management.*

Beginning at the bottom poses risks that the goals and objectives will be too narrow to actually give sufficient guidance for effective operation of the public relations department. Related to this is the tendency for objectives written at this level to be too limited to the present, rather than be oriented to the future. This probably stems from the daily concern or necessity of completing tasks by deadline.

Middle approach advantages and disadvantages

Advantages to using the middle approach emerge from the meeting and probable blending of goals and objectives coming from two different perspectives. *Out of a healthy clash of ideas should evolve goals and objectives that contain the concerns of both public relations manager and staff member.* A shared perspective for operating under PR-MBO is possible. Another advantage is the feeling that PR-MBO can become a relatively democratic form of managing as differences are discussed and compromises are reached.

A serious disadvantage is that sometimes compromise cannot be reached between different perspectives, and chaos may prevail. Also, the middle is likely to be the most time-consuming of the three approaches because more employees are involved and you have to develop communication and planning for compromises.

Before you turn to a logical question suggested by the trait of public relations professionals to take the initiative by becoming the first to explore change, consider the counsel of Paul Watzlawick of Stanford University and his co-authors in their discussion of "utopia" problems:

> Change can be implemented effectively by focusing on minimal, concrete goals, going slowly, and proceeding step by step, rather than strongly promoting vast and vague targets with whose desirability nobody would take issue, but whose attainability is a different question altogether.[9]

A FOURTH OPTION: YOU

Ideally, the next question should not have to arise. Realistically, you may discover that none of the three options you have just reviewed for a beginning point prove feasible. Some public relations professionals create a fourth option by asking: *What if I am the beginning point?*

In special circumstances, you may decide to begin PR-MBO quietly with yourself as the only participant. This decision may be a sound one for several reasons.

You may decide to do this by yourself *so that you can become familiar with PR-MBO before asking others to join.* Or your executive may show little interest in PR-MBO initially, and you may decide to become the experimental volunteer for implementation. If you are successful, then you have *persuasive evidence* to support the feasibility of PR-MBO in your particular set of circumstances.

By becoming a private model for PR-MBO, you have a unique opportunity to master the objectives system.

A good place to begin is to set some professional goals and objectives concerning how effectively you do your job. Think about what you would like to accomplish during the next year. Then set goals and write objectives as discussed in earlier chapters. Establish evaluation criteria, and you are on the way to operating under PR-MBO.

You may decide to gain expertness in a particular area of public relations. PR-MBO can easily be used as a framework for gaining knowledge and experience.

Or you may decide to apply PR-MBO to a specific project for which you are responsible. Again, you alone decide to meet the requirements of the project through the use of goals and objectives. The final format as originally called for stays the same, but you have the satisfaction of knowing the utilitarian role played by PR-MBO during the project. *Professionals have found this a very pragmatic use of PR-MBO and an excellent way of utilizing and learning the approach.*

An unusual but perfectly acceptable place to begin your efforts can be at a trouble spot. Simply take some public relations problem that has been particularly troublesome for you and apply PR-MBO. Through goals and objectives, you may be able to focus more clearly on what has to be done to reach a solution. For example, PR-MBO may help you break any tendency of "doing more of the same" so common to repetitive problems, or help you do something differently and more effectively when attacking the problem.

Nathaniel H. Sperber, retired CEO of the agency bearing his name, and Otto Lerbinger of Boston University provide in their 1982 book pragmatic assistance in complementing PR-MBO with techniques for managing a wide range of projects and problem solving activities. *Manager's Public Relations Handbook* offers 56 mini-chapters with detailed planning checklists. [10]

PR-MBO AND "ORDERS OF REALITY"

By carefully reading and answering the questions in this chapter, you should have a more comfortable feeling toward implementing objectives. You previously learned the importance of making your public relations objectives specific so they can be measured. And you have reviewed several beginning points or strategies for implementing PR-MBO. Thoughtful and complete answers to the questions on implementation should point you toward the best strategy for implementing PR-MBO in your organization.

That strategy should take into account what a futurist termed "orders of reality" as he counseled public relations professionals on implementation of PR-MBO. Hank E. Koehn, vice president in charge of futures research for Security Pacific National Bank, suggested the heading for this section as the title for a chapter in *PR-MBO*. In his interview, Koehn said:

> PR-MBO is a fine concept if you separate the concept from . . . the reality as MBO is sometimes practiced:
> Although MBO is based on a participative management model in which different levels of management are supposed to come in with open minds to mutually determine objectives, the model of appropriateness of what they will accept from their employees may be predetermined. . . .[11]

That works both ways, of course. The public relations manager may approach objectives setting sessions with a higher executive with a less than flexible agenda. And when public relations managers themselves discuss objectives with members of their staffs, it may be tempting to predetermine what will be accepted.

Not to be discounted is the extension of benefits to other members of the public relations staff, including secretaries and interns, who may increase productivity, creativity, and conscientiousness as they propose and follow through on their own objectives in support of public relations department objectives.

Koehn recommended *an honest participative management model of MBO to develop ideas for objectives and to create initiative for follow-through.* He said this works by making those who deliver the results part of the process in deciding what should be achieved.[12]

And in a subsequent speech to public relations professionals, the futurist reviewed some of the projections of Alvin Toffler in *The Third Wave*.[13] Koehn said the United States is trying to shift to "high tech industrial," and he projected that 76 percent of the population would *not* be in manufacturing or farming by the year 2000.[14]

He said the country already is "simultaneously and dangerously" moving into a postliterate phase in which people think in terms of visual images rather than the written word, a phase in which the barriers between education, information, and entertainment are being dissolved and in which the focus is shifting from sequential communication to simultaneous. And this presents a challenge to public relations professionals as part of the management team:

> The '80s are the beginning of the overture to the 21st century. Many will be too little informed about too much.
> Are you prepared for it? You're in a very powerful position. . . .[15]

To prepare for it and strengthen that position, you may wish to begin by reviewing such literature as *Megatrends*[16] or reading an overview in the October 1982 issue of a publication named *Inc.*[17]

Then consider several strategies for involvement of your executive in the PR-MBO process and for gaining additional respect as a vital member of the management team.

INVOLVING THE CEO

You may start the process of involving your chief executive officer in implementation of PR-MBO with an investigation of the goals, policies, and objectives of the board of directors, CEO, and other members of top management as they perceive them. Sometimes the approach may be to modify the perception of reality, rather than reality per se. At times, even top management may have unclear or contradictory purposes in mind.

STRATEGIES FOR INVOLVEMENT

Gaining Access to Reports, Proposals

Gaining access to the CEO's or board's own reports on organizational goals and the objectives for the fiscal year will allow you, as public relations officer, to study style, approach, and substance in gaining a prerequisite understanding for developing and polishing your own. It will be especially helpful if the person to whom you report shares with you copies of past proposals and year-end progress reports.

Similarly, because public relations and other parts of the organization are interdependent, because public relations programs support the objectives of other divisions, and because resources in any company or institution are finite, it proves beneficial to secure and study copies of other departments' proposals and reports.

Interviewing as a Strategy

If others do not put their goals, objectives, and progress reports on paper, you may have the opportunity to use the interviewing skills developed by most public relations professionals.

Even if written documentation is available, interviewing others on their approaches, desires, goals, objectives, and interests may be valuable in other ways:

1. The mere seeking out of information on what board, upper management, and other departments want and achieve and how they go about it will speak well of public relations as a member of the organizational and management team.

2. It helps public relations counselors to plan and develop priorities when they investigate how they best fit into the whole operation.

3. Mutual understanding may be developed through interviewing. This is done by weaving into the interview questions on how public relations may support the purposes and meet the needs of the other person's part of the organization. And it is done by weaving in, when and where appropriate, comments on what public relations can do—or has done—to help.

Following Through with Progress Reports

After you have worked out objectives and priorities to the mutual satisfaction of all, public relations follow-through in the form of monthly and annual progress reports may reinforce your reputation with your executive while maintaining top management involvement in the process.

Objectives with monthly follow-through progress reports remind management of what the public relations counselor contributes to the organization. So do annual reports on results achieved. They show how the public relations professional, with a record of achieving objectives, proposes to accomplish more in the future.

PR-MBO also enhances the credibility of the public relations staff to other members of the management team who operate from similar results-oriented, data-based perspectives.

PR-MBO breathes life into the principle that public relations programs should include management involvement. You may secure commitment, understanding, and support, including involvement of other members of the management team, by making it clear that the programs back up key organizational objectives and pay dividends on investments made in public relations functions.

RCA BOARD CHAIRMAN AND PR-MBO

When Dr. Thornton F. Bradshaw, chairman of the board of RCA, moved to New York as CEO of the multibillion-dollar communications conglomerate, he took with him a reputation as an executive who devoted much of his time and creative energies to public relations in the classic sense of public relations as a management function complete with goals, objectives, research, and action.

Earlier in this book, a case study featured the issues identification program that was part of Bradshaw's legacy when he left the presidency of ARCO in mid-1981.

As indicated in his 1982 report at the annual meeting of RCA shareholders, Bradshaw turned around the communications conglomerate and set it on a new course within his first 10 months of leadership.[18] In so doing he exemplified, as well as communicated, the application of a number of PR-MBO principles and practices.

One indicator of his effectiveness has been increased investor confidence in the value of RCA. Although a share of common stock sold for as low as 15 ¾ in 1982, on the day Bradshaw addressed the 1982 meeting of shareholders, the stock closed at 20 ⅞. Shares were to trade as high as 27 in stock market rallies during the year.

Bradshaw places strong confidence in what he calls "real professionals" in a statement prepared for this book:

> Public relations is extremely important to a major corporation. It is vital that people know what the facts are about a company and that they do not deal with something less than the facts.
> When you deal with less than the facts, you deal with rumors and the entire company becomes a rumor mill. Then morale starts slipping.

So it is very important to bring in real professionals in the field of public relations and make sure that they are part of the CEO's inner circle.[19]

In the section that follows, review the Bradshaw address to RCA shareholders with particular attention to where he directly and indirectly refers to goals, objectives, priorities, research, action, strategies, planning of resources, communication, and evaluation.

RCA

63rd Annual Meeting of Shareholders 1982

RCA REPORT TO SHAREHOLDERS

Good morning and welcome to the 63rd annual meeting of RCA shareholders. This is my first meeting as your Chairman, and I look forward to your questions, comments, and suggestions during the discussion period.

When I assumed the job as RCA's Chief Executive Officer last July, it was with great expectations and high enthusiasm. Those expectations and that enthusiasm remain undiminished. My belief in RCA and the men and women who make it one of the most promising business enterprises in America is as strong today as it was when I first moved into David Sarnoff's former office.

I quickly realized, however, that there was a considerable difference between RCA's promise and its reality. Closing that gap became my first priority. As I immersed myself in RCA's operations and traditions, it became clear to me that the company had gotten away from its roots—roots that are intertwined with the history of the electronics industry. This company shaped the radio industry in the 1920s. It formed the first national broadcasting network. It introduced black-and-white and color television. And, in the early days of the electronics industry, RCA research became a driving force, accounting for nearly one-fourth of all private electronic research in the United States. Of course, RCA had its failures, but it had more successes than most companies—as long as it stuck to the things it knew best.

Somewhere along the line, the company became enamored with diversification. It was the trendy thing to do, and many companies—not just RCA—believed that the path to improved profits lay in acquiring companies far removed from their basic businesses. Pretty soon, our executives were managing not only electronics and communications businesses, but frozen chickens, carpeting, and greeting cards as well. Not that there is anything wrong with frozen chickens or carpets. The companies that RCA acquired were fine companies. But our technically oriented managers, a basic resource of this company, had to learn the fundamentals of entirely new industries, and catching up on these fundamentals became increasingly difficult as economic conditions changed radically.

The underlying assumptions of RCA's diversification program—a strong economy and relatively low interest rates—proved to be way off the mark. In mid-1980, the nation's economy began to soften. Six months later, we were in a deep recession, and interest rates were at record levels. Demand for many of the products and services of our acquired companies declined.

The impact of the economic conditions hit RCA's balance sheet hard. When I joined RCA, the company's short-term debt totaled $1.3 billion. An increase of just one percentage point in the prime rate resulted in a decrease of $13 million in pretax profits. Employee morale had been shaken as a consequence of the turbulence and turnover in top management. Several of RCA's key businesses were in trouble. NBC was in turmoil. Our picture-tube operations were squeezed by a combination of reduced demand and overcapacity. A recession was cutting deeply into Hertz's car-rental and truck leasing operations.

These factors combined to make 1981 one of the most difficult years in RCA's history. My immediate goals were to contain RCA's problem areas, chart new directions for the company, and strengthen its balance sheet. This was a full and challenging agenda that only could be approached with a sense of urgency and an eye toward lasting results. . . .

During the next few months, I worked closely with senior management in an intensive review of operations. Our objective was to clear out those business activities whose prospects for growth did not justify their high operating costs. . . .

So RCA ended the year with sales of approximately $8 billion. Earnings were down to $54 million from the $315 million reported in 1980. After payments for preferred and preference dividends, the company lost $.19 a share of common stock.

It would serve no useful purpose for me to say that RCA's earnings would have been higher, for example, had our short-term debt been lower. RCA got into difficulties in 1981 largely as the result of a diversification program that exposed its balance sheet to the corrosive effects of external economic conditions, high interest rates, continuing inflation, and a deepening recession.

In response to those economic conditions, we initiated a comprehensive cost-reduction program. During the latter part of 1981 and the first quarter of 1982, RCA reduced its work force by nearly 1,000 jobs. It extended the interval between merit increases, froze senior-management salaries, and limited hirings. We eliminated 103 corporate staff positions and reduced floor space at our 30 Rockefeller Plaza headquarters by some 66,000 square feet. These and related cost-reduction measures held the cost of our operations in the first quarter to about the same level as in the first quarter of 1981.

The paring down of our corporate staff headquarters has prompted some to say that RCA was preparing to move out of New York City. This is not so. As long as I am Chairman, there will be a glowing RCA logo at the top of 30 Rock. This building is, and will continue to be, the site of RCA's corporate headquarters. I don't think I can say it more emphatically than that.

In March, the Board of Directors took a further step toward conserving capital by reducing the quarterly dividend on common stock from $.45 to $.225 a share. This reduction in the dividend payout will save an additional $68 million this year. I realize the hardship imposed on shareholders and employees by these measures. It is particularly difficult for those retirees who rely on dividends as the primary source of income. But the Board believes that it is in the ultimate best interests of shareholders and employees alike to take those difficult actions now so that we can strengthen the Corporation's performance for the future. . . .

Now, I'd like to turn more specifically to plans for the future and what has been done to get them under way. One of my first priorities as Chairman was to evaluate RCA's current mix of businesses in terms of the emerging new communications, electronics, and information technologies. Major studies were made to determine where the new technologies are heading, which ones will dominate, and how RCA could tailor its future to meet them. After all, we still have our technological base of 6,200 scientists and engineers. In 1980, for example, more patents were issued for RCA inventions than for those of any other company in America except General Electric, more even than for the Bell System.

So it was a question of refocusing on our core businesses, getting back to our roots—and that is what we are doing now. Our recently completed studies convince us of the validity of this decision. We know where we are going. We have a strategic concept of what the future holds for the markets that our industry serves.

Our first conclusion is that the electronics and entertainment industry is poised for the greatest growth era in its history. The decade ahead will see a major change in the way entertainment and information are produced and delivered to the American home. All the new electronic media and services—communications satellites, video cassettes, video discs, teletext, cable, video games—are even now beginning to shift the consumer's viewing and spending habits. And this shift in viewing and spending will accelerate. RCA is ideally positioned to participate in these emerging growth markets.

Now, what kind of growth do we expect? Last year there were 80 million television homes in the United States. We see this population growing to 96 million by the end of the decade and home viewership increasing from 47 hours a week to 54 hours a week. If you think that's a lot to expect, bear in mind that in homes that subscribe to pay television today the set is on more than 54 hours. By 1990, we expect that 60 percent of all television households will subscribe to cable and that roughly three-quarters of those will opt for paid programming. The implications of this growth for the entertainment industry are absolutely enormous.

Last year, the total video market—broadcasting, cable, VCRs [video cassette recorders], discs, games—accounted for $20 billion in revenues. Cable's share of that was about $4 billion. By 1990, the total video market will generate $70 billion in revenues, and cable's share will rise to $28 billion. . . .

We've also set our sights on a second growth market—telecommunications. In telecommunications, we see an era of new opportunities and new challenges as a result of changing government regulation and technological advances. Deregulation is erasing the distinctions between domestic and international services, between voice and non-voice, between communications and data processing. New technology can integrate voice, record, and data services and can transmit them at higher speeds and with better quality. It can allow higher frequency transmissions, thus opening up frequency space for new services and expansion of established services.

The rise of data processing and office automation is also stimulating the need for greater communications capacity and new non-voice services. They represent an emerging business that we believe will grow at a rate of more than 45 percent a year.

So there are two major growth areas—entertainment, with its related electronics and communications; and telecommunications, standing on its own. Both of these areas correspond neatly to RCA's basic strengths and competences.

What, then, is RCA's strategy? Our strategy is twofold. We will consider joint ventures and acquisitions, depending upon prevailing financial and market conditions. We also plan to strengthen our core electronics and communications businesses through a phased redeployment of the company's assets.

As a part of this strategy, we are currently . . . considering selling other of our nonelectronic businesses [that] are not compatible with an RCA whose future lies in electronics and communications. . . . We did, at one time, consider the possible sale of C.I.T. Financial, but the consideration was short-lived.

C.I.T. continues to perform impressively. Its debt is not a part of RCA's balance sheet, and its prospects for growth are too promising for it not to remain a part of our portfolio of businesses.

In the weeks and months ahead, RCA will make the transition

from a diversified organization to one tightly focused on its newly defined core businesses. Steps have already been taken toward creating a new organizational structure.

The new look at RCA will also extend to the makeup for the Board of Directors. The Nominating Committee of the Board has indicated its desire to add several new outside directors to the present seven. It will seek individuals of national stature whose knowledge and skills in differing areas will contribute to the policymaking process of the Board. . . .

I'm also very sensitive to the issue of employee morale at RCA. The morale of any organization depends upon its leadership. People must be confident that an organization's leadership knows where it is going and that there is a place for people within the organization's goals. And, finally, there must be evidence of success. Without these key factors, morale is likely to be low. . . .

Our performance over the remainder of the year will depend in large measure on the nation's economy. We are faced with a deep recession and continuing high interest rates, and no one can predict with certainty when the recovery will begin to take shape. But the recovery will come—and with it a resurgence of RCA's prospects. Everything is in place. We have a plan, we have the goals, and we have the people. Now we must get on with the job of restoring magic to those letters "RCA."

Thank you.[20]

PR-MBO SELF-TEST

1. What were Bradshaw's objectives in developing the style and points of his speech?

2. What corporate objectives did these support?

3. Who were the primary and secondary publics he was addressing? (Consider the coverage of the meeting by financial media and circulation of the reprint of the speech as well as the persons who actually attended.) Include publics and subpublics you would target.

4. What methods would you counsel for evaluation of his communication strategies, of the tools of communication employed, of the impact of the actions reported in the speech, and of the presentation itself?

5. What would you want to measure in each case?

6. What research would you have wanted to do as public relations consultant before this speech was drafted?

7. What follow-through, if any, would you program beyond arrangements for media coverage and distribution of the speech reprint in July 1982 to RCA shareholders?

8. If you could go back to when the speech was still in draft form, what counsel would you give Bradshaw on how and *why* to improve the content and style?

9. Upon what data would you base this counsel?

10. What options would you recommend for future public relations actions to support the objectives and goals he mentioned in the speech?

11. What were Bradshaw's greatest strengths in public relations actions reflected in his report?

12. What have you learned from those actions, the substance of the speech, and Bradshaw's style that would be of particular value to you as a professional?

A TIME TO UPGRADE HUMAN RELATIONS

Another question, a challenge to public relations professionals and their executives the world over, was voiced by Göran Sjöberg, 1983 president of the International Public Relations Association. He asked whether the evolution to new technologies and new strategies would lead into confusion and disorder or into upgraded human relations.

> One of the paradoxes of the communications world today is this: The Global Village means that the whole world may be reached by our message on an instant basis; but simultaneously people will be subject to such a variety of conflicting and competing messages that their picture of what is happening around them is scattered. *Multiplying the number of media available does not automatically mean multiplying understanding or sharing of ideas.*
>
> The further you get in your breakdown of target groups for your communication, the vaster the number of messages aimed directly at each individual will be! . . . The ultimate result of all this is that (the individual) might get drowned by this Operation Overkill from all communicators—and here comes the other side of the paradox: The professional communicators who want to reach people personally see to it that individuals do *not* listen to *any* of them; there are too many messengers and too many messages competing for interest. . . .

We must fight the exaggerated flow of non-essential or useless information, to reduce the noise in the communication network all over the world, so that meaningful, fruitful dialogue may make itself heard. . . . We must upgrade human dialogue and create truly confident relations among individuals, groups, and nations—based on reciprocal respect for intelligence and mutual understanding.[21]

NOTES

1. W. Thomas Duke, interview, Salt Lake City, May 13, 1983. The October 25, 1983, National Conference program for Corporate was scheduled to feature as panelists Robert A. Kelly, APR, Vice President, Public Relations and Communication, Olin Corporation; H. Darden Chambliss, Jr., APR, Senior Vice President: Aluminum Association, Inc.; Norman Nager, APR, one of the authors of this book.
2. PRSA National Assembly, transcript of adopted motion, San Francisco, November 6, 1982.
3. Samuel H. Armacost, "The Environment of the '80s" (tape of panel remarks, PRSA National Conference, San Francisco, November 8, 1982).
4. Ibid.
5. Craig E. Aronoff and Otis W. Baskin, Public Relations (St. Paul: West, 1983), p. 135.
6. Robert R. Updegraff, All the Time You Need (Englewood Cliffs, N.J.: Prentice-Hall, 1958), p. 6.
7. George L. Morrisey, Management by Objectives and Results for Business and Industry (Reading, Mass.: Addison-Wesley, 1977); and Dale D. McConkey, How to Manage by Results (New York: AMACOM, 1967).
8. Dale D. McConkey, "How to Succeed and Fail with MBO," Business Quarterly (Winter 1974), p. 60.
9. Paul Watzlawick, John H. Weakland, and Richard Fisch, Change (New York: Norton, 1974), p. 159.
10. Nathaniel H. Sperber and Otto Lerbinger, Manager's Public Relations Handbook (Reading: Mass.: Addison-Wesley, 1982). For a number of other sources of value in public relations management, please review the Notes at the ends of chapters throughout this book.
11. Hank E. Koehn, interview, Los Angeles, August 21, 1981.
12. Ibid.
13. Alvin Toffler, The Third Wave, (New York: Morrow, 1980).
14. Hank E. Koehn, in a speech to the Public Relations Society of America, Los Angeles Chapter, August 21, 1981.
15. Ibid.
16. John Naisbitt, Megatrends (New York: Warner, 1982).
17. Tom Richman, "Peering into Tomorrow," Inc., October 1982, pp. 45–48.
18. Thornton F. Bradshaw, "Chairman's Report to Stockholders" (63rd annual meet-

ing of shareholders, New York City, May 4, 1982) and shareholders' reprint, distributed by RCA Corporation, July 1982.

19. Thornton F. Bradshaw, telephone interview remarks, Dec. 21, 1982.
20. Bradshaw, "Chairman's Report," excerpted for length.
21. Göran Sjöberg, "Communication Among the Nations" (closing address, Communications Week 1983, Fullerton, California), April 29, 1983.

APPENDIX A

GLOSSARY OF RESEARCH TERMS

accidental/convenience sampling   A form of nonprobability sampling. Happenstance examples (rather than planned sampling) that include a handful or more of data that could range from good to poor representation of the population under study.

analysis of variance   Compares the differences of mean scores from three or more groups. *See* mean and ANOVA.

ANOVA   Acronym for analysis of variance, a computer program for assisting you in finding the difference of means of scores from three or more groups. *See* SPSS.

attitude   Predisposition to behavior as indicated by observation and/or responses to questions. If scientifically measured, helps predict how persons might act under circumstances presently influencing them.

average   *See* central tendency, mean, median, and mode.

baseline or benchmark   Data that measure "the way things were" at a given point in time and against which you compare future surveys or study results. This may be the first scientific survey results for a company or the "base" survey against which you measure any change after particular public relations happenings. This serves as a starting point in comparisons of attitudes or behavior over time to give early warning of dangerous trends or to monitor progress.

behavior   Observable actions; what persons *do* as opposed to what they *say* or *think* they might do. This is generally the most sought after measure of public relations effectiveness.

bias   In research sense, this may be unintentional distortion in data base or collection because of defects allowed in survey design or procedure.

census   An actual counting of all subjects or elements in the population.

central tendency   Three different measures at the center of data: mean, median, mode. One or all three may be referred to as "average," a word that may lend itself to misinterpretation.

chi square   This test of significance is used when data are assigned to categories. It is usually noted by the symbol X^2. Chi square is used to detect differences, if any, between observed (actual) frequencies and expected (theoretical) frequencies.

CIPP model   Acronym for an approach that combines four kinds of evaluation: Context, Input, Product, Process.

cluster samples   Groups or clusters of elements, such as cities or districts of cities, from which smaller samples are taken. The population is divided into clusters or groups reflecting various traits before the sample is drawn.

cohort study   Longitudinal survey in which different samples are drawn from the same population for subsequent surveys. A survey that tends to focus on a more specific population than a trend study. *See* longitudinal and trend.

comparison   A way to gauge effectiveness by analyzing changes and patterns in awareness, level of understanding, attitudinal predisposition to behavior, and actual observed behavior.

confidence level   Refers to the accuracy of a sample when drawn from the larger population. Basically a measure of how confident you are that your sample reflects the population's traits. Normally expressed as a percentage level of confidence; 95 percent usually acceptable. *See* population and sample.

construct   Conceptual building block, part of a theory.

content analysis   An observation technique for analyzing language meaning. Frequently used for examining content in news releases, media reports, speeches, videotapes, slide shows, correspondence, public relations publications, and so forth. Allows the setting of numerical values and objective measurement for descriptive or analytical ends.

control group   A group of persons similar in as many respects as possible to the experimental group in pre- and posttest studies, except that it is *not* exposed to the treatment, such as a public relations campaign, and is compared over the same before-and-after time interval with the experimental group. *See* experimental group, pretest, and posttest.

correlation   Degree of interdependence among several factors. Relationship in which reciprocity is studied.

correlation coefficient   Test of significance that examines relationship between two measures to determine if both move together in the same or different direction and with what, if any, degree of significance. The symbol for correlation coefficient is *r*.

cost-benefit ratio   Used to indicate the ratio of resources (fiscal and human) invested in a public relations program or activity compared to the benefits derived. Investment of human resources can be translated into dollars by computing the hourly costs of salary *plus* approximately another 25 percent for fringe benefits and related costs *plus* pro-rated organizational overhead.

cross-impact matrix   A futures research methodology for revealing and examining the impacts or interaction among anticipated future events for which a person or panel of experts assigns probabilities. This method typically involves use of a matrix of possible events and impacts upon one another. *See* futures.

cross-sectional survey   A survey in which data is collected at only one point in time, a one-time "photograph" of key publics. This "snapshot" of opinions reflects attitudes only on the day of survey.

data   Another word for evidence. (Data is plural; datum is singular.) In Chapter 6, data refer to information normally in numerical form that help describe, explain, or predict phenomena and that are derived from systematic observations or surveys of publics.

degree focus   As opposed to simple "for" or "against," "favorable" or "unfavorable," "positive" or "negative," "supportive" or "opposed," and similar either-or dichotomies, public relations officers increasingly focus on the degree of intensity of feeling or the degree of difference.

delphi technique   A futures research methodology aimed at provoking interaction of ideas from a panel of experts and arriving at consensus through several rounds of mailings of questionnaires in which responses from the earlier survey are reported but not attributed to individuals.

demographics   Statistics describing a population, such as age, geographical distribution, voter registration.

dependent variable   The condition or factor affected or influenced by independent variables. This is the variable watched for change when independent variables are manipulated. See independent variable and experimental.

descriptive   Concerned with description of some event, occurrence, or other phenomenon. Also, could involve measurement of dependent variables.

discriminant analysis   SPSS DISCRIMINANT computer program procedure helps identify factors that distinguish one group from another.

elements   Units of whatever population you are studying.

empirical   Based upon actuality and physical observation.

evaluation   As cited in text, "to determine the operations and effects of a specific program—relative to the objectives it set out to reach—in order to contribute to the decision making surrounding the program."

evaluation-research   A process in which the two are intertwined in ongoing study that begins with the first search for information at the inception of an idea or concern, continues with investigation and testing at the preliminary planning stages, backstops professional in monitoring progress and checking effectiveness throughout campaign, and provides for assessment of both end results and the campaign and its parts. The latter part of the process may serve as the beginning of the search for data as you come full circle.

expected frequencies   Unlike the observed or actual frequencies with which an answer is given in a survey or something happens in a study, these are what the public relations researcher will propose in the research hypothesis. They will be compared with observed frequencies. *See* hypothesis.

experimental group   Members of a public exposed to a treatment, such as a public relations campaign, while a similar or "control" group is not exposed. Both are measured at the same times before and after for comparison.

explanatory study   Explores relationships between dependent and independent variables, paired or in groups.

fact, truth, and reality   As commonly used in the English language, these vary from individual to individual depending on the way people selectively perceive the world and are affected by conditions of the moment. For the public relations professional, as for the scientist, what is fact, truth, or reality is a matter of *probability* based on painstaking measurement and analysis *and* precise procedures that are replicable—able to be reproduced and verified by others.

factor analysis   SPSS FACTOR computer program procedure helps correlate each variable with every other variable in a search for patterns of intercorrelations that might explain other findings. Compares the correlation among all variables.

factors   Synonym for variables.

field setting   Natural setting for public relations activity and experiments or studies as opposed to laboratory settings in university classroom or research facilities.

field study   Observation or survey done in natural setting, such as everyday work or living environment.

field test   Normally, trials of public relations strategies, tools, and/or campaigns with limited populations under field conditions before full-scale implementation.

focus group   Up to several dozen persons selected for a test panel as fairly representative of critical publics on whom you may wish to test ideas or interview in depth.

formative evaluation   As cited in the text, such evaluations provide information for developing and implementing new or revised programs. *Also see* summative.

futures   Plural form refers to alternatives.

futures research   Research that attempts to anticipate and shape the future. Employs waves of questioning of same or different panels to bring together best estimates in a consensus on future events that may affect your organization. Futures research is a policy making tool of particular value to the organization sensitive to changes in the environment.

givens   Aspects of a situation that cannot be changed.

hypothesis   Hunch, proposition; if X this, then Y that. On a more complex level, if A and B conditions exist in a certain way, then. . . . The hypothesis is a tentative explanation.

independent variable   Variable or factor that may be involved in causing something to happen or that has an effect of some kind on a dependent variable. An independent variable may be manipulated.

intercoder reliability   When several persons code, interpret, or rate materials in content analysis or responses to open-ended questions ("why do you feel that way?") in survey research, intercoder reliability testing and measures provide for greater assurance of objectivity by comparing how coders score comparable materials. Some case studies call this interrater reliability.

laboratory setting   Setting that allows control over the environment as opposed to little control in the field. A typical laboratory setting could be a college classroom or research center facilities relatively isolated from factors that might intervene in the field and confuse the picture of the effects of a given treatment.

longitudinal survey   Collects data at different time periods unlike the cross-sectional survey. See trend, cohort, and panel studies.

manipulate variables   Change one or more variables (factors) with some measure of control to see if and how other variables may be influenced.

Mann-Whitney U test   Test of significance that focuses on rankings of group members rather than means of scores. May be used, for example, to test rank ordering of opinions between two groups.

matrix   A table of columns and rows of events, used in cross-impact analysis or in reports of survey or experiment results to help graphically make clear the relationships or interactions of events. Plural is matrices.

mean   This central tendency measure is the mathematical "average" calculated by dividing the sum of the values of scores by the total number of scores. Commonly thought of as average score of a set of data.

measurement component   As attributed, quantifiable, time-bound, and cost-bound.

median   This central tendency measure is the exact midpoint, the figure above which 50 percent of scores will lie and below which you will find the other half of the scores.

mid-course evaluation   Sometimes mistaken for evaluation done once in the middle of a campaign or project. Refers to evaluation/research ongoing process between initial factfinding and end result assessment. Includes monitoring of progress and testing of tactics, strategies, and tools. Also may include systematic observation of changing public, media, or environmental conditions during the campaign.

mode   This central tendency measure is the most common or frequently found score in the data set.

multiple regression   Allows the correlation of one characteristic with a set of others.

nonprobability sample   No estimate is available for the chances of the subject being included in the sample. This runs high risk of over- or underrepresentation. *See* probability sampling and accidental/convenience, purposive, and quota sampling.

null hypothesis   There is no statistical significance. The opposite of the research hypothesis.

observed frequencies   Actual frequencies of scores found as compared to expected (or theoretical) frequencies.

obtained values   Term for numerical scores calculated from empirical, real-world evidence such as survey responses or experiment data. Obtained values are calculated for certain tests of significance and then compared with recorded tables of values in computer programs or appendices of research books. *See* tabled values.

operational definition   Precisely written step-by-step procedures that could be followed by persons seeking to analyze research results or reproduce the survey, experiment, or situation themselves. *See* scientific method.

opinion   Expression of attitude orally or in writing as the person perceives his or her thoughts, feelings, and beliefs under the conditions present at that particular time.

panel study   A longitudinal survey in which the same individuals are surveyed each time.

PARTIAL CORR   SPSS name for the partial correlation computer program procedure for showing correlation between two measures when a third factor believed to influence the relationship is accounted for or otherwise controlled.

participant observation   A research method that allows the researcher to participate in the actual research setting. This calls for systematically recording observations as data.

population   The whole of all elements (including but not limited to persons) being studied that share a particular set of characteristics.

pre- and posttest design   Pretest means to question or observe subjects of study in control and experimental groups before the treatment begins for the experimental group. Posttest means to measure control and experimental groups after the treatment is given to the experimental group and withheld from the control group. *See* control, experimental, and treatment.

probability sampling   Sampling in which you can gauge the chances of your sample accurately representing the population from which it was selected. *See* nonprobability sampling, sampling error, confidence level, and random selection.

problem   Used not only in the conventional sense but also as public relations officers may consider positive situations or needs in which options may be researched and opportunities seized or in which challenges may be explored and met.

purposive   Nonprobability sampling in which elements are selected for the sample based upon judgment and experience of surveyor. May include large unintentional bias factor.

Q-sort technique   A technique for measuring attitudes toward a subject by having an individual or panel of individuals assign values of their preferences to a number of choices on a particular subject. Q-sorting is also used to help public relations professionals or others make decisions when confronted with a number of options.

quantify   To use numbers.

quota sampling   Nonprobability sampling in which you set quotas to make sure various subgroups with certain sets of characteristics are included in your sample in whatever proportions you set.

r   Symbol for correlation coefficient.

random   Each person or other element in a population has same chance of being chosen for sample. Usually assured through use of table of random numbers generated by a computer or in a statistics book.

random selection   A method for selecting sample subjects or elements such that only chance alone determines the final choice. Also an attempt to free the sample of unintentional bias.

research   Strategy for gathering information based on systematic observation.

research design   The procedures and conditions under which you collect information or data in a study.

research-evaluation   *See* evaluation-research. The authors' way of stressing the close relationship and process.

research hypothesis   Proposes that a significant difference will be found, for example, in the group subjected to a campaign as compared to the control group that was not. If such a difference is not found, this glossary and text refer to the null hypothesis as being supported.

sample   Representative portion of population's elements. A sample may be thought of as a mirror image or facsimile of the population under study.

sample size   Number of elements sufficient for scientific validity; 1,200 to 1,500 for many surveys of American voters.

sampling   Data collected from a group of subjects in order to make inferences about a larger parent population.

sampling error   Actual differences in characteristics of the sample and those found in the population. Normally expressed in terms of plus or minus a specified percent. This means actual population value may be, for example, within range of 5 percent more or less than what sample reveals.

scenario analysis   A futures research methodology in which a person or panel develops *what if* approaches to create and explore alternate scenarios for projecting what might happen if a policy or program was changed or allowed to remain the same. It starts with givens (unchangeable conditions) and moves to what can change.

scientific method   Thinking about a problem, need, or opportunity based on reasoning and empirical observation. Description of what exists based on data from observation according to precisely defined and repeatable methods that can be used by others to verify or support the findings. *See* empirical and operational definition.

setting   Place where you do research.

simple random sample   The basic probability sample, with each subject in the population having the same probability of being selected for the sample.

SPSS   *Statistical Package for the Social Sciences*, a computer software package for doing complex calculations.

standard deviation   A measure of sampling variance, computed by taking the square root of the variance. Variance in this sense represents a formula for determining how much scores vary from the mean of scores in a set.

stratified samples   The population is divided into various strata (sections or groups with common characteristics) and the sample contains the same proportion of the population strata.

summative evaluation   As contrasted to formative evaluation, this mode is aimed at developing data on the overall effectiveness of an ongoing program.

survey   A field method for collecting data, usually relying on a questionnaire or interviewing.

systematic samples   Every *n*th element, in which *n*th is an arbitrarily set sampling interval selected systematically for the sample, such as every 10th newspaper issue or every 50th voter.

tabled values   Data in tables built into computer programs or found in appendices to research reference books against which you can compare obtained values calculated from empirical real-world evidence such as survey responses or experiment data. Obtained values are calculated and compared with tabled data in certain tests of significance.

tests of significance   *t* test, chi square, Mann-Whitney U, and other tests tell how frequently scores would be expected to occur by chance alone, and how much you can rely on the groups being alike, such as before an experimental treatment.

***t* test**   Test of significance used to determine any significant difference between sample means of two sets of scores such as the means for the two groups—experimental and control. *See* control, experimental, and tests of significance.

treatment   Something withheld from a control group but to which an experimental group is exposed in pre- and posttest studies. Example: a public relations message, action, or campaign.

trend study   A longitudinal survey that focuses on a particular sample at different time periods. *See* longitudinal.

unobtrusive measures   A method that uses physical evidence to reach research conclusions. Unobtrusive, in the sense that persons being observed are unaware of it. Also can include observation of records, archives, or media coverage.

variables   Factors or elements that change (vary). *See* dependent and independent variables.

variance   *See* standard deviation.

χ^2   Symbol for chi square.

APPENDIX B

ORGANIZATIONS AND PERIODICALS

*indicates case study material used.

ABC's "20/20", Chapter *8
American Hospital Association,
    Chapter 7
American Management Association,
    Chapter 7
American Medical International,
    Chapters 5, 6, 8
American Neurochemical Society,
    Chapter 8
Anderson Communications, Chapters
    5, 7
Apple Computer, Chapter 5
Apple Computer's Apple II Plus,
    microcomputer used throughout
    manuscript and in coding
    diskettes to be typeset by
    computer
ARCO, Chapters *1, 5, 6
Aspen Institute, Chapter *8
Associated Press, Chapter *8
Association for Education in
    Journalism and Mass
    Communication, Chapters 4, 5
Atlanta Bar Association, Chapter *1
AT&T, Chapters 3, 6
Avco, Chapter 5
N W Ayer Public Relations Services,
    Chapter *3

Bahamas Ministry of Tourism,
    Chapter *3
Ball State University, Chapter 1
Bank of America, Chapters 6, *9

Bechtel Power Corp., Chapter 5
Beckman Instruments, Chapter *8
Bell System, Chapter 3
Billboard, Chapter 1
B'nai B'rith, Chapter *8
Boston University, Chapters 1, 5, 9
Botsford Ketchum Public Relations,
    Chapter *1
Boy Scouts of America, Chapter *7
Bradley University, Chapter 5
Brigham Young University, Chapter 5
Bronson Methodist Hospital,
    Chapter *8
Chester Burger & Co., Chapter 1
Burson-Marsteller, Chapters *1, *6, 7,
    *8, 9
Business Horizons, Chapter 1
Business Periodicals Index, Chapters
    5, 9
Business Quarterly, Chapter 9
Business Week, Chapter 1
Carl Byoir & Associates, Chapters *1,
    *6, 8

California Bankers Association,
    Chapter *8
California Prune Board, Chapter *1
California State Legislature, Chapter 1
California State University,
    Dominguez, Chapter 5
California State University, Fullerton,
    Chapters *5, *6, *7, *8
Cambridge Reports, Chapter 1
Canadian Post Office, Chapter 1

INDEX

1983 SILVER ANVIL AWARD WINNERS

Selected and Edited from *1983 Silver Anvil Awards Presentation*,
courtesy of the Public Relations Society of America.

"THE TYLENOL STORY FROM CRISIS TO COMEBACK"
Category: Special Award
Winner: Johnson & Johnson and McNeil Consumer Products Company with
Burson-Marsteller

In late September 1982, an unknown murderer laced Extra-Strength Tylenol
capsules with cyanide and killed seven people in Chicago. The Tylenol tragedy
was unprecedented in American business.

Extensive consumer surveys showed that the company was held blameless
and confidence in the product was still high.

J&J's massive public relations effort not only made Tylenol's comeback
possible, but engendered new respect for the public relations profession.

"AMFAC'S SUGAR INFORMATION AND EDUCATION
CAMPAIGN IN HAWAII"
Category: Community Relations—Business
Winner: Amfac, Inc., Honolulu, Hawaii

Evaluative research validated the dramatic success of Amfac's campaign,
which resolved a shared business and community issue with public
participation. Resultant community support for the company's sugar
consolidation moves helped Amfac reduce sugar losses from $30 million in 1981
to $2.6 million in 1982.

"ENGINEERING SUPPORT FOR YOUTH, SUMMER 1982"
Category: Community Relations—Government
Winner: U.S. Army Corps of Engineers, Memphis District, Memphis

The U.S. Army Corps of Engineers, Memphis District, in support of Youth
Service USA, provided jobs, motivation, and recreation at minimum cost for
200 disadvantaged, inner-city youth. The District was assisted by active duty
and reserve, National Guard and Army recruiting units.

"HYDE PARK COMMUNITY RELATIONS PROGRAM"
Category: Community Relations—Nonprofit Organizations
Winner: Hyde Park Partnership, St. Louis, Missouri with Aaron D. Cushman

The Partnership, one of only a handful in the nation formed by a special
ruling of the U.S. Comptroller of the Currency, aimed to renew and redevelop a
declining neighborhood through positive changes in attitude and perceptions,
sharing and coordination of communication and limited resources.

The program emphasized research, then used organized but flexible six-
month public relations-marketing support outlines and calendars to develop
and implement ongoing media publicity, collateral, special events, special
projects and counsel.

"STAKEHOLDER PROCESS WINS BUDGET SERVICE OK"
Category: Institutional Programs—Business
Winner: Mountain Bell, Phoenix, Arizona

Protests and angry letters greeted Mountain Bell's first proposal for measured local telephone service. The Corporation Commission said public understanding and acceptance were necessary before approval. A dialogue emerged, with thousands of meetings to explain the plan and determine customer concerns. The program resulted in three significant changes: simplified distance bands; off-peak discounts; and a new name—Budget Service. In December the new plan was approved without opposition.

"CAMDEN—LOOK BEFORE YOU LAUGH"
Category: Institutional Programs—Nonprofit Organizations
Winner: City of Camden, New Jersey

Middle-class home owners abandoned Camden in the 1960s exodus to the suburbs. More fled after urban riots in 1969 and 1971. A multimedia campaign to lure buyers to 2,000 abandoned, vandalized homes was launched in October. More than 4,000 interested people responded, and some 200 vacant homes were sold during the program's first five months. Brisk sales continue.

" CRACKER JACK OLD TIMERS BASEBALL CLASSIC"
Category: Special Events and Observances—Business
Winner: Cracker Jack Company, Borden, Inc., Consumer Products Division,
Columbus, Ohio with Ketchum Public Relations, New York, New York

The Classic was created to stimulate trade interest in a special Cracker Jack aisle exhibit that featured consumer premiums and balloting to help choose the game's starting lineups.
As a result of the program, display activity increased 45 percent and 75,000 premiums were redeemed.

"CENTURY IV CELEBRATION"
Category: Special Events and Observances—Government
Winner: City of Philadelphia, Pennsylvania with The Philadelphia Convention
and Visitors Bureau

Philadelphia's Century IV Celebration involved over 200 programs commemorating the city's 300th birthday in 1982.
Proof of the public relations campaign's success: Tourism increased 14.3 percent in 1982 over 1981; unsolicited daily mail increased 103 percent; and coupons and toll-free telephone responses increased 116 percent.

"INTERNATIONAL SYMPOSIUM ON ALCOHOL AND DRIVING"
Category: Special Events and Observances—Trade Associations
Winner: American Insurance Association, Washington, DC and Insurance
Information Institute, New York, New York

Some 600 attendees, including media representatives, from all 50 states and several foreign countries, represented a broad cross section of interests.

Their goal: to review ways to fight drunk driving and to bring together special interest groups concerned with a problem that kills 25,000 people each year. Result: new insights for many, a broad-scale communication program that includes national advertising, a motion picture, print materials and action.

"BOYS CLUBS OF AMERICA—DIAMOND JUBILEE"
Category: Special Events and Observances—Nonprofit Organizations
Winner: Boys Clubs of America, New York, NY

Diamond Jubilee projects—planned and directed by a volunteer committee of leading public relations, marketing and media executives—were carried out over an 18-month period.

Extensive exposure was generated and documented. A subsequent Gallup poll showed a significant increase of seven percentage points in awareness of Boys Clubs among people earning over $20,000 annually.

"THE JUAREZ CONNECTION—AN EDUCATIONAL MODEL"
Category: Public Service—Business
Winner: Illinois Bell, Chicago, Illinois with the Chicago Board of Education

Attendance at Benito Juarez High School, in the Mexican-American community of Pilsen, had been below average among Chicago high schools.

Illinois Bell managers jointly studied problems with Juarez administrators, teachers, students, parents, community leaders and central staff of Chicago public schools. Approximately 125 company employees volunteered to help. The result was a 4.54 percent increase in average daily attendance.

"VOLUNTEER NORTH CAROLINA"
Category: Public Service—Government
Winner: Governor's Office of Citizen Affairs/State of North Carolina, Raleigh

Guided by an intensive communication effort, the program helped encourage more than three million adults—a 20 percent increase—to volunteer. The verifiable dollar value of volunteer contributions to state government alone in 1982 exceeded $307 million. Public schools, one of the focal points of the program, now involve almost 95,000 volunteers—a 20 percent increase over the previous year.

"RIDERS WANT RIDER TRAINING"
Category: Public Service—Trade Associations
Winner: Motorcycle Safety Foundation, Chadds Ford, Pennsylvania with Carl Byoir & Associates, Inc., New York, New York

"Riders Want Rider Training" was designed to increase state-funded rider education programs, increase the number of motorcyclists taking courses and decrease motorcycle fatalities.

402

Results: Eleven states passed legislation to fund rider courses; the number of trained riders on the roads doubled; and motorcycle fatalities declined for the first time since 1973.

"PETITION TO THE U.S. INTERNATIONAL TRADE COMMISSION"
Category: Public Affairs—Business
Winner: Harley-Davidson Motor Company, Milwaukee, Wisconsin with Bozell
    & Jacobs Public Relations, Milwaukee, Wisconsin

The comprehensive public affairs program developed to support the petition included research; publicity and media relations; employee, dealer, customer and vendor communications; Congressional testimony and liaison; and posters. On February 1, 1983, in a landmark decision, the Commission recommended that record tariffs be imposed on imported heavyweight motorcycles. On April 1, President Reagan imposed the recommended tariffs.

"THE WOMEN'S HOSPITAL: THE OTHER SIDE"
Category: Public Affairs—Nonprofit Organizations
Winner: Baptist Medical Centers, Birmingham, Alabama with Sankey 2, Inc.

An investor-owned hospital in Birmingham launched a campaign to gain public support for a proposed women's hospital. Baptist Medical Centers of Birmingham, a not-for-profit hospital system, formed a consortium of nine not-for-profit hospitals and planned and implemented a public relations program to inform publics of existing quality health care for women and to document lack of need for a women's hospital.

    The certificate of need for the women's hospital was unanimously denied by the Alabama State Health Planning and Development Agency. An evaluation survey showed that awareness of the issue increased by 8.5 percent; 43 percent opposed the new hospital; and 26 percent were undecided.

"THE LAUNCH OF DISC PHOTOGRAPHY"
Category: Promotional Publicity—Business
Winner: Eastman Kodak Company, Rochester, New York

Kodak had to persuade consumers and its other publics world-wide to change their concept of amateur photography and adopt a revolutionary system.

    Publicity resulted in some 500 million consumer impressions in less than a month. More than 8 million cameras were shipped in 1982 alone, and disc cameras were given as Christmas gifts in 1 out of 13 American homes. *Fortune* named the disc camera one of its "Top Ten New Products of 1982."

"BUREAU NATIONAL INTERPROFESSIONEL DU COGNAC"
Category: Promotional Publicity—Trade Associations
Winner: Bureau National Interprofessionel du Cognac, Cognac, France with
    Carl Byoir & Associates, New York, New York

Intensive placement efforts were carried out with national and local media to educate the broadest possible audience. A Cognac Library and Tasting Center was established. Other activities included a key-market media tour, promotion of a documentary and television news film, and a series of tasting events for journalists and private groups. The program achieved an estimated 400 million audience impressions and helped boost sales 27 percent.

"PROMOTIONAL COMMUNICATIONS FOR OBSTETRICS"
Category: Promotional Publicity—Nonprofit Organizations
Winner: Unity Medical Center, Fridley, Minnesota

In 1982 Unity Medical Center, faced with a declining in-patient census, low visibility in its service area, and other increased competitive pressures, responded with a marketing communication program for one of its strongest, most successful services—obstetrics.
Specific evaluation mechanisms were established for each part of the campaign. Overall, the project generated 150 referrals of pregnant women— representing nearly a 10 percent increase in new business.

"MANVILLE CHAPTER 11"
Category: Internal Communications—Business
Winner: Manville Corporation, Littleton, Colorado

On August 26, 1982, Manville Corporation declared Chapter 11 bankruptcy because litigation by employees claiming asbestos-related illnesses threatened the company's finances. Manville's chairman designated employees as a top communication priority. An extensive internal and external communication effort aimed at employees and mostly implemented within hours or days after the filing succeeded in assuaging fears, maintaining productivity, encouraging loyalty, and creating ambassadors for the company's point of view.

"EFFECTIVELY COMMUNICATING THE 'BAD' NEWS TO THE INVESTMENT COMMUNITY"
Category: Special Public Relations Programs—Investor Relations
Winner: Clark Equipment Company, Buchanan, Michigan with Burson-Marsteller, Chicago, Illinois

Preserving a corporation's carefully nurtured reputation, credibility and positive relationships with the investment community is, at best, hazardous when the company announces major losses, multiple plant closings and permanent layoffs.
Extensive planning and preparation ensured simultaneous communication to all vital audiences. This minimized negative perceptions and helped Clark win understanding and support for the corporation within the investment community and among other key publics.

"GE DUAL WAVE MICROWAVE OVEN INTRODUCTION"
Category: Special Public Relations Programs—Customer or Member Relations
Winner: General Electric Major Appliance Business Group, Louisville, Kentucky with Burson-Marsteller, New York, New York

Editors of six appliance industry publications toured GE's state-of-the-art manufacturing plant and enjoyed a luncheon prepared in Dual Wave™ ovens. Their visit was documented in a videotape and brochure, which also announced upcoming consumer-oriented activities. GE sales force used the tape and brochure as sales tools.
As a result of the program, 4,000 dealers—more than double GE's original goal—agreed to carry Dual Wave™ ovens.